Distributed Operating Systems

Concepts and Practice

Doreen L. Galli, Ph.D.

Prentice Hall
Upper Saddle River, NJ 07458

Publisher: *Alan Apt*
Editorial supervision/page composition: *Scott Disanno*
Editor-in Chief: *Marcia Horton*
Executive Managing Editor: *Vince O'Brien*
Managing Editor: *Eileen Clark*
Director of production and manufacturing: *David W. Riccardi*
Cover design director: *Jerry Votta*
Cover design: *Heather Scott*
Manufacturing buyer: *Pat Brown*

Cover art: Blanchard, Andy. (www.andyblanchard.com) Detail of *Astral Forest*, 1998. Acrylic on Wood, 40"x24". Private Collection. © 1998 Galli Enterprises, Atlanta Georgia.

ISBN 0-13-079843-6

Prentice-Hall International (UK) Limited, *London*
Prentice-Hall of Australia Pty. Limited, *Sydney*
Prentice-Hall Canada Inc., *Toronto*
Prentice-Hall Hispanoamericana, S.A., *Mexico*
Prentice-Hall of India Private Limited, *New Delhi*
Prentice-Hall of Japan, Inc., *Tokyo*
Prentice-Hall (Singapore) Pte. Ltd., *Singapore*
Editora Prentice-Hall do Brasil, Ltda., *Rio de Janeiro*

To my loving husband, Marc and my little ones, Marc Jr. and Steven

Preface

This book examines concepts and practice in distributed computing. It is designed to be useful not only for students but for practitioners and corporate training as well. Over the past decade, computer systems have become increasingly more advanced. Most computers are connected to some type of network on a regular basis. The installation of LANs at smaller businesses is even becoming commonplace. LANs are also being installed in custom homes at an ever-increasing rate. Software technology must keep up and so must our future and current practitioners! At the current pace, it is only a matter time before a working knowledge of distributed systems is mandatory for all computer scientists, because this technology pertains to a majority of all computers and their applications.

INTENDED AUDIENCE

While the study of standard operating system concepts is extremely important for computer science undergraduates, there is a significant and ever-increasing demand to extend this knowledge in the graduate and fourth-year undergraduate curriculum as well as for the practitioner out in industry. Therefore, there is a great need to study distributed operating systems concepts as well as practical solutions and approaches. This book is intended to meet this need for both students and practitioners.

OBJECTIVE

The objective of this book is to describe in detail each major aspect of distributed operating systems from a conceptual and practical viewpoint. Thus, it includes relevant examples of real operating systems to reinforce the concepts and to illustrate the decisions that must be made by distributed system designers. Operating systems such as Amoeba, Clouds and Chorus (the base technology for JavaOS) are utilized as examples throughout the book. In addition, the case study on Windows 2000™ provides an example of a real commercial solution. Technologies such as CORBA, DCOM, NFS, LDAP, X.500, Kerberos, RSA, DES, SSH, and NTP are also included to demonstrate real-life solutions to various aspects of distributed computing. In addition, a simple client/server application is included in the appendix that demonstrate key distributed computing programming concepts such as the use of INET sockets, pthreads, and synchronization via mutex operations.

In summary, this book focuses on the concepts, theory and practice in distributed systems. It is designed to be useful for practitioners, fourth year undergraduate as well as graduate level students and assumes that the reader has taken a basic operating system course. It is hoped that this book will prove to be invaluable not only for those already active in industry who wish to update and enhance one's knowledge base but also for future reference for those who have used it as a course text.

ORGANIZATION AND PEDAGOGICAL FEATURES

This book is divided into two parts. The first part, Chapter 1-6, presents the base foundation for distributed computing. The second part, Chapter 7-11, expands on these topics and delves more heavily into advanced distributed operating system topics. The pedagogical features included in this book are the following.

1. Detail Boxes to further enhance understanding. These boxes contain information such as complex algorithms and more in depth examples.

2. More than 150 figures and tables to help illustrate concepts.

3. A case study of Windows 2000™ to demonstrate a real life commercial solutions.

4. Project oriented exercises (those with italicized numbers) to provide "hands on" experience.

5. Exercises that build upon concepts covered in earlier chapters.

6. Reference pointers to relevant sources including:

   A. *overview* sources for further in-depth study,
   B. *research* papers, and
   C. *'core' web & ftp sites*.

7. A simplified distributed application program to demonstrate key distributing programming concepts.

8. Comprehensive glossary of terms (**boldfaced** words appear in the glossary) to provide a centralized location for key definitions.

9. Complete list of acronyms to aid readability and provide a centralized location for easy reference.

10. Chapter summaries.

11. Comprehensive index, primary references in **bold**.

12. Book website located at www.prenhall.com/galli.

SUGGESTIONS FOR INSTRUCTORS

This book is designed to provide maximum flexibility to instructors and has pedagogical features inherent within the text to allow you to customize the coverage to best meet the needs of your class and your institution's mission statement. In preparing this book, the only assumption made is that a basic introductory to operating systems course has been taken by the reader. Select topics that may be included in an introductory operating system course but are sometimes omitted, covered lightly, often not grasped or may have been forgotten but nonetheless are key to distributed operating systems, are included where appropriate. This material need not be presented in the classroom but is included in the book so that you can be assured that the students have the basis necessary for the more advanced distributed topics. Below are suggestions on how this book may be used for those requiring additional practical emphasis as well as for those desiring additional research emphasis. A graduate course desiring to add both types of emphasis may wish to use suggestions from both categories. Additional information may be available at the author's Prentice Hall website, www.prenhall.com/galli.

Adding Practical Emphasis

The following are a few suggestions for adding practical emphasis to a course utilizing this text.

1. Have the students, either individually or as a group complete one or more of the 'Project Exercises', those indicated by an italicized exercise number at the end of relevant chapters. Additional practical experience may be achieved if their design and implementation is orally presented to the class.

2. Cover all Detail Boxes related to real-life implementations.

3. Spend class time covering the Windows 2000™ Case study.

4. Create an individual or group project working with the distributed features of Windows 2000™.

5. Have the students expand or change the Surgical Scheduling Program. This may be as simple as changing the type of interprocess communication employed or as complex as creating another program utilizing the same distributed concepts.

Adding Research Emphasis

The following are a few suggestions for adding a research emphasis to a course utilizing this book.

1. Have the students, either individually or as a group, prepare a paper on a topic relevant to distributed operating systems. Reference papers cited at the end of each chapter should serve as good starting points. These projects may include an oral presentation.

2. Present lecture material from the relevant RFCs or research papers cited at the end of each chapter that are available on the web and include it the list of required reading for the students.

3. Have the students seek the relevant RFCs or research papers cited at the end of each chapter that are available on the web and prepare a summary.

4. Select a subset of the reference papers cited at the end of each chapter and create a spiral bound accompaniment to be used in conjunction throughout the course with the book. A large number of bookstores at research institutions have the ability to perform the copyright clearing necessary for this purpose.

Contents

Acknowledgments

As Sir Isaac Newton once said, "If I have seen further, it is by standing on the shoulders of Giants." To that I would like to add, "and I have always tried to find the tallest giants." To those giants I say thank you. A book such of this could not exist without the help of others, and I would like to thank all of those who have assisted me, including those giants whose contributions have advanced and continue to advance distributed computing as well as the computer science field as a whole. Their contributions are far reaching and have affected this book even though I may have never met or worked with them.

I would like to thank those giants who let me stand upon their shoulders possibly never knowing how much they had given me or that it could lead to this project. I would like to thank Mark Fishman, Ed Gallizzi, and the rest of the faculty at Eckerd College, who first sparked my interest in and love for computers. I would like to thank all of the wonderful faculty and students at the University of Waterloo, including my graduate supervisor, Charlie Colbourn. You taught me more than I ever realized from consistent formatting to advanced research techniques. You were the best supervisor one could have ever hoped to have worked with in graduate school.

I would like to thank all of those involved in the IBM CORDS (Consortium of Research in Distributed Systems) project, one of my greatest source of tall shoulders, including Gopi Attaluri, Michael Bauer, Dexter Bradshaw, Neil Coburn, Mariano Consens, Pat Finnigan, Masum Hasan, James Hong, Paul Larson, Kelly Lyons, Pat Martin, Gerry Neufeld, Jon

Pachel, Wendy Powley, David Rappaport, Avi Silberschatz, Jacob Slonim, David Taylor, Toby Teorey, Yachiam Yemini, and all others who spent so much time and energy on this project. In addition, I would like to thank all of the engineers as well as those in operations at Premiere Technologies, our strategic partners with whom I have had the privilege of working, and all of Premiere's customers, who enjoy using the distributed real-time products that have resulted.

I would like to extend a huge thank you to John Fritz who performed the implementation of the appendix, as well as his wife, Victoria, who inspired the application domain. I believe this example will provide a great deal of assistance to those wishing to go beyond concepts and into the actual programming. I am very grateful for all of the time John spent carefully preparing (and debugging!) this appendix.

I would like to thank Andy Blanchard, the amazing Atlanta-based particle vision artist whose work is featured on the cover. It never ceases to amaze me how Andy manages to create such incredible works. For those who would like to enjoy viewing additional Blanchard creations, a selection can be found at his Web site, www.andyblanchard.com. I can only hope our distributed systems present as cohesive of a picture as Andy's particles manage to achieve. I also hope that this book will allow the readers to see the forest through the trees on their quest to learn about distributed operating systems. I wish Andy continued success and the continued luxury of endless hours of painting his particle visions that bring so much pleasure to so many. It is a pleasure and honor to know such a talented artist and kindhearted person.

I would like to thank my first contact at Prentice Hall, Carole Horton, and all of those at Prentice Hall who have been involved with this project and whose work has helped bring it to fuition. In particular, I would like to extend my gratitude to Alan and Toni for their unwavering support. It is wonderful to work with such a great team!

I would like to express my gratitude to my reviewers. Their thoroughness is appreciated and their comments were exceptionally helpful. Each of my reviewers greatly contributed to the quality of the book and its mission of covering key concepts in a practical manner. Specifically, I would like to thank Dr. Tracy Camp from the Colorado School of Mines; Dr. Ed Gallizzi from Eckerd College; Dr. Michael Godfrey from Cornell University; Peter Kortmann from Tri-Pacific Software, Inc.; Jacky Mallet from Nortel Telecommunications; Dr. Klara Nahrstedt from the University of Illinois; and Dr. Clifford Neuman from USC Information Sciences Institute. In addition, I would like to thank the initial anonymous reviewers. Each of their perspectives has helped to ensure the best quality in the final product. I would also like to thank Mary Ann Telatnik and Nick Murray, my developmental editors, who greatly assisted me by compiling the feedback from my reviewers. The overview perspective was exceptionally helpful. Of course, despite all good intentions, typos and minor errors are one of those examples of an infinitely-long decreasing sequence and I alone take responsibility for any that remain. In that respect, I apologize in advance and appreciate reader feedback.

I would like to thank all of my students at SPSU who always inspired me to find the best ways to communicate ideas in the classroom and always reminded me of the great rewards of teaching. Specifically, I would like to extend a huge thank you to all of my students who helped me class test the material. In particular, I would like to extend a special thank you to my students who won the Submit the Most Suggestions - Find the Most Typos contest, John Fritz (the winner with an exceptional talent for proofreading), Moji Mahmoudi, and Haoyuan Chen. The quality of the material is greatly increased due to their due diligence, and I am confident that all readers will benefit from their unique insight as someone learning from this book. I sincerely welcome suggestions and comments from all readers as it is only with readers' insight that continual improvement for future revisions is possible. Readers can contact me through my Prentice Hall Web site, www.prenhall.com/galli.

I would like to thank my family for supporting me during this quest. Thank you Jr. and Steven, who gave up "Mommy time" and cheered me on to the finish line. Most of all, I would like to thank my husband and best friend, Marc. Thank you for your inspiration and the many hours of your invaluable assistance, including the times you let me read the chapters out loud to you in order to identify and correct any awkward wording as well as your assistance in smoothing out the rough spots. You made it fun; and yes, I'm sure it took a lot of patience, too. It is great to have a family that comes first yet appreciates and supports me in endeavors such as this. I'm very fortunate to have been so blessed with each of you. May you always be inspired and have the support necessary to chase and catch all of your dreams as well.

Doreen L. Galli, Ph.D.
August, 1999

Introduction to Distributed Systems

Never before have there been such rapid advances in computer systems. The development and creation of distributed computing. Thus, the demand is quickly increasing for all computer scientists to have an in-depth understanding systems, once left to specialists, has begun to take an unprecedented role in everyday of this advanced technology [Nev95]. In the basic centralized computing environment, a simple understanding of operating system concepts suffices. In contrast, developers in distributed environments are often required not only to understand the concepts of distributed, real-time, and sometimes even parallel systems but also to implement them on a much larger scale [SHFECB93]. Personal experience has shown that it is not uncommon for development teams to spend over 50% of their time implementing these advanced operating system concepts to develop an application in an advanced environment.

1.1 WHAT IS AN OPERATING SYSTEM?

An operating system is the computer's project manager. It controls, regulates, coordinates, and schedules all the processes and their utilization of the resources. Resources include, but are not limited to, the following.

- ◆ CPU(s)
- ◆ Memory modules(s)

- Media storage (disk drive(s), DVD[1], CD-ROMs, etc.)
- Sound and video boards
- Bus(es) or interconnection networks
- Modems and network adapters
- Monitors, terminals, printers, and other output devices
- Keyboards, pointing devices, scanners, and other input devices

Managerial tasks of the operating system include, but are not limited to, the following.

- Process (or object) management
- Communication
- Memory access/management
- Resource scheduling
- Information and resource security
- Integrity of data
- Meeting deadlines

    With all of these tasks and components, we only hope our system can create a unified and cohesive view or "picture" as the Blanchard original on the cover of this book achieves with each of the individual "particles". Traditionally, each of these managerial operating systems tasks was taken care of in software. This, however, is not necessarily true in a distributed system. We examine the major fundamental operating system concepts, even if they are currently implemented in a hardware component within a distributed environment.

    To visualize the magnitude and complexity of the problem posed to a computer scientist, we might think of the operating system as a musical conductor. Of course, the more complex the piece, the amount and complexity of work is greatly increased for the conductor. The conductor's job becomes even more complex if there is an attempt to conduct multiple orchestras at the same time, playing different pieces. Moreover, the orchestras may not be in the same location, and there may be time constraints! It is easy to see that this could be viewed as an overwhelming task; but as with any complex task, we will focus on one issue at a time, thereby overcoming one hurdle at a time, and eventually we will reveal the forest amidst the trees. Before you know it, the whole picture becomes clear and the result is music and beauty, not chaos, noise, or a clump of dots. As a first step, let's define distributed, real-time, and parallel computing in Sections 1.2 through 1.4 respectively.

1.2 WHAT IS A DISTRIBUTED SYSTEM?

A **distributed system** is a collection of heterogeneous computers and processors connected via a network, as depicted in Figure 1.1. This collection works closely together

---

[1] DVD once stood for Digital Video Disk as well as Digital Versatile Disk. The formats combined into what is now known as DVD, which is no longer an acronym although it is frequently thought to imply one of its hereditary acronyms.

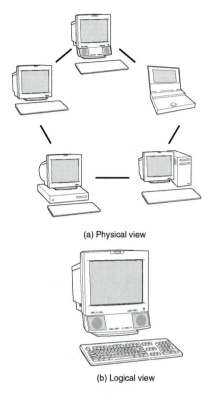

(a) Physical view

(b) Logical view

Figure 1.1 Computers in a Networked Environment.

to accomplish a common goal. The goal of a distributed operating system is to provide a common, consistent global view of the file system, **name space**, time, security, and access to resources. To provide this common view, there are numerous constraints and requirements on all participating systems; thus, distributed systems are generally referred to as a tightly coupled system (there are exceptions to every rule!). If the heterogeneous computers are connected by a network and are not tightly coupled, they are generally referred to as a **network system**. A network system does not attempt to provide a common global view, nor does it place significant demands on the participating systems. Components in a distributed or network system may be simple centralized system components; components with real-time constraints, as presented in Section 1.3; or more complex parallel systems as introduced in Section 1.4. Furthermore, it is not uncommon for a distributed system to incorporate components centralized in nature, realtime in nature, and parallel in nature at the same time, as can be seen in the sample distributed application presented in Section 1.5.

Both network and distributed systems have grown in popularity due to the rapid increase in PCs' computing power per dollar. Section 1.2.1 presents an introduction to popular networks. Section 1.2.2 presents the Open System Interconnection (OSI) reference model defined by the International Standards Organization (ISO). Section 1.2.3 introduces distributed computing models. Section 1.2.4 discusses issues involved in deciding between distributed versus centralized solutions within a distributed system. Finally, Section 1.2.5 describes the various computing models utilized in a distributed environment.

1.2.1 Popular Network Topologies and Features

While entire books have been written and entire courses have been taught on networks, this section provides only a brief introduction to networks. It is hoped that the minimal basics of networks presented provide a sufficient basis for understanding the operating system concepts we study in this book.

There are two basic categories of networks: local area networks (LANs) and wide area networks (WANs). Local area networks are typically owned by a single entity and are only a few kilometers in area. Prior to the mid 1990s, it was not uncommon for the error rate on a LAN to be as much as 1000 times lower as compared to a WAN, although more modern WANs, such as ATM networks, have dramatically reduced the relative error rate. A given site may employ several subnets or smaller LANs that make up the larger LAN. The smaller LANs may be connected in one of the following manners, whose algorithms are presented in Detail Box 1.1.

1. **Repeater**: An unintelligent device that simply repeats everything from one network to another network. Both networks must employ the same protocol, i.e., they are the same type.

2. **Bridge**: An intelligent device that only transfers data from one subnet to another if its destination is on that subnet or it must travel on that subnet to reach its destination. Both networks must implement the same network protocol.

3. **Router**: A router is even more advanced than a bridge in that it can also connect LAN segments that possibly employ different protocols. Routers are capable of connecting more than two networks at a time.

4. **Backbone**: A LAN that does not contain users on the network but rather other networks, as depicted in Figure 1.2.

DETAIL BOX 1.1
CONNECTING LAN SUBNET ROUTER ALGORITHMS

Let P1 and P2 be two ports on the device.
Let OUTPUT (a,b) put the contents of the message received on port b out onto
    the network connected to port a.
Let DESTINATION(a,b) return true IF and ONLY IF the message received on
    port a must use port b to reach its destination where a and b are ports.
Let DIF_PROTOCOL(a,b) return true IF and ONLY IF port a and port b utilize
    a different network protocol and DESTINATION(a,b) is true.

Let CONVERT(a,b) convert a message received on port a to a message utilizing the protocol employed on port b and send out on port b.

The Repeater Algorithm.
While()
{
OUTPUT(P1, P2);   //All messages received on P2 are output on P1
OUTPUT(P2, P1);
}

The Bridge Algorithm
While()
{
If DESTINATION(P1,P2);
        Then OUTPUT(P1,P2);   //Only forward if required to reach destination
If DESTINATION(P2,P1);
        Then OUTPUT(P2,P1);
}

The Router Algorithm
While()
{
If DIF_PROTOCOL(P1,P2);   // Only forward if required to reach destination
        Then CONVERT(P1,P2);   //Only convert if necessary
        Else If DESTINATION(P1,P2);
            Then OUTPUT(P1,P2);   //Only forward if required to reach destination
If DIF_PROTOCOL(P2,P1);
            Then CONVERT(P2,P1);
            Else If DESTINATION(P1,P2);
                Then OUTPUT(P1,P2);
}

A LAN may be wired or wireless. Wired LANs are connected physically with cables, while wireless LANs are connected via nontangible communication channels such as infrared light or radio frequency. There are three common topologies for wired LANs, which are depicted in Figure 1.3. Two of the most common protocols for wired LANs are Ethernet (formally known as CSMA/CD as specified in the standard IEEE 802.3 [IEEE85a]) and token ring (formally specified in the standard IEEE 802.5 [IEEE85b]). Since these protocols provide radically different types of operational service, they are not considered direct competition. The Ethernet is similar to putting a stamp on an envelope, while the token ring is similar to sending next day delivery with return receipt requested. Basic Ethernet runs at 10 Mbps with popular variations such as fast Ethernet running at 100 Mbps and the Gigabit Ethernet running at 1000 Mbps. Ethernet tries its best to send a message; however, it does not provide any acknowledgement that the message was received correctly. In addition, the standard Ethernet protocol does not support message priorities nor does it guarantee delivery times. Nevertheless, for many applications it does function in a satisfactory manner up until it reaches 50% capacity. At this point, it slows considerably, and almost all CSMA/CD networks will collapse and fail to deliver any messages once they exceed approximately 60% capacity.

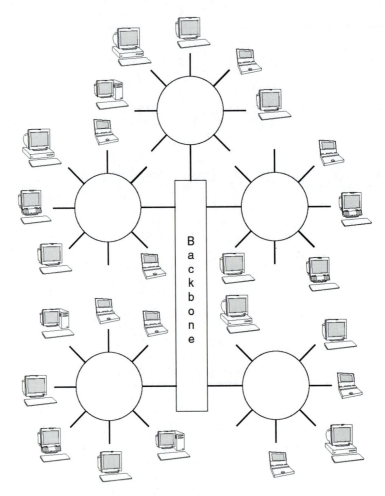

Figure 1.2   Connecting LAN Subnets with a Backbone.

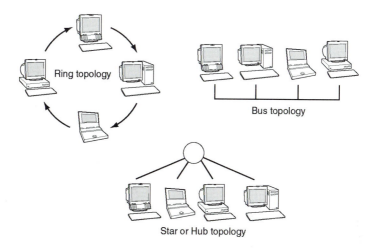

Figure 1.3 Common Wired LAN Topologies.

The token ring, which is analogous to next day delivery with return receipt, acknowledges the correct delivery of all messages. It allows priorities and has a guaranteed delivery time which makes it particularly attractive to real-time applications. Unlike the Ethernet, it does not collapse under high loads but rather continues successfully sending messages. This protocol is totally fair with respect to priority. Depending on the variation being employed, it runs at 4 to 16 Mbps and in comparison with the 10 Base[2] Ethernet, it costs about twice as much to implement.

Fiber Distributed Data Interface (FDDI) is another common network protocol. It is frequently utilized as a backbone or as a high-speed LAN. FDDI operates at 100 Mbps. It is implemented on two counter-rotating rings. The protocol is designed to support synchronous traffic; thus, it is attractive to real-time applications.

Wireless LANs are becoming more popular due to the increased desire for mobility and the expenses involved in constant reconfiguration of wired LANs. Wireless LANs generally have a greater initial installation cost but a much lower maintenance cost. Wireless LANs may be either frequency based or infrared based. Frequency-based wireless LANs can currently achieve up to 4 Mbps and are easier to install since radio signals can generally travel through opaque substances. While this ability to travel through opaque substances may allow for easier installation, it also means that the network signals can travel outside a building's confines. Thus, frequency based wireless LANs are sometimes thought of as being less secure than wired LANs or infrared-based wireless LANs. However, due to the utilization of spread spectrum technologies that either spread the signal in such a manner that it appears as noise or force the signal to hop channels constantly, frequency-based LANs are considered secure. In addition, all the security measures employed on a wired LAN, including encryption as described in Chapter 11, may also be employed for wireless LANs. Infrared wireless LANs today can achieve up to 10 Mbps and infrared signals cannot travel through opaque substances. The inability to travel through opaque substances makes

---

[2] 10 (ten) Base Ethernet is a common way to refer to Ethernet networks that operate at 10 Mbps.

infrared wireless LANs more difficult to install since the transmitters and receivers must be in direct line of sight of each other. In addition, infrared signals can suffer from light noise, which can affect their reliability.

Many distributed systems are not centered on a LAN but rather a WAN. To connect a LAN to a WAN, a gateway must be employed. The information is divided into smaller pieces, referred to as frames or packets, before it is sent out on the network. Two general methods may be utilized to send these packets out over a WAN. The first method is circuit switching and is employed on the public-switched telephone network (PSTN). This type of network provides a fixed data rate channel that is totally dedicated and reserved prior to any data transmission taking place. This method incurs a lot of set-up time and reduces throughput on the network but does ensure that such a message only incurs propagation delay during its transmission. The second major type of WAN is that of packet switching. In packet switching, every message is again divided into a smaller unit known as a packet. These packets have a tight upper bound on their size. They may be sent in a connection-oriented manner, utilizing a virtual circuit, or in a connectionless manner, utilizing datagrams. Virtual circuits require that each packet from a particular message travel along the same exact path and in proper order. This usually requires a set-up packet to be sent first. In contrast, datagrams place no constraints on the transmission path or order of related packets. The datagram packets are then rearranged into the proper order and reassembled into the original message at the destination. This is considered less reliable but more robust and efficient.

Popular network protocols utilized on WANs include frame relay and asynchronous transfer mode (ATM) networks. Frame relay allows network messages to include information on congestion control and a rating as to if that message should be thrown out if the network is too busy. ATM networks are known for their speed and support of transmitting multimedia files, although this characteristic is not unique to ATM networks. Each packet on an ATM network is exactly the same size, 53 octets. ATM networks refer to these 53 octet packets as cells. The ATM adaptation layer (AAL) allows support for constant bit rate and variable bit rate traffic as well as connection and connectionless-oriented traffic through various frame formats. It was designed knowing that it needs to support real-time multimedia applications. Of course, a WAN such as the Internet uses a combination of all network types.

1.2.2 ISO/OSI Reference Model

The ISO/OSI Reference model [ISO84] describes how one might divide all the tasks necessary to compute in any type of network model. This reference model is divided into seven layers as depicted in Figure 1.4. The lower the number of the layer, the closer the layer is to the network. Layers 1 through 3 are network dependent. These layers are highly involved with the exact network protocol with which the system is directly interfacing. Layers 5 through 7 are application oriented, while layer 4 is a transition layer between the network and the application. Operating system concepts begin at the interface to layer 4 and involve layers 5 through 7. The relationship of this reference model to the popular Transmission Control Protocol/Internet Protocol (TCP/IP) suite employed on the Internet can be found in Detail Box 1.2. We now briefly define and describe each of the seven layers in the ISO/OSI reference model.

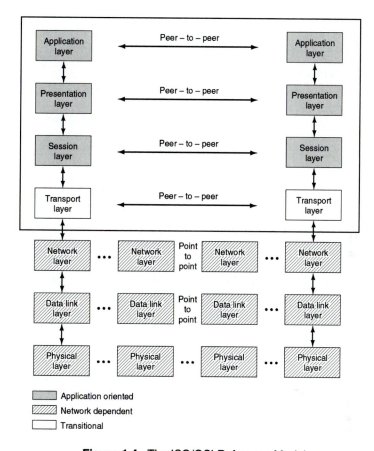

Figure 1.4   The ISO/OSI Reference Model.

1. **Physical layer**: The physical layer is the lowest layer. It is in charge of placing the bits on the wire and all protocols regarding how many connectors on an adapter. This layer is of particular interest to electrical engineers.

2. **Data link layer**: The datalink layer is divided into two sublayers for LANs: medium access control and logical link control. The logical link control is not exclusive for LANs and employs protocols for acknowledging and retransmitting frames as a form of error control. The data link layer is also responsible for flow control that involves controlling the amount and speed of information transmitted on the network. Thus, flow control helps prevent "overwhelming" the network and its resources. Since LANs are a shared, broadcast communication medium, we must employ protocols for efficient and effective utilization. Popular protocols include CSMA/CD (Ethernet) and the token ring protocol described in Section 1.2.1.

3. **Network layer**: The network layer's dominating function is that of routing a message from the source to the destination. Since routing is unnecessary on a LAN, this layer is a null layer in that environment and performs no functionality.

4. **Transport layer**: The primary function of the transport layer is to determine the class of service necessary for communication over the network. The highest class of service is considered connection oriented and provides full error control and acknowledgment services. The lowest class of service is connectionless and does not provide such error recovery services in this layer.

5. **Session layer**: The session layer is predominantly concerned with the organization and synchronization between the source and destination throughout their communication.

6. **Presentation layer**: This layer is responsible for the syntax of the message data and performing the appropriate conversions. This includes but is not limited to conversion between the American Standard Code of Information Interchange (ASCII) and the Extended Binary-Coded Decimal Interchange Code (EBCDIC), compression, and encryption.

7. **Application layer**: The user interface and establishing authority and availability for resource usage are the dominating functions of the application layer.

Another important feature of the ISO/OSI reference model is the concept of layers that are **point-to-point layers** versus **peer-to-peer layers**. Functions in point-to-point layers are performed at each and every location between the source and destination as well as being performed at the source and destination. Since there may be thousands of nodes between the source and destination, point-to-point functions may be performed thousands of times while a message is traveling from its source to its destination. All functions defined in layers 1 through 3 are point to point. Functions in peer-to-peer layers (layers 4 through 7) are only performed at the source and destination: two times in all. For an example of a point-to-point function, let's look at the *function* of examining the address on the envelope of a letter. This function is performed at the source, at the local post office branch, and at every post office branch between the source and destination. In addition, the post office branch closest to the destination performs the function of looking at the address as well as the delivery person. Finally, the destination performs the function of examining the address to determine the exact recipient. In contrast, the *function* of reading the contents of the letter is (hopefully!) only performed by the sender and receiver; thus, it is an example of a peer-to-peer function.

DETAIL BOX 1.2
TCP/IP PROTOCOL SUITE & THE ISO/OSI REFERENCE MODEL

The TCP/IP protocol suite is a group of protocols designed to be utilized for computing across heterogeneous networks or internets (an abbreviated contraction of interconnection networks). While TCP/IP was initially designed for the government-funded advanced Army research projects network (ARPANET) in the 1960's (well before the ISO/OSI), it did not take on its current form that is the basis for the most popular internet until 1978 (the original ARPANET protocol was network control program -NCP). When the term internet is written with an upper case I, it refers to the worldwide Internet or simply the Internet. In 1983, the first release of UNIX incorporating TCP/IP was released and the first release of Windows (Windows 95) to incorporate TCP/IP for the home PC environment was in 1995. TCP/IP is divided into four layers. Figure 1.5 depicts the relationship of these four layers to the ISO/OSI reference model. We now describe each of these four layers.

Link layer: The link layer is the lowest layer and incorporates the functions of the two lowest ISO/OSI reference model layers. Literally, this implies that the network card and the operating system device drive for the card are included in this layer.

Network layer: The network layer is the second lowest layer and directly maps to the ISO/OSI's network layer. This layer includes the Internet Protocol (IP), Internet Control Message Protocol (ICMP), and Internet Group Management Protocol (IGMP).

Transport layer: The transport is related to the ISO/OSI's transport layer. In this layer reside theTransmission Control Protocol (TCP) and User Datagram Protocol (UDP). TCP provides reliable transmission that includes acknowledgments and is a high class of service. UDP, on the other hand, just sends packets and lets higher layers worry about the reliability. While providing a lower class of service, UDP is known to be much more efficient and is sometimes the preferred method for real-time applications. In this circumstance, the application must perform any reliability functions desired itself.

Application layer: The application layer relates to the three highest layers of the ISO/OSI reference model. Services included in the protocol include telnet for remote sessions, File Transfer Protocol (FTP), e-mail via Simple Mail Transfer Protocol (SMTP), Name Server Protocol (NSP), and Simple Network Management Protocol (SNMP).

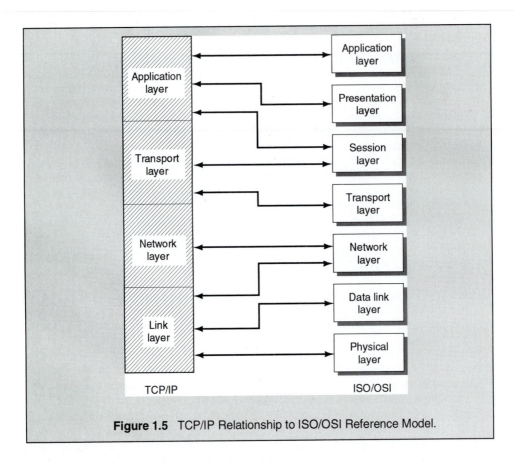

Figure 1.5 TCP/IP Relationship to ISO/OSI Reference Model.

 ## 1.2.3 Distributed Computing Models

There is an old saying, "too many cooks spoil the broth." So the big question in distributed computing is, how do we manage all these cooks so we do not spoil the broth? There are two primary approaches to distributed computing: the client/server model and the peer-to-peer model. The client/server model is very popular due to its simplicity, and the peer-to-peer model is a more advanced model that is gaining popularity as time progresses.

The Client/Server Model

The client/server model is much like a manager/subordinate model in the work force. The client is the manager and the server(s) are the subordinates. The client wants something accomplished and gives the task to the server, who then completes the task and notifies its boss, the client. Clients make requests to servers and servers reply to clients, as depicted in Figure 1.6. This operation takes place in the ISO/OSI Session layer. It is implemented through interprocess communication, as discussed in Chapter 4. In the client/server model, there may be several clients making requests to several servers. Likewise, a given server may be satisfying the requests of several clients. In a local environment, there are two basic methods for implementing the client/server model. This includes the workstation model and the processor pool model.

The workstation model allows each of the local users to have a small workstation, which in itself does not have enough computing power to complete all of the tasks that the user would require of it. When more power is needed, the user's workstation makes a request through the network in hopes of finding another workstation to assist that is currently being underused. This creates its own set of problems and concerns as discussed in Chapter 7.

In the processor pool model, each user is only provided with a simple terminal and all of the processing power is kept at one centralized location, as is the case with a mainframe. When resources are needed, the user makes a request to the server, who controls all of the processing power and other services as well as controlling their distribution. This is also further discussed in Chapter 7.

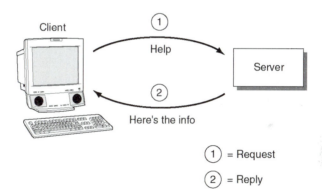

Figure 1.6 Client/Server Model.

The Peer-to-Peer Model

The peer-to-peer model is a natural evolution of the client/server model. It is similar to a group of colleagues working together. Each member of the computing team may make a service request of other members. Thus, the client/server model may be thought of as a simplification and predecessor of the peer-to-peer model. Some applications dictate the necessity of a peer-to-peer model that provides a many-to-many relationship. As pointed out in [BCEF94], a distributed system may require a large database system to store information from all the devices and hosts. The management component needs to manage and optimize the system that requires the utilization of the database system. Likewise, the database system requires the management component to optimize the distributed queries. Which is the client and which is the server? Neither. They both need to work together as colleagues in a peer-to-peer environment, as depicted in Figure 1.7. Observe that if an environment supports peer-to-peer cooperation, it does not eliminate the client/server model for those implementations that do not need the team work approach. The peer-to-peer model is supported by what is referred to as a balanced configuration.

Examples of peer-to-peer architectures include the High Level Data Link Control protocol that implements the Logical Link Control sublayer of the ISO/OSI's datalink layer. This protocol supports the peer-to-peer model when operating in asynchronous balanced mode and is implemented in a standard known as X.25. IBM's Advanced Peer-to-Peer Networking (APPN™) also supports peer-to-peer computing. Since further details on these architectures are beyond the scope of operating systems, we do not discuss the details here, but interested readers may find more information on X.25, High Level Data Link Control, and APPN in a textbook such as those listed in Section 1.7.

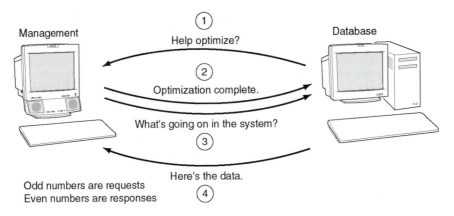

Figure 1.7 Peer-to-Peer Model.

1.2.4 Distributed versus Centralized Solutions

Solutions to the various tasks in a distributed environment offer a choice between distributed or centralized solutions. Centralized solutions place the entire decision and all information related to the decision in one location. This type of solution is the simplest solution and is the easiest method to adapt algorithms intended for nondistributed systems; however, there are several disadvantages. First, this central authority becomes a critical element. If this critical element fails, the entire distributed system is subject to failure. Second, network traffic around this centralized authority is increased since all participants in the system will have to communicate with this single location. On the positive side, application software upgrade is quite simple in a centralized architecture since there is only one system that requires the new software.

In comparison, distributed solutions do not suffer from a critical element but do have their own weaknesses. Distributed solutions frequently increase traffic throughout the entire network since many distributed solutions involve broadcasting information. In addition, it is more difficult for several locations to maintain consistent information. Some locations may receive information, whether it be data updates or software upgrades, prior to other locations due to network delays. Optimal solutions may not be possible due to incomplete information. Furthermore, distributed solutions generally require cooperation among the various participants.

1.2.5 Network Versus Distributed Operating Systems

The primary factors distinguishing a network operating system from a distributed operating system are the level of transparency provided and the requirements put on the participating systems.

System Requirements

A distributed system requires that all participants each run their own copy of the same distributed operating system; however, this distributed system is quite often running locally on top of different base or centralized operating systems. Distributed operating systems that run on top of a base operating system are often referred to as **midware**. A network operating system does not require participants to run the same system, only that they all agree upon the same network protocols for operations such as copying files and remote logins. Thus, the biggest difference between a network operating system and a distributed operating system is that a network operating system does not attempt to hide the fact that you are operating on different systems. That is, it does not make remote operations transparent to the user or support any of the following transparencies.

Transparencies

We now examine various types of transparencies that may be supported by a distributed operating system. Some are more desirable than others.

- ♦ **Name transparency**: The name of the resource does not indicate where in the distributed system the file, data, or process is physically located. Furthermore, if users change location, their view of the system would not change since the name is not tied to a particular location. Overall, this implies some sort of global naming scheme.

- ♦ **Location transparency**: When location transparency is provided, users cannot tell where the resources they are utilizing are physically located. This implies the support of name transparency and access transparency. This is beneficial when speaking of files and processors, assuming that the utilization of each has no additional cost. However, resources such as printers generally do not desire location transparency. When users wish to print a document, they like to know exactly where it will be printed!

- ◆ **Access transparency**: Access transparency takes location transparency even further in that a user cannot distinguish a local resource from a remote resource. The interface, command, and timing (the most difficult aspect) are all consistent for local and remote access to resources. The time constraint is generally only obtainable for local (within the same LAN) distributed systems. One of the most difficult aspects of access transparency is supporting secure access, as described in Chapter 11, without interfering with access transparency.

- ◆ **Migration transparency**: Migration transparency implies that users cannot notice if a resource or their job has been migrated to another location within the distributed system. Name transparency is necessary for this to occur. This issue is discussed in detail in Chapters 4 and 7.

- ◆ **Replication transparency**: Replication transparency allows multiple copies of files and servers to exist throughout the system. Furthermore, the existence of multiple copies is transparent to the users with replication transparency and all changes and updates must be made simul-taneously to all replicas. For more information on replication transparency see Chapters 8 and 9.

- ◆ **Concurrency and parallelism transparency**: Multiple processes may utilize the same resource or a process may utilize multiple resources at the same time without interference or awareness. These tasks are automatically and efficiently handled to take full advantage of the distributed system. This issue is discussed in detail in Chapter 10.

- ◆ **Failure transparency**: If a link or system within the distributed system fails, the entire system should not fail. Failure transparency is a key benefit to distributed computing over centralized computing in that you cannot help but notice if your one and only computer crashes. This issue is discussed in detail in Chapter 9.

 ## 1.3 WHAT IS A REAL-TIME SYSTEM?

A real-time must satisfy bounded response time constraints or suffer severe consequences. If the consequences consist of a degradation of performance but not failure, the system is referred to as a **soft real-time system**. If the consequences are system failure, the system is referred to as a **hard real-time system**. In a hard real-time system, system failure may result in death or other life-threatening consequences. If one can tolerate a low probability of missing a deadline, the system is referred to as a **firm real-time system**. Multimedia applications across networks are examples of firm real-time systems. It may have already crossed your mind that most computer systems must satisfy some time constraints or suffer consequences, and you are correct. Most systems are soft real-time systems. In this book as in most, when we refer to real-time systems, we mean hard real-time systems and firm real-time systems, where the consequences are severe. The classic teaching tool for real-time computing is the use of computer-controlled trains. If the programmer fails, the trains crash. If this was not practice, lives could be lost. This is one area in which we all hope that practice makes perfect! Traditional real-time applications are abundant in the tele-communications, aerospace, and defense industries.

There are two types of real-time systems: reactive or embedded. A **reactive real-time system** involves a system that has constant interaction with its environment. This reaction may involve a pilot constantly pressing control functions or a person constantly pressing on keys or buttons. An **embedded real-time system** is used to control specialized hardware that is installed in a larger system. An example would be the microprocessor that controls the fuel-to-air mixture for your automobile.

Additional information concerning real-time systems is presented in the following two sections. Specifically, real-time event characteristics are discussed in Section 1.3.1. Network characteristics that affect distributed real-time systems are presented in Section 1.3.2.

1.3.1 Real-Time Event Characteristics

Real-time events fall into one of three categories: asynchronous, synchronous, or isochronous. **Asynchronous** events are entirely unpredictable like the exact location lightning will strike during a storm. Generally, asynchronous events are caused by external sources. For example, telephone calls are asynchronous as a telecommunication application has no way to know when users of the application will use their telephone to connect to the system. In contrast, **synchronous** events are predictable and occur with precise regularity if they are to occur. Synchronous events are usually generated by an internal source such as an embedded component. If an event can be subjected to any type of propagation delay, such as a network connection, the event is not synchronous. If an event occurs with regularity within a given window of time, it may be considered **isochronous** (pronounced eye-sock-run-us); however, this category, technically a subcategory of asynchronous events, is not always accommodated by applications. An example of an isochronous event is the receiving of audio bytes in a distributed multimedia application. These audio bytes must be received within a given window for the application to function in the acceptable range. While predictable, these bytes may not be received at precisely predictable moments in time since they experience network delay and are subjected to network errors.

It might be helpful to point out that these terms also have meaning within the discipline of networks. Specifically, asynchronous describes a network or network protocol that transmits every packet of data independently in a noncontiguous manner. In contrast, a synchronous network or network protocol sends a message as a contiguous stream of bits.

1.3.2 Network Characteristics Affecting Distributed Real-Time Applications

The following are four facts of life about the underlying network that can affect real-time applications operating in a distributed environment:

1. NetworklLatency,
2. Bandwidth versus cost,

3. Routing optimization, and

4. Micronetwork characteristics.

The first fact is that basic network latency cannot be ignored. Latency is the delay experienced due to the requirement of the data to travel from the source to the destination. In a centralized system, the latency experienced while communicating within the system is unnoticed. In contrast, basic physical limitations may cause the latency in distributed systems to become an issue, particularly for distributed real-time applications such as telecommunications. For example, even at the speed of light, it would take 20 ms for information to travel across the United States. Using a highway analogy, this assumes no red lights (delays at various hops), congestion, or traffic accidents (data errors causing retransmission). If the application is forced to perform massive communication to components severely geographically distributed, it may not meet its real-time constraints. Furthermore, network latency forces all distributed events to become asynchronous (or isochronous) as precise timing predictability is no longer possible.

The second fact of life is the bandwidth versus cost tradeoff. Distributed real-time applications require constant bandwidth. Currently, it costs approximately one-half million dollars per month for a 155-Mbps connection (such as an OC3 Sonnet) between Osaka and Tokyo. Thus, while it may be technically achievable to send real-time video, it may not be financially viable. The good news is that chances are that bandwidth will become less expensive as the years go by, although it is difficult to determine when massive bandwidth will be truly affordable for the masses and the world wide wait (www) will be truly over. History has shown many times to many people that no matter how much resources are available (whether the resources are physical computer resources or even money), we always seem to find a way to use the resources and dream of a need for more. It is hard to imagine how the early satellites with only 16 kbytes of memory functioned or how a 300-baud modem for home use was a prized possession (not for its value in a computer museum either!).

The third fact of life for distributed real-time systems is that they must reside on a network and therefore be subject to its topology and its effect on distribution and routing. In theory, networks are designed to minimize the number of hops (network nodes) between the source and destination, but this theory does not hold true in life (see Exercise 1.8). As an analogy, think of traveling in your automobile from downtown in a metropolitan area to a suburban town during rush hour. The physically shortest path is not always the shortest path in terms of time (i.e., the fastest path). The physically shortest path may be slower for a number of reasons, including the speed limit or data transfer rate of the path, the amount of traffic on the path, or the number of lanes or capacity of the path. If the city has toll roads, the shortest path may not be the least expensive. All of these sorts of issues also play in the Information Highway and therefore the overall performance of the distributed real-time applications is generally at the mercy of the underlying infrastructure.

The fourth fact of life for distributed real-time systems is that they are subject to micronetwork characteristics, such as buffer size on the network switches, the queue sizes, as well as the packet sizes allowed on the network. Theoretically, these characteristics should be transparent to the upper layers and applications; in practice, however, they are often very visible due to ignorance on the part of a programmer and perhaps the lack of supporting standards when software is written. A colleague of mine came across a video streaming program (which will go unnamed) that is unusable and cannot take advantage of high-speed WANs because the video programmer hard coded a 65-kbyte UDP packet size. The moral of this fact of life is that applications are subject to micronetwork characteristics, and these aspects of applications should be left to the lower-level software. One never knows how many years a given application will be used (as is evident by the September 9, 1999[3] and year 2000 software crisis) and what type of technology will desire to run it (as was the case for the video streaming program). The more flexible the code, the better the usability of the application.

1.4 WHAT IS A PARALLEL SYSTEM?

Much like a distributed system, a **parallel system** consists of multiple processors; however, the multiple processors are (predominantly) homogeneous and located within the same computer. In addition to multiple processors, parallel computers may be designed in which each processor has its own local memory. Such parallel computers are referred to as **multicomputers**. If the parallel processors share memory, they are referred to as **multiprocessors**. These multiprocessors are often classified in terms of the cost for accessing the shared memory. If the access time is the same for all processors, the multiprocessor's memory is referred to as Uniform Memory Access (**UMA**); otherwise, the memory is referred to as Non-Uniform Memory Access (**NUMA**). Multiprocessors that do not share memory (each processor has its own local memory) are referred to as **NORMA** multiprocessors (NO Remote Memory Access). Section 1.4.1 presents some of the various architectures utilized to organize the numerous processors into a single computer. Section 1.4.2 presents some of the software paradigms employed in a parallel computing environment. Since parallel computers are often utilized to solve the most complex problems and are considerably more expensive than a uniprocessor, they are often referred to as supercomputers. Efficiently utilizing all of these resources to solve these complex problems and increase the speed of computations is the job of the parallel operating system.

1.4.1 Parallel Architectures

We now present some of the popular parallel architectures. Detail Box 1.3 describes a popular architectural taxonomy from [Fly72]. The interconnection network that is utilized to join processors largely determines the architecture of a parallel system. If the parallel system is a multiprocessor, the interconnection network is also utilized to join processors and shared memory modules, as depicted in Figure 1.8. The interconnection networks may be designed to allow either synchronous or asynchronous communication. Data and messages between the

---

[3]September 9, 1999 can be represented as 9999. This number has been used to create an exception by some programmers in some applications therefore creating a dilemma when clocks hit this date unless the problem was identified and addressed prior. Fortunately, this problem was generally identified in the Y2K certification process at most locations.

processors and memory modules must be routed. Some interconnection networks support distributed routing control, while others employ centralized routing control. In addition, the basic topology of the interconnection network may be static or dynamic. Dynamic topologies allow the interconnection network to be reconfigured during operation to allow various connections through the use of switches. When an inter-connection network can achieve every possible connection, it is referred to as having 100% permutation capability. We now examine the various topologies of interconnection networks.

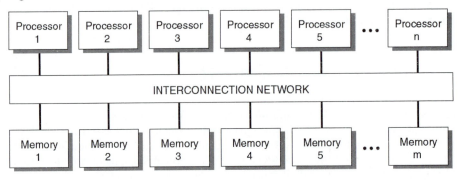

Figure 1.8 An Interconnection Network in a Multiprocessor.

Bus

The simplest interconnection network is a bus. A bus is static and does not require any type of routing. Every processor and memory module is connected to the bus, and all transactions and movement of data take place over this common shared bus, as depicted in Figure 1.9. The Sequent™ parallel computer utilizes a bus as an interconnection network. While this is a simpler interconnection topology, the bus limits intermodule bandwidth and creates a communication bottleneck.

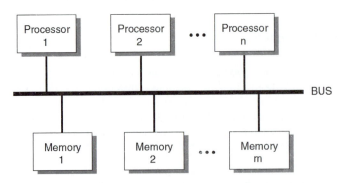

Figure 1.9 A Bus Used as an Interconnection Network.

DETAIL BOX 1.3
FLYNN'S ARCHITECTURAL TAXONOMY

Flynn segregated the various architectures based on how they handled the machine instructions and the data. The following are the four categories [Fly72].

SISD

The first category is for architectures with a single instruction stream and single data stream (SISD). Such computers follow the traditional von Neumann model. Examples include the traditional uniprocessor, such as simple PCs or a mainframe in the early 1980s.

SIMD

The second category is for architectures with a single instruction stream but a multiple data stream (SIMD). This architecture is useful for performing the same instruction on a large set of data. As an example, consider the operation on a matrix of data of multiplying row i by a value v. The single instruction is that of multiplication; however, this instruction is applied to every element of the row. One parallel architecture model known as a vector-array processor, such as the CRAY™ supercomputer, is a SIMD architecture. Vector machines arrange the multiple (typically a few thousand) processors in a grid. Vector-array processors specialize in computations on data types that are (surprise surprise!) vectors. Other examples of SIMD machines include the Illiac IV, and the Connection Machine CM-2. Unfortunately, the architecture on SIMD parallel systems evolved faster than operating system technology; thus, SIMD systems typically utilize a front-end computer that employs a conventional uniprocessor operating system for control. The SIMD computer is then treated as a device by the 'front-end' computer.

MISD

The third category is multiple instruction stream and single data stream (MISD). Flynn included this category for completeness, but no systems of this type exist.

MIMD

Finally, we have parallel computers with multiple instruction stream, multiple data stream (MIMD) architectures. Both distributed and parallel systems may be classified as MIMD architectures, but we only focus on parallel machines in this section. MIMD architectures utilize multiple processor fetching, and instructions tend to be executed asynchronously. Examples of MIMD architectures include the Sequent, hypercubes, and transputers.

Crossbar Interconnection Network

One of the simplest interconnection networks that allows dynamic configuration is the crossbar network. A crossbar network of size $n*n$ connects n memory modules with n processors. This network requires $O(n^2)$ switches, as depicted in Figure 1.10. The large number of switches means that this is an expensive interconnection network to implement. This dynamic configuration has 100% permutation capability. Furthermore, as long as the

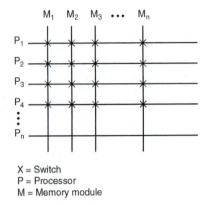

X = Switch
P = Processor
M = Memory module

Figure 1.10   A Crossbar Interconnection Network.

same exact crossbar switches are not being utilized, multiple processors can utilize the network at the same time.

Hypercube

A well known static interconnection network is the hypercube. The hypercube is defined in terms of its dimension; specifically, a k-cube is a network with 2^k switches. Since the number of switches is a power of two, the cubes are sometimes referred to as binary hypercubes. The switches are numbered 0 to 2^k-1, as depicted in Figure 1.11. Two switches in the network are connected by a link if and only if the switch numbers in binary representation differ by exactly one bit. Thus, switch 0100 is connected by a link to switch 0110 but not to a switch numbered 0111. The benefit of this topology is that the distance between two switches is easy to calculate. In this topology, a single processing element is located at each switch.

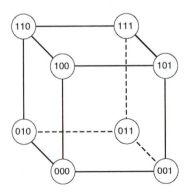

Figure 1.11   A Hypercube Interconnection Network of Order 3.

Shuffle-Exchange Interconnection Network

One of the most dynamic interconnection networks is the shuffle-exchange network. The switches allow dynamic reconfiguration and have four modes of operation, as depicted in Figure 1.12. The control bits determine the exact mode of operation for the switch box. This type of interconnection network obtained its name from behavior that resembles shuffling a deck of cards. Specifically, a perfect shuffle is achieved if the higher destinations are perfectly interleaved with the lower destinations, as depicted in Figure 1.13. A multistage shuffle-exchange interconnection network is depicted in Figure 1.14. This example utilizes eight inputs. The routing on this network is simple since any source can locate the destination by its address. Specifically, the highest-order bit determines action to take at the first stage of the network, the second highest order bit for the second stage, and so on. A 1 bit indicates that the action is to take the bottom output, and a 0 bit indicates that the top input should be taken. Other interconnection networks based on the shuffle-exchange network include the Benes, Banyan, Omega, and Theta interconnection networks.

1.4.2 Parallel Software Paradigms

There are three basic categories on which a parallel system may divide the work among its many processors. This division may be accomplished by the programmer, or the system, or it may be dictated by the architecture.

1. *Replicated code, Partitioned data.* In this scenario, each processor is given the same exact task to accomplish but each is working on a different set of data. For example, each processor may be given a sort routine but one processor may have to sort all the IEEE journals by title and date and another processor may have to sort all the ACM journals by title and date.

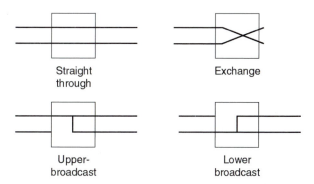

Figure 1.12 A 2x2 Switch Box in a Shuffle-Exchange Interconnection Network.

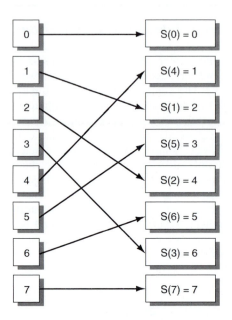

Figure 1.13 A Perfect Shuffle.

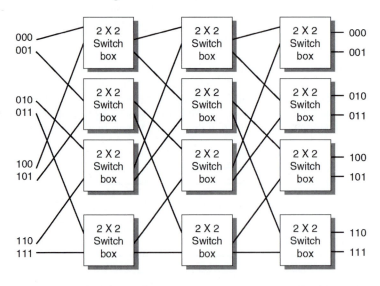

Figure 1.14 A Multistage Shuffle-Exchange Interconnection Network.

2. *Assembly line*. In this scenario, each server is given a task that builds upon the task completed by the previous processor, much like an assembly line. The task is not completed until the final processor completes its job. This

approach is modeled after the same observation that Henry Ford made when manufacturing automobiles. The total function is divided into distinct processing phases, and each processor is given its own phase to complete and pass on to the next processor.

3. *Tree structured.* This scenario is similar to the top-down design approach used in writing algorithms. The first processors have a task to complete. This task may consist of several subtasks. These subtasks are then passed on to other processors to complete, who in turn pass part of the task on to other processors, and so on.

1.5 SAMPLE DISTRIBUTED APPLICATION

A distributed system frequently has components that are not only the once traditional centralized machines but also has real-time components as well as parallel components. Figure 1.15 depicts such a system in the telecommunications application domain. While this is not representative of any specific system architecture necessarily in production by any given company, it is representative of what one may typically find in such a system. We now examine each of its components.

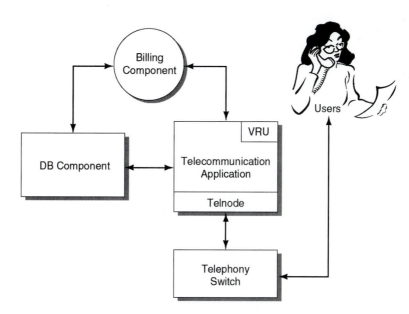

Figure 1.15 Distributed System Example.

The users represent the multiple application users desiring access to the telecommunications system. When they dial in, they access the telephony application through the telephony switch that receives the calls based on what numbers the users dialed on their telephone. The user expects prompt continual service, thereby making this distributed system a distributed real-time system with harsh time constraints. While one may think the real-time constraints are placed on the system strictly for the purpose of customer satisfaction, one must keep in mind that telephony applications connect customers to 911 as well as to their doctors' office, poison control centers, and other locations that make the real-time constraints potentially life critical.

The telephony switch in this application is capable of handling multiple concurrent calls. It is a parallel hardware component containing many incoming and outgoing telephone lines. The switch performs concurrent operations on the numerous concurrent calls. Switches are expected to have less than one-minute downtime per year and therefore must be very tolerant of faults and have built-in redundancy. Typically, a switch is an example of an embedded real-time component.

A telnode is a generic term for a computer with telephony boards, such as a fax board enabling the computer to accept faxes or a conference board enabling the computer to handle conference calls. A telnode only runs telecommunication-based applications. In a commercial atmosphere, there would be a group of telnodes that run the application software. These telnodes may be organized in a fully distributed manner as a distributed subsystem of the telecommunication system. It is also common that this component may be a parallel component, primarily for the sake of redundancy and fault tolerance, since telecommunication applications are not tolerant of downtime (neither are customers!). Any of the software paradigms described in Section 1.4.2 may be employed for this component of the application. The least popular paradigm for telnodes is the replicated code, partitioned data since this paradigm would require each telnode to have full replication of all hardware boards, thereby substantially increasing the hardware cost of the system.

The telnode component typically functions as or interacts with a voice response unit (VRU), which plays prerecorded messages to the user based on what is happening with the user's telephone call. An example of a prerecorded message would be, "I'm sorry. The call cannot be completed as dialed. Please hang up and try the number again." The VRU frequently provides interactive voice response (IVR) capabilities. An example building on the previous would be, "If you would like operator assistance, please press '0' now." Upon the user entering the 0, the caller would be transferred to a live operator. IVR is an example of a reactive real-time component.

The billing component is a real-time application that keeps track of the cost incurred by the actions of the user. In particular, the billing component in this scenario is involved in the continual checking of how much money the customer spent and comparing that to the amount allowed to be spent. For example, if the product is a prepaid card, the application must ensure that the user does not use more resources than are allowed by the amount on the prepaid card. This involves interaction with the database component. If this component is not accurate, the telecommunications company hosting the user loses money.

The database component can be involved in many aspects of the application. Typically, the hosting telecommunications company serves a large number of customers, thereby requiring the database to be fully distributed to spread out the load and minimize the wait for the user. In addition, components within the database component may be implemented on parallel architectures to increase speed. This component must deal with all of the issues discussed in several chapters of this book, including distributed memory as presented in Chapter 4, concurrency control as presented in Chapter 5, distributed files as presented in Chapter 8, as well as transaction management as presented in Chapter 9.

While there are many more details that could be communicated, it is apparent that even with the simplified view of a telecommunications application, this application is required to have components of all types of systems, including realtime and parallel. While the telecommunication industry may be one of the more obvious application domains for complex distributed applications, such systems exist and are being created in every aspect of the computer industry.

 1.6 SUMMARY

Distributed systems are becoming increasingly dominant within the computer industry and everyday life. Distributed systems often include real-time and parallel components. Each component presents the operating system with its own set of challenges and problems to handle and overcome. Both parallel and distributed systems employ multiple processors. A parallel system involves tightly coupled homogeneous components as compared to the vast array of different components present in a common distributed system. A network system does not attempt to hide the fact that multiple remote resources are being utilized. Thus, while a distributed system may employ a remote processor without the user's knowledge, a user would have to command all remote actions when utilizing a network operating system. Real-time systems have inherent strict time constraints. These time constraints in themselves are challenging and become even more so when dealing with network delays in distributed real-time systems.

In this book, the fundamental topics of distributed computing are presented in Part 1. Part 1 contains some material occasionally present in introductory courses but relevant and necessary when studying distributed systems. The material in Part 2 builds upon the topics of Part 1, expands these fundamental issues, and focuses on the more in-depth, advanced, and sometimes more difficult to understand issues particular to distributed systems. The Windows 2000 case study in Chapter 12 presents a comprehensive look into a single system attempting to solve many of the issues presented to a distributed operating system. Through all of this, it is hoped that you will be able to see the forest through the trees and venture into the world of distributed computing, creating and seeing a cohesive system despite all of its individual, dissimilar components.

1.7 REFERENCES FOR FURTHER STUDY

The following references can provide more general information on distributed, real-time, and parallel systems as well as networks and parallel computers: [Akl97, Ber92, Bla96, DDK94, Hal96, Hun95, Kop97, Kri89, Lap92, Sin97, SSF97, Sta97, Ste94, Tan95, and

Tan96]. Some appropriate traditional research papers concerning information in this chapter include [BCEF94, BrJo94 (a collection of papers), CaMu94 (a collection of papers), Mul93a (a collection of papers), SHFECB93, and Son95 (a collection of papers)].

We now list some great starter points for sources on the Internet concerning advanced operating systems useful for information on topics presented in this chapter and through-out this book. The IEEE Computer Society's Technical Committee on Real-Time Systems home page contains extensive list of links on real-time at http://cs-www.bu.edu/pub/ieee-rt/Home.html. A collection of links for papers of very large scale integration (VLSI) and parallel architectures can be found at http://rtlab.kaist.ac.kr:80/ ~yunju/wavelet-papers.html. The Internet Parallel Computing Archive can be found at http://www.hensa.ac.uk/parallel/. The University of Pennsylvania Distributed Systems Technical Document and Research Library contains numerous research papers and can be found at http://www.cis.upenn.edu/ ~dsl/library.html. A collection of computer science bibliographies including over 13,000 entries on operating systems, 32,000 entries on parallel processing, 28,000 entries in distributed computing, and over 22,000 links to technical reports, can be found at http://liinwww.ira.uka.de/bibliography/index.html. The Network CS Technical Report Library provides extensive links to computer science technical reports from research labs and universities around the world at http://www.ncstrl.org. The WWW Virtual Library has a computing category that is also helpful at http://src.doc.ic.ac.uk/bySubject/ Computing/overview.html. The Virtual Entity of Relevant Acronyms (VERA) location is at http://userpage.fu-berlin.de/~oheiabbd/veramain-e.cgi. IEEE's general home page at http://www.computer.org/ and Association for Computing Machinery's (ACM) home page at http://www.acm.org/ provide helpful search engines for their perspective related publications and even include some abstracts. The Computer Online Research Repository (CORR) can be found at http://www.acm.org/corr/. Proceedings from the Special Interest Group in Operating Systems (SIGOPS) can be found in the ACM's digital library at http://www.acm.org/pubs/contents/proceedings/ops/.

EXERCISES

1.1   Why is it necessary for today's computer scientists to understand advanced operating system concepts?

1.2   What are the primary differences between a network operating system and a distributed operating system?

1.3   What LAN and WAN protocols are best suited for real-time computing?

1.4   Why are wireless LANs gaining popularity?

1.5   Why is it advantageous to have distributed operating systems performing in the peer-to-peer ISO/OSI layers?

1.6   What are the advantages of using the peer-to-peer distributed computing model over the client/server model?

1.7 For each of the seven distributed transparencies presented in this chapter, name and describe an application that would benefit from its support in a distributed system.

1.8 Traceroute is a utility that prints out the exact route taken on a network from a source to a destination. Perform a traceroute from your location or from one of the Web-based traceroute gateways such as Yahoo's at http://net.yahoo.com/cgi-bin/trace.sh, a multiple traceroute from http://www.tracert.com/, or any of those found when performing an Internet search on the word *traceroute*. Perform and record the results of a traceroute during three separate times of the day for one week straight from your university (or home Internet site) to five separate destinations of your choice. You should use the same set of source and destination combinations for each series of traceroutes.

   a. Do you get the same results each time?

   b. Are the routes always minimal? Why or why not?

   c. What does this mean for distributed real-time applications, assuming optimal routing?

1.9 Describe an example for each of the following.

   a. Soft real-time system

   b. Firm real-time system

   c. Hard real-time system

   d. Reactive real-time system

   e. Embedded real-time system

1.10 Describe an example for each of the following. (Do not use the same examples provided in this book.)

   a. Synchronous event

   b. Asynchronous but not isochronous event

   c. Isochronous event

1.11 Describe the difference between a multicomputer and a multiprocessor.

1.12 For each of the following, list a potential advantage and disadvantage of its use in a parallel architecture for interconnection.

   a. Bus

   b. Crossbar interconnection network

   c. Hypercube

   d. Shuffle-exchange interconnection network

1.13 Describe a potential application for each of the following parallel software paradigms.

   a. Replicated code, partitioned data

   b. Assembly line

   c. Tree structure

CHAPTER 2

The Kernel

One of the most influential portions of an operating system is the kernel. Actually, the kernel is the head cook of the computer and ensures that all of the cooks don't spoil the broth! The **kernel** is the privileged portion of the operating system that, unlike other programs, can execute with complete access privileges for all resources on all systems under its complete control (distributed system kernels generally do not have control over every participant and in fact may only control the local system). The kernel controls process management, including process migration (Section 2.3), process scheduling (Section 2.4), the memory management, and the address space (the latter two are discussed in Chapter 4). These functions operate in a protected and separate address space to prevent interference and manipulation, whether accidental or malicious, by applications. We begin by examining the two basic kernel types in Section 2.1. Section 2.2 introduces the concepts involved with processes, while the various tasks and solutions performed by the kernel are discussed in Sections 2.3 and 2.4.

2.1 KERNEL TYPES

Kernel designs fall into two general categories based on the size of the kernel and what it includes. The first category is monolithic kernels as used by UNIX™, OS/360™, and VMS™. As the name implies, monolithic systems have large kernels that include most operating system services, including process, memory, file, name, and device management as well as interprocess communication. In other words, the monolithic kernel is the complete operating system. System-supplied shared memory or message-based communication, as discussed in Chapters 4 and 5, respectively, is generally utilized for communication among processes to implement their functionality. There are no protection boundaries within the kernel. The lack of security along with the size and complexity of monolithic kernels are generally to blame for their earned reputation for being difficult to debug, validate, and, of course, modify. Not only are monolithic kernels difficult to debug, but debugging support is virtually nonexistent. In distributed environments, not all operating system functions are necessary in every copy or every location participating in the distributed environment, thereby making the proximity of the hardware to the kernel an issue for distributed systems. Thus, distributed environments prefer the second type of kernel, a layered kernel.

Layered kernels focus on divisible modular designs. One of the most popular types of layered kernel is the microkernel. Microkernels aim to keep the kernel as small as possible. Distributed real-time systems generally employ microkernels; in fact, for embedded real-time systems, the microkernel is the entire operating system. These types of kernels only provide minimal services, such as interprocess communication and limited device, process, thread, and memory management. All other services are implemented above the kernel as user-space operating system services. These services rely on (hopefully!) efficient interprocess communication mechanisms. Microkernels tend to be modular and are generally easy to design, implement, install, extend and reconfigure. Part of the modular design includes keeping all architecture-dependent portions in one location, as depicted in Figure 2.1. This assists in enhancing portability. This also makes microkernels attractive to distributed systems such as Chorus (the base technology for JavaOS™), described in Chapter 6, Mach, described in Chapter 7, and Windows NT™, as described in the case study on Windows 2000 (built on NT technology) in Chapter 12.

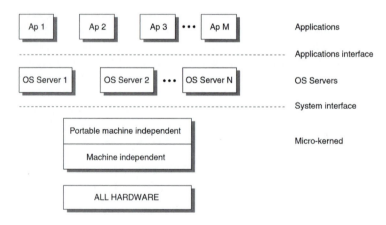

Figure 2.1 Microkernel Design.

2.2 PROCESSES AND THREADS

A program in execution is frequently referred to by its abstraction, the **process**. The concrete counterpart of a process is the systems view is commonly referred to as a **job**. The idea of a process originated in the days of centralized systems; but this concept has become more difficult to define in advanced systems. The complication arises from the fact that in a distributed or parallel environment, a single process may utilize several threads of control to take advantage of the expanded resources available. Regardless of what environment one is operating in or what application one is running, everything boils down to running processes. These processes may need to perform several computations. Some environments, particularly distributed and parallel environments, allow each individual computation to run as an independent **thread** of execution representing a path through the program allowing the program, to take advantage of the multiple processors available. When an operating system allows more than one thread of execution, it is referred to as multithreaded. Section 2.2.1 introduces multithreaded processes. Organization of multiple threads is discussed in Section 2.2.2, while Section 2.2.3 discusses the various types of support for multithreaded processes. Detail Box 2.1 presents the POSIX language support for multithreaded programming most commonly utilized by C and C++, while Detail Box 2.2 presents Java™ support for multithreaded programming. In addition, the surgical scheduling program in the appendix is programmed to operate in a multithreaded environment.

2.2.1 Introduction to Multithreaded Processes

In a traditional operating system, each process runs independently utilizing a single **address space** and single thread of control for each process. In distributed and parallel environments, processes are allowed to run multiple threads of execution. These threads are sometimes referred to as lightweight processes. Each thread has its own program counter and stack but shares the address space as well as global variables with its sibling threads, as depicted in Figure 2.2. In all nonparallel environments and in parallel environments that do not implement shared memory, threads will also share the same CPU. There is no protection barrier in the shared address space from other threads belonging to the same parent process (if the general concept of threads is appealing but the loss of protection of memory space is not acceptable, it might be best to utilize true lightweight processes instead of threads). Each thread of execution is allowed to run quasi-parallel and thus increase throughput by taking advantage of the extra resources available. Just like processes, a thread may spawn a child thread. Since the creation and destruction of threads may be time consuming, many applications create a thread pool and reuse threads when creating new threads or child threads. We now examine the various methods for organizing multithreaded processes.

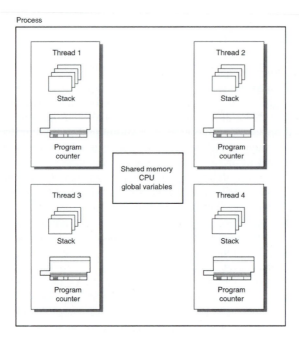

Figure 2.2   A Multithreaded Process.

2.2.2 Multithreaded Process Paradigms

There are three common paradigms to utilize for structuring threads belonging to the same parent process, as depicted in Figure 2.3.

1. *Specialist Paradigm.* In the specialist paradigm, all threads are equal but may implement their own specialized service for the parent process; in other words, all threads can be but are not required to perform a unique specialized service. Requests for service for each thread originates directly from the parent process.

2. *Client/Server Paradigm.* In the client/server paradigm, the client receives all requests from the parent process or thread and then passes the request to an appropriate server thread. This structure is based on the client/server paradigm for distributed processes.

3. *Assembly Line Paradigm.* In the assembly line paradigm, the output of one thread process is the input to the next thread process much like an assembly line. The input to the initial thread is the input to the process while the output of the final thread is the output of the process. This structure is based on the assembly line parallel software paradigm.

A. Specialist Paradigm

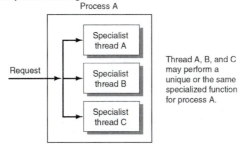

Thread A, B, and C may perform a unique or the same specialized function for process A.

B. Client/Server Paradigm

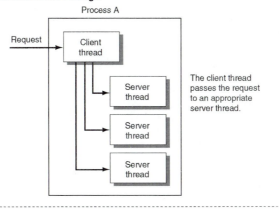

The client thread passes the request to an appropriate server thread.

C. Assembly Line Paradigm

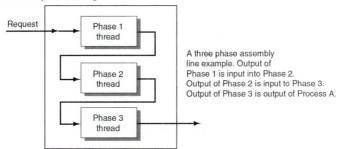

A three phase assembly line example. Output of Phase 1 is input into Phase 2. Output of Phase 2 is input to Phase 3. Output of Phase 3 is output of Process A.

Figure 2.3 Multithreaded Process Paradigms.

DETAIL BOX 2.1
POSIX SUPPORT FOR MULTITHREADED PROGRAMMING

The IEEE Society formed a special task force in the 1980s called POSIX to form a set of standards for operating system interfacing. In particular, the POSIX.1c standard specifies the multithreaded programming interface. While most people view the POSIX standard as being UNIX oriented, there are many non-UNIX, POSIX-compliant operating systems, including IBM's OS/2, Microsoft's Windows-NT, and DEC's (Digital Equipment Corporation) VMS. Threads are an optional feature in POSIX that are almost always found in UNIX and its variations but were traditionally less common in other environments. As a standard, the use of its threads should enable greater portability to all applications employing the standard.

All programs utilizing POSIX threads must include the library pthread.h. It is common when programming multithreaded code to use basic template programs and modify them to suite your needs. In addition, most multithreaded programs require concurrency control, which is the subject of Chapter 5. While entire books have been written on the subject of thread programming and too much detail would be far beyond the scope of this book, we discuss four primary functions necessary for thread management and utilization. Section 2.6 presents some references for multithreaded programming. An example of a multithreaded application, a surgical scheduling program, utilizes multithreading and is written in C can be found in the Appendix.

As is standard, a return value of '0' indicates a successful function call.

```
int pthread_create(pthread_t* tid,
    const pthread_attr_t *attr,
    void* ((*start)(void*), void* arg));
```

The `tid` argument contains the process id of the created thread. If the attribute argument, `attr`, is null, the thread will have the default attributes. The final argument is the name of the function with which that the thread will begin its execution.

```
int pthread_exit (void* status);
```

The exit function is used to terminate a detached thread. If a thread is not detached, it is *joinable*. Such threads are terminated with a function call to `pthread_detach` with the same arguments. The argument status is the address of the variable containing the exit status code of the terminating thread that must persist after the thread exits; thus, it cannot be a variable local to the thread.

```
int pthread_join (pthread_t tid, void** statusp);
```

The function `pthread_join` waits for `pthread_t` to exit and then stores its completition status in the location pointed to by `statusp`.

```
int pthread_self
```

This function returns the process ID for a given thread. NOTE: This is also returned in `pthread_create`.

DETAIL BOX 2.2
JAVA SUPPORT FOR MULTITHREADED PROGRAMMING

Java provides extensive support for threads, which are considered an important integral part of the language. Once an object is created as a thread, it is pretty much treated like any other object. There are two classes supporting thread utilization: `Thread` and `ThreadGroup`. `Thread` is utilized for creating independent threads while `ThreadGroup` is utilized for creating a group of threads. Operations may be performed on this group as a whole. System-level programs most commonly utilize `ThreadGroup`.

The Java class `Thread` contains seven constructors.

```
public Thread();
public Thread(Runnable target);
public Thread(ThreadGroup group, Runable target);
public Thread(String name);
public Thread(threadGroup group, String name);
public Thread(Runable target, String name);
public Thread(ThreadGroup group, Runnable target,
        String name);
```

No matter how you instantiate a thread, it must be passed a runable object. In Java, a runnable object is an object that defines a `run()` method. If you do not instantiate the thread with a runable object, you must subclass your thread and have it define its own run() method.

Some of the other methods contained in the `Thread` class include the following.

```
public final void join()throws InterruptedException;
public synchronized void start() throws
        IllegalThreadState Exception;
        //Starts a Thread
public final void stop();
        //Stops a thread
public final void suspend();
        //Suspends a thread
public final void resume();
        //Resumes a suspended thread
```

2.2.3 Multithreaded Support

The kernel may support threads or a system may provide user-level support for threads. When the kernel supports threads, the kernel maintains a thread-status information table within the protected memory space of the kernel. This fixed-size status table maintains the state of all threads. It has one entry per thread and has fields for the thread's state, priority, register values, and other pertinent information. Whenever a thread blocks, the kernel utilizes a single-level scheduler to select another thread to run. This new thread may be related to the original thread or may be unrelated and therefore come from a different process.

When threads are implemented in the userspace, they run on top of the runtime environment that manages the threads. Thus, the runtime system maintains the status information table. The complete functionality of the threads is controlled by the runtime environment, including scheduling, which allows users to have control over the specifics such as the selection of what thread to execute. User-level support makes it possible to support multithreaded programs even if the underlying operating system does not support multiple threads of execution.

We now compare the two implementations of threads. The location of the status table influences the flexibility and scalability of thread utilization. Since the kernel-level thread implementation has a fixed-size status table, it is less flexible and, more important, less scalable. Scheduling is another important issue. Kernel-level thread support forces the programmer to use the kernel implemented. In contrast, if threads are implemented above the kernel at the user level, a programmer may be able to control if a sibling thread or a thread from another processes is selected to execute. If speed is important, then one must consider that a kernel-level thread context switch implies the use of a (slow) kernel trap.

With all of these issues in mind, one might be led to believe that user-level threads could do no wrong; however, they too have some drawbacks. In particular, any process above the kernel, including a user-level thread support process, does not have the same control as the kernel. Unlike a kernel implementation, if one of the threads gets control of the CPU, the user-level implementation cannot force the thread to relinquish its position to allow other threads to run. Even if a protocol is established for threads to request a time quantum to execute, a user-level implementation cannot enforce the protocol the same way as the kernel. Finally, the user-level implementation must be aware that if any thread implements a command that causes the thread to be blocked by the kernel, the entire process (i.e., the user-level thread implementation process) is blocked. One work-around is to use a jacket routine that catches each system call executed by a thread. These jacket routines first check to ensure that the executing thread will not block the user-level thread management process before passing it on to the system. One must keep in mind, however, that any seemingly innocent command could cause a page fault and thus cause the entire thread package to block. The case study in Chapter 13 describes how OSF's DCE™ (Open Software Foundation's Distributed Computing Environment) implements user-level threads. DCE is also able to take advantage of a kernel-level thread implementation if it is running on top of a system with kernel-level support. Scheduling issues are further discussed in Section 2.4.

2.3 PROCESS MANAGEMENT

Process management is employed to control a process and all its components. Process management refers to the management of a process and all related components, which includes the following.

- ◆ Address space contents
- ◆ Registers
- ◆ Program counter
- ◆ Stack pointer
- ◆ State of system call(s)

◆ All related threads of execution

◆ All files from the process and their state (open or closed)

When a process gives up control of a processor, either voluntarily or forcefully, the entire state must be switched out and saved. The state of a process involves information as to the current status of all related components of the process (as in the preceding list). If a process is only going to be blocked for a short time, this may be more overhead than it is worth. In this situation, a process may be put into a busy spin or tight loop that is executed while the process is waiting for whatever blocked it. Unfortunately, it is difficult for the system to determine how long a process will be blocked; however, there are heuristics available. Some of the choices include never spin or always spin. If you never spin, the system may implement a context switch that consumes more processing time than the length of time necessary for the block. If you always spin and the process ends up being blocked for an extended period of time, a lot of processor time is wasted. This control may be utilized by the system or by a parent process. Process management includes the following responsibilities.

◆ Creating a process

◆ Identifying the type of process (discussed in Section 2.3.1)

◆ Process migration (changing the location of a process's execution to a different processor or host as discussed in Section 2.3.2)

◆ Scheduling (when a process will run as discussed in Section 2.4)

◆ Querying a process about its status

◆ Process status reporting (e.g., I just crashed or I just exited)

As depicted in Figure 2.4, a process may be in one of three states: blocked, running, or waiting (runable but not currently executing). A process may be blocked because it is waiting for input, access to a resource, or to be synchronized with a cooperative process. A process may be waiting because it is a new process, it just became unblocked, or it utilized the maximum time slice and had to be switched out. Detail Box 2.3 describes the process management system in Amoeba. Finally, more in-depth information on distributed process management, including distributed and real-time process scheduling, is contained in Chapter 7.

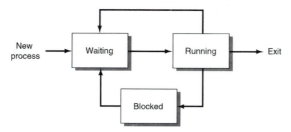

Figure 2.4 Process States.

DETAIL BOX 2.3
AMOEBA PROCESS MANAGEMENT

Amoeba is a distributed object-based operating system developed at Vrije Universiteit in The Netherlands by Andrew Tanenbaum and his students. The Amoeba microkernel and its process management is described in [MVTVV90, TaAn90, and Tan95]. Since Amoeba is object based, a process in Amoeba is an object. A key feature to assisting in process management is the *process descriptor*. A process descriptor has the following fields.

1.   A field to define what CPU architecture for which the executable is prepared

2.   A field to communicate exit status to the owner

3.   A platform-dependent thread descriptor including (at least) a program counter and a stack pointer

   There are three significant functions related to process management. The first function is that of exec. This function creates a new process, including the process descriptor, through a remote procedure call (see Chapter 3) to the processor who is requesting the process to be executed. The second function is getload. This returns information to assist in migration by locating a processor able to execute the process. In particular, it returns information on the CPU speed as well as the current load and free memory space available. The final function is that of stun. Stun can operate in emergency and normal mode and is utilized to suspend a process or stun it. With a normal stun message, the process must finish its work immediately and reply. An emergency stun stops processes immediately and does not wait for a reply. If the stunned process had any child processes, they are left hanging as orphans.

2.3.1 Types of Processes

In the view of schedulers, there are two general categories of processes in distributed and parallel environments. The first category involves **indivisible processes**. In this category, all processes are independent, indivisible, and may be of different sizes. For these processes, it is not possible to divide the processing load, and the entire process must be assigned to a single processor. These processes are not able to take advantage of the additional resources available in a distributed and parallel environment.

   The second category involves **divisible processes**. In this category, a process may be subdivided into smaller subprocesses or tasks (which we know as threads) based on the characteristic of the algorithm. The entire job is complete only when all tasks are complete. Each task is treated as an independent process. These related tasks of a given process can be represented as a graph whose vertices are the tasks and whose edges represent the interaction of the processes. This graph is commonly known as a **task interaction graph (TIG)**. The edges of the graph may be directed (have arrows) if the processes have a precedence relationship; that is, some processes must complete prior to other processes being able to execute. Furthermore, the relationship of this group of processes may require that all run concurrently. Detail Box 2.4 presents an example of a divisible process and the use of a TIG.

2.3.2 Load Distribution and Process Migration

The primary goal of load distribution is to obtain results and utilize resources efficiently. The goal may be stated in terms of **load balancing**, which strives for an equal load throughout the system, or **load sharing**, which only strives to assist overloaded resources. There are several issues involved in the distribution of a processing load that involves utilizing processors at remote locations. Load distribution is accomplished through **process migration**, the relocation of a process and all related state information to another processor. If the process is indivisible, then the entire process may be migrated to another location; however, if a process is divisible, then only portions may be migrated. Due to a usual dependence on changing shared data in a divisible process, one must be particularly careful if only portions of a divisible process are distributed to remote locations. Of course, once a process is migrated it is then scheduled locally.

There are two components to a load-distributing algorithm that may or may not be implemented together. All components may be solved with centralized algorithms or distributed algorithms. The first is the *information-gathering* component and the second is the *process selection* component. The information-gathering component is responsible for deciding what information to gather, gathering the information, and selecting a suitable migration partner. The most successful information-gathering algorithms collect information on demand or when a given location changes its status by a predetermined amount (my CPU is now down 10%) or changes load **status states**. Depending on the exact algorithm, a system may have two or three load status states. The two state algorithms consider a location either overloaded or underloaded. The three state algorithms have an additional suitably loaded state.

The identification of available resources can be a complex task. Identification algorithms may also be centralized or distributed. A centralized algorithm involves a single processor (or location) to be responsible for all information on all the systems regarding their current load and available resources. If a process wishes to migrate, it can then contact this centralized authority for information on the entire system. This centralized authority must operate efficiently and be kept up to date; thus, the most effective solutions maintain minimal information to streamline the entire operation. The following is a list of questions that identification algorithms must answer.

♦ Are all processes considered equal or do some processes have higher priority?

♦ Do resources identify themselves as idle or is availability determined by identifying a CPU being idle for x microseconds?

♦ How do we know how long a resource will be idle? In a distributed system, did the user of the system with an idle CPU go for a coffee break or go home? What happens when a user returns?

♦ If we do not seek or find idle processors, how do we estimate the load of a particular location? Is this estimate statically or dynamically calculated?

♦ Will the migration improve the local performance of other processes? Will it negatively affect the remote location?

♦ Is the regular user of the remote resource able to kill migrated processes? Is the regular user able to force a process to migrate to another location?

◆ What is the risk of system failure during process migration? How expensive is it to defend against system failure during process migration?

◆ Is participation in load distribution voluntary or mandatory?

DETAIL BOX 2.4
A DIVISIBLE PROCESS AND ITS TIG

Let us look at a common everyday process: making and presenting dinner. This may be divided into tasks as follows.

    T1. Prepare main course.
    T2. Prepare side dishes.
    T3. Prepare dessert.
    T4. Set table.
    T5. Serve meal.
    T6. Serve dessert.

This process has a precedence relationship, as depicted in the TIG in Figure 2.5.

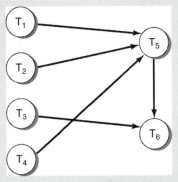

Figure 2.5 TIG Revealing Precedence Relationships.

As depicted and expected, the food must be prepared prior to its being served to the table. Likewise, the table must be set before one can serve the meal. Finally, it is tradition to serve the meal prior to serving dessert.

A distributed solution generally involves broadcasting the needs or the availability of resources. Thus, a location may send out a message such as, "I have a free CPU. Let me know if you need it." To spare the system from the constant bombardment of broadcast messages, a location could broadcast "I need another processor. Can you help me?" and those with available resources can exclusively contact the location in need of assistance. With this information, a migration partner is then selected.

Now that we have located a migration partner, we must decide which process to migrate; thus, as previously mentioned, the second component is the *process selection* component. This component must consider several issues, including the amount of overhead necessary to transfer a particular process, the dependence of a given process on a given computer architecture, and the expected length of execution of a given process. If the overhead is high and the process will not execute long, that process would not be a good migration choice. Alternatively, if a process is newly created (maybe the process that caused the system to seek a migration partner) it can be migrated and execute from start to finish at the remote location. Complete execution at the migration site reduces overhead that would accompany a process that was preempted to be migrated. The following is a partial list of points to consider regarding the overhead of migrating a process.

♦ What is the initial communication delay for migrating a process?

♦ What is the final communication delay for returning process results to the home location?

♦ What is the communication cost for an intermediate communication between separate sub-divided parts of a process if all parts were not migrated to the same location?

♦ Is the total turn-around time better than if I do not migrate the process?

♦ What is the processing power of each processor?

♦ How do we maintain consistency of shared changeable data between separate sub-divided parts of the process if all parts were not migrated to the same location?

♦ How do we transfer the virtual memory with the migrating process (discussed in Chapter 4)?

♦ How do we accommodate the differences if heterogeniality exists in the system?

An additional issue in process migration involves the complexities of operating in a heterogeneous environment. Heterogeniality includes the utilization of different types of computers. This implies that migration must be able to handle different processors with their various speeds, software configurations, and, even more difficult, data representations. Different data representation means that migrating a process may also involve data translation. Maguire and Smith [MaSm88] presented a proposal to use an *external data representation* (EDR). This common representation could be utilized by all participating members in the distributed system and reduce the amount of translation required. Figure 2.6 shows that with only 5 different types of computers, there are 20 different translations that can occur. As displayed in Figure 2.7, with a data translator to common external data representation, there are only 10 translations. This greatly reduces the amount of software required to implement cross-platform process migration. One of the most important issues that the translator must handle includes the representation of numbers since different systems use different representations for the mantissa, exponent, and negative numbers (zero representation).

One final question remains: When do we utilize the centralized algorithms and when do we utilize the distributed algorithms? In a parallel system or a distributed system utilizing a pool of processors and remote terminals, knowledge of the entire system is easy to obtain; therefore, a centralized algorithm is generally employed. Otherwise, the distributed solutions work best.

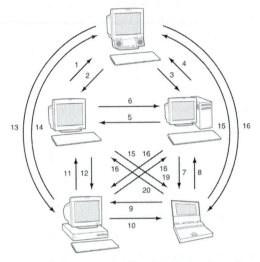

Figure 2.6   Data Translation without External Data Representation.

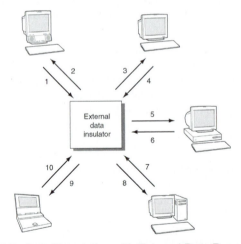

Figure 2.7   Data Translation with External Data Representation.

2.4 PROCESS SCHEDULING

In an environment with multiple processors (parallel or distributed), scheduling becomes an interesting task. In a real-time environment, time is not always a matter of convenience; rather, it could mean life or death. Thus, distributed real-time environments have to account for communication delays and be accountable to their time constraints. We look at two methods for identifying a process to be scheduled in Section 2.4.1. Section 2.4.2 examines the various organization methods for schedulers. A more in-depth look at distributed scheduler algorithms is presented in Chapter 7, with additional related information in Chapter 9.

2.4.1 Identifying Processes for Scheduling *(What to do next?)*

The simplest method for identifying schedulable tasks is that of a **polled loop**. In a polled-loop design, the scheduler has a complete list of everything that may need the system's services. As the name indicates, its overall design is that of a loop. This loop continuously asks each process if it needs the system. If the answer is yes, the request is met. If the answer is no, the loop continues on to the next process. Since this method is not reactive, its design is most popular for special purpose scheduling rather than for overall system scheduling. A special-purpose scheduler may control access to a network or other I/O device. Detail Box 2.5 depicts an example of using a polled loop for scheduling access to a network gateway.

As with centralized systems, advanced systems may be **interrupt** based. An interrupt is a simple signal to the system that some sort of service is required; thus, these interrupts are utilized as a means to identify schedulable processes. Unlike polled-loop systems, interrupts do not necessarily guarantee that you will have immediate access to your desired system service. Quite the contrary, the interrupt allows the process to be put into the appropriate scheduling queue depending on the priority of the process and the type of request (as communicated by the type of interrupt). In addition, there is a third concept of timed interrupts that involves the use of a timer. Each time a particular interrupt occurs, the timer is reset. If an interrupt does not occur but the timer expires, an interrupt is generated.

2.4.2 Scheduler Organization

There are two methods for organizing the overall function of the scheduler. With divisible processes with a precedence relationship, the scheduler generally is organized in a state-driven manner. The organization of the various states is dependent on the particular precedence relationship of the process and its components. If the precedence relationship is not observed, the end result may be incorrect and the data may be irrevocably corrupted. The existence of a precedence relationship in a group of processes may require that all run concurrently. If even one process is not scheduled at the same time, the entire job may take as much as twice as long to execute. Thus, the application programmer must have access to the scheduling algorithm to employ smart scheduling. Without this knowledge, the scheduler is blind. All related processes scheduled together is often referred to as **gang scheduling** [Ous82]. An example of the advantages of smart scheduling over blind scheduling is presented in Detail Box 2.6.

In a distributed system, if the load is divisible, the scheduler must be aware of all related costs. One of the most important related costs is the latency due to the time necessary for communications. This includes the time for sending the process and all its parts to the assigned processor. In a distributed system, there could be a significant time factor involved in transmitting the process information. In NUMA systems, the scheduler must also consider the communication cost for getting or moving the data if they are not at the same location that the process is assigned to execute.

State-driven schedulers are frequently implemented using co-routines. In particular, all aspects of the process for a specific state are scheduled. When a state is complete, the scheduler then schedules the appropriate processes for the next state. An example of a state driven scheduler is IBM's OS/2 Presentation Manager™. This program utilizes co-routines to schedule its processes and maintain the precedence relationship necessary to coordinate and schedule user's windows. The topic of precedence relationship is further addressed in Chapter 9.

If no precedence relationship exists, the scheduler organization reflects the same methods you studied for centralized operating systems. In particular, it may employ such algorithms as round-robin scheduling, shortest-job-first scheduling, or priority scheduling (including derivatives such as foregound/background and preemptive priority scheduling).

2.5 SUMMARY

The kernel is a very important part of an operating system. In this chapter, we have been introduced to some of the basic underlying concepts; many of these concepts are further expanded upon in Chapters 3 and 4. Parallel and distributed systems tend to be constructed as microkernels. This design is particularly appealing to distributed systems that require portability and flexibility. Real-time systems, which require efficiency, also utilize microkernels. The kernel is responsible for many things. In this chapter, we focused on the concepts of processes and threads, process management, and scheduling. Processes may be divisible and consist of many tasks and have several threads of execution. In a distributed system, the kernel not only has to determine where a process will execute but is also responsible for local scheduling. For the processes to communicate with the kernel and other processes, interprocess communication is employed. This topic is expanded upon in Chapter 3. The kernel is also responsible for memory management, which is the topic of Chapter 4.

DETAIL BOX 2.5
A SAMPLE POLLED LOOP ALGORITHM

Let's look at a simple example of a few computers connected to a gateway. The gateway utilizes the following polled-loop algorithm to identify which process/machine will be granted access to the gateway as depicted in Figure 2.8.

```
current_machine =0
Repeat
          If offer_service(machine[current_machine])
                                                    // if system needs access
          Then
            service(machine[current_machine]);
                                                    // gets access to gateway
                    Endif;
          current_machine=(current_machine +1)
                          mod total_number_of_machines;
Until (eternity)
```

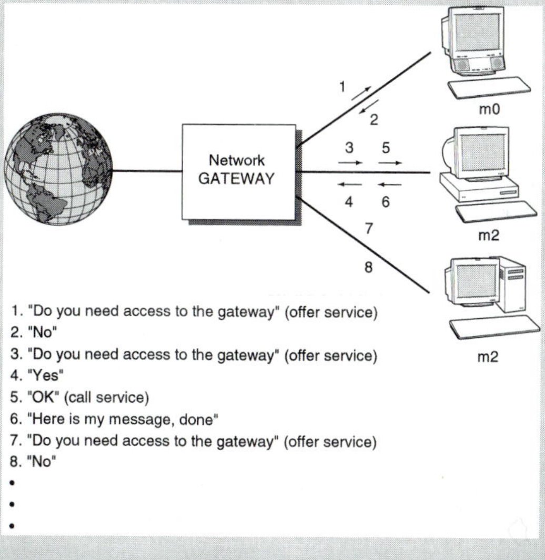

1. "Do you need access to the gateway" (offer service)
2. "No"
3. "Do you need access to the gateway" (offer service)
4. "Yes"
5. "OK" (call service)
6. "Here is my message, done"
7. "Do you need access to the gateway" (offer service)
8. "No"
•
•
•

Figure 2.8 Polled-Loop Example.

DETAIL BOX 2.6
CONCURRENT PROCESS SCHEDULING

Phase Process	0	1	2	3	4
1	W	R	R	R	E
2	W	R	R	R	E
3	W	R	R	R	E
4	W	R	R	R	E
5	W	R	R	R	E

Key: R = Running
     W = Waiting
     B = Blocked
     E = Exited

Processes 1 – 5 are related.

Figure 2.9   Smart Concurrent Scheduling.

Phase Process	0	1	2	3	4	4	4
1	W	R	B	B	R	R	E
2	W	R	B	B	R	R	E
3	W	R	B	B	R	R	E
4	W	W	R	B	R	R	E
5	W	W	W	R	R	R	E

Key: R = Running
     W = Waiting
     B = Blocked
     E = Exited

Processes 1 – 5 are related.

Figure 2.10   Blind Concurrent Scheduling.

The above example depicts the benefits of proper scheduling for related processes. In smart scheduling, knowledge of the processes is obtained from the application programmer, who has access to the scheduling routine. In blind scheduling, no information from the application programmer is provided to the scheduler.

Suppose we have five related processes. These processes all produce information that is then utilized by the same processes in the next stage. The information for one stage of execution is dependent on all processes finishing the previous stage. This type of relationship is referred to as a producer/consumer relationship. We assume there are three basic stages of execution for these five related processes. Figure 2.9 depicts the results of smart scheduling while Figure 2.10 depicts the results of blind scheduling. As you can see in Figure 2.10, processes 1 through 3 are forced to block and cannot proceed to their second and third stage of execution until processes 4 and 5 are also scheduled.

2.6 REFERENCES FOR FURTHER STUDY

The following references can provide more general information on kernels and their functionality along with their implementations [Akl97, BGMR96, Cha97, Cou98, Fla96, Kri89, KSS97, Lap97, LeBe96, and RoRo96]. Some appropriate traditional research papers concerning information in this chapter include [ABLL91, ArFi89, BrJo94, CaKu88, Cve87, EAL95, ELZ86, Esk89, Fer89, FeZh87, GeYa93, KrLi87, Kun91, LHWS96, Lo88, Mul93b, PTS88, SKS92, SWP90, TaKa94, VLL90, WaMo85, and Zay87].

   The following provide some great starting points for sources on the Internet concerning issues related to kernels. The Anderson, Bershad, Lazowski, and Levy paper [ABLL91] is available on the Internet at http://www.cs.berkeley.edu/~brewer/ cs262/Scheduler.pdf. Sun Microsystems™ maintains a Web page dedicated to threads at http://www.sun.com/ software/ Products/Developer-products/sig/threads/index.html. The Sun site also includes examples of programs utilizing threads. These example programs can be found at http://www.sun.com/ workshop/sig/threads/Berg-Lewis/examples.html. Another Web page on threads can be found at http://www.mit.edu:8001/people/proven/ pthreads.html. The Amoeba home page can be found at http://www.am.cs.vu.nl.

EXERCISES

2.1   Name and describe three primary advantages to designing an advanced system kernel utilizing a microkernel versus a monolithic kernel.

2.2   For each of the following thread structuring paradigms, list a possible application.

   a.   Specialist paradigm.
   b.   Client/Server paradigm.
   c.   Assembly line paradigm.

2.3   Name and describe the advantages of kernel-supported threads.

2.4   Name and describe the advantage of user-level supported threads.

2.5   When is it not advantagous to switch out a blocked process?

2.6   Suppose you have a process you wish to migrate. Your process has been compiled to execute in a UNIX environment. Describe the benefits and complications of migrating your new process to each of the following locations.

   LOCATION 1

   ◆   UNIX environment
   ◆   Communication cost 150 time units for each direction
   ◆   Processor current utilization 80%
   ◆   Processor speed of 100 MHz.

LOCATION 2

♦   UNIX environment
♦   Communication cost 250 time units for each direction
♦   Processor current utilization 60%
♦   Processor speed of 60 MHz

LOCATION 3

♦   Windows 98™ environment
♦   Communication cost 50 time units for each direction
♦   Processor current utilization 30%
♦   Processor speed of 200 MHz

LOCATION 4

♦   Windows-NT environment
♦   Communication cost 1000 time units for each direction
♦   Processor current utilization 20%
♦   Processor speed of 260 MHz

LOCATION 5

♦   Windows 3.1™ environment
♦   Communication cost 10 time units for each direction
♦   Processor current utilization 0%
♦   Processor speed of 60 MHz

2.7   Implement a program to make migration decisions. The program should accommodate the type
      of OS environment, communication cost, processor utilization, and processor speed. In addi-
      tion, the user should be able to enter the weight of importance for each of these factors. Based
      upon the user's requested weighting of importance (total weighting for all factors is 1.00), what
      location(s) are the best choices to migrate the process described in exercise 2.6. Your program
      should utilize the following formula:

```
Total_Weight =[ Env_WT * (1/0)] + [1-(Com_WT * Com_Cost)] +
        [1-(Util_Wt * Util)] +  [Speed_Wt * Speed]
```

For environmental weighting (1/0), if the environment matches, it is multiplied by 1. If the environment does not match, it is multiplied by 0.

Test the program with the five locations from exercise 2.6 and the following weightings and two
more of your choice.

WEIGHTING 1

♦   Environment .25

- ◆ Communication cost .25 (the lower the better)
- ◆ Processor current utilization .25 (the lower the better)
- ◆ Processor speed .25 (the higher the better)

WEIGHTING 2

- ◆ Environment .75
- ◆ Communication cost .25 (the lower the better)
- ◆ Processor current utilization 0 (the lower the better)
- ◆ Processor speed 0 (the higher the better)

WEIGHTING 3

- ◆ Environment .55
- ◆ Communication cost .15 (the lower the better)
- ◆ Processor current utilization .20 (the lower the better)
- ◆ Processor speed .10 (the higher the better)

WEIGHTING 4

- ◆ Environment .15
- ◆ Communication cost .55 (the lower the better)
- ◆ Processor current utilization .20 (the lower the better)
- ◆ Processor speed .10 (the higher the better)

2.8   Suppose a migration policy allows the owner of a resource to immediately (without warning) kill any process executing on the owner's resources (such as a user returning from a coffee break). What are some possible affects on each of the following?

1. The progress of the executing process
2. The state information of the executing process
3. The data of the executing process that is residing in that systems memory
4. The overall efficiency of the entire distributed system

2.9   How many data type translations are necessary in a heterogeneous environment with seven different architectures without using EDR? With using EDR? Optional: What is the formula for the number with EDR and without?

2.10   Suppose a system provides a two-level priority system for threads to be scheduled: low priority for user-level threads and high-priority for kernel threads. The scheduler utilizes shortest-job-first scheduling with priority preemption (any job arriving with a higher priority immediately preempts a lower running job). Calculate the total weight time for each thread as well as the average wait time for each type of thread. All threads labeled with a U are user-level threads, while threads labeled with a K are kernel-level threads. Threads of equal priority are scheduled on a first-come first-served basis.

Arrival Time	Thread Number	Required Processing Time
0	U1	12
3	K2	5
9	K3	3
11	U4	5
27	K4	7
27	U5	2

2.11 Write a program to implement the shortest-job-first scheduling with priority preemption described in Exercise 2.10. Test the program with the data provided in Exercise 2.10 as well as with your own test data.

2.12 Describe two disadvantages of utilizing a polled-loop scheduler for system scheduling.

Interprocess Communication

One of the essential elements to achieving group success is establishing an effective means of communication. Thus, if we are to achieve the benefits of having multiple processes working on the same problem in any type of advanced environment, we must also achieve an appropriate and effective means of communication; in particular, interprocess communication (IPC). This is a fundamental concept and is even utilized in the simplest of computer games to allow users to play across a network. In this chapter, we examine the various types of interprocess communications methods. The methods may be implemented at a low level and involve system calls, or they may be implemented through language support. We discuss four major types of interprocess communication. Section 3.1 presents some factors that can influence what mechanism is selected when implementing interprocess communication with a distributed system. Section 3.2 presents message passing, Section 3.2 examines pipes, Section 3.4 discusses the details of sockets, and Section 3.5 presents information on remote procedure calls. An additional method for communication is through the use of shared memory, which is discussed in Chapter 4. Finally, CORBA and DCOM provide a means for communication among objects and are described in Chapter 6.

3.1 SELECTION FACTORS

There are many factors that affect what method of interprocess communication the programmer selects for a given application selects. The following are some of the issues that should be considered.

- ◆ Programmer's current skill set (not a sound technical reason for selection of a particular method but one that has influenced many systems). It is easier to implement a method for IPC that you have implemented previously.

- ◆ Desire for transparency of the IPC mechanism to the programmer. The less details the programmer is exposed to, the lower the chance of error. However, generally this entails overhead to abstract away the details and handle them automatically.

- ◆ Methods supported on the systems that make up the distributed system. Obviously; a method that is not supported on required environments cannot easily be selected unless the organization custom implements the infrastructure.

- ◆ Desire for future growth of the system. Will this application always operate in a client/server mode? Will we desire communication to go beyond the scope of a single machine and/or file space? If you make a selection that limits your ability to go beyond your current file space, future scalability could be sacrificed. (Remember, many prototypes are put directly into production so it is best not to assume there will be a major rewriting of the code.)

- ◆ Desire to support process migration. If an IPC method prohibits communication across different file systems, a process cannot be migrated beyond the domain of the file system.

- ◆ Is the mechanism standardized, thereby allowing maximum flexibility for the types of systems that may be added to the distributed system and have the ability to conduct communication?

- ◆ Efficiency of the mechanism. This is particularly true of distributed real-time systems with time constraints.

With these points in mind, we now examine the various methods of IPC.

3.2 MESSAGE PASSING

Message passing allows two processes to communicate by physically copying the shared data to the other process's address space. This is accomplished by sending a message to the other process containing the shared data. This form of communication is most common when two processes do not share memory space, whether they are on physically different systems or the same system where each process has its own memory. Message passing communications involve send and receive primitives similar to the following.

```
send (b,msg);
receive (a, msg);
```

These primitives can be blocking or nonblocking. To understand the difference between blocking and nonblocking primitives, let us first examine a hypothetical scenario. Suppose Susan telephones and leaves a message for Steven. The message includes a question and requests a return call. At this point, Susan has two choices. First, she may sit by the telephone and wait for Steven to call back or she may work on another project until she receives said call. The first choice is parallel to a **blocking primitive** while the second is a **nonblocking** message-passing primitive. Each choice has its own advantages and disadvantages, which are described in Sections 3.2.1 and 3.2.2 respectively. Furthermore, the messages may be addressed to an individual process or to a group of processes, as described in Section 3.2.3.

3.2.1 Blocking Primitives

Suppose the message Susan left for Steven was concerning a surprise party they are throwing for Lynn. Susan and Steven decided to split up the work for this party as follows.

Susan's List of Tasks

1. Order the cake
2. Pick up the cake.
3. Let Steven know she has picked up the cake.
4. Receive telephone call from Steven that Lynn is surprised by the party.
5. Bring cake to party after Lynn is surprised.

Steven's List of Tasks

1. Telephone Lynn.
2. (Acknowledge message that cake is picked up.)
3. Bring Lynn to the party.
4. Let Susan know that Lynn is at the party and the "coast is clear."

If Susan had not waited for Steven's return call, she might have ruined the surprise by running into them in the hallway prior to entering the party room. Thus, Susan and Steven not only needed to communicate but they also needed to synchronize their efforts.

Much like Susan and Steven, when multiple processes are working on the same task, they may not only desire to communicate but also to synchronize. Thus for these processes, a blocking message-passing primitive, also referred to as a **synchronous primitive**, accomplishes both. Blocking primitives do not return control to the process immediately. In particular, a `send` blocks until an acknowledgment for the send has been received and a blocking receive blocks until the message has been received. When a process is blocked, it cannot continue to execute further until it is unblocked. Thus, the two processes have not only been allowed to communicate, but also synchronize. If you desire synchronization, this can be helpful; however, it does inhibit concurrency.

The blocking primitives may utilize a buffer or may operate in a bufferless fashion. When utilizing a buffer that is also referred to as a mailbox, the acknowledgment for the send or the message that has been received is put into a buffer until the respective process is unblocked. This buffer may reside in the kernel's address space or in the process's address space. In a distributed environment, the receiver's location is responsible for the buffer. This can create a problem if the receiver has not issued the `receive` command since the kernel may not know where to put the message!

When the blocking primitives operate without a buffer, the send is blocked until its kernel notifies it of a `receive`. Upon receiving this notification, it reexecutes the send and continues.

For a process to realize it should no longer be blocked, there are two general methods. The first method involves polling. When a process utilizes polling, it executes a test primitive to determine if the relevant information is in the buffer as indicated by the buffer status. This involves continuously checking the buffer and, thus, utilizing CPU resources. This action is referred to as a busy wait. While many applications may not be affected by busy waits, they are not particularly desirable for real-time applications. In addition, polling is generally not recommended at intervals less than 1 minute or it would impede system performance. The second method involves the use of an interrupt. Interrupts may also be utilized for nonblocking primitives. Interrupts are more efficient since the process does not continually waste time checking the buffer.

For the message-passing system to be considered synchronous, both the send and receive primitives must be blocking. Regardless of the method employed, if the test continues to fail or the interrupt never occurs, the process could be blocked indefinitely. Thus, a timer is often utilized. This timer may have a default value or may be controllable by the programmer. In a bufferless implementation, each time the send primitive is executed, a timer is started. If there is no notification from the kernel when the timer expires, the process retries for a finite number of times, as depicted in Figure 3.1. In a distributed environment, it is not practical to resend a message continuously across the network; therefore, distributed environments generally operate with at least a single buffer. Detail Box 3.1 describes a blocking send and a blocking receive utilizing a buffer, as depicted in Figure 3.2.

DETAIL BOX 3.1
BLOCKING SEND & BLOCKING RECEIVE USING A BUFFER

In general, a blocking send is equivalent to the following.

```
Procedure A
Begin                          //Procedure A begins
Instructions
...
send (b, message,...)          //Where b is the destination
                               //waiting for acknowledgment
                               //received send acknowledgment

next instruction
...
End                            //End procedure A
```

In general, a blocking receive is equivalent to the following.

```
Procedure B
Begin                          //Procedure B begins
Instructions
...
receive (a, message,...)       //Where a is the source
                               //waiting for message
                               //received message

next instruction
...
End                            //End procedure B
```

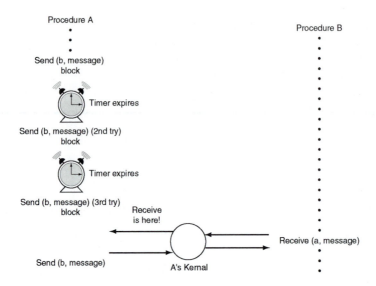

Figure 3.1   Blocking Send and Receive Primitives: No Buffer.

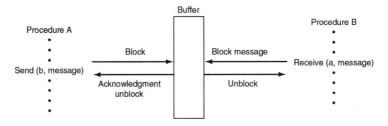

Figure 3.2   Blocking Send and Receive Primitives with Buffer.

3.2.2 Nonblocking Primitives

In the same manner that most people would find it inefficient to wait by the telephone for a return call and cease all other productive activities, processes may not desire to block and inhibit concurrency. Thus, synchronization is sometimes unnecessary and undesirable. When **nonblocking** primitives execute send and receive primitives, control is immediately returned to the process to execute further statements. The process is then notified when it can complete its primitive via an interrupt that is generated when the response is received. Nonblocking primitives are also referred to as **asynchronous primitives** since this method does not provide any means of synchronization.

Much like the blocking primitives, the sending process is usually informed that it may reuse the buffer via a message or an interrupt. This helps alleviate the problem of the sender inadvertently overwriting its own message prior to being sent. Again, processes utilizing nonblocking primitives are allowed to be productive and execute statements during this time that is nonproductive for blocking counterparts. This is one reason that nonblocking message passing is very popular for real-time applications.

3.2.3 PROCESS ADDRESS

Addressing in a message passing system may fall into two general categories. The addressing may be for one-to-one communication or it may involve group addressing.

One-to-one Addressing

One-to-one addressing may be explicit or implicit. **Explicit addressing** requires the process you are communicating with to be explicitly named as a parameter, as depicted in Figure 3.3. **Implicit addressing** only requires the service name to be included as a parameter in a send message but not a particular process and is depicted in Figure 3.4. Thus, any (but only one) server involved in a client/server relationship may respond to the message communicated. A `send` primitive with implicit addressing is also referred to as a `send_any` command. Likewise, implicit addressing in a `receive` primitive indicates that the server is willing to communicate with any client. A receive primitive with implicit addressing is commonly referred to as a `receive_any` command.

Figure 3.3 Implicit Addressing for Interprocess Communication.

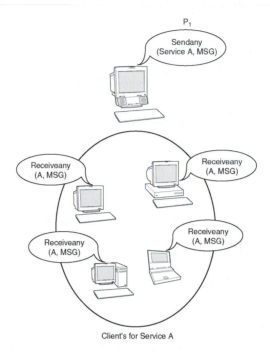

Figure 3.4   Explicit Addressing for Interprocess Communication.

Group Addressing

Group addressing is designed to support group communication and is particularly useful in parallel and distributed systems. Group communication may further be divided into three groups.

1. **One-to-many.** In this scenario, there are multiple receivers for a message but only a single sender. Communication using this type of addressing is also known as multicast communication. If all receivers are on the network and all members of the network are receivers, you may also refer to communication utilizing this addressing type as broadcast communication. Unlike one-to-one implicit addressing, all members of the receiving group receive the message. This type of addressing is useful for many applications, including locating an available server or notifying a group of a problem. One-to-many group addressing is depicted in Figure 3.5.

2. **Many-to-one**. In this scenario, there are multiple senders but only one receiver. Like implicit one-to-one addressing, the solitary receiver may receive from a single sender of a group. In addition, the receiver may receive from several or all the members of a group.

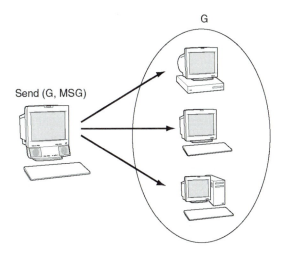

Figure 3.5 One-to-Many Group Addressing.

3. **Many-to-many**. In this scenario, there are multiple receivers and multiple senders. The most difficult task involved with this type of addressing involves ordering the messages, as described in Detail Box 3.2.

3.3 PIPES

Pipes are the earliest and most primitive type of interprocess communication mechanism. Pipes allow two processes to communicate through a finite size buffer implemented by the kernel, as depicted in Figure 3.7. The data communicated is stored in first-in-first-out (FIFO) order. This type of communication primitive is implemented through a system call. Pipes provide one-to-one communication and exist only during the duration of the communicating processes. Traditionally, UNIX™ pipes were unidirectional, although current versions operate in full duplex or are bidirectional. Pipes are considered synchronous as they cause a process to block when the buffer is full. There are two types of pipes: unnamed pipes and named pipes.

3.3.1 Unnamed Pipes

Unnamed pipes allow two related processes, such as those created by a fork operation, to communicate. Related processes include parent/child and sibling processes. This type of pipe can be created in UNIX with a system call to `pipe` or on the command line with the vertical bar (`|`), such as `ls|more`. Pipes are also common in a Windows™ environment.

DETAIL BOX 3.2
MANY-TO-MANY MESSAGE ORDERING

When communicating using many-to-many addressing, many applications require that all messages be received in an acceptable manner. We now describe three basic ordering semantics from the least structured to the most rigid semantic.

1. **Incidental Ordering**. The least structured but fastest of all ordering semantics, this ensures that if messages are incidentally related then the messages are received in the correct order. This is related to Lamport's algorithm, which is described in Chapter 10.
2. **Uniform Ordering**. This mandates that all messages are received by all receiver processes uniformly; that is, they are received by all in the same order. However, this order may be different from the order sent, as depicted in Figure 3.6.
3. **Universal Ordering**. The most rigid semantic, this mandates and ensures that all messages are received in exactly the same order as sent. There must be one universal time; that is to say, the clocks of the processes involved (if they are not on the same system) must be synchronized or use global timestamps, as discussed in Chapter 10.

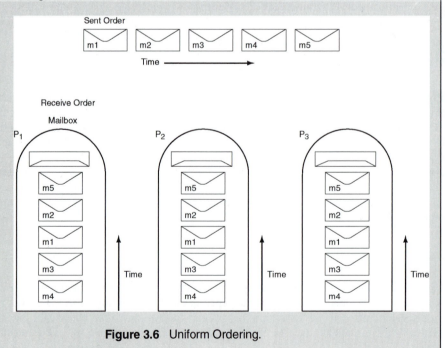

Figure 3.6 Uniform Ordering.

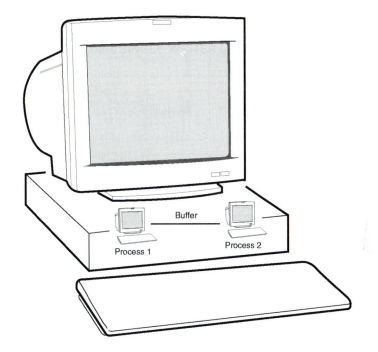

Figure 3.7   Interprocess Communication Using Pipes.

3.3.2 Named Pipes

Named pipes allow unrelated processes to communicate. While the processes do not need to be related, they do need to share a common file system. Since this name pipe is a shared data structure, access to this buffer must be inside a critical region, as described in Chapter 5. Detail Box 3.3 describes how to use named pipes in a UNIX environment.

3.4 SOCKETS

To achieve interdomain interprocess communication, or communication across a network involving systems that do not share a data structure or a file, one must use a mechanism above the transport services. One of the most widely used mechanisms is the socket. All **sockets** are managed by the transport service. A socket consists of two endpoints for communication. Each endpoint belongs to one of the processes involved in the communication. Each socket has a local endpoint address and a global endpoint address. The local address refers to the address from the transport service while the global address refers to the network host address. These two addresses must be bound together through a system call. Both addresses are necessary to communicate unless, prior to communicating,

---

DETAIL BOX 3.3
UNIX NAMED PIPES

In UNIX, the creation of a named pipe generates a directory entry. The file access permissions on this entry allow the involved processes to communicate through this commonly known named buffer. Like unnamed UNIX pipes, named pipes can be created on the command line through the `mknod` command. Specifically,

```
% mknod MYPIPE p
```

where `mknod` is the command, the first argument is the name of the named pipe (`MYPIPE`), and the second argument (`p`) indicates it is a named pipe. It is tradition for pipe names to be in all uppercase letters to alert users that this is a special file. Once created, a user can utilize the UNIX unmask command or `chmod` to change the access privileges. Pipes in UNIX are also known as FIFOs. The `mknod` command often requires superuser privileges; however, UNIX systems include a C library function called `mkfifo` to assist in generating a named pipe and do not require such privileges. The function header for `mkfifo` is as follows.

```
int mkfifo(const char *path, mode_t mode);
                            //POSIX.1 Spec 1170
```

`Path` is the pathname of the named pipe to be created. `Mode` specifies the access permission for the user, group, and others for the pipe that is being created. The return value is 0 for success and -1 for unsuccessful attempt.

The following code segment allows a program to create a named pipe that is (only) readable by everyone.

```
#include <sys/stat.h>
#include <sys/types.h>
mode_t fifo_perms =
        S_IRUSR | S_IWUSR | S_IRGRP | S_IROTH;
if (mkfifo("MYPIPE", fifo_perms) == -1)
        perror("Couldn't create MYPIPE");
                        //Created named pipe named MYPIPE
```

a connect socket call is placed. This call can bind your local address to the remote global address address and simplify future communications. Both endpoints must perform the bind. A socket exists until every process referring to it dies or a process closes the socket. Information on the secure socket layer (SSL), which provides a secure socket implementation, is provided in Chapter 11.

There are six general steps involved in utilizing a socket, as depicted in Figure 3.8 and as can be seen in the surgical scheduling program in the Appendix that employs sockets. We now describe each of these steps using the telephone as an analogy. Step 1 is creating a socket. This is analogous to installing a telephone jack. You must have a telephone jack before you can use the telephone; likewise, you must create a socket before you can communicate using a socket. Step 2 involves binding your socket to a port. This is analogous to getting a telephone number from the telephone company that is associated with your telephone jack. Only once we have bound our socket to an address or bound our telephone jack to a telephone number can we use it to communicate. The third step is to listen for the telephone to ring, or to listen on the socket for someone to communicate with us. Once we realize someone has tried to reach us, we can accept the communication, which is the fourth step. Furthermore, while telephones frequently have the call-waiting feature, sockets can determine how many "calls" they can accept. Step 5 is communication: we may now commence communication. For sockets, this is generally through read and write commands. Finally, step 6 is the disconnect or hang-up, when the communication is completed.

There are two primary domain types of sockets. The first type is a stream socket (implemented in TCP/IP) and is used for highly reliable connection-oriented communication. The second type is a datagram (implemented in UDP/IP), used for (potentially) unreliable connectionless communication. The fact that datagrams do not incorporate the necessary overhead to ensure reliability makes this type more efficient and thus more attractive to real-time applications. The implementation of sockets in a Windows™ environment utilizes Winsock, which is based on UNIX's BSD implementation as described in Section 3.4.1. Section 3.4.2 presents the details of implementing sockets using Java™.

3.4.1 UNIX Sockets

The first UNIX socket interface originated with 3.1 BSD UNIX in 1981. To compile a program and utilize the UNIX socket libraries, you must use the `-lsocket` option. UNIX socket primitives are available through C libraries and include `socket`, `bind`, `connect`, `listen`, `send`, `receive`, and `shutdown`. UNIX allows two types of sockets, UNIX sockets and Internet sockets. The interfaces are as follows.

```
SOCKET
#include <sys/types.h>
#include <sys/socket.h>
int socket (int domain, int type, int protocol);
```

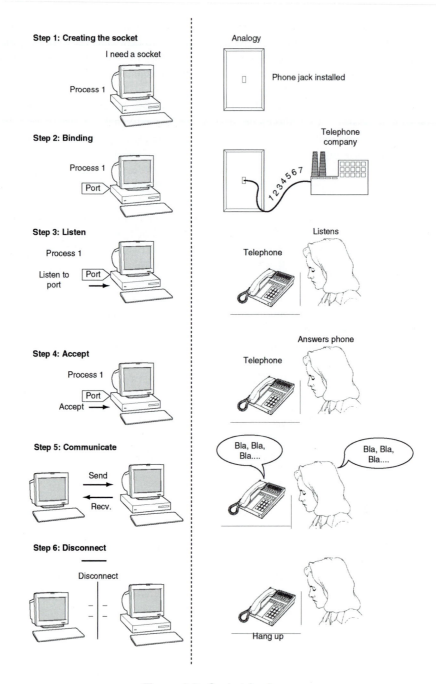

Figure 3.8   Socket Analogy.

The domain parameter can have the values AF_UNIX for UNIX domains and AF_INET for Internet domains. The UNIX domain dictates that both processes must reside on a single UNIX system. The type parameter can have the values SOCK_STREAM for reliable connection-oriented communication using a stream and SOCK_DGRAM for unreliable connectionless communication using datagrams. Streams are generally implemented with TCP while datagrams are generally implemented with UDP. Generally, only one of the protocols is available for a particular type, and thus the protocol value is usually 0 for the default value.

```
BIND
    #include <sys/types.h>
    #include <sys/socket.h>
    int bind(int s, const struct sockaddr *address, size_t address_len);
```

The parameter *s* is the return value from the function call to socket and is the file descriptor: address_len is the number of bytes in the *address structure, which contains the family name and protocol-specific information. When using the Internet domain, sockaddr, defined as follows, is utilized for struct sockaddr.

```
    struct sockaddre_in
        {
        short       sin_family;
        u_short     sin_port;
        struct      in_addr sin_addr;
        char        sin_zero[8];
        };
```

For use in the Internet domain, the sin_family parameter has the value AF_INET as in the socket function. The port number is stored in the variable sin_port. If you wish to allow communication with any host, then sin_addr is set to INADDR_ANY. To make the structure the same size as sockaddr, the structure is filled out with sin_zero.

When using the UNIX domain, sockaddr, defined as follows is utilized.

```
    Struct sockaddr
        {
        short   sun_family;
        char    sun_path[];
        };
```

In the UNIX domain, the sun_family parameter should be defined as AF_UNIX as in the socket function. The UNIX path name is assigned to the field sun_path.

```
LISTEN
    #include <sys/types.h>
    #include<sys/socket.h>
    int listen(int s, int backlog_size);
```

This function is only used to establish a connection-based socket. Once again, s is the return value from the function call to socket. The field backlog_size allows one to limit the number of pending client requests that can be backlogged before a connection is refused (call waiting). This allows a server to process multiple communications requests.

```
ACCEPT
    #include <sys/types.h>
    #include <sys/socket.h>
    int accept(int s, struct sockaddr *address, int *address_len);
```

Observe that these parameters are very similar to bind with one exception: *address will contain information about the client making the connection. Thus, for use in the Internet domain, *address_len of accept specifies the size of the buffer before the call and the size of the information filled in after the call. The return value is a file descriptor for use with communication to the client.

```
GETHOSTBYADDR
    #include <sys/types.h>
    #include <sys/socket.h>
    struct hostent *gethostbyaddr(const void *addr, size_t len, int
type);
```

This function is quite valuable as it converts the address received in the function call to accept to a name.

```
SEND
    #include <sys/types.h>
    #include <sys/socket.h>
    int send(int s, const char* buf, int len, int flag);
```

The message contained in buf of size len bytes is sent to a socket designated by s.

```
RECV
    #include <sys/types.h>
    #include <sys/socket.h>
    int recv(int s, char* buf, int len, int flag);
```

Once again, a message is received by the socket s and copied to buf . The maximum size is specified by len. All messages are received in FIFO order. If flag is set, then you are accepting out-of-band messages that do not respect this order (they cut in line). This type of message should be used on an emergency basis only.

```
CLOSE
     #include <sys/types.h>
     #include <sys/socket.h>
     int close(int s);
```

This function is used to close the socket s.

Finally, since all systems are slightly different, we may have to convert the form of the data prior to sending. In particular, some machines use ASCII while others use EBCDIC. Machines also use different byte order. Some functions available include the following.

```
htons(): host to network short integer
ntohs(): network to host short integer
htoni(): host to network integer
ntohi(): network to host integer
htonl(): host to network long integer
ntohl(): network to host long integer
```

3.4.2 Java Support for Sockets

Java provides two classes to support Internet sockets. The class `java.net.ServerSocket` is for use by the clients and the class `java.net.Socket` is for use by a server. As you can see, this is perhaps the simplest method of programming using sockets. The Client class is defined in Detail Box 3.4.

Using this class, the client first attempts to open a connection to a server by constructing a socket. To accomplish this, the user must specify the hostname and port number of the appropriate server. The default mode for this class is utilizing a stream socket; however, one may specify the use of a datagram.

The following code fragment attempts to connect a socket to port 25 of the host rose.myuniversity.edu. As commented in the specification, if you prefer, you can replace the hostname with the actual IP address, which is useful for communicating with parties who do not have static IP addresses.

```
Try  {Socket sock = new Socket
          ("rose.myuniversity.edu",25);
             }
catch (UnknownHostException e)
             {
              System.out.println("Unable to locate host.");
             }
catch (IOException e)
             {
              System.out.println("Host Connection Error.");
             }
```

DETAIL BOX 3.4
JAVA CLIENT SOCKET CLASS

```
Public final class Socket extends Object{
//                      Public Constructors
//
        public Socket(String host, int port)
                throws UnknownHostException, IOException;
//                              uses hostname and default data streams
        public Socket(String host, int port,
                boolean stream)throws IOException
//                              uses hostname and nondefault datagrams
        public Socket(InetAddress address, int port)
                throws IOException;
//                              uses IP address and default data stream
        public Socket(InetAddress address, int port,
                boolean stream)throws IOException;
//                              uses IP address and nondefault datagrams
//
//Class Methods
//
        public static synchronized void
                setSocketImpIFactory(SocketlmpIfactory
                fac)throws IOException, SocketException;
//
//Public Instance Methods
//
        public synchronized void close()
                throws IOException;
        public InetAddress getInetAddress();
        public InputStream getInputStream()
                throws IOException;
//                              for reading from socket
        public int getLocalPort();
        public OutputStream getOutputStream()
                throws IOException;
//                              for writing to socket
        public int getPort();
        pubic String toString();
//                              Overrides object.toString()
    }
```

If the connection is successfully completed, a user may now send and receive information by retrieving the input and output streams with

```
Socket getInputStream() & Socket getOutputStream()
```

as specified in the methods.

After the client has established a connection, the server may then use the Java server class for sockets defined in Detail Box 3.5 for communication to the client.

DETAIL BOX 3.5
JAVA SOCKET SERVER CLASS

```
Public final class ServerSocket extends object{
//
//Public Constructors
//
        public ServerSocket(int port)
                throws IOException;
        public ServerSocket(int port, int count)
                throws IOException;
//
//Class Methods
//
        public static synchronized void
                setSocketFactory (SocketImpIFactory fac)
                throws IOException, SocketException;
//Public Instance Methods
        public Socket accept() throws IOException;
//                                          accepts a call
        public void close() throws IOException;
//                                          closes a socket
        public InetAddress getInetAddress();
        pubic int getLocalPort();
        public String toString();
//                                     Overrides object.toString()
}
```

The `ServerSocket` created listens for connections on a specific port for a specified amount of time utilizing the method *accept*. The port number should be larger than 1024 since standard, well-known, and system processes utilize ports of lower numbers. The server then utilizes `getInputStream` and `getOutputStream` to send and receive data. The server socket can accept many connections once `ServerSocket` is created.

3.5 REMOTE PROCEDURE CALLS

Most computer scientists are comfortable programming in a procedural paradigm. **Remote procedure calls** (RPCs) allow processes to communicate with remote processes connected via a network by a simple (familiar) procedure call. Observe that in all the previous interprocess communication techniques presented, only simple messages have been passed between the communicating processes. Like the procedures of many popular languages, RPCs not only allow the programmer to communicate by sending a message, but also allow more complex data structures as parameter values as well as a return value. The caller is blocked while waiting on this return value. Thus, RPCs do provide synchronization at the cost of concurrency much like blocked message-passing primitives. However, since RPCs' calling function is waiting on a return value, not just an acknowledgment, the calling function is blocked for a longer duration. We now examine the various issues involved in remote procedure call implementations (Section 3.5.1 through 3.5.6). Section 3.5.7 discusses how these issues are handled in SUN's ONC RPC.

3.5.1 Parameter Type

It is just as important to understand parameter types in remote procedure calls as it is for local procedure calls since it affects your expectations on the results. There are three basic parameter types for remote procedure calls.

1. *Input only*: This type of parameter can only pass information to the server and is parallel to call-by-value.

2. *Output only*: This type of parameter can only pass information from the server to the client. The client cannot utilize this parameter to send information to the server.

3. *Input and output*: This type of parameter can pass information to a server and the server can use this same parameter to pass information back to the client. This parameter type is generally implemented as call-by-value/result.

3.5.2 Data Type Support

Data type support relates to the data types that can be used as arguments in a remote procedure call. Just as various programming languages may limit the complexity of arguments, RPC may limit the complexity as well. More common is for RPC to limit the number of arguments and allow data types that are more complex. For example, if you are limited to a single parameter but the parameter may be a complex structure, a programmer may get around this limitation with a minor inconvenience.

3.5.3 Parameter Marshalling

For efficient communication to take place, these parameters and larger data structures must employ RPC marshalling. **Marshalling** involves flattening or packing the information in a compact manner to minimize the amount of information sent across the network. The method must be precise so the recipient is able to unpack the information correctly. This marshalling is carried out by a stub function that is called each time an RPC function call is made, as depicted in Figure 3.9. This stub requires the use of an extensive library, which not only relieves the programmer of this task but aids in the promotion of transparency (transparency issues are discussed in detail in Chapter 8). Some RPC implementations are more generous in providing you with all the stubs necessary than are others [NIST93a]. In practice, RPCs are utilized to hide the underlying interprocess communication methods being employed, such as sockets (discussed in Section 3.4).

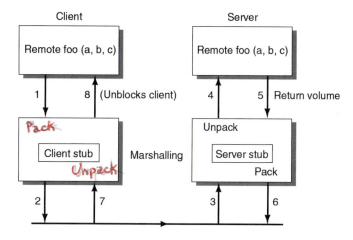

Figure 3.9 Remote Procedure Call Stubs.

3.5.4 RPC Binding

Prior to utilizing remote procedure calls, a client and server must first establish communication. Similar to sockets, before a client can send an RPC to a server, that server must exist and be registered. Registration involves requesting a port to the kernel's port mapper. (If the server is unknown, then a directory server like those presented in Chapter 8

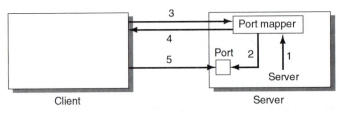

1. I need a port
2. Here is your port
3. I need a handle
5. Communicate using handle

Figure 3.10   Establishing Communication for RPC.

must be contacted.) This identifies which port the server will be listening on in order to communicate with the client. The client must then contact the port mapper and receive a "handle" for accessing the server, as depicted in Figure 3.10. This handle is then utilized to conduct the underlying socket binding. This overall process that is transparent to the programmer and user is known as binding and can occur at three different times.

1. *Compile time*: This requires the server's address to be known and compiled into the client's code. This is not the most flexible method but can be convenient if the application's configuration is expected to remain static.

2. *Link time*: The client requests the handle just before making a service request. In this case, the handle is put into the client's cache for use during future requests.

3. *Run time*: The client is bound to the server when the first call is made. The server sends the handle back along with the other RPC return values.

A word of warning: The handle provided to the client is valid as long as the server is running. If the server has several clients and wishes to revoke the privilege of only a single client, it must exit and obtain a new port. This new port must then be rebound to the remaining valid clients, who are provided with a new handle. In conclusion, a server is not able to deny access to a client with a valid handle.

3.5.5 RPC Authentication

In a distributed system, you may wish to verify the identity of either the server you are utilizing or the server may wish to verify the identity of the client. Is this really Alice withdrawing the money from the account? More information on distributed authentication and digital signatures can be found in Chapter 11.

3.5.6 RPC Call Semantics

Call semantics determine what happens to a repeat procedure call. Since network errors occur, a return value or the original procedure call may be lost or corrupted or delayed long enough to making the calling procedure believe that the call was lost. In these instances, the procedure call may be repeated. This may seem harmless; but what if the procedure call involved removing $300 from your bank account? If the call is repeated, you would not be pleased if the system recorded an additional $300 withdrawl (but did not give you the money!). Precisely how these semantics are implemented depends on if the system is utilizing a stateful or stateless server. Stateful servers maintain client state information in a table. Thus, subsequent calls can utilize information from previous calls without retransmitting significant information. This information reduction reduces the load on the network and the total transmission time. This, in turn, increases the speed of request handling; however, if the server crashes and loses information, the client would be unaware. Some semantics are easier to implement on stateful servers while others are easier to implement on stateless servers.

The following are the four popular RPC call semantics.

At-Most-Once

At-most-once semantics are usually implemented on stateful servers. This semantic requires a guarantee that repeat invocations of the same RPC will not be processes by the server. A server generally checks its state information table to identify repeat procedure calls.

At-Least-Once

At-least-once semantics guarantee that the remote procedure call will be executed at least once and maybe multiple times. This semantic does not specify or guarantee which invocation of the procedure call will return a value but that some value will be returned.

Last-of-Many-Call

Last-of-many-call semantics require each invocation of a remote procedure call to contain an identifier. The client only accepts the return value of the most recent invocation.

Idempotent

Idempotent semantics are used by RPC applications utilizing stateless or stateful servers. While this semantic does not guarantee that remote procedure calls won't be invoked multiple times, it does guarantee that there will be no undesirable effects as a result. For stateful servers, this implies that the server state cannot be corrupted by multiple client invocations.

3.5.7 SUN's ONC RPC

The first commercial implementation of RPC was SUN^{TM}'s Open Network Computing (ONC) RPC, which is often and originally referred to as SUN RPC. The original implementation was highly dependent on the SunOS, whose success is now known as the Solaris^{TM} operating system. ONC also has a Transport Independent RPC (TI RPC), which can use different transport layer protocols and more complete client/server stubs.

ONC RPC supports both at-most-once and idempotent call semantics. In addition, it provides support for broadcast RPC (multiple recipients) and no-response or batching RPC. A batching RPC does not require a return value and it is commonly utilized to update logs. The implementation of parameter types seems to be limited since ONC only allows two parameters: one input parameter and one output parameter. However, since almost all scalar and aggregate data types in the C language are supported, one can combine the desired parameters into a structure and pass them to the remote procedure. ONC RPC supports three levels of authentication; the highest level is referred to as Secure RPC and utilizes the Data Encryption Standard (DES), as described in Chapter 11.

3.6 SUMMARY

Interprocess communication is a critical aspect for multiple processes trying to accomplish a common goal. There are various techniques available to a programmer. Table 3.1 summarizes the methods described in this chapter in relation to which type of advanced components in a distributed system can employ them. Interprocess communication implementation is further addressed in the Chapter 12 case study. When utilizing interprocess communication, one must be aware of the advantages of each as well as their shortcomings. Message passing may be employed in distributed or parallel systems in either a blocking or a nonblocking mode. Pipes utilize a buffer; therefore, they also provide synchronization. Pipes may be used as long as the processes can share a directory space, but the programmer must realize that this inhibits future expansion of the application and its scalability. Generally, this limitation is severe enough that it is best to avoid pipes and use sockets. Sockets are perhaps the most powerful mechanism for interprocess communication due to the level of control provided to the programmer. However, this added control comes with the responsibility of dealing with many additional details. Until one has some practice and develops proficiency, sockets can be somewhat messy. Java's support of sockets through the classes defined in Detail Boxes 3.4 and 3.5 offers a lot of promise, but only time will tell. Remote procedure calls are useful in distributed systems, but many of the implementations available require the programmer to implement stubs since they may come with poor stub support [NIST93a]. It is also good to keep in mind that underneath RPC you will generally find our friend sockets. Research and development continues in this area to enhance this critical aspect of computing with multiple processes.

IPC Method	Distributed Components	Real-Time Components	Parallel Components
Message Passing	Yes	Yes	Yes
Pipes	No	Yes	Yes
Sockets	Yes	Yes	Yes
RPC	Yes	Yes	Yes

Table 3.1 Summary of IPC Mechanisms and Their Use in Distributed System Components.

3.7 REFERENCES FOR FURTHER STUDY

The following references can provide more general information on interprocess communication and their implementation: [Blo92, Cha97, Fla96, Gra97, Lap92, NiPe96, RoRo96, and QuSh95]. Some appropriate traditional research papers concerning information in this chapter include [BaHa87, BALL90, BeFe91, BiJo87, Bir85, BLPv93, Cla85, Fer95, GaSp91, Gen81, Gib87, GiGl88, HuPe91, KiPu95, KJAKL93, NeBi84, NIST93a, RaSh92, ScBu89, SrPa82, Sun88, TaAn90, and WuSa93].

The following provide some great starting points for sources on the Internet concerning interprocess communication and synchronization issues. Information on Winsock2 can be located at http://www.intel.com/ial/winsock2 as well as at the FAQ (frequently asked questions) sight for Windows Sockets Version 1.1 at ftp://SunSite. UNC.EDU/pub/micro/pc-stuff/ms-windows/winsock/FAQ. A general Winsock FAQ site can be found at http://www.well.com/user.nac/alt-winsock-faq.html. The online version of [NIST93a] can be found at http://nemo.ncsl.nist.gov/nistir/5277/. The online version of [Sun88] can be found at http://ei.cs.vt.edu/~cs5204/rpc/rfc1057.html.

EXERCISES

3.1   For each of the selection factors (not including first factor) presented in Section 3.1, evaluate the IPC mechanisms presented in this chapter.

3.2   Describe an application scenario where a program requires synchronous communication.

3.3   Describe how you might simulate blocking message passing with nonblocking primitives.

3.4   Describe how you might simulate nonblocking message passing with blocking primitives.

3.5   Describe an application scenario that requires asynchronous communication.

3.6   Describe the advantages and disadvantages of blocking versus nonblocking message passing.

3.7   Describe a use for each of the following message-passing address categories.

   a.   One-to-one addressing
   b.   One-to-many addressing
   c.   Many-to-one addressing
   d.   Many-to-many addressing

3.7   Describe a possible approach to implement each of the following message-passing address schemes.

   a.   One-to-one addressing
   b.   One-to-many addressing
   c.   Many-to-one addressing
   d.   Many-to-many addressing

3.8   Describe a situation where incidental ordering for many-to-many message passing could create a problem.

3.9   Write a client and a server program that share a UNIX named pipe. The client program should accept input from the user and write it to the named pipe. The server program should read from the named pipe and print the information to the screen.

3.10   Discuss the relative advantages and disadvantages of sockets versus pipes.

3.11   Blackjack is a popular card game. A deck of cards consists of 52 individual cards. There are four suits: hearts, diamonds, spades and clubs. Each suit has an ace, 1, 2, 3, 4, 5, 6, 7, 8, 9, 10, jack, queen, and king. The jack, queen and king are considered face cards. Points are assigned to cards in the following manner:

Face cards: 10 points,

Ace to 10:   1 to 10 points respectively.

The game begins with the dealer presenting each player with one card. The dealer then presents each player with a second card. Each player is then given the opportunity to receive additional cards. Players may receive as many cards as they like until they either (a) ask to stop or (b) go over a total of 21 points.

Consider that there is a single dealer and up to five players. For simplification, we only allow an ace to be worth 1 point and we will not allow the dealer to play.

The winner is determined in the following order:

a.   The first player to reach 21 without going over,
b.   The player who comes closest to 21 without going over 21, or
c.   The group of players who tie for the highest score without going over 21.

The players are allowed to play multiple games but the (single) deck of cards is shuffled (Hint: Use random number generator) after each game. There is a finite time that players are allowed to join a game at the beginning of each new game.

OPTION 1: Implement this game utilizing a named pipe.
OPTION 2: Implement this game utilizing a UNIX socket.
OPTION 3: Implement this game utilizing an Internet datagram socket.
OPTION 4: Implement this game utilizing an Internet stream socket.
OPTION 5: Implement OPTION 3 and OPTION 4.

3.12   A lightweight RPC allows RPC calls within the same host system. Describe why this might be beneficial.

3.13   Describe an application that might benefit from nonblocking RPCs.

3.14   ONC RPC only allows two parameters: one input-only parameter and one output-only parameter. What are some of the potential benefits associated with this decision?

Memory Management

*A*s mentioned in Chapter 2, memory management is generally part of the kernel's responsibility. It is a crucial element in all systems since all executing programs and their data reside in and require memory. Memory management is generally not only dependent on the operating system but also on the underlying machine architecture. Some of the more recent research in this area involves separating memory management from the computer architecture.

In this chapter, we first briefly review relevant centralized memory management issues in Section 4.1. For further information, please see your favorite introductory operating systems text. We then progress to a discussion of memory management in advanced systems. Memory has several parts: cache, main memory (random access memory - RAM), and secondary storage. Secondary memory storage is commonly implemented on a magnetic tape, hard/floppy disk drive, CD-ROM, or DVD. Cache, including flash memory, is the fastest (and most expensive) type of memory but it is volatile; data stored on it will not endure a power outage. Cache located directly on a CPU is faster than cache connected via a bus (generally on the motherboard). Main memory is the next fastest type of memory and is also volatile. Secondary storage is slower and cheaper but is not volatile. The seek, access, and transfer speeds greatly depend on the storage/memory type and are continually improving.

A parallel computer with a single memory space will utilize the simple memory model presented in Section 4.2. With NUMA architectures, the shared memory model discussed in Section 4.3 is often utilized. Small-scale distributed systems may also utilize this model. In addition, distributed systems may employ an extended virtual memory or distributed shared memory model, as discussed in Section 4.4. Finally, Section 4.5 discusses implementation issues related to memory migration that are of particular importance in distributed memory management.

4.1 REVIEW OF CENTRALIZED MEMORY MANAGEMENT

To understand advanced memory management, it is essential to understand centralized memory management. In particular, it is not uncommon in distributed systems for the distributed memory manager to reside on top of the centralized memory manager. Real memory refers to the actual physical main memory. Most centralized systems not only utilized the main physical memory but also provide virtual memory. In this section we briefly review the basic concepts of virtual memory (Section 4.1.1), pages and segments (Section 4.1.2), and page replacement algorithms (Section 4.1.3).

4.1.1 Virtual Memory

Virtual memory dominates modern centralized systems. With virtual memory, a process believes it actually has access to more main memory than is available (whether to the system or to the process). The portion of virtual memory that is not stored in main memory is located on disk. The memory manager provides each process with a virtual address that is within the system's virtual address space. It is also responsible for knowing which parts of virtual memory are located in the physical memory versus disk. This mapping of virtual memory to physical memory or disk is accomplished by the MMU, the **memory management unit**.

4.1.2 Pages and Segments

For ease of movement and addressing, memory is often divided up either into **segments** or **pages**. Segments vary in size according to the data but are generally rounded up to the nearest power of two. Pages are always the same exact size. Pages of memory are placed into frames within the physical memory that are the same size as the pages. There are two types of wasted memory space: **internal fragmentation** and **external fragmentation**. Internal fragmentation is wasted space within a block of memory while external fragmentation is wasted space between the various blocks of data in main memory. It is not uncommon for a system to have 30% of its memory wasted by fragmentation. Figure 4.1 displays external versus internal fragmentation in a page-based memory and a segment-based memory.

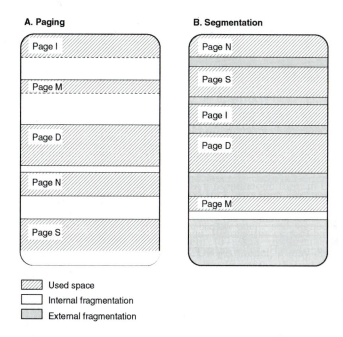

Figure 4.1 Fragmentation in Page-Based Memory versus a Segment-Based Memory.

Segments suffer from external fragmentation and occasionally minor internal fragmentation. The external fragmentation results from the movement of segments in and out of memory. While the initial segments may be brought in to fit nice and neat, when a segment is moved out of the physical memory, the probability is extremely high that the new segment brought in will not be the same size. This creates a "hole" between segments. As segments are continually brought in and out of the physical memory, multiple holes exist.

These holes are external fragmentation. The common algorithms for choosing a hole to place a segment in are first fit, best fit, and worst fit. First fit places the segment in the first feasible hole it finds. Best fit places the segment in the smallest hole possible. Worst fit places the segment in the largest hole available, assuming the hole is large enough for the segment to fit. These algorithms are depicted in Figure 4.2.

Since all pages are the same size but a process's need for memory may vary, pages suffer from internal fragmentation. The uniform sizing of pages does, however, eliminate external fragmentation. When a page is removed from the physical memory, the "hole" left is the perfect size for another page. Pages are most commonly used in virtual memory systems. The data structure maintaining information on the pages is referred to as a page table. This table stores the virtual address of pages (in particular, a virtual page number and the offset within this page). The virtual page number is simply an index into this page table.

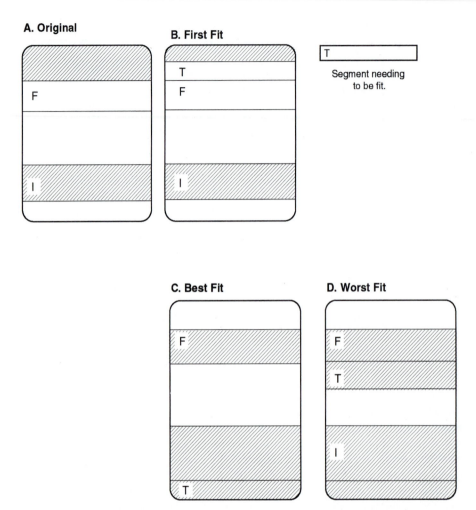

Figure 4.2   Algorithms for Choosing Segment Location.

4.1.3 Page Replacement Algorithms

A **page fault** occurs when a process requires a page that does not currently reside in the physical memory. Page replacement algorithms are utilized to decide what page in the physical memory will be "ousted" to bring in this new required page. The replacement algorithm may utilize the algorithm on the physical memory of the entire system, the memory allocated to the same user that caused the page fault, or the physical memory of the process causing the page fault. It is an important decision since moving pages requires overhead. An important goal of any page replacement algorithm is to make the right choice. Ideally, the right choice is any page that will never be utilized again. The worst choice is a page that is about to be accessed; this would cause another page fault! If the system is constantly fetching and refetching pages to a point where performance is seriously hindered, it is considered to be **thrashing**. While thrashing may be the result of a poor page replacement algorithm, it is usually indicative of too high of a degree of multiprogramming for the resources available. If the system were to reduce the degree of multiprogramming, it would reduce the number of processes it is trying to serve. This, in turn, increases the amount of physical memory available per process and reduces the number of page faults. Poor programming practices can also result in unnecessary page faults (i.e., accessing an array in column major order when the programming language stores arrays in row major order).

The first page replacement algorithm is first in first out (FIFO). In this algorithm, replacement is based on the time a page was brought into memory. The first page brought into memory is the first page removed when a page fault occurs and no frames are available. This algorithm's weakness is due to the fact that the first pages brought in are generally important pages that are frequently used and will be needed again. The second replacement algorithm is not recently used (NRU). This algorithm discards pages that have not been used recently. Recently may be a static threshold, thereby making several pages equal candidates for discarding. The third replacement algorithm is similar to NRU and is known as least recently used. This algorithm removes the page that has not been accessed for the longest time, figuring it is no longer necessary. Consider that you have a closet full of clothes with no room for another item. If you bought a new outfit and wanted to put it in your closet, you would most likely choose to remove clothes that you have not worn for a year or two versus an outfit you wore last week. This is the basis of this algorithm. This is a very popular algorithm. Variations to the algorithms include second chance algorithms. Second chance algorithms mark a page the first time it is chosen for removal but do not remove the page unless it already has been marked. When a page of memory is accessed, it clears the mark (if any). The page replacement algorithm continues to search for a page that meets the particular criteria and is already marked. Other algorithms take into consideration the cost of removing a page. This type of "lazy" algorithm strives to find a page that it will not need to rewrite back to disk. This is accomplished by keeping track of what pages have data that have been changed ("dirty pages"). It is faster to throw out a clean page than a dirty page.

4.2 SIMPLE MEMORY MODEL

The **simple memory model** is utilized for memory management in parallel UMA systems. In the simple memory model access times are equal for all processors. Thus, our main concern is the degree of parallelism in global memory. Recall that when a centralized system has too high of a degree of multiprogramming, no single task has adequate memory space to operate. Thus, each task is constantly calling for pages of memory that are not loaded into main memory and thrashing results. This causes a large degree of overhead. Likewise, parallel systems must have sufficient memory to service each of the processors efficiently. Of course, high memory solutions become more attractive as they become more financially feasible, thereby taking advantage of memory when it is less expensive.

High-performance parallel systems often choose not to utilize virtual memory or cache. Virtual memory requires additional overhead to manage. This overhead can reduce performance in a system designed for and requiring optimal performance. Due to the type of programs implemented on high-performance parallel systems, there is a large amount of data required for computations. This would require an enormous amount of cache. Furthermore, since these data typically are not reused, the benefits of providing cache are further diminished so providing cache becomes impractical.

4.3 SHARED MEMORY MODEL

When computing in a small distributed or multiprocessor (NUMA) environment, one can either utilize the message-passing model or utilize a **shared memory model**. As mentioned in Chapter 3, the shared memory model is an additional method for accomplishing interprocess communication. In fact, shared memory may be one of the most popular methods as it is a fast way to accomplish tasks such as passing information between a modem and a network interface on a dial-up router box. The shared memory model extends the concept of virtual memory to multiple physical memories, their local cache, as well as their secondary storage. When utilizing message passing (or remote procedure calls), difficulties can be encountered since it is not an effective or efficient way to manipulate large complex data sets. The biggest advantages of shared memory over message passing are the ease with which data may be partitioned as well as the ease with which load distribution can be performed through migration. The shared memory model functions by allowing multiple processes to read and write to shared data structures in memory common to all. Such a system must employ some type of concurrency control (discussed in Chapter 5) and transaction management (discussed in Chapter 9). An additional benefit of shared memory systems involves the utilization of workstations with local cache that share the same memory. The workstations are then connected via a bus to form the common shared memory. This design works best for multiprocessors or local distributed systems. It allows a significant increase in performance and computing power while keeping the financial burden to a minimum. One of the difficulties encountered is the constant demand for access to memory over this single bus. In other words, the workstations often experience **bus contention**. This bus contention causes a bottleneck, and thus this implementation is traditionally not recommended for more than 32 processors on a single bus. Detail Box 4.1 describes Amoeba's memory management system while Detail Box 4.2 describes UNIX System V support for shared memory.

> **DETAIL BOX 4.1**
> **AMOEBA**

The microkernel of the Amoeba distributed operating system is described in [TaKa94]. The microkernel contains the memory management system. This memory management system is simply designed to provide for performance, simplicity, and economics. It requires the entire process to reside entirely in memory to enhance the speed of RPC operations. A given process is not limited to the number of segments it may utilize. A process, which starts with one segment, can create and destroy segments it utilized while it is running. When a process creates a segment, it is given a capability to utilize this segment. The hardware memory management unit (MMU) is utilized and segments are not swapped or paged; they may be located anywhere within virtual memory. Furthermore, they must be entirely located within the virtual memory or they cannot be executed utilizing Amoeba. These segments may be shared between various processes on the same system; however, they may not be shared over a network.

> **DETAIL BOX 4.2**
> **UNIX SYSTEM V SUPPORT FOR SHARED MEMORY**

UNIX System V supports shared memory as part of the interprocess communication facility. To utilize this shared memory support in a C or C++ program, you must utilize the following include statement.

```
#include <sys/shm.h>
```

The function call for creating shared memory is `shmget`. The functions `shmat` and `shmdt` attach and detach shared memory to a user's memory space. A complete listing of all details is available in the man pages (online UNIX manual) on your local system (type in `man shmget`, `man shmat`, or `man shmdt`). In addition, a list of all support for shared memory on a UNIX system can be found with the keyword search option (type in `man -k shared memory`).

4.3.1 Shared Memory Performance

With processor speeds constantly increasing, the memory bottleneck becomes even more significant; that is, the system spends most of its idle time waiting to retrieve information from memory. Systems always advertise their performance; but this performance is peak performance and not average performance. Some of the biggest problems that prevent taking full advantage of the fast processors and the many resources available are memory speed, memory access, and communication delay. This is particularly true in shared memory systems. One of the fundamental questions in utilizing shared memory regards the scalability, how well the system maintains its performance if the number of processors and the amount of memory increased. When one increases the memory and processing power of a parallel or distributed system, one would think that performance would linearly increase. Unfortunately, the old saying, "too many cooks spoil the broth" takes on a whole new meaning. Generally, it is not the number of cooks but how they are coordinated and utilized!

Performance is important to all applications but is of particular importance to real-time applications. Generally, supercomputers and real-time applications will not utilize any type of virtual memory. The phrase commonly heard is, "If it ain't real [meaning it is virtual], it ain't fast." For less time critical applications, Sun and Zhu presented two important factors that can increase the performance of shared virtual memory [SuZh96]. First, the system should overlap communication with computations. A system that does not allow overlap cannot be utilizing resources as efficiently as a system that can provide communication and computation overlap. Second, the system should perform automatic prefetch of data whenever possible. If the instructions to fetch remote data are able to be executed one step prior to the system needing the data from memory, the delay for remote data will be eliminated or minimized at the least. Software development technologies allow for the identification of such information ahead of time. This identification may be performed automatically either during runtime or approximated by the compiler.

Two additional factors may affect the performance of a shared memory system. First, recall that nonlocal memory references are more expensive in NUMA architectures (by definition) than local memory references. In addition, it is customary for the nonlocal to local memory reference ratio to be as high as 10 : 1. Thus, one can increase performance by monitoring nonlocal references; when a certain threshold is reached, the algorithm migrates this page to local memory. This task is generally performed by a system daemon process called a **page scanner**. This scanner will monitor the appropriate statistics and migrate the page. If the system is a homogeneous system, migration is simply handled as a page fault. Section 4.5 discusses issues related to migration.

4.3.2 Cache Consistency

If it is necessary to prefetch data, an important factor to a successful shared memory implementation is maintaining cache consistency. **Consistency** is a term used to describe the function of ensuring all data copies are the same and correct. There are three popular methods for realizing cache consistency. The first employs software to enforce critical regions, protected regions of code where a given process is changing shared data, as discussed in detail in Chapter 5. The second utilizes software to prevent a processor from ever caching shared memory. The third method for maintaining cache consistency is ref-

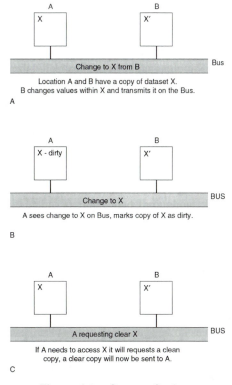

Figure 4.3 Snoopy Cache.

erred to as **snoopy cache** and is depicted in Figure 4.3. In this method, every processor constantly snoops or monitors the shared bus, relying on the fact that all processors are connected via a common bus. If a processor detects information on the bus regarding a change to data that the processor has locally cached, that portion of the cache is marked as "dirty". If the processor goes to access memory from the cache that is dirty, it must request a clean copy from the shared memory system. Snoopy cache does reduce bus traffic by an order of magnitude but does not help increase the maximum number of processors that may be connected to the system. Variations of snoopy cache are also utilized on systems that employ multiple buses, which further complicates the algorithm and the process of maintaining cache consistency. Information on the various types of data consistency is presented in Chapter 9.

4.4 DISTRIBUTED SHARED MEMORY

The distributed shared memory model was first introduced by Li and Hudak in 1989 [LiHu89] and has been widely discussed in literature since that time. A system employing distributed shared memory (DSM), commonly referred to as a multicomputer, consists of independent processors with their own local memory. These processors are connected via an interconnection network, as discussed in Chapter 1. The primary difference between a message passing and distributed shared memory is that DSM presents a logical view of shared memory. Thus, the DSM system implements the necessary communication and maintains data consistency for the application. Much like the shared memory model, most participants in DSM maintain a local cache for the sake of efficiency. Some portion (or all) of the local memory of each participant is mapped to the DSM global address space. The DSM system maintains a directory service to store complete state and location information for all data residing within the system. There are many models for implementing this directory service. The method utilized should be determined and is dependent on the type of consistency required of the system (see Chapter 8 for information on distributed directories and Chapter 9 for a discussion of the various types of consistency models). Regardless of how the actual internal directory is implemented, the DSM system maintains complete information by utilizing a single directory or several distributed directories.

4.4.1 Methods for Distributing Shared Data

To manage shared data, the following decisions must be made.

1. How will the shared data be distributed?
2. How many readers and writers are allowed for a given set of data?

There are two approaches to distributing shared data: replication and migration. Replication involves maintaining multiple copies; each participating location requiring the data has its own local copy. Migration involves moving the copy of data to various locations that require it. With migration, only one location is allowed to have a copy. If another location is utilizing the data, any request for this data will not be granted until the data are relinquished by the current holder. If multiple requests are received, the DSM system determines which request is honored based on the received order of requests or based on priority.

Managing shared data involves determining the number of readers and writers that will be allowed concurrent access to a given set of data. Systems allowing multiple writers are much more complicated than those limiting the number of writers to one. We now look at three approaches: single reader/single writer, multiple reader/single writer, and multiple reader/multiple writer.

Single Reader/Single Writer

As the name indicates, this type of method only allows one reader or one writer for a particular data set; thus it inhibits concurrent use of the shared information. Replication is not allowed. Solutions may be centralized or distributed. As with all centralized solutions, this type of DSM system requires a centralized server, a potential bottleneck as well as a critical element. A distributed solution generally requires a static distribution of the data. Thus, the distributed solution may require a process to contact two different locations to obtain two different data sets; however, the same data set will always be controlled from the same location. If the distributed solution does not allow migration, a given data set will not only be controlled from the same location but will also always be at that location. Single reader/ single writer distributed DSM algorithms that allow migration are called "hot potato" algorithms [KeLi89].

Multiple Reader/Single Writer

As the name indicates, this type of method allows multiple readers but only allows permission to write to a single location. When multiple readers have a copy of a data set and the single writer changes the data, the readers' copies are no longer accurate. To handle this scenario, most implementations provide some sort of invalidation process to the locations possessing read-only copies. This invalidation process requires a **copy set**, a list of system participants who have a copy of each piece of data. The multiple reader/single writer method may be implemented with a centralized solution, a combination centralized and distribution solution, or a distributed solution.

The centralized solution requires a single (critical element) server to process all requests and to maintain all data. This server is also responsible for sending all invalidation notifications, as depicted in Figure 4.4. As we have seen with every centralized solution, this isn't the most efficient solution because it increases network traffic around the server and requires excess work from the server.

An alternative approach to the centralized solution involves partial distribution. In particular, the centralized server receives every request for information. All of the data are statically distributed throughout the system. After receiving the request, the centralized server then passes the information to the distributed location in charge of that particular piece of information. Each location is responsible for handling the requests forwarded by the centralized server as well as notifying readers when their data become invalid. Figure 4.5 depicts an example of invalidation in this implementation.

There are two basic distributed approaches for the multiple reader/single writer method of DSM. The first distributed approach is dynamic, and the information may change locations. To locate the owner of a data set, all requests are broadcast throughout the system, as in Figure 4.6.

This method increases the amount of messages being transmitted throughout the system; thus, it creates more overhead and places an additional burden on the entire distributed system. Detail Box 4.3 presents the dynamic algorithms. The second approach statically distributes the data. The owner of the data (i.e., the location maintaining a particular data set) for responsible to receiving and handling all requests regarding that information as well as notifying readers of any invalid data. Since this design involves a static distribution, every participant has knowledge of where each piece of data is stored. The static algorithms are presented in Detail Box 4.4. One variation of this solution that allows dynamic allocation of data involves sending a request to the probable or last-known owner of the data set. If this is the owner, the problem is solved. If the data have been relocated, the receiver of the request forwards the request to the location it believes to be the current owner. This algorithm is depicted in Figure 4.7. Detail Box 4.5 describes the DSM system of Chorus.

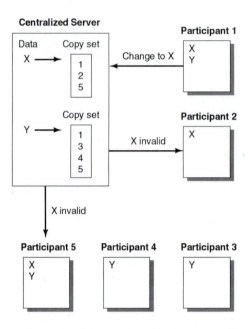

Figure 4.4   Centralized Server for Multiple Reader/Single Writer DSM.

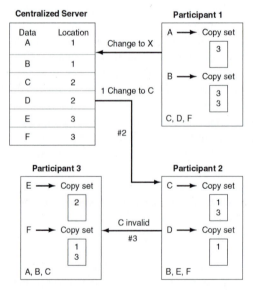

Figure 4.5   Partially Distributed Invalidation for Multiple Reader/Single Writer DSM.

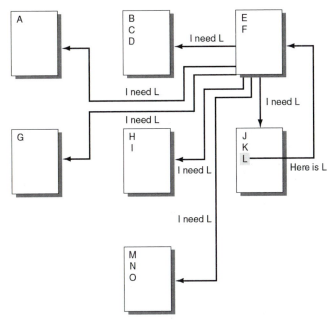

Figure 4.6 Dynamic Distributed Multiple Reader/Single Writer DSM.

Multiple Reader/Multiple Writer

To understand the complexity of the multiple reader/multiple writer approach to DSM, consider yourself part of a group working on a written project. If each takes a copy of the program home on disk and makes individual changes, how would you automatically integrate each of the individual changes? This is exactly the scenario presented to this type of DSM. The solution requires a sequencer that is in charge of time ordering all read and write requests. Algorithms for time ordering in a distributed environment are presented in Chapter 10. After the sequencer receives a request and attaches sequencing information, the request is then broadcast to sites holding a copy of the data set. The recipient of the broadcast updates its copy of the data set in the order dictated by the sequencer. Algorithms for the sequencer may be centralized or distributed. Multiple reader/multiple writer DSM algorithms are also known as full replication algorithms.

4.4.2 DSM Performance Issues

With all systems, everyone desires efficient implementations. As we have frequently mentioned, efficiency for real-time is not only desired but also required. In particular, we examine the issues of thrashing, data sharing, selection of the block size, and implementation location of a DSM system.

DETAIL BOX 4.3
DYNAMIC MULTIPLE READER/SINGLE WRITER DSM DISTRIBUTED
ALGORITHMS

Dynamic Distributed Request Page
```
Broadcast Request Page(Page Number);
```

Dynamic Service Request Page
```
If receive(Broadcast Request Page (Page Number,
        read write status)& Owner(Page Number);
```
                                    // We own the data being requested
```
Then
            {
        If write(Page Number)r=0;
```
                                    // If no current writer for page
```
        Then
        {
        return(Page Number, read write status);
```
                            // Releases page when satisfies
                            // single writer constraint
                                        // with requested read/write status
```
                If read write status=write
```
                            // If request is to write
```
                Then  write(Page Number)=1;
```
                            // update write flag for page
```
                Else Add to copy set (requester);
```
                            // add readers to copy set
```
        }                           // end no current writer
        Else                        // there is a current writer
        {
        Wait for writer release;
        return(Page Number, read write status);
                If read write status=write
                Then  write(Page Number)=1;
                Else Add to copy set (requester);


        }                           // end was a current writer
    }                               // end received request
```

Dynamic Invalidation
```
If receive(change, page Number)
Then forall in copyset(page number)
    Send invalid(page_number);
```

DETAIL BOX 4.4
STATIC MULTIPLE READER/SINGLE WRITER DSM DISTRIBUTED
ALGORITHMS

Static Distributed Request Page
```
Owner=look up owner(page number);
Send (owner, Request Page(Page Number));
```

Static Service Request Page
```
If write(Page Number)r=0;
```
                                     // If no current writer for page
```
Then
        {
        return(Page Number, read write status);
```
                                     // Releases page when satisfies
                                     // single writer constraint
                                     // with requested read/write status
```
        If read write status=write
```
                                     // If request is to write
```
        Then  write(Page Number)=1;
```
                                     // update write flag for page
```
        Else Add to copy set (requester);
```
                                     // add readers to copy set
```
        }
```
                                     // end no current writer
```
Else
```
                                 // there is a current writer
```
        {

        Wait for writer release;
        return(Page Number, read write status);
        If read write status=write
        Then write(Page Number)=1;
        Else Add to copy set (requester);


        }
```
                                   // end was a current writer

Static Invalidation
```
        If receive(change, page Number)
        Then forall in copyset(page number)
            Send invalid(page number);
```

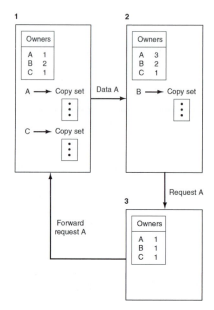

Figure 4.7   Dynamic Data Allocation for Multiple Reader/Single Writer DSM.

DETAIL BOX 4.5
CHORUS™

Chorus is a distributed real-time operating system that began as a research project in 1980. It reached its third version and a commercial product and was purchased by Sun Microsystems in late 1997. Chorus has since been established as the foundation for Sun's JavaOS and is individually marketed by Sun under the name ChorusOS.

Chorus utilizes a dynamic distributed DSM algorithm. The unit of shared memory is a segment. A given segment may either be possessed by several participants in the system for read-only access or by a single location for read and write access (multiple readers/single writer). Memory management is performed in the kernel. When a page fault occurs, the kernel checks its local cache for the page. If this page is not found locally, it then contacts the mapper to determine who maintains this page. The next step is to contact the owner. If the owner is not using the segment that contains the requested page, it updates the memory management unit to adjust the page tables and sends the page. While the page is being fetched, the process that caused the page fault is halted. Finally, the mapper will request the kernel to return the "dirty" pages so it may update its cache. Once the cache is updated, it decides whether to write it back to disk or leave it in the cache. Additional information on Chorus may be found in [AAO92, AGGL86, ARS89, BGGLOR94, and LJP93].

We remember the term **thrashing** from the more standard operating systems where the degree of multiprogramming is too high and the system is forced constantly to change pages in main memory, thereby degrading performance. In distributed operating systems, thrashing refers to a DSM when multiple locations desire to modify a common data set. This causes the data set to travel constantly between the locations as they play tug-of-war over the network to control the data set. If the data set spends more time traveling up and back than at a given location, it is not able to make progress on its execution with the data. Performance then degrades and we have the advanced version of thrashing. If the game of 'tug-of-ware' involves a page but there is not any sharing of the data structures within a page, the problem is referred to as **false sharing**. One solution for thrashing is to ensure that each location has a set of data for a minimum amount of time. This is referred to as temporarily freezing a page.

The best solution to thrashing is utilizing proper block sizes for data migration. If the block size is too large, the probability that multiple locations desire that same block of data increases. Large block sizes may also cause two or more pieces of data to be stored in the same block when they are fundamentally unrelated and should be stored in separately. When they are stored in the same block, the probability of multiple locations desiring that same block increases. Of course, if the block size is too small, the amount of overhead necessary for the directory server managing the data increases as the server has more blocks and thus more entries in its status information table. Large blocks also reduce the amount of overhead since each block of data must be individually requested and transferred to its desired location.

This brings up the question of what is the best block size for efficiency. Generally, the best compromise is for a DSM system to utilize data blocks the same size as the underlying system, such as the page size. This allows the DSM to be integrated easily on top of the existing system, utilizing the same page faults and access control mechanisms. These page-sized blocks should be guaranteed to a given location for a fixed minimum length of time to make some progress on computations. On the other hand, since the distributed system resides on top of a network, there are performance enhancements to having the block sizes as well as the page sizes connected to the underlying packet size the network utilizes to transmit the information. While this issue should be transparent to the application developer, since distributed real-time applications have been known to self-destruct when this issue is ignored, it is something the system programmer may wish to address.

An additional performance issue is that of memory wait states and the careful choosing of a location for data elements. This issue is easiest to address in the simple memory model for a parallel architecture but should not be ignored in a distributed environment. As long as there is some form of synchronization, data access patterns can be identified and possibly optimized to minimize the delay of memory access. This problem is becoming most noticeable in real-time applications as processor speeds rapidly increase. Additional information on this topic can be found in [ErCo92, ErCo93a, ErCo93b, Erick93b, GaCo95].

The final efficiency question involves where the DSM is implemented: the algorithms may be implemented in hardware, software, or a combination. Generally, the more expensive and sophisticated computers utilize hardware implementation, the most efficient implementation. Less expensive systems such as personal computers implement DSM in software while workstations utilize a combination of hardware and software.

4.5 MEMORY MIGRATION

One task that is often necessary in memory management is transferring virtual memory, or memory migration. Memory migration is the most time-consuming aspect of process migration, which was presented in Chapter 2. There are two fundamental decisions to be made regarding memory migration.

1. When in the migration process will we migrate memory?
2. How much memory will we migrate?

We now discuss the three basic methods for implementing memory migration.

The first method is **stop-and-copy**. This is the simplest and most straightforward approach but unfortunately is the least efficient solution. When migrating a process utilizing this type of memory migration, the execution of the process at the original location is immediately suspended. Next, the entire virtual memory having to do with this process is transferred to the migration destination. Once all other pertinent information related to the process has been migrated, the process resumes execution. This method is terribly unattractive to interactive and real-time applications. The inefficiencies introduced by completely halting process execution (referred to as **freeze time** [Esk89]) until total migration occurs as well as the potential wasted time in transferring all related virtual memory are simply not acceptable in such environments. The stop-and-copy method is depicted in Figure 4.8.

The second method is **concurrent copy** and is depicted in Figure 4.9. This method attempts to alleviate the inefficiencies of totally halting the process execution while migrating the process. Thus, when a process is designated for migration, the process continues to execute at its original location while it concurrently copies the entire virtual memory and other information related to the migrating process to the destination. As the process continues to execute at its original location, some of the pages that have been already migrated may become dirty; that is, they may not contain the same information as the migrated pages due to this continual execution. These dirty pages are repeatedly transferred to the migration destination. The question then arises as to when we should stop the execution at the original location, recopy these dirty pages, and finally complete the execution of the process at its migrated location. Stopping execution and completing the migration is performed when a particular limit is reached. Algorithms to determine limits may be based on a particular dirty to clean page ratio, a nonchanging number of dirty pages for a fixed amount of time criteria, or a combination of both. This method effectively reduces the freeze time but, like stop-and-copy, still may waste time and resources by copying all related virtual memory. Concurrent copy is also referred to as precopy and is utilized in the V-Distributed System [TLC85].

The third method is **copy-on-reference**. When a process is identified for migration, the process is stopped and all state information except the related virtual memory is transferred to the migration destination. The process then resumes execution at its migration site and the pages from memory are only transferred when the process requires the individual pages. The pages related to the migrated process may either remain at the original

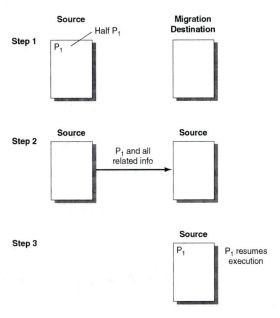

Figure 4.8 Stop-and-Copy Memory Migration.

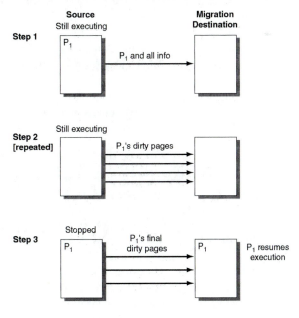

Figure 4.9 Concurrent-Copy Memory Migration.

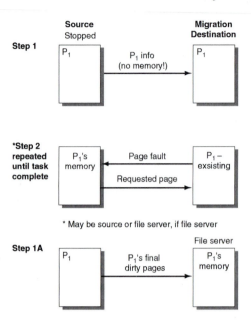

Figure 4.10   Copy-on-Reference Memory Migration.

location or be transferred to a file server. If the pages remain at the original location, resources at that location are still being utilized and are not as freed as when the virtual
memory is transferred to a server. When utilizing a server, all virtual memory is still being
transferred across the network but not all pages may have to travel to the migration destination. This transfer occurs prior to any state information being transferred to the migration destination and consequently allows the memory resources at the originating location
to become freed immediately. Finally, the utilization of the server removes all dependencies between the original location and the migration location. Copy-on-reference is depicted in Figure 4.10.

4.6 SUMMARY

Memory management is an extremely important aspect of all operating systems. Every
process executing and all data that are being manipulated must reside in memory. Table
4.1 presents the various models discussed in relation to what type of advanced system can
utilize them. Real-time systems can take on any of the architectural forms listed; therefore,
they are excluded. Memory management does, however, provide many opportunities to
increase performance for real-time systems. Table 4.2 summarizes the choices listed
throughout this chapter that will enhance system performance.

Fine-tuning distributed memory management will remain an active research area, as
it has with centralized systems. As we have discussed, much of memory management performance focuses on executing and manipulating data within a *limited* memory space.

Therefore, one might be led to believe that as memory size increases due to advances in technology and increased affordability, the issue of memory management would become less critical. This is not necessarily true because of the expanding demands of systems and the resulting increased size of programs. Remember, at one time many centralized systems had only 16K of RAM and no virtual memory!

Memory Management Models	Advanced Systems Component Type		
	Parallel UMA	Parallel NUMA	Distributed
Simple Memory Model	yes		
Shared Memory Model		yes	Best for small scale
Distributed Shared Memory			yes

Table 4.1 Memory Management Choices Available for Advanced Systems.

Method/ Concept	Performance Choice
Simple Memory Model	Works well but avoid thrashing.
Shared Memory Model	Overlap communication and computation.
	Prefetch data.
	Utilize snoopy cache.
Distributed Shared Memory	With multiple reader/single writer: static distributed algorithm.
	With multiple reader/single writer: centralized algorithm.
	Multiple reader/multiple writer (good concurrency).
	Temporary freezes allowed.
	Block size = page size.
	Hardware implementation (at least partial).
Memory Migration	Concurrent-copy.

Table 4.2 Performance Choices for Memory Management.

4.7 REFERENCES FOR FURTHER STUDY

The general references provided in Chapter 1 can provide more general information on memory management, as can [PTM98]. Some appropriate traditional research papers concerning information in this chapter include [AAO92, AGGL86, ARS89, BGGLOR94, ErCo92, ErCo93a, ErCo93b, Erick93b, Esk89, Esk95, Fu97, GaCo95, KeLi89, LaEl91, Lee97, LEK91, LiHu89, MoPu97, PTM96, StZh90, SuZh96, and TLC85].

The following provide some starting points for sources on the Internet regarding the two systems presented in the detail boxes. In particular, the CHORUS home page can be found at http://www.sun.com/chorusos/ and the Amoeba Web pages can be found at http://www.am.cs.vu.nl. The University of Pennsylvania's Distributed Systems Technical Report and Research Library at http://www.cis.upenn.edu/~dsl/library.html contains some research papers regarding the efficiency of DSM in terms of latency. The general Web sites from Chapter 1 will provide pointers to specific documents that may also contain information on memory management.

EXERCISES

4.1   For secondary storage on a personal computer, answer each of the following. (Hint: Check current trade journals, Web sites for manufacturers, and Web sites for vendors.)

    a.   What are the various types of hard drives available today?
    b.   Explain the difference between each type of hard drive.
    c.   What is the current price for the various types of hard drives?
    d.   What are the current access, seek, and transfer rates for various types of hard drives?
    e.   What is current maximum capacity for hard drives? Why is there a limitation?
    f.   What are the current access, seek, and transfer rates for read-only CD-ROM?
    g.   Are rates different for writeable versus read-only CD-ROM? Why?
    h.   What is the current price for a CD-ROM? writeable CD-ROM?
    i.   What is the current price for DVD?

4.2   Describe an advantage of segments over pages. Describe the advantages of pages over segments.

4.3   What are the advantages of utilizing larger page sizes? disadvantages? What are the advantages of utilizing smaller page sizes? disadvantages?

4.4   Write a program to implement FIFO page replacement and FIFO second chance page replacement. Your program should report what frame each page is being placed into as well as the total number of page faults. You may assume that each frame is empty at the beginning. (Note: Every time a page is loaded into a frame, a page fault occurs.) Test your program with four memory frames and each of the following page access sequences.

    a.   1,2,3,4,5,2,6,2,7
    b.   1,2,3,4,5,2,1,4,2,3

4.5   Prefetching data can assist in optimizing performance in the shared memory model. Discuss one potential problem in implementing automatic data prefetch.

4.6   Describe and discuss one advantage and one disadvantage for each of the following types of
      access for distributed shared memory.
      a.   Single reader/single writer
      b.   Multiple reader/single writer

4.7   Write a program to implement multiple reader/single writer DSM with a centralized server.
      Your solution should include a program for a single centralized server and a program for
      participating clients. The server and the clients should utilize interprocess communication. In
      addition, the server and the clients should record all actions taken and all messages received
      in a file. Test your program with four participating clients and the following request sequence
      as well as with your own test data.

      a.   Clients 1 through 3 request Page 1 for reading.
      b.   Client 4 requests Page 1 for writing.
      c.   Client 4 writes to Page 1.
      d.   Clients 2 through 4 request Page 2 for reading.
      e.   Client 1 requests page 1 for writing.
      f.   Client 1 requests page 2 for writing.
      g.   Client 1 writes to pages 1 and 2.

4.8   Discuss the relative advantages and disadvantages for the following methods of implement-
      ing memory migration.
      a.   Stop-and-copy
      b.   Concurrent-copy
      c.   Copy-on-reference, data maintained at origin
      d.   Copy-on-reference, data maintained at file serve

Concurrency Control

Whenever you have multiple threads of control or multiple processes accessing shared data and resources, you must ensure that access is conducted in an orderly fashion or inaccurate results will occur. In this chapter, we focus on the issues of concurrency control. Concurrency control keeps processes out of each other's way and ensures a smooth and proper execution in a distributed and parallel environment. It is often considered the most important issue in distributed computing; therefore, it is presented in its entirety even though some aspects are often presented in introductory operating systems texts. Section 5.1 introduces the concepts of mutual exclusion and critical region as well as the three-point test for evaluating solutions. Sections 5.2 through 5.6 present various solutions to mutual exclusion; specifically, Section 5.2 presents semaphores, Section 5.3 presents monitors, Section 5.4 presents the basics of locks, Section 5.5 presents software lock control, and Section 5.6 presents a token-passing approach. This chapter concludes with a discussion of a possible consequence of mutual exclusion; in particular, issues related to deadlocks are presented in Section 5.7. In Part 2 of this book, Chapter 9 expands on issues related to multiple access to data with the concept of transaction management while Chapter 10 discusses information related to ordering and synchronization.

5.1 MUTUAL EXCLUSION AND CRITICAL REGIONS

Mutual exclusion ensures that multiple processes that share resources do not attempt to share the same resource at the same time. Users of a distributed system would not be happy if they went to a printer to pick up their output only to realize that the document is intertwined with several of their colleagues' documents, on each page. Users want their document to print exclusively and consecutively on its own pages of paper. Exclusive access through mutual exclusion is necessary for resources such as tape drives, printers, and files. If we are to ensure peak performance, we would not want to stop a process in execution when it is not necessary. The portion of code or program accessing a shared resource is referred to as a **critical region**. Only such a region needs to prohibit concurrency. This is referred to as concurrency control and is realized by semaphores (Section 5.2), monitors (Section 5.3) or any of the other concurrency control mechanisms discussed in this chapter (Sections 5.3 through 5.6). These controlling mechanisms assist in ensuring mutual exclusion through a means that makes a process stop and wait its turn for resource access. Figure 5.1 displays two processes accessing and changing a variable 'foo' and the utilization of a critical region. A basic mutex operation is employed in the Surgical Scheduling Program in the appendix.

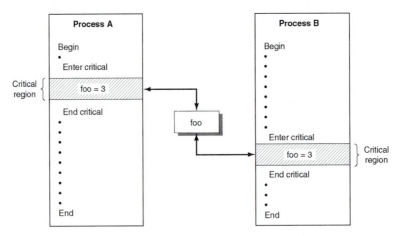

Figure 5.1   Critical Regions Protecting a Shared Variable.

We now look at a basis for evaluating the various solutions presented throughout this chapter. In particular, solutions to the mutual exclusion problem must pass the following three-point test.

Point 1. Does the solution ensure that two processes will not enter their critical regions at the same time?

Point 2. Does it prevent interference from processes not attempting to enter their critical regions?

Point 3. Does it prevent starvation? (Starvation results from a process waiting forever to enter its critical region, also referred to as indefinite waiting.)

We now examine some of the solutions available to solve the mutual exclusion problem.

5.2 SEMAPHORES

The idea of utilizing semaphores to achieve mutual exclusion was suggested by Dijkstra in 1965 [Dij65] and implemented in the programming language Algol 68. A semaphore is a type of integer variable whose value indicates the status of the protected resource. There are only two operations allowed on a semaphore: `raise` and `lower`.[1] When a process wishes to enter a critical region of code, it must execute a `lower`. When a process leaves a critical region of code, it must execute a `raise`. Both `raise` and `lower` check the value of the semaphore and either increase it by 1 or decrease it by 1, respectively. The checking and changing of the semaphore is completed as an **atomic action**; that is, the action is indivisible and uninterruptable. The algorithms for semaphores are presented in Detail Box 5.1. An example of processes using a semaphore to access a shared resource is presented in Detail Box 5.2.

DETAIL BOX 5.1
SEMAPHORE ALGORITHMS

```
    Let
            Semaphore SEM;
                            //initial value is 0.
            SEM=my_favorite_shared_device;


    LOWER
            SEM=SEM-1;
            If SEM >=0
                    Return(true);
            ELSE
                    Wait (until_raise);
                    Return(true);
    RAISE
            SEM=SEM+1;      //If more than one process is
                            //waiting, system chooses which
                            //process will receive a raise
    USING SEMAPHORE
            Bla Bla Bla;    //execute non-critical region
                            //code
            lower(SEM);     //waits for return of true
            critical_region_code;
                            //accessing shared resource
            raise(SEM);
            Bla Bla Bla;    //executing non-critical region
```

---

[1] P and V were the names of the original operations originating from words in the Dutch language.

5.2.1 Semaphore Weakness

The weakness of semaphores involves their reliance on the programmer. Semaphores rely on a programmer issuing a `lower` to enter and a `raise` to leave a critical region. However, what would happen if the programmer accidentally issued another `lower` to leave the critical region? (You know, the programming at 2A.M. trying to make a deadline type of error we have all made and been driven crazy by!) The semaphore would remain in a protected state, no process would be raised, and no further progress could be made. The system with regard to this resource would be deadlocked! Such a deadlock could also occur if the process had an untimely crash (that is, after the lower is executed but prior to the execution of the raise operation). Issues regarding deadlocks are discussed in Section 5.5.

5.2.2 Semaphore Evaluation

We now evaluate semaphores according to the three-point test. First, do semaphores ensure that two processes will not enter their critical regions at the same time? Yes. Second, do semaphores prevent interference from processes not attempting to enter their critical region? Yes, with proper utilization. Only processes that have expressed their desire to enter a critical region decrement the semaphore. However, if the semaphore is used incorrectly, as pointed out in Section 5.2.1, then a process that is no longer interested in entering the critical region would be able to interfere with processes still waiting to enter their critical region. Finally, do semaphores prevent starvation? Yes. There is nothing inherent in semaphores, with proper utilization, that would cause a request to suffer eternal postponement. However, as we have discussed, improper use may result in a deadlock. In conclusion, with proper use a semaphore can pass the three-point test. A description of support for semaphores available in UNIX System V is presented in Detail Box 5.3. Finally, it is important to note that semaphores are difficult to implement in a truly distributed environment and are generally best avoided since absolute consistency of the semaphore data must be maintained. Additional related information regarding the maintenance of consistency is contained in Chapter 9.

5.3 MONITORS

Monitors are a higher-level synchronization primitive proposed by Hoare [Hoa74] and Brinch Hansen [Bri75]. A monitor is a compiler supported programming language construct that allows a group of procedures, their variables, and data structures to be grouped together in a package or module; in other words, it is an abstract data type. Other non-monitor processes may call the procedures within the monitor but may not access the internal data structures. To ensure mutual exclusion, monitors do not allow more than one process within the monitor to be active at any given time. If a monitor has an active process and another call to a procedure within that same monitor is received, the new call to the procedure is blocked until the other, active process that is using the monitor relinquishes control. Underneath the monitor, the compiler frequently utilizes a binary semaphore. Binary semaphores are semaphores with a restriction on the values of the semaphore to 2. With the compiler and not the programmer utilizing the semaphores, the 'opportunity' for the programmer to misuse the semaphore is removed. The programmer is only left to worry about compiler bugs and memory corruption (the biggest nightmare for all programmers that increases with the complexity of the system).

DETAIL BOX 5.2
EXAMPLE UTILIZING SEMAPHORES

Let processes A, B, C, D, and E desire access to the shared resource protected by the Semaphore SEM. We now show an example by tracing the values of SEM. We assume they are all using the algorithm for USING SEMAPHORE presented in Detail Box 5.1. The actions are depicted in Figure 5.2.

```
0.   SEM =0;        //initial value
1.   SEM=-1;        //Process B issued a lower, entered critical region
2.   SEM=-2;        //Process A issued a lower, waiting for a raise
3.   SEM=-3;        //Process C issued a lower, waiting for a raise
4.   SEM=-2;        //Process B issued a raise, left critical region
5.                  //System chose to raise Process C, C enters critical region
6.   SEM=-1;        //Process C issued a raise, left critical region
7.                  //Process A is raised, A enters critical region
8.   SEM=-2;        //Process D issued a lower, waiting for a raise
9.   SEM=-1;        //Process A issued a raise, left critical region
10.                 //Process D is raised, D enters critical region
11.  SEM=0;         //Process D issued a raise, left critical region
12.  SEM=-1;        //Process E issued a lower, enters critical region
13.  SEM=0;         //Process E issued a raise, left critical region
```

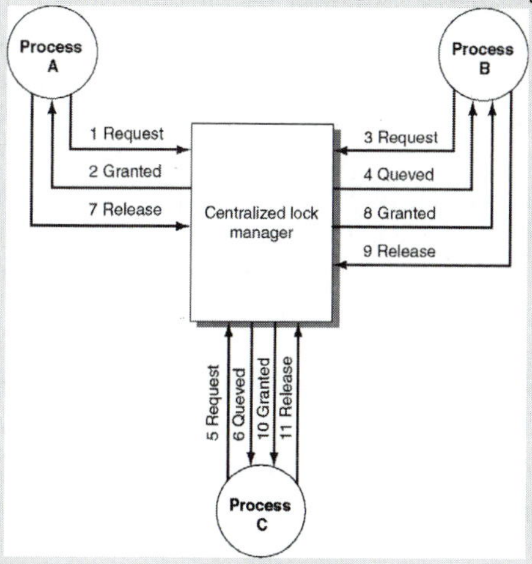

Figure 5.2   Example Utilizing Semaphores.

DETAIL BOX 5.3
SEMAPHORE SUPPORT IN UNIX

UNIX System V supports semaphores as part of the interprocess communication facility. To utilize semaphores in a C or C++ program, you must utilize the following include statement.

```
#include <sys/sem.h>
```

The function call for creating semaphores is `semget`, while `semop` performs the various semaphore operations. A complete listing of all details is available in the man pages (online UNIX manual) on your local system (type in `man semget` or `man semop`). In addition, any hardware support for semaphores on a UNIX system can be found with the keyword search option (type in `man -k semaphore`).

5.3.1 Condition Variables

As currently defined, a monitor contains several procedures and variables. This raises the question of what happens if Process A, in control of the monitor, needs Process B to perform a particular action in order to proceed. If B's action does not utilize any procedures or variables in the monitor, there is not a problem. However, if Process B needs to utilize procedures within the monitor to perform the necessary action for Process A to continue, this creates a dilemma. Remember, more than one process is not allowed to be active inside the monitor at any given time. To accommodate this circumstance, monitors have **condition variables**. These condition variables are global to the monitor and are included within the monitor. Much like semaphores, condition variables have two operations: `wait` and `signal`. The `wait` operation suspends the calling process while `signal` resumes a single process. `Wait` is similar to the `lower` operation of a semaphore, but the `signal` operation differs from the semaphore `raise` operation. In particular, if no process is suspended, the `signal` operation will have no effect.

Let us now examine what happens if Process A executes a signal and Process B is waiting to be allowed to become active within the monitor. The following is a list of the two choices available along with their relative benefits.

1. Process A continues to remain active until it leaves the monitor. When it leaves the monitor, Process B becomes active. Benefits of this approach include no context switch and thus efficiency. One potential problem arises due to the fact that time has elapsed and computations occur between when Process B executes a wait and receives a signal. This is the approach proposed by Brinch Hansen [Bri75].

2. Process A is suspended and allows Process B to become active (context switch). When Process B has completed, Process A is allowed to become active once again (another context switch). While this method does involve more context switching, it lends itself to behavioral correctness proofs. This is the approach proposed by Hoare [Hoa74].

5.3.2 Monitor Evaluation

We now evaluate monitors with the three-point test. First, do monitors ensure that two processes will not enter their critical regions at the same time? Yes. Second, do monitors prevent interference from processes not attempting to enter their critical regions? Yes. This allows only one process to be active in a monitor at a time. Only the process that is currently active or a process waiting to become active can influence when a waiting process is allowed to become active. Finally, do monitors prevent starvation? Yes, since the compiler implements the underlying semaphore utilized to provide mutual exclusion. However, there is one significant shortcoming for monitors in any advanced environment that does not employ shared memory: specifically, the compiler implementation relies on shared memory to implement the semaphores. In conclusion, without shared memory you cannot utilize monitors. Detail Box 5.4 presents an overview of the use of monitors in Java.

DETAIL BOX 5.4
MONITORS IN JAVA

Java implements monitors. Java handles the set-up and acquisition of all locks. A programmer only needs to indicate what resources require concurrency control by utilization of the word `synchronized` in the object or method definition. The condition variables have two operations in Java: `wait()` and `notify()` (signal). The condition variables' behavior follows Hoare's recommendation, previously discussed. If multiple methods are asleep in a `wait()`, Java wakes objects on a first come first served basis. When threads are synchronized, only one thread will execute at a time. Java also contains a `notifyall()` to awaken all waiting threads.

5.4 LOCKS

Mutual exclusion, as we have seen, involves a process utilizing a shared resource and needs to ensure that the process is the only one utilizing the said resource. Locks are used in everyday life to keep people out; likewise, a lock can be utilized to keep other processes from utilizing a shared resource. A lock can have two states—locked and unlocked—thereby providing concurrency control and mutual exclusion to a resource. If a process wants to utilize a shared resource, it checks to see if it is locked. If the resource is not locked, the process locks the resource and proceeds. This seems quite simple! However, consider the scenario in Detail Box 5.5. Two resources both desire to enter their critical region and both determine that it is unlocked. This can result in what is commonly known as a race condition and may allow two processes to enter their critical region at the same time! Obviously, this is not the desired outcome of concurrency control and it does not provide mutual exclusion. In this section, we examine the various approaches for successful lock implementations that avoid this race condition.

DETAIL BOX 5.5
RACE CONDITION EXAMPLE

Consider Process A and Process B executing the following steps.
1. Check lock state.
2. Find the lock in an unlock state.
3. Set lock.
4. Execute critical region.

Now consider the following scheduling scenario that results in a race condition as both processes race to set the lock. What results is improper execution.

1. Process A checks lock state.
2. Process A finds the lock in an unlock state.
3. Process A is sent to the waiting queue by the scheduler (blocked due to maximum   processing time).
4. Process B checks the lock state.
5. Process B finds the lock in an unlock state.
6. Process B sets locks.
7. Process B executes critical region.
8. Process B is blocked by scheduler.
9. Process A sets lock. (Remember, it checked prior to its block and it was unlocked!)
10. Process A executes critical region.

5.4.1 Taking Turns

Taking turns is something most of us were taught in our toddler and preschool years. The concept is simple. If multiple processes want to share resources, then let them share by taking turns. The catch involves that a process is not allowed to pass up a turn. Suppose that once again, Process A and Process B shares a resource. If Process A utilizes the resource, then the next process to utilize the resource must be Process B. Process B cannot pass up its turn. This is also referred to as strict turn alteration since passing up a turn is not an option. Taking turns is implemented with a variable. If two processes share the resource, the variable may have the value 0 or 1. The value is initialized to 0 for Process A. When Process A completes its critical region, it must change the value of the variable to 1. The value of this variable will not and cannot be changed except by Process B entering its critical region and at the conclusion changing the value to 0. If Process A wishes to enter a critical region, it checks the value of the variable. If the value is 0, it may proceed; otherwise, it must wait its turn. At this point, Process A will continuously check the variable for a value of 0. This process of continuous checking is referred to as a **busy wait**. This busy wait wastes system resources, which are consumed by constantly checking the value of the variable. This continuous checking is referred to as **spinning** and the variable being continuously checked is referred to as a **spinlock**. In other words, a busy wait implements spinning on a spinlock.

We now evaluate this method by the three-point test. First, does it ensure that two processes will not enter their critical regions at the same time? Yes, a process can only enter the critical region based on the status of turn. Both processes cannot change the variable at the same time. Second, does it prevent interference from processes not attempting to enter their critical regions? No. If Process B never desires to enter a critical region, it will be able to interfere with Process A's ability to enter its critical region. Finally, with regard to the prevention of starvation, this method fails. Look at a scenario where Process A does not attempt to enter a critical region to change the value of the variable. In this situation, Process B would be permanently forbidden to enter its critical region and thereby suffer resource starvation. In conclusion, this proposed solution as presented would not pass the three-point test. However, varying this approach by incorporating polling, as presented in Chapter 2, would correct the deficiencies in the proposed solution to taking turns. Evaluating this variation by the three-point test is left as an exercise.

5.4.2 Atomic Operations and Hardware Support

One series of solutions to the mutual exclusion problem utilizing locks involves atomic operations. The first of these solutions prevents the race condition presented in Detail Box 5.5. This is accomplished by implementing an atomic (indivisible) check-and-set operation. Since the operation is atomic, it would be impossible for another process to perform any operation intertwined within the checking of the lock and the setting of the lock. This operation, also referred to as test-and-lock, is frequently supported by the hardware to ensure its atomic operation. With hardware support, if two processes attempted to check-and-set at the same time, the system would decide which process's operation would be performed first.

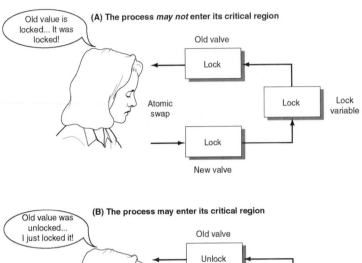

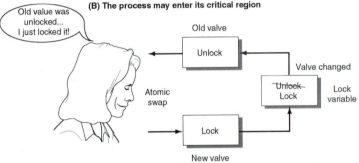

Figure 5.3   Atomic Swap.

The second solution involving atomic operations is a swap. A swap generally executes three statements and utilizes a temporary variable. The atomic swap is able to swap
out the current value of the lock state with a value indicating that the shared resource is
now in a locked state. At this time, the process examines the value of the variable with
which it swapped. If the value indicates that the state was already locked, the process cannot continue and the variable remains in the locked state. However, if the value the process
received in the swap was unlocked, the process may now enter its critical region since the
variable is now in a locked state (due to the swap), as depicted in Figure 5.3. Once again,
with hardware support, if two processes attempted to swap at the same time, the system
would decide which process's operation would be performed first.

We now evaluate the atomic operations solution by the three-point test. First, we observe that it will ensure mutual exclusion. Second, it does prevent interference from processes not currently attempting to enter their critical regions. Third, a process desiring access to a shared resource that is protected by these atomic actions will not starve but will
eventually be scheduled and thereby receive an opportunity to enter its critical region.
Evaluating this solution for advanced systems is difficult. Atomic actions are very difficult
to implement in hardware for parallel computers; nevertheless, they are available on some

systems. Distributed systems, which by nature involve multiple physical computers, need to rely on software implementations.

5.5 SOFTWARE LOCK CONTROL

When hardware support for locks is not available, utilizing locks requires a software implementation. Distributed solutions often utilize software and provide different types of locks to coincide with the memory management schemes discussed in Chapter 4 (specifically, read locks and write locks are available). Solutions to distributed lock control may employ a centralized lock manager or a distributed lock manager. We now examine the two basic approaches.

5.5.1 Centralized Lock Manager

As with every solution in distributed computing utilizing a centralized control of authority, employing a centralized lock manager creates a single critical element and single point of failure, thereby making this approach unviable for distributed real-time applications. If the lock manager were to crash, the entire system would suffer. There is an increase in network traffic around the centralized authority, and if the demand is high enough, a system bottleneck results. The lock manager performs much of the same function performed in hardware for centralized systems. This server maintains information concerning what processes have requested to enter their critical region and what process has been granted access. In centralized lock manager solutions, there are three required messages involved and one optional message.

1. *Request.* This message travels from the requesting process to the centralized lock manager. Its purpose is to request entry into its critical region.

2. *Queued.* This message is optional and is sent by the centralized lock manager to a requesting process. It is utilized when the request cannot be granted immediately. It can be used to notify the process that the request has been received and to expect a message when it can proceed. Requests that cannot be granted immediately are placed into a queue and serviced in a first come first serve basis. If this optional message is not employed, it may be difficult for participants to distinguish a dead centralized lock manager from a busy centralized lock manager.

3. *Granted.* This message is sent to a requesting process from the centralized lock manager. It is sent *only* when it is time for that process to enter its critical region. If a request is received that cannot be granted, the requesting process receives nothing or the optional "Queued" message.

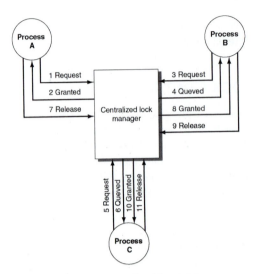

Figure 5.4   Centralized Lock Manager.

4. *Release.* This message is sent to the centralized lock manager from the requesting process that has been serviced. This message indicates that the
   process has completed its critical region and is releasing the lock. At this
   time, the centralized lock manager sends a "Granted" message to the next
   process in the queue.

Figure 5.4 depicts a centralized lock manager functioning with three processes all requesting to enter their critical region. This example utilizes the three required messages as
well as the optional "Queued" message.

   We now evaluate the centralized lock manager by the three-point test. First, does it
ensure that two processes will not enter their critical regions at the same time? Yes. The
centralized lock manager will only permit one process to enter its critical region at a time,
thereby successfully guaranteeing mutual exclusion. Second, does it prevent interference
from processes not attempting to enter their critical region? Yes. Only a process in its
critical region or other processes that have been queued can affect when a given process
enters its critical region. Finally, does it prevent starvation? Yes. This algorithm will service requests in the order they are received, so it is fair and will service all processes that
make a request at some point in time.

5.5.2 Distributed Lock Manager

Distributed solutions to implement a lock manager have two required messages and one
optional message. While there are similarities to a centralized lock manager solution, there
are several differences including the following.

- ♦ Who receives such messages
- ♦ Who sends such messages
- ♦ What is necessary to enter a critical region

We now examine each of these messages, including information on the senders and recipients.

1. *Request.* This message travels from the requesting process to all participants in the system. This message may be individually sent to each participant or it may utilize a group communication mechanism. Its purpose is to request entry into its critical region. All requests contain a timestamp from the source. Chapter 10 presents algorithms for employing timestamps in a distributed environment.

2. *Queued.* This message is optional and is sent by recipients of a "Request" message to a requesting process. It can be used to notify the process that the request has been received and to expect a message when the process can proceed to the next step. It is utilized whenever the request cannot be granted immediately. A participant will not grant a request when executing its critical region or if it has made its own earlier request (determined by timestamps) that is still outstanding. Any denied requests are placed into a queue until the location has completed its critical region and appropriate outstanding requests. If this optional message is not employed, it may be difficult for participants to distinguish a dead participant from a busy participant.

3. *Granted.* This message is sent to a requesting process from all participants in two circumstances. First, if that location is not in its critical region and does not have a request with an earlier timestamp, it will send the "Granted" message. Second, when a location has queued messages it will send a 'Granted' message to every location in its queue upon completion of its critical region. This situation is roughly the equivalent of the "Release" message in the centralized approach. If a "Request" is received that cannot be granted (i.e., the process is in its critical region or has a request with an earlier timestamp), the requesting process receives nothing or the optional "Queued" message.

We now examine the issue of permission. In the centralized approach, there was one lock manager and a "Granted" message was absolute authority to enter a critical region. In the distributed lock manager algorithms, "Granted" is a vote to grant permission. It is not absolute permission. Earlier solutions utilizing a distributed lock manager required a unanimous decision: A participant must receive a "Granted" vote from each and every participant to enter its critical region. This created complications. It is often difficult to know who is participating in the distributed system and how many participants exist at a given moment. Participants in a distributed system come and go due to lunch breaks, crashes, and network failures. If a unanimous decision is necessary, any and every system participating is a critical element. This is simply not acceptable! An alternative solution requires a majority vote; a participant must receive a "Granted" message from a majority of the participants to enter its critical region.

We now test the distributed lock manager solution by the three-point test. First, does it ensure that two processes will not enter their critical regions at the same time? Yes. With a unanimous decision, everyone has decided together to allow a given process to proceed. With the majority vote, the majority has decided who shall be permitted to proceed and enter the critical region. There is only one majority since multiple majorities would require the support of overlapping members and members check for the presence of earlier requests prior to sending a "granted" message. Therefore, more than one process cannot receive proper permission to enter a critical region. Second, does it prevent interference from processes not attempting to enter their critical region? No and yes. In the unanimous decision implementation, a process cannot continue without a "Granted" vote from all participants. If a given participant crashed, no other participants would be able to continue. The crashed participant interfered with others attempting to enter their critical region. Thus, the unanimous implementation fails. In contrast, since the majority vote approach allows for individual system failures, the solution passes Point 2 of the test. Finally, evaluating by Point 3, does it prevent starvation? Since requests are serviced in an ordered fashion, all requests will eventually be serviced and a process does not suffer from starvation. In conclusion, the unanimous approach fails and the majority approach passes the three-point test.

5.6 TOKEN-PASSING MUTUAL EXCLUSION

The token-passing solution to mutual exclusion is intended for use with multiple processors connected via a network (parallel or distributed). The solution consists of a single token and a path traveling through all of the processors: a logical ring. To enter a critical region, a process must possess this token. Since there is one token, there may only be one process in a critical region. When a process exits its critical region, the token is released back into the system. If no process wishes to enter a critical region, the token continually circulates. While this solution seems ideal, there are complications.

1. How do you determine if the token is lost or is just being used for a long time?

2. What happens if the location possessing the token crashes for an extended period of time?

3. How do we maintain a logical ring if a processor drops out (voluntarily or by failure) of the system?

4. How do we identify and add processors joining the logical ring?

Some of these concerns can be resolved by designating one or two locations as a monitor. These monitors will occasionally send messages requesting the identification of the token holder. If no one responds, they can place a new token on the network. New members can register with the monitor and lost members can be recorded. The easiest method for identifying lost members is through their neighbor. When a processor attempts to pass the token along, it waits for an acknowledgment. If no acknowledgment is received, it attempts a second time. If there is still no acknowledgment, the neighbor can be considered lost. The neighbor then notifies the monitor, who then records the information and assigns a new neighbor.

We now evaluate this solution by the three-point test. First, does it ensure that two processes will not enter their critical regions at the same time? Yes, there is only one token on the ring at a time. Even with the utilization of two monitors, in the event the token is lost, there will only be one new token placed into the system. Second, does it prevent interference from processes not attempting to enter a critical region? Yes. A noninvolved process will simply pass the token along and will not interfere. Finally, does it prevent starvation? Yes. All processes receive fair and equal treatment.

5.7 DEADLOCKS

Thus far, this chapter has focused on providing mutual exclusion. In this section, we examine a possible side effect of mutual exclusion. In particular, mutual exclusion is one of the four allocation conditions that contribute to **deadlocks**. If the following four allocation conditions hold, you will have a deadlock?

1. *Mutual exclusion:* As we have seen, this is a type of resource allocation used to provide a process with exclusive access to the resource. It is utilized to prevent the concurrent sharing of a resource.

2. *Non-preemptive resource allocation:* A resource access is provided to a process by the system but the system cannot force the process to relinquish control of the resource.

3. *Hold and wait:* A process holds one resource and is waiting on another resource.

4. *Cyclic wait:* There exists a cyclical path in the resource allocation graph. Each process involved holds at least one resource. This resource will not be released until the process obtains a resource currently held by another member in this cycle. Observe that a cyclic wait cannot occur without the hold and wait condition.

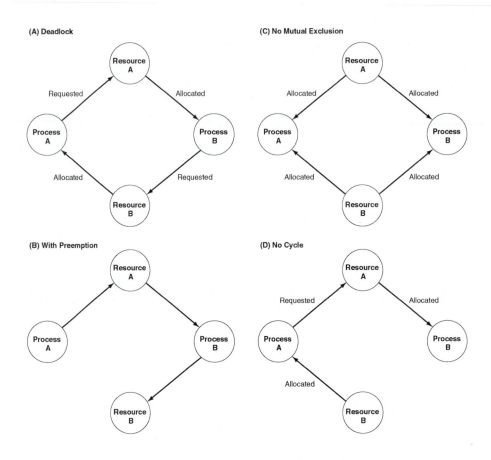

Figure 5.5   Resource Allocation Graph.

Thus, a deadlock is a system state that involves an inappropriate resource allocation resulting in two or more executing processes being unable to change states and complete
execution. If any of these conditions do not hold, you will not have a deadlock.

Let's look at a simple deadlock example with two processes and two resources as depicted
in the resource allocation graph in Figure 5.5(A). All arrows into resources are requests and all
arrows from a resource represent an allocation. Each process has one resource and wants the
other resource. In addition, each process will not give up its currently held resource until it obtains and utilizes the other resource (cyclic hold and wait). Observe that if we introduce preemption, processes can be forced to give up a resource and the cycle breaks. Therefore, there is
no deadlock, as depicted in Figure 5.5(B). If the processes can concurrently share the resource
(no mutual exclusion) then the cycle does not present a problem. Again, there is no deadlock as
in Figure 5.5(C). Finally, look at an example where there is no cycle, as in Figure 5.5(D). With
no cycle, no process is prohibited from successful execution and there is no deadlock. A dead-

lock will only occur when a process controls a resource exclusively, cannot be preempted, *and* is involved in an allocation cycle.

If the resource is buffer space in a distributed system, the deadlock is commonly referred to as a **communication deadlock**. If the communication deadlock only involves two locations, it is referred to as a **direct store-and-forward deadlock**. If multiple locations are involved in the deadlock, it is referred to as an **indirect store-and-forward deadlock**.

How do we deal with deadlocks? We use the mnemonic PAID to remember the relevant approaches: Prevent, Avoid, Ignore, or Detect. We now examine each of these approaches.

5.7.1 Prevent Deadlocks

To prevent a deadlock, we must prevent one of the aforementioned allocation conditions. This entire chapter has discussed mutual exclusion, the first allocation condition. This allocation condition is necessary for resources such as a printer, so it is not an option to avoid deadlocks. The printer also presents why a system would not want to force preemption, the second allocation condition, for that would allow multiple print jobs to be interleaved, possibly on the same page. Since a cyclic wait cannot occur without a hold and wait, we are left with one allocation condition to break. There are a few options to break this condition, but each has disadvantages. We now present these options.

1. *Only allow single resource holding.* If a process only holds a single resource and it is not allowed to hold multiple resources, there cannot be a cycle! This solution can be quite cumbersome. Some processes simply need simultaneous access to multiple resources.

2. *Preallocation of resources.* This solution forces every process to gain access to all resources prior to initiating execution. The question of efficient resource utilization arises. Suppose you have a process that will take three weeks to complete execution. At the very end of this execution, it may need a resource. Preallocation would force this process to gain exclusive access to this resource and let it sit idle for three weeks prior to its utilization! This is not very efficient.

3. *Forced release to request.* This solution forces every process to release all allocated resources before it can make additional resource requests. This allows any and all processes waiting for the previously held resources to continue and thus prohibits the cyclic hold and wait. For some applications, this may not be practical.

4. *Acquire in order.* This solution numbers all resources. A process can only request a resource that is numbered higher than all resources it has previously been allocated. Since you cannot go to a lower number resource, you cannot create a cycle and therefore you can avoid deadlock; however, num-

bering all the resources in a distributed environment in this manner would not be an efficient or enjoyable task. Particularly, no one would want to be the location assigned the highest numbers.

5. *Seniority rules.* This solution utilizes a timestamp method (discussed in Chapter 10) to ensure unique timestamps on the processes. Any process holding a resource must relinquish a resource if an older process (based on the timestamp) requests that resource. The senior process always wins. The younger process must take careful steps to preserve its own integrity and die (see Chapter 9 for more details on transaction management).

5.7.2 Avoid Deadlocks

Recall the deadlock avoidance algorithms for centralized systems. All the algorithms forced a process to present all its needs up front. After presenting its needs, the avoidance algorithms (which are exceptionally slow due to NP completeness) determine if a safe allocation can be made. If such a safe allocation can be made, the process is allowed to continue and is allocated its desired resources. There are several problems. First, no processes can predict exactly what they need. Second, the algorithms are so slow that they are never utilized in a centralized environment. Thus, not many people are anxious to add a network communication delay to already slow algorithms. Utilizing these algorithms in a distributed environment could only make a slow solution slower. Thus, we continue and discuss ignoring deadlocks.

5.7.3 Ignore Deadlocks

Ignoring deadlocks is the approach taken by UNIX and is the favorite of many. It coincides with the philosophy of "Don't worry, it will be fine." In particular, this method simply chooses to ignore the problem. If the system administrator notices the system having problems or gets a complaint from a user, then the administrator investigates (or delegates someone to investigate) the problem and attempts to fix it. Frequently, the human owner of a deadlocked process (who thinks it is just "slow") becomes frustrated. This frustrated user generally proceeds to cancel the process. The cyclic hold and wait is now broken and the problem is solved! This approach is also referred to as recovery.

5.7.4 Detect Deadlocks

Of all PAID solutions for handling deadlocks, detection is the solution area receiving the most research attention (how many grants could be issued on the study of ignoring?). Detection solutions do not worry if a deadlock occurs but focus their concern in finding a deadlock after it has occurred. Once found, appropriate steps will be taken to remove the deadlock. Approaches for deadlock detection, like many problems we have examined previously, are available in the centralized and distributed variety with all the usual advantages and disadvantages. There are two frequently cited surveys in this area: [Kna87] and [Sin89]. We are going to focus on an unusual and very successful solution. This is a distributed solution proposed by Chandy, Misra, and Haas [CMH832]. Their solution is based on probing messages. These special messages are sent whenever a process fails to receive a resource or times out. The probes contain the following three fields.

1. Identification of the blocked process
2. Identification of the process sending this message
3. Identification of the process to whom this message is being sent

The process for sending a probe is as follows.

1. The blocked process (A) initiates a probe. This probe is sent to the holder of the resource for which it is waiting (B). This originator (A) places its identification in fields 1 and 2 of the probe and the holder of the resource (B) in field 3.
2. The holder of the resource receives the probe. If this location (B) is not waiting on another location for a resource, it terminates the probe. However, if this location (B) is waiting on another location(s) (C) for a resource, it forwards the probe according to step 3.
3. Forward the probe to (C) (for all locations). The probe is modified as follows. Field 1 is unchanged. Field 2 becomes its own process identification (B), Field 3 identifies the new recipient (C).
4. If field 1 = field 3, there is a deadlock. Otherwise, repeat (starting at step 2).

If field 1 ever equals field 3, there is a deadlock. That is, the probe is sent back to the originator of the probe. For a simple example, consider a direct store-and-forward deadlock situation. The first probe is sent with (A,A,B). Location B receives the message and sends it to A with (A,B,A). The cycle is identified and thus the deadlock is found.

Now that the deadlock is identified, there are three choices to eliminate the deadlock. First, we can enlist the system operator for assistance. Second, we could terminate the process ourselves (just like the ignore method!). The third option is to roll back the system, a feature of transactions that are discussed in Chapter 9. Suppose you are the system operator; you then proceed to select a process (or two) to terminate. The obvious choice is a process of low priority that hasn't utilized a significant amount of system resources and, of course, does not belong to your boss. To prevent starvation in the future, the terminated process is often raised one priority level so it will not continue to be a victim if future deadlocks should occur.

5.8 SUMMARY

Concurrency control is imperative when computing with multiple processes or multiple threads of control. Without concurrency control, an application cannot take full advantage of the resources available in a distributed or parallel environment. We have seen that concurrency control benefits from the cooperation of the hardware, the operating system, as well as the application development language, as summarized in Table 5.1. The most popular modern languages provide some sort of mechanism to support mutual exclusion and access to critical regions. The methods presented are generally utilized by any multi-threaded application. The Surgical Scheduling Program in the Appendix provides an example of a multi-threaded application utilizing concurrency control.

Level of Support	Tools Provided
Hardware	Atomic operations
	Spin locks
	Mutex hardware operations
	Cache concurrency control
System Support	System Libraries utilizing hardware support
	System support for concurrency with multi-threaded applications
	Lock Manager
	Token Passing mutual exclusion
Language Support	Semaphores.
	Critical regions
	Monitors
	Mutex operations using system libraries

Table 5.1 Summary of Support for Concurrency by Hardware, System, and Languages.

We have also examined deadlocks, a potential problem when allowing mutual exclusion in accessing shared data. Of all PAID approaches, detection is the most popular and feasible. Deadlock detection is always difficult. With more resources available, the problem becomes even more complicated. With regular network delays, it is difficult to determine if something is "hung up" or just slow. Perhaps that is the attraction of ignoring! If we are not to ignore the problem in a distributed environment, the probe solution of detection is by far the most popular as well as the most elegant.

5.9 REFERENCES FOR FURTHER STUDY

Additional overview information on concurrency control can be found in most introduction to operating systems textbooks. Resources for programming utilizing concurrency control include [Cha97, Cou98, DeDe94, DeDe98, and RoRo96]. Some appropriate traditional research papers concerning information in this chapter include [AgAb91, Bri75, CaRo83, CMH83, Dij65, Fu97, Hoa74, Joh95, JoHa97, Kna87, RiAg81, Sin97, and Tho79].

The SUN Microsystems Web site includes examples of programs utilizing threads with concurrency control. These example programs can be used as templates and are found at http://www.sun.com/workshop/sig/threads/Berg-Lewis/examples.html. Otherwise, the general Internet sites provided in Chapter 1 are the best sites to utilize to locate information concerning concurrency control.

EXERCISES

5.1 Mutual exclusion is often necessary to protect shared data. Name three applications that require mutual exclusion for data access.

5.2 Data mutual exclusion can be utilized for different levels of granularity. The unit of data to be protected may be an individual piece of data, an individual record, or a set of records. Discuss the relative advantages and disadvantages for the different levels of granularity. Provide examples.

5.3 The accidental execution of a semaphore `lower` operation when exiting a critical region is a common programming mistake. Describe one possible change to the semaphore operations, `raise` and `lower,` that could help alleviate this problem.

5.4 Suppose an application allows processes to be assigned priorities. These priorities would be utilized to determine which process receives a raise in a semaphore operation when multiple processes are blocked. Would this solution pass the three-point test? Explain your answer and any necessary assumptions.

5.5 Describe an alternative to a busy wait. What are the relative advantages and disadvantages to your approach?

5.6 In Chapter 2, we studied the use of polling for scheduling. Consider a solution to mutual exclusion utilizing locks. This solution utilizes a continuous loop that polls users of a resource it guards. When a process is polled, it may accept the opportunity to lock the resource or it may pass until the next time it is polled. Provide a short discussion evaluating this solution according to the three-point test. In addition, discuss the strengths and weaknesses of this approach.

5.7   What are the potential difficulties involved if the "Queued" message is not utilized in the centralized lock manager system?

5.8   When utilizing a Centralized Lock Manager, what happens if a process is granted access to its critical region and then dies? Propose a solution to prevent this problem.

5.9   Registration for courses is something that all students have endured. For a given course, there is a finite number of spaces. Registering more students for a course than there are spaces is not allowed. In addition, registration would take forever if only one process was allowed to access the data required to register students. Therefore, the data regarding each course must be protected via concurrency control. Write a program to perform course scheduling. You must assume that multiple copies of this program may be executing and that all executing copies access the same data. You may also assume that you were hired by the world's smallest university and that there is only one course. Test your program thoroughly. Choose one of the following options.

Option A.   Implement your solution utilizing semaphores.

Option B.   Implement your solution utilizing monitors.

Option C.   Implement your solution utilizing locks.

5.10   Automatic teller machines are a part of everyday life. Implement a simulation program for a simplified automatic teller machine. Make sure you protect the account balance using a form of concurrency control as more than one person may have an access card for a given account. Your solution should focus on the issues of concurrency control, and you may utilize one of the following options.

Option A.   Implement your solution utilizing semaphores.

Option B.   Implement your solution utilizing monitors.

Option C.   Implement your solution utilizing locks.

Object-Based Operating Systems

Object-based technology has appeared in nearly every aspect of computer science, including operating systems. In this chapter, we introduce objects and related terminology (Section 6.1). We examine how objects are used in operating systems by discussing the most pertinent implementation details of object-based operating systems. In particular, Section 6.2 presents how Clouds implements objects, threads, and the overall design of their memory storage system. In Section 6.3, we discuss the architecture of Chorus's object-oriented subsystem COOL. Section 6.4 presents Amoeba, focusing on its treatment of objects in terms of identification, protection, and communication. The two dominating object models are presented in Sections 6.5 and 6.6. Specifically, Section 6.5 provides details on the Distributed Component Object Model known as DCOM, originated by Microsoft but currently managed by an independent group and available for all UNIX and Windows platforms. Section 6.6 examines a popular object-based standard, the Common Object Request Broker Architecture, known as CORBA.

6.1 INTRODUCTION TO OBJECTS

Operating systems are programs and are frequently written in everyday languages such as C and C++. While objects have appeared everywhere in computer science, an agreed upon, exact, and consistent definition of objects and all related terminology does not exist. In this section, we focus on the definitions most widely accepted. We present these common definitions in Section 6.1.1. In Section 6.1.2 we present the benefits of object-based systems.

6.1.1 Object Definitions

An **object** is a development abstraction that encapsulates all related services and data as depicted in Figure 6.1. Object services are defined in terms of functions. In object-based systems, functions are also referred to as methods or member functions. In this chapter, we simply use the term **method**. Methods cannot be independently accessed; rather, these methods are accessed only through their object. The overall concept is based on the view that methods mean little without the objects. Take, for example, walking. What does walking mean? If we provide a further description, such as a person walking or a dog walking, walking now has some meaning. The method only has meaning due to the owner-object. A method is accessed when a client makes a **request** to an object. Thus, objects service requests from clients. A request can accept information through arguments and may return results. The complete collection of methods that can be performed by a particular object defines the **object's behavior**. For example, a person's behavior is the collection of all the "methods" such as walking, talking, singing, whispering, shouting, thinking, eating, drinking, sleeping, running, sitting, dancing, and so on.

It is common in object-based systems to allow multiple definitions for methods. This allows generic requests whose exact behavior is determined by the set of parameters of the request, provided the parameters match up with a defined method. When multiple method instantiations are allowed, the method instantiations are commonly referred to as **constructors**. The allowance of multiple method definitions by the same name is traditionally referred to as **function overloading**. We saw an example of this in Chapter 3, Detail Box 3.4. This Java example has multiple constructors for the socket object, including some default parameter values.

Object-based systems frequently allow multiple instances of an object. This feature allows objects to share a common implementation. For example, if we have a person object, we can have Steven and Sue as two independent instantiations of this object. The abstract definition of an object is often referred to as a **class**. When this term is utilized, the actual instantiations are then referred to as objects. An instance of a programming class is often referred to as a **servant** in Java and CORBA.

In addition, objects may partially share implementation details through **inheritance**. Inheritance allows objects to define themselves in terms of existing objects. When inheritance is allowed, the object-based system is defined as an object-oriented system. Some implementations allow objects to inherit characteristics from multiple objects. This type of inheritance is referred to as **multiple inheritance**.

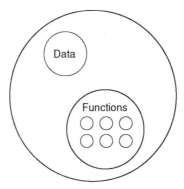

Figure 6.1 An Object.

6.1.2 Evaluation of Objects

Objects have many benefits. One of the greatest benefits of utilizing objects is data abstraction and encapsulation. This encapsulation encourages strong modularity and clean interfaces. In addition, objects encourage strong scope and type checking, which in turn provides enhanced security by means of forbidding inappropriate data manipulation and object actions. In object-based systems, the unit of distribution for migration as well as the unit utilized in shared memory is the object. In an object-oriented system, the inheritance feature encourages incremental design and development. Detail Box 6.1 presents a variation on the pure object model, subject-oriented programming (SOP), that shows potential for use in large-scale systems, including distributed operating systems and applications.

While the benefits of using objects are well regarded, the benefits of object orientation in advanced environments are a little more controversial. Does the use of objects have any drawbacks? Yes, although most concern object-oriented and not object-based systems. Object inheritance, particularly multiple inheritance, is difficult to manage. Any change to a parent object affects objects derived from it. Designing and managing a large design with multiple inheritance is difficult to represent and document. In addition, an object's behavior is dependent on the parent objects from which it was derived. Frequently, to understand the behavior, you must understand the behavior of the parent. This implies total knowledge of the complete system (not a desirable characteristic in a massively distributed environment). However, the operating system is usually developed by a controlled group of people. In addition, object-based operating systems do not dictate the methodology of applications developed on top of the system. Object-based systems and languages are historically slower. In a distributed environment with network delays or a real-time environment with tight time constraints, utilizing known slower technology generally is not desirable. However, despite the drawbacks there are some successfully designed object-based and object-oriented operating systems.

DETAIL BOX 6.1
SUBJECT-ORIENTED PROGRAMMING

Subject-oriented programming is described in many papers, including [HaOs93, OsHa95] and evaluated in terms of its potential for use in a distributed environment in [MDGM99]. The research group at IBM's T. J. Watson Research Center designed SOP to support programming in the large (that is, the development of massive software projects). SOP is designed to allow sub-development teams to program using traditional object-oriented techniques. The difference between the classic object oriented paradigm and SOP is when the results of these smaller teams are brought together to create the larger product resulting from the work of all teams. Each development group has its own subjective view of the larger system. At the subject view, collections of classes (or fragments of classes) defining and implementing a particular point of view form the subject. A collection of subjects that are composed together, along with the resulting composed subjects, forms a universe. With the use of the concept of different universes, a given class may be used multiple times in different universes. The behavior of the class depends on how it was composed (according to rules known as composition rules) into the universe. Essentially, the structure of each universe is encapsulated and then isolated from other universes once the collection of all of the universes begins to come together.

Formally, a subject represents a subjective view of the classes comprising the problem domain. One could think of object-oriented programming as restricting the user to one subject view, thereby increasing the reliance of the developer on global knowledge or increasing the chance of possibly unwanted side effects. Likewise, SOP allows multiple subject views of the same object. With these views, there may be different interfaces. The developer only needs to know and understand the universe in which the developer works. The subject-oriented paradigm requires us to consider the interface *our* application requires of an object. A different application may require a different interface. We need not concern ourselves with the other applications as they exist outside our space and time. Utilizing SOP, one must still identify the objects but only for the immediate domain, and these objects have no requirement to know about all objects in the system (i.e., those outside the subject's universe). Furthermore, one need have knowledge only of the messages that an object supports applicable to the context in which the object will be used. This behavior may be provided by the object, or the behavior may be added to the object by the application developer. Therefore, the need for communication between application developer and "class owners" is greatly reduced [OsHa95].

The significance of this type of system is that each local universe is unaffected by changes in the global universe. Therefore, this type of model can increase the location, migration, and concurrency transparency of the resulting system. While this approach is still in the research stage and is not aimed at operating systems, it would be interesting to see this model employed for a massive system such as a distributed operating system. SOP does present many advantages over object-oriented programming in a distributed environment, as detailed in [MDGM99]. In addition, similar methodologies are also being explored in the context of language support [LoKi97].

6.2 THE CLOUDS OBJECT APPROACH

Clouds is an object-based distributed operating system developed at the Georgia Institute of Technology and described in [DLAR91]. Clouds is a general-purpose operating system with a native kernel (that is, it does not run on top of another operating system). The kernel kernel is called Ra[1] and is an example of a layered kernel that is not a microkernel. It can be utilized for centralized and distributed applications that can be written in object-oriented and non-object-oriented languages. Section 6.2.1 presents Clouds's objects while Section 6.2.2 presents Clouds' threads. The discussion of Clouds concludes in Section 6.2.3, which presents Clouds' memory storage system.

6.2.1 Clouds Objects

Clouds is based on a popular object-oriented programming model, the object-thread model. In this section, we introduce the Cloud object. Each object consists of data and methods. An entire Cloud object is persistent and contained in a virtual address space. Multiple inheritance is not allowed. Objects communicate via messages, which in turn invoke the execution of a method. This process is referred to as an invocation. This method may then change the value of data or cause other objects to receive messages. Objects have the capability to reply to the sender of a message, when the invoked method has completed, through reply parameters. Messages result from a thread of execution and thus the origin of the model's name. These messages pass into the object by invoking an entry point with its input parameters. Parameters are utilized strictly for data, not the address of the data. All addresses are meaningless since they are relative for a given object. A user can invoke a Clouds object by specifying the object, entry point, and arguments to the Clouds' shell.

Cloud objects are considered "heavyweight" and are best suited for large grain programs. A Cloud object is passive as it does not contain a process or thread. In particular, a cloud object consists of the following items.

- ♦ User-defined code
- ♦ Persistent data
- ♦ Volatile heap for temporary memory allocation
- ♦ Persistent heap for allocating memory

All objects are physically stored in data servers, but Clouds provides location transparency; therefore, all are accessible from any system server. Transparency is further enhanced since each object has a unique global system-level name. A user is not responsible for determining the object system name but rather can assign any name and allow the naming service to translate the name into a unique system name.

---

[1]Ra is the Egyptian sun god.

Clouds maintains orthogonality of computation and storage by providing objects to support an abstraction of storage and threads, thereby decoupling the two. Clouds's implementation of the object-thread model has allowed for a unified treatment of I/O, interprocess communication, information sharing, long-term storage, as well as atomic and reliable computations.

6.2.2 Clouds Threads

Threads traverse a path through objects and execute the entry points to an object. As the threads traverse, they execute the code within the objects. Thus, the various threads represent all user activity with each thread, thereby representing a logical path of execution. A thread can be created in one of two ways: by a user or by a program. Clouds threads are not bound to a single address space as were the threads described in Chapter 2. When the execution of an object results in the invocation of another object, the thread temporarily leaves the first object to enter the newly called object. Upon completion, the thread returns to the original object. Object invocations may be recursive or nested. A thread terminates when it completes execution of the entire operation, as depicted in Figure 6.2.

Threads are allowed to execute concurrently within an object thus permitting multiple simultaneous threads within an object. When multiple threads exist within an object, they share the contents and the object's address space. Clouds supports locks and semaphores for concurrency control within an object. All application objects must be written to support concurrent executions. The actual level of concurrency is specified when creating concurrent threads at execution time.

6.2.3 Clouds Memory Storage

In traditional systems, persistent storage consists of files and the memory associated with a process is volatile. Clouds objects are utilized to unify persistent storage and memory to create a complete, persistent address space. Messages and files are not supported but can be simulated. For objects to share data, they must invoke the object where the data exists. From the memory manager viewpoint, Clouds objects are composed of segments that are mapped in virtual memory. All segments are a multiple of the physical page size. System objects called partitions maintain the segments. These partitions are responsible for creation, maintenance, and storage. A segment belongs to the partition that created it.

6.3 CHORUS V3 AND COOL V2

Chorus V3 (version 3) is a distributed real-time microkernel operating system and is described in [LJP93]. It was originally developed as a research project at the French research institute INRIA. Since that time, it has evolved into a commercial product family, including a variety that is CORBA compliant. In particular, CHORUS V3 included an object-oriented

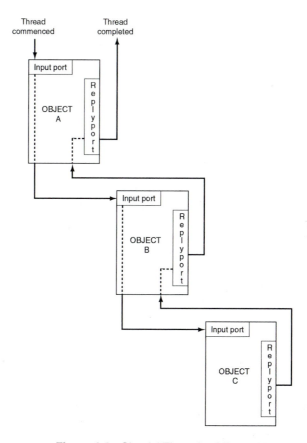

Figure 6.2 Clouds' Threads of Execution.

subsystem. This subsystem is known as COOL (Chorus Object-Oriented Layer) and is now part of the distributed real-time commercial product Chorus/COOL ORB, which is CORBA compliant. Since the third version was released as a commercial product, Chorus was purchased by Sun Microsystems in late 1997. Chorus has since been established as the foundation for Sun's JavaOS and is individually marketed by SUN under the name ChorusOS.

The COOL subsystem runs on top of the Chorus microkernel. One significant goal of Chorus V3 was system responsiveness in terms of process control and telecommunications. This was considered very important to realize a distributed real-time executive kernel.

COOL objects consist of two segments, a data segment and a code segment. The object methods, referred to as methods, are contained within the code segment. This code segment is shared by all instantiations of the same object.

In this section, we focus on COOL V2 (version 2). The COOL architecture consists of the following three layers.

1. Base layer
2. Generic runtime system
3. Language runtime systems

User programs reside on top of the language runtime system. We now discuss each of these layers.

6.3.1 The Base Layer: COOL Memory Management

This layer provides a set of services for user processes. It spans the entire system and extends the (process-based) microkernel. The object-oriented equivalence to DSM is provided in this layer as well as message-passing support. The underlying Chorus DSM was presented in Detail Box 4.4. Memory management in COOL is based on clusters. Clusters are persistent, and the base layer is able to locate nonactive clusters. Each cluster is a set of regions, which in turn consist of segments. Members of clusters are normally related objects that belong to the same class. Higher layers in the architecture determine actual cluster assignments. These clusters are mapped to arbitrary address space and are logically a collection of virtual memory regions. The distributed virtual memory mapper manages the relationship between virtual memory and secondary storage. Distributed virtual address spaces are referred to as a context space. This context space allows clusters to share threads of execution belonging to a particular context space. The binding of the actual mapping of the context space may be changed and thereby remapped to a different set of addresses when needed. This unique approach allows a cluster to be mapped into several contexts concurrently but does not require all contexts to be mapped. Thus, contexts that are not currently being utilized can remain unmapped.

6.3.2 The Generic Runtime System Layer: COOL Objects

Objects are implemented in the generic runtime system layer. COOL objects consist of a state and a set of methods. These objects are intended to service application development. Two types of object references are available. The first is a domain-wide reference that is persistent and globally unique. The second is a language reference that is valid in the current context of an object and is a reference to virtual memory.

One component of the generic runtime system layer is the object management component. Object management includes the following operations.

- ◆ Object creation
- ◆ Dynamic linking
- ◆ Dynamic loading
- ◆ Transparent invocation (mapping into contexts and location on secondary storage)

This layer supports an execution model and a language-level model. The execution model maps object activities to Chorus threads and jobs. Threads of execution result when an object launches an activity. Threads are supported by the underlying microkernel and jobs are utilized to model distributed execution. Each job represents a single distributed application. In particular, jobs organize a collection of contexts. Each context can support several clusters while a cluster can contain many objects, as depicted in Detail Box 6.2. In addition, a cluster can support concurrent activities. Concurrency is supported locally by synchronization primitives and nonlocally by a distributed token manager, as discussed in Chapter 5. Local synchronization primitives include semaphores and multiple reader/single writer locks, as presented in Chapter 5.

The language-layer model is designed to support the varied semantics of different language models; in particular, this portion implements ORB. This model supports persistence, invocation and address space remapping. In general, it allows this layer to function in a language-specific manner for multiple languages in a distributed environment. Normal method invocation is automatically replaced by remote invocations utilizing a proxy service called an interface object. This proxy service replaces the language communication primitives with remote procedure calls by marshaling and unmarshaling the parameters. It allows, and in fact implements, the distributed execution of objects.

6.3.3 The Language-Specific Runtime System Layer

This layer is responsible for mapping language-specific objects to a generic runtime model through the utilization of preprocessors, thereby implementing ORB's IDL as described in Section 6.6.1. A programmer can use the generic language COOL++, a variation on C++ or program in standard C++ and explicitly utilize system calls to the generic runtime layer. The primary advantage of employing COOL++ is a transparent programming model due to its CORBA compliance, as described in Section 6.6.

6.4 AMOEBA

Amoeba is based on the processor pool model, which allows a dynamic number of processors. Amoeba's process management and memory management system were introduced to you in detail boxes in Chapters 2 and 4 respectively. In this section, we focus on Amoeba's object technology. Amoeba objects may be client objects or server objects, and multiple inheritance is allowed. We pay particular attention to the identification and protection of Amoeba objects in Section 6.4.1 and object communication in Section 6.4.2. The Amoeba system is described in [MVTVV90, TaAn90, and Tan95].

DETAIL BOX 6.2
COOL MEMORY EXAMPLE

In this example, we use two locations: locations A and location B, as depicted in Figure 6.3. Three contexts exist: Context 1 and Context 2 at location A and Context 3 at location B. In addition, there are three clusters, which, we have learned, can be contained in multiple contexts. In particular, Cluster 1 is mapped to three virtual memory regions as it is mapped to Contexts 1, 2, and 3. Cluster 2 is mapped to two virtual memory regions, as it is mapped to Context 1 and Context 3. Cluster 3 is also mapped to two virtual memory regions as it is mapped to Context 2 and Context 3.

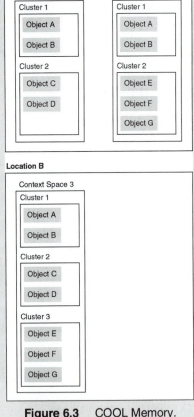

Figure 6.3   COOL Memory.

6.4.1 Identification and Protection of Amoeba Objects

Identification of objects is based on a structured capability that has four primary fields.

1. Service port
2. Object number
3. Rights field
4. Check field

The service port is an encoded representation of the server process that manages that particular object. Like Clouds' objects, Amoeba's objects have a unique name that is chosen randomly. This is represented as the object number. This number is mapped to an ASCII name by the directory service. The operations that may be performed (e.g., read, write, execute) on an object are mandated by the contents of the rights field. Finally, this capability is also responsible for protecting objects, which is carried out by the check field. This field provides cryptographic protection designed to prevent one from guessing an object's capability. This protection also allows capability management to occur by a user process, outside of the kernel.

6.4.2 Amoeba Object Communication

Objects communicate through remote procedure (object) calls. In total, there are three primitive types of remote procedure calls.

```
1.Do_operation
2.Get_request
3.Send_reply
```

A `do_operation` originates from a client thread. It is utilized to send a request from the object's managing service for the object to perform operations. If a server is willing to accept remote procedure calls at a particular port, it utilizes the `get_request` to announce this to the system. When a `do_operation` is received, the server carries out the request and returns a reply through a `send_reply`, as depicted in Figure 6.4. These basic communication primitives are further enhanced to the same level as most operating systems as they are inherited by other classes.

Messages are received on an object's port, a 48-bit number known only by the service and its clients. Public services such as the file system publicize their port. Private services' ports are kept secret as the knowledge of a port number represents permission to utilize the service. In addition to the port number, a client must have proper capabilities to utilize the service for the intended request. Thus, the communication mechanism includes security measures; ports protect access to servers and capabilities protect objects. In addition, servers can utilize asymmetric cryptography (described in Chapter 11) to enhance security further.

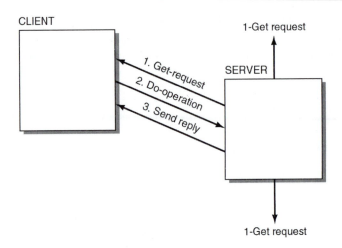

Figure 6.4 Amoeba Object Communication.

Recall from Chapter 3 that remote procedure calls require parameter marshalling. In Amoeba, parameter marshalling (and unmarshalling) is performed by the Interface Language Compiler. After marshalling a request, the Amoeba transport mechanism is called to deliver the message. A message consists of a header and a buffer. While the buffer generally contains the data, the header has a fixed format. Specifically, the header contains addressing information, operation code, and other information that is dependent on the type of message. Operation codes are utilized to select an object that will service a particular message.

6.5 Distributed Component Object Model (DCOM)

The Component Object Model was the basic Microsoft Component Object Model. DCOM, for Distributed COM, provides a programming model, binary standard, as well as interoperability standard for distributed object computing. DCOM is available since Windows NT 4.0, has had versions downloadable for Windows 95, is included in Microsoft Internet Explorer 4.0, and Windows 98, and is available for all major UNIX platforms from a company by the name of Software AG. Although initiated through Microsoft, COM and DCOM are no longer proprietary to Microsoft; rather, the independent ActiveX Consortium is responsible for their management. Some information contained within this section is abstracted from the Microsoft white paper series on NT [Micr98].

The basic COM model includes the ability to allow logical elements to be considered independent. It also allows flexible binary components for adaptability to different configurations and machines. COM is most widely recognized as the core technology within ActiveX. Any software tools that support COM components automatically support DCOM, the distributed extension to COM. There are four ActiveX Server Framework services that are particularly useful to DCOM: transactions including rollback and recovery capabilities; queuing with reliable store-and-forward queues to enable operations on networks with intermittent inaccessibility; server scripting to allow easy integration with HTML-based Internet Applications; and access to production legacy systems. DCOM takes COM one step further and enables software components to communicate directly across networks. Some highlights of DCOM including the following.

- *Transport neutral*. DCOM can enable components to communicate whether they are connection oriented or connectionless and can support TCP/IP, UDP/IP, IPX/SPX, Apple Talk, and HTTP.

- *Open technology*. DCOM technology is an open technology and is available for UNIX, Apple, Windows, and some legacy environments; however, it is most common in Windows-based environments.

- *Common Web browser and server components*. Since DCOM includes ActiveX and ActiveX components, it can be embedded into browser-based applications. DCOM can enable distributed Internet applications that support browser technology.

- *Security*. DCOM can integrate Internet certificate-based security, as described in Chapter 11, into standard-based applications.

- *Distributed Computing Environment's (DCE's) RPC mechanism extension*. The extensions to this mechanism by DCOM, which are layered upon DCE's RPC mechanism, are also the subject of a proposed Internet standard.

The basic DCOM architecture allows applications to be designed and developed in a manner that automatically allows future distribution and scalability. Generally, it is less expensive and more practical to add a server to a system than to be in the constant state of upgrading a system. So what does this have to do with DCOM? Applications designed using DCOM come with an inherent ability to enable flexibility in deployment. An application may originally be deployed as a centralized solution on a single server. The demands on the application may outgrow the current capabilities of the server. Generally this would require a rewrite of the application or upgrading the server. With a DCOM application, an additional server may be added to the system and allow different components to run on the new server. This greatly increases the scalability of the application and very likely decreases the engineering maintenance cost since changes to the application were not required. The exact degree of scalability of the application is dependent on the architecture of the application. Of course, if the original application is not designed appropriately, it may not be able to take advantage of this aspect of DCOM.

To communicate with a component that is nonlocal, DCOM employs an interprocess communication mechanism that is completely transparent to the application. Specifically, DCOM replaces the local communication mechanism with a network protocol. In this regard, DCOM provides location independence and location transparency to the applications.

6.5.1 Monikers

Instance names in DCOM are referred to as **monikers**. Monikers are themselves objects and allow extreme flexibility. Identifiers ranging from a database name and server to a uniform resource locator (URL) and hypertext markup language (HTML) page and may characterize object instances. Monikers contain the necessary information and logic to locate a currently running instance of the object they are naming. The standard interface to a naming object is known as an IMoniker. This IMoniker can be employed to bind to a named object instance.

Generally, object instances name themselves. In the naming process they create a moniker object that is provided to clients interested in reconnecting to them. In addition, object instances register their moniker objects with the COM libraries. Currently running monikers are listed in the running object table (ROT). This ROT is used by monikers to find running object instances quickly. When a moniker object needs to bind to an instance, the ROT attempts to find a match; when a match is found, a pointer to the appropriate active object that is stored in the ROT is returned. If there is no running instance, or the moniker is not registered, the moniker uses the object creation mechanism to create an uninitialized instance. Upon creation, the moniker stores the object's state through the appropriate mechanism for that particular object. This entire process is transparent to the application.

Monikers contain reference information to an object's persistent state. This information is typically stored in a file or a database. An object can indicate to a moniker what should be activated when this state has been stored. Thus, a data-intensive operation may prevent a potential bottleneck if the object is run at the same server that stores that data. If multiple clients need to access the object, the object should execute in a location accessible by all clients.

Monikers also have the ability to have their binding operation overridden. Specifically, it is programmatically possible to override the remote server name that should be used in a moniker bind operation. This is accomplished through the inclusion of an optional pointer to the COSERVERINFO structure within the moniker. This structure is employed by the CoCreateInstanveEx structure for creating object instances.

The file moniker is employed as part of COM. This portion encapsulates the file protocol for the object instantiation. This can be used for mapping the COM file moniker to the URL file protocol, for accessing persisted data in the native file system, for initializing a file protocol to access the given file name, or as a detection mechanism for indentifying of the type of storage file. A URL moniker encapsulates IP protocols such as http, ftp, and gopher.

6.5.2 Remote Method Calls

DCOM performs remote method calls when a client wants to call an object in another address space. As mentioned, DCOM's Interface Description Language (IDL) was built on-top of DCE RPC standard IDL. As is common in RPC, all parameter information is marshalled into a flag memory buffers, as discussed in Chapter 3. The recipient re-creates the parameter information by re-creating the stack contents through an unmarshalling process. As the remote procedure call returns, any return values and output parameter need once again to be marshalled from the local stack and sent back to the client. The client then unmarshalls the values and the process for this round of communication is completed. The client side code is referred to as the proxy, while the server code for conducting the remote method calls is referred to as the stub.

An additional data type not included in DCE RPC is the interface pointer. These types of pointers can appear as a result of a `CoCreateInstance` or a parameter to a method call. To handle this new data type, the creation of a proxy/stub pair was created that is capable of handling this data type in all methods in the interface. As is traditional in most areas of COM and DCOM, the process of marshalling an interface pointer may be extended or overridden through the use of a custom proxy/stub pairs.

6.5.3 Garbage Collection

The primary mechanism for controlling a given object's lifetime is maintaining a reference count. An object reference count is increased by using `AddRef` and decreased through the method Release. Since it is not feasible to expect all remote clients to terminate normally and perform a Release, Pinging is employed. Pinging is a well-known mechanism for detecting when clients terminate abnormally. Each exported object has a `pingPeriod` time value and a `numPingsToTimeOut` count. In combination, these values determine the overall amount of time known as the "ping period". If the amount of time in the "ping period" passes without a ping for the given object ID, the remote references are considered expired; in effect, the reference counter is decreased as if the process terminated normally. When an object has no active references, garbage collection of that object's resources may occur.

6.5.4 Thread Models Supported in DCOM

COM and DCOM operate with the multithreading capabilities of the native operating system, as discussed in Chapter 2. Since DCOM interprocess communication requires DCE RPC, which in turn requires RPC messages to be processed on an arbitrary thread, this requirement holds true for DCOM. The COM and DCOM programming model scales with the needs of current applications and thus the needs of application developers by providing totally free-threaded method invocations. In addition, DCOM provides automatic synchronization of method invocations to a single thread.

DCOM utilizes the apartment model with regard to threads. From a marshalling perspective, one may think of each thread as a separate process. Same thread access is direct access while access from a different thread is indirect, possibly through proxy/stub code. An object may support any of the following three threading models.

1. *Single-threaded apartment, main thread only.* In this model, all instances are created on the same single thread associated with that object.

2. *Single-threaded apartment.* In this model, an instance is tied to a single thread; however, different instances can be created on different threads.

3. *Multithreaded apartment.* In this model, instances can be created on multiple threads and can be called on arbitrary threads.

Any object implemented as local servers controls the kind of apartment used for its objects. The local server, through CoInitializeEx on one or more threads, registers the class or multiple class factories from the appropriate thread to the appropriate thread apartment model. When an object is being created, COM needs to know if the object is compatible with the threading model of its parent object. If the child object is not compatible, COM attempts to load the object into a different apartment that is compatible. If this is possible, the appropriate proxy/stubs are placed between the client and the object to enable communication. Since DCOM aims to maintain full flexibility for the application developer, it is possible to customize threading models.

6.5.5 DCOM Security Policies

As with any system supporting distributed computing, DCOM must also address security issues within itself. With this in mind, DCOM identifies four aspects of security that it is designed to handle.

1. *Access security.* Ensures that an object is only allowed to be called successfully by objects with appropriate permission.

2. *Launch security.* Ensures that only appropriate objects are allowed to create new objects in a new process.

3. *Identity.* The principle of how an object identifies itself.

4. *Connection policy.* This encompasses issues such as when a message may be altered and if a message is capable of being intercepted by another objects. In addition, the authentication of the object's identity is considered to fall under this category.

Access security may be conducted on a per-object basis, per-method basis, per-parameter basis, or on the higher process level. Access security may even be configured to accommodate different security checks for different callers. DCOM objects are able to configure their security policy and allow new objects to be developed without explicit security information or awareness.

Launch security is conducted from within the COM libraries. These libraries validate callers in terms of privileges for the given requested operation. This privilege information is configured in the registry that is external to the object.

In terms of providing security identity, DCOM supports many forms, from the low level per object that could be cumbersome for an application with a large number of users to the more convenient but less configurable group level. Security identity may be further complicated by the fact that every account may not be limited to a single dedicated user thereby making secure access based on a given user more difficult. Each approach has its strengths and weakness, but many varieties are possible within DCOM.

For connection security, DCOM once again provides many options to the application thereby allowing developers to select whatever level is most appropriate for their application. The greater the number of links between the source and destination over a network, the greater the possibility of interception. Keep in mind that the higher the level of security, the more overhead necessary to perform the desired communication. The exact level can be dynamically chosen. One of the best preventive measures is to take advantage of DCOM's ability to support the transfer of encrypted data. In this situation, the privacy and integrity of the contents can be protected.

When mechanisms for checking access, checking launch permissions, and protecting data are employed, they require some method for determining the security of the client's identity. Several security providers may be utilized. These security providers return a unique session token for ongoing authentication throughout the connection.

Since objects often are required to perform operations on behalf of their parent objects, measures also have been taken to incorporate four different levels of impersonation. The first level is Anonymous (`SecurityAnonymous`) and prevents obtaining the identity of the caller. The second level is Identity (`SecurityIdentification`) and allows the object to detect the security identity of the caller. The object is not able to impersonate the caller. The third level is Impersonate (`SecurityImpersonation`) and allows the object to impersonate and perform local operations as the caller. Despite these abilities, the object is not able to call other objects on behalf of the caller. The fourth level is Delegate (`SecurityDelegation`). In this level, the object can impersonate the call and perform method invocations using the identity of the caller. Within the Windows 2000 operating system, DCOM is allowed full system access and can take advantage of the basic Windows 2000 security infrastructure (presented in Chapter 12). Observe that full system access in general may allow for a breach in the confidence and security of a participating system.

6.6 CORBA™ OVERVIEW

The Common Object Request Broker Architecture, CORBA, is defined by the Object Management Group, OMG. The purpose of CORBA is to provide interoperability between applications in a heterogeneous distributed environment. It is sometimes referred to as middleware since it does not perform the lowest-level functions required of an operating system. While it must reside on top of a traditional operating system, it performs many operations traditionally considered in the operating system domain for a distributed environment. CORBA was originally defined by a committee including representatives of the following companies: Digital Equipment Corporation, Hewlett-Packard Company, HyperDesk Corporation, NCR Corporation, Object Design Inc., and SunSoft Inc. The CORBA 2.1 specification involved over 750 participating companies and vendors. This version of the specification was adopted in August of 1997. It is defined in [OMG97]. In this section, we present a brief overview of key concepts, as the complete formal specification is nearly twice as long as this entire book. Finally, it is important to note that the information and figures in this section are based upon information from CORBA specification 2.1 [OMG97] and 2.2 [OMG98a] and are used with the permission of the Object Management Group™.

As we have seen, CORBA's design is comprehensive yet flexible. The contribution and purpose of CORBA is to simplify and make possible heterogeneous computing, including heterogeneous systems and languages. The heart of CORBA is the Object Request Broker (ORB™), as discussed in Section 6.6.1. The other prime feature of CORBA is the definition of object adapters, described in Section 6.6.2. CORBA messaging is discussed in Section 6.6.3. Finally, Mapping CORBA to COM is discussed in Section 6.6.4.

6.6.1 CORBA's ORB

ORB provides a transparent interface, as depicted in Figure 6.5. In particular, the interface is independent of the object's location and implementation language. Thus, ORB can allow a Smalltalk object to communicate and work with a C++ object even if they physically exist at the other side of the world from each other. ORB is responsible for taking care of all translations. This is made possible by utilizing a common Interface Definition Language (IDL) that interfaces with object adapters. Interfaces consist of specific operations and their parameters. There are three categories for interfaces.

1. *Common.* Common interfaces apply to operations that are the same for all ORB implementations.

2. *Object type.* This interface applies to operations that are specific for only particular types of objects.

3. *Object style.* This interface applies to operations that are specific only for particular styles of object implementations.

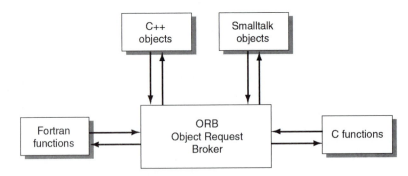

Figure 6.5   The Function of ORB.

6.6.2 CORBA Object Adapters

CORBA 2.1 [OMG97] specifies the following responsibilities for object adapters.

♦ Generation of object references

♦ Interpretation of object references

♦ Method invocation

♦ Security of interactions

♦ Object and implementation activation and deactivation

♦ Mapping object references to object implementations

♦ Registration of all object implementations

Object adapters can delegate responsibilities to the ORB core. They are responsible for maintaining their own state. While they are responsible for invocation, they are actually interfaced through something referred to as a skeleton using the IDL. An example of an object implementation receiving a request and how the skeleton fits into the ORB architecture is depicted in Figure 6.6. The IDL is a higher-level object language very similar to C++. Every instantiation of an object adapter must have the same interface on all ORB implementations. With adapters, ORB provides programming language mapping for object-as well as non-object-oriented programming languages. Thus, C and Fortran programs may utilize the CORBA ORB to work together with C++ and Smalltalk programs.

While a basic object adapter (BOA) meets all of these responsibilities, not all adapters perform each of these responsibilities. For example, a library object adapter is designed to support objects with library implementations. Since such objects are assumed to be client programs, the library implementation does not support activation or verification of identity. In addition, a database object adapter would not need to provide state information since this would be stored in the persistent storage of the object-oriented database.

Prior to CORBA 2.2, the BOA was the only standard object adapter defined. As a result, each vendor implemented its own BOA and in the process revealed ambiguities and shortcomings in its specification. As one might suspect, this led to customized proprietary BOA implementation; thereby, interoperability between ORBs was compromised. CORBA 2.2 sought to alleviate this problem through the specification of a portable object adapter (POA).

A server object must obtain a POA object prior to implementing an object that will use the POA. The root POA is the distinguished POA object managed by the ORB. This root POA is provided to the application using the ORB initialization interface. As long as the default policies are suitable, an application developer may create objects using the root POA. There are a total of seven policies associated with a root POA.

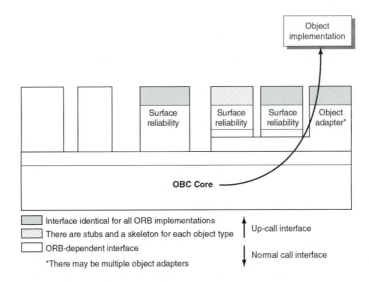

Surface
reliability

Surface
reliability

Surface
reliability

Object
adapter*

OBC Core

Object
implementation

▨ Interface identical for all ORB implementations
▨ There are stubs and a skeleton for each object type
☐ ORB-dependent interface
  *There may be multiple object adapters

↑ Up-call interface

↓ Normal call interface

Figure 6.6   An Object Implementation Receiving a Request.

1. *Thread policy*: This policy provides the ability to support thread choices in-cluding multithreading (for more information, see Detail Box 6.3).

2. *Lifespan policy*: The ability to support transient objects in addition to the previously supported persistent objects. The life of a transient object is bounded by the lifetime of parent POA whereas a persistent object's lifetime persists across the lifetime of multiple servers. This new option is beneficial for eliminating orphan objects or objects whose parent objects have termi-nated execution and thereby no longer require the child object to continue execution.

3. *Object ID uniqueness policy*: This policy is necessary to identify each object uniquely.

4. *ID assignment policy*: The ID assignment may be obtained from the applica-tion or the POA. This results in a value in system_id.

5. *Servant retention policy*: If the POA has the retain policy, it invokes the servant associated with the object ID value from the request. If the POA has the non-retain policy, the POA may use the default servant or a servant manager to lo-cate an active agent. The servant is active only for the duration of the singular request. There is no record kept of the servant-object association.

6. *Request processing policy*: If there is no servant associate with or located for the given object ID, the POA then follows the USE_DEFAULT_SERVANT, USE_SERVANT_MANAGER, or USE_OBJECT_MAP_ONLY policy to re-quest processing. If none of the above policies exist, the appropriate excep-

tion is raised. This provides the ability to dispatch object request to multiple incarnations of the object increasing its ability to distribute a workload.

7. *Implicit Activation Policy*: This allows a POA to be created with a policy that indicates that objects may be implicitly activated. An implicit policy requires a retain policy as well as a `system_id`. Operations are provided to support implicit activation. A POA has the ability to perform explicit object registration in addition to implicit registration. This allows an object to create instantiations to receive requests through the POA prior to making requests within a system.

DETAIL BOX 6.3
CORBA POA THREAD MODELS

When an application creates a POA within the CORBA model, it may choose one of two thread models for the underlying ORB implementation. If a single-threaded model is selected, a single thread handles every object request from that POA. One effect of this selection is sequential processing. In contrast, a POA may choose the ORB-controlled model. In this scenario, the ORB selects the model and, therefore, may be implemented in a multithreaded manner if the underlying environment supports multithreading. Due to the possibility of multi-threading, all POAs implemented in this manner should be able to handle multiple threads, including concurrency, possible re-entrance, and multiple instantiations, that may occur as a result.

6.6.3 CORBA Messaging

Traditional CORBA messaging provided three models for message invocation. The first model is synchronous, where a client would invoke the operation and then block, waiting for a response. The second model is a blocking model. Specifically, a client invokes an operation and continues. The response is retrieved at a later time via a poll or by blocking and waiting for a response and was only available for dynamic invocation. The third messaging model is that of unacknowledged communication. This model ensures a best effort to complete the communication, but the originator does not wait or check or expect a response or acknowledgment. This model was designed to allow CORBA support of UDP.

6.6.4 CORBA Compliance

For a system to be considered CORBA compliant, it must adhere to the specification in CORBA Core and provide at least one mapping. The languages specified in the standard are C, C++, Smalltalk, COBOL, Ada, and Java. For each of these languages implemented at a particular site, it must adhere to the CORBA specifications for the mapping to that language to be called CORBA compliant. In other words, a system is either entirely compliant or it is not. If a vendor supports C++, its ORB must comply with the OMG IDL to C++ binding specified in the standard.

6.6.5 CORBA to COM Mapping

The CORBA specification 2.2 presents information on data type mapping from CORBA to COM in Section 16. The ability to interoperate between standards is essential in successfully building and deploying a distributed system in heterogeneous environments, which may find it necessary to incorporate both standards. This is no easy task. For example, both CORBA and COM employ interface identifiers to identify object interfaces uniquely. Through the identifiers, client code is able to retrieve information about the object, including information about other interfaces to the object. Both specify a textual name for the interfaces, which are for convenience and are not guaranteed unique by either. However, the CORBA interfaces use a RepositoryId that is capable of uniquely identifying interfaces, while COM uses a structure known as IID. CORBA and COM handle exceptions differently. While CORBA uses exceptions to report errors and allows complex structures to communicate information about the exception, COM only reports errors if an operation uses a return result of type HRESULT. This result is then converted to a 16-bit code. Unfortunately, it is not possible to conduct a complete mapping of CORBA's exceptions to these bit codes. While CORBA specifies best effort at-most-once semantics for one-way operations, as discussed in Chapter 3, COM does not guarantee at-most-once semantics. These are just a few examples of the many differences and difficulties encountered when attempting to interoperate between the two standards. Despite these difficulties, interoperation is possible and hopefully over time it will become an easier task.

6.7 SUMMARY

In this chapter, we have studied the object approach to designing an operating system. We have seen how concepts such as communication, threads, synchronization, and memory management are handled in select object-based operating systems.

Not all object approaches allow inheritance or multiple inheritance. When inheritance is allowed, one must be cautious. Despite the possible drawbacks, this approach has been successful, and there is continuous research concerning this topic. DCOM and CORBA are also rapidly evolving as they define models for efficient object-oriented distributed computing. In addition to basic CORBA, there are additional CORBA architectures being defined for specialized areas of interest, such as CORBAMed for medical profession applications and CORBAtelecoms [OMG98b] for the telecommunications industry. There are products on the market based on CORBA, such as Chorus COOL, which implement the ideas behind the ORB. DCOM, once started in the Windows world, is widely deployed in the Windows and UNIX world and also dominates object technology within the distributed arena.

While we have examined three operating systems in addition to two dominating protocols, the reference section contains additional pointers to other object-based operating systems and related work. Both Chorus COOL and Amoeba can support participants in the distributed system that are multiprocessors (parallel). The Chorus microkernel supports real-time applications, although this support is not related to its object-based design but rather its utilization of priorities in its scheduling algorithms. Based on the success of these systems and the constant trend toward object orientation, do not be surprised if more and more object-oriented operating systems are developed not only as research projects, but also as commercial products.

6.7 REFERENCES FOR FURTHER STUDY

Overview information on real-time object-based systems can be found in [AKZ96]. Some appropriate traditional research papers concerning information in this chapter include [ARJ97, BSCEFHLS93, CIRM93, DLAR91, GhSc93, HaSe98, Hen98, Her94, Kim97, Lin95, LJP93, LoKi97, Micr98, MVTVV90, OMG97, OMG98a, OMG98b, OSH95, Sch98, Sie98, and Vin98].

The following provide some starting points for sources on the Internet concerning object-based operating systems. The home page for CORBA can be found at http://www.omg.org/omg00/wicorba.htm. A list of publications including the latest specification, white papers, and reference books specifically related to CORBA can be found at http://www.omg.org/store/pub.htm. The Amoeba home page can be found at http://www.am.cs.vu.nl. The Chorus homepage can be found at http://www.Chorus.com/. Choices is another object-oriented distributed operating system. The Chorus homepage with references to publications can be found at http://choices.cs.uiuc.edu/choices/index.html. A list of papers on SUN's object-oriented operating system, Spring, can be found at their Spring Papers Web page at http://www.sun.com/tech/projects/ spring/papers.html. Software AG that has commercial implementations for DCOM on all major UNIX platforms can be found at www.sagus.com.

EXERCISES

6.1   What are the benefits of allowing multiple method constructors? What difficulties could they cause?

6.2   What are the advantages and disadvantages of allowing multiple inheritance versus simple inheritance?

6.3   Define and describe the advantages and disadvantages of employing an object-based model in a distributed environment.

6.4   In Chapter 2, we examined the various issues involved in migration. What are the advantages and disadvantages of utilizing objects as a basis for migration?

6.5   Does CORBA assist or interfere with migration? Explain.

6.6   Name and describe the benefits of CORBA in a distributed environment.

6.7   Why is it important to only allow access to Clouds' objects via their entry point?

6.8   Why is data sharing in Clouds only allowed by invocation of an object?

6.9   What are the benefits of Clouds' segments being a multiple of a page size?

6.10   Why is it necessary for COOL to allow contexts to be remapped?

6.11   All of the operating systems described support persistence. Why might persistence be an important feature in a distributed system?

6.12   Name and describe some of the advantages of the proxy service supported by COOL's generic runtime system layer.

6.13   In Amoeba, why is knowledge of the port not sufficient protection for Amoeba services? Describe a situation that could occur without the requirement of client capabilities.

6.14   Both Clouds and Amoeba provide globally unique names. What are some of the possible advantages of globally unique names? What are potential problems and difficulties if globally unique names are not utilized?

Distributed Process Management

*I*n this chapter, we focus on the various issues related to process management in a distributed environment. This includes expanding on topics discussed in Chapter 2 related to general process management. In particular, we focus on distributed scheduling algorithm choices in Section 7.1. Section 7.2 examines a variety of approaches for scheduling algorithms, including an example for each approach. Section 7.3 focuses on the issue of coordinator elections, a process that is necessary for all solutions to any problem within distributed systems utilizing a centralized server. Section 7.4 examines issues of managing processes. In particular, this section addresses issues related to a child process within a distributed system whose parent process has terminated due to a system crash.

7.1 DISTRIBUTED SCHEDULING ALGORITHM CHOICES

Casavant and Kuhl [CaKu88] present a taxonomy for classifying the various available types of scheduling algorithms. We examine the various choices related to scheduling algorithms based on this taxonomy in Sections 7.1.1 to 7.1.4. Each choice can be utilized to classify a scheduling algorithm. Figure 7.1 presents a scheduling decision chart reflecting the various choices for scheduling algorithms. Detail Box 7.2 presents an overview of choices for global schedulers.

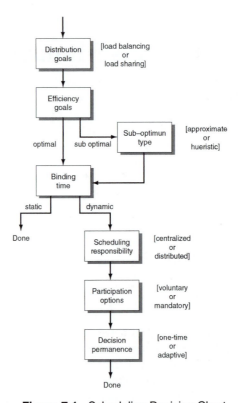

Figure 7.1   Scheduling Decision Chart.

7.1.1 Level of Scheduling

Distributed systems must make a choice regarding the level of scheduling; this choice is not valid in a centralized system. In distributed systems there are two levels for process scheduling: local and global scheduling. **Local scheduling** involves allocating a process to the actual processor while global scheduling involves choosing which processor at what location will execute a given process. **Global scheduling** is also referred to as processor allocation in the literature. The global decision must be made prior to making the local decision. In a distributed environment, both choices must be made at some point but not necessarily the same point in time. In this chapter, we are strictly concerned with global scheduling. Some issues relevant to local scheduling were presented in Chapter 2.

7.1.2 Load Distribution Goals

As we learned in Chapter 2, there are two load distribution goals. One goal is that of load balancing, which strives to maintain an equal load throughout the entire distributed system. Load balancing requires extensive overhead and constant system-performance evaluation. The second and more popular goal is simple load sharing. Load sharing strives to prevent any given location from becoming overly busy. Load sharing is a much easier goal to obtain as compared to load balancing. Figure 7.2 depicts the goals of load distribution based upon three load status states, as described in Chapter 2.

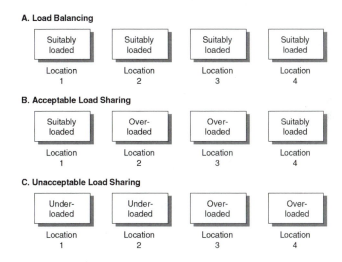

Figure 7.2 Load Distribution Goals.

7.1.3 Scheduling Efficiency Goals

Algorithms may provide two levels of efficiency goals; in particular, they may provide for an optimal or suboptimal scheduling solution. To have an **optimal scheduling algorithm**, the state of all competing processes and all related information must be available to the scheduler. Optimality may be measured in terms of completion time, resource utilization, system throughput or any combination thereof. Since computing optimal solutions may not be feasible since they are generally **NP-Hard**[1] for more than two processors, **suboptimal** solutions are often utilized. Suboptimal solutions fall into two categories: those that approximate and those that utilize heuristics. Detail Box 7.1 describes some of the metrics utilized for determining optimal scheduling algorithms.

DETAIL BOX 7.1
EFFICIENCY METRICS FOR SCHEDULING

There are a number of metrics utilized for determining and measuring scheduling efficiency. Algorithms may employ one or more of the following metrics.

One of the most common metrics is that of communication cost. Algorithms employing this metric may take into consideration the amount of time spent transferring a process to and from a given location. More important, they must also take into consideration the communication cost for a particular process location assignment. This cost will be low if the process is not required to communicate with any other process. It may also be low if the process is at the same location as the other processes it is required to communicate with during the execution of its computations.

Execution cost is another popular metric. This metric reflects the expense of assigning a process to a given location based upon the environment. If the environment is the same as the process's home environment, the execution cost would be zero. If, however, a given location runs a different operating system or has a different architecture utilizing a different character encoding scheme, zero representation, mantissa representation, and so on, the execution cost would be fairly high due to the amount of translation necessary.

Resource utilization metrics attempt to identify a proper location to schedule a process based on the current load of the various participants of the distributed system. Resource utilization metrics may be based upon the load status state. A more detailed metric may include a load index providing a wider scale as compared to the two- or three-level status states. Resource utilization metrics may also be based upon the resource queue lengths, memory usage, or any metric thought to reflect all resources at a given location.

Suboptimal Approximate Solutions

Suboptimal approximate solutions frequently utilize the same algorithms as optimal solutions but don't follow all the steps through to a complete solution and the identification of the best possible scheduling solution. Instead, they attempt to find a very good

---
[1] NP-hard problems are computationally intractable and no known polynomial-time algorithms exist.

solution as quickly as possibly by limiting the search space. To determine an acceptable suboptimal scheduling solution, there must exist some notion of what the optimal solution would yield according to some metric. In addition, the optimal solution must lend itself to intelligent shortcuts. While these shortcuts may employ heuristics, approximate solutions imitate optimal solutions and then employ heuristics.

SubOptimal Heuristic Solutions

Suboptimal heuristic algorithms employ rules of thumb or basic intuition regarding scheduling. These **heuristics** may not be provable and may be off base or completely wrong in certain circumstances but are generally considered to work in an acceptable manner. The following is a list of possible scheduling heuristics.

1. Dependent processes that involve many interprocess communications should be located in close proximity, generally at the same location.
2. Independent processes that change shared files should be located in close proximity, generally at the same location.
3. Divisible processes with little or no precedence relationships can be easily distributed, so distribute them.
4. If a system's load is already heavy, do not schedule another process at that location.

These rules as well as all heuristics may not directly, or quantitatively affect system performance but are intuition-based rules for what could assist in increasing system performance. While approximate solutions may employ heuristics to achieve shortcuts, heuristic suboptimal schedulers employ heuristics throughout the scheduling algorithm.

7.1.4 Processor Binding Time

This category determines at what point the scheduling algorithm decides when and where a process will execute as determined by binding a process to a particular processor group, a memory unit with one or more tightly coupled processors. Algorithms may provide **static binding** or **dynamic binding**. In a static scheduling algorithm, each process's executable image has a static assignment to a particular processor group that is assigned at link time. Such algorithms are considered static. Contrary to static binding algorithms, dynamic scheduling algorithms do not determine when/where a process will run when the executable image is created. Instead, the image is created in a relocatable form, thereby allowing binding to a particular processor (and location) at some later point in time. Dynamic scheduling algorithms must also determine scheduler responsibility and the permanence of the decision.

Scheduler Responsibility

Scheduler responsibility can be determined in a centralized or distributed manner. This scheduler decision can apply to distributed as well as parallel systems, although it is most common in distributed systems. In addition, scheduler responsibility only applies to schedulers with dynamic binding. It involves the determination of whether the responsibility for scheduling resides in a single processor at a centralized server or if the algorithm for determining scheduling is physically distributed among various processors (possibly at different locations). If the scheduling algorithm is centralized, the processor making all the scheduling decisions becomes a critical element in the system. If there does not exist a means to provide for a back-up processor to take over if the scheduling processor experiences failure, the entire system can be brought to a halt if this centralized server crashes or becomes unavailable.

Distributed, dynamic, global scheduling algorithms must also make decisions with regard to participation options. Participation options include the choice to make participation voluntary or mandatory. In **voluntary scheduling algorithms**, each local scheduler has a greater degree of autonomy over its resources and their utilization. A processor is not and cannot be forced to participate and cooperate. In contrast, a **mandatory scheduling** algorithm forces each processor to carry its weight and each processor is obligated to perform its portion of the scheduling task to meet the common system-wide performance goal. Regardless of the scheduler responsibility decision and participation status, the algorithm may choose to employ optimal, suboptimal heuristic, or suboptimal approximate solutions.

Scheduler Decision Permanence

A dynamic scheduling algorithm may employ permanence (that is, all assignments are one-time assignments) or it may be adaptable and allow dynamic reassignment. One-time assignments are nonchangeable once the scheduling decision is made; conversely, dynamic reassignment allows for process migration and reassignment after a process has begun execution. **One-time assignment schedulers** frequently rely on user information when making assignments while **adaptive schedulers** using dynamic reassignment take advantage of information created while a process is executing to possibly change the initial scheduling decision and migrate an executing process. Thus, dynamic reassignment allows the scheduler to adapt constantly. Of course, frequent changes would hinder system performance due to the migration overhead as we have learned in Chapters 2 and 4. Most algorithms are not inherently one-time or adaptable; rather, they can be used in either manner, although some systems inherently utilize only one method or the other.

DETAIL BOX 7.2
GLOBAL SCHEDULING ALGORITHMS

The following is a list of the various types of global schedulers that can result based on the number of decisions involved in the designing of a scheduling algorithm as presented in this chapter. Each of these schedulers may be employed for load balancing or load sharing; thus, it follows that there are 42 possible types in all!

- Optimal static scheduler
- Optimal one-time centralized dynamic scheduler
- Optimal adaptive centralized dynamic scheduler
- Voluntary optimal one-time distributed dynamic scheduler
- Mandatory optimal one-time distributed dynamic scheduler
- Voluntary optimal adaptive distributed dynamic scheduler
- Mandatory optimal adaptive distributed dynamic scheduler
- Suboptimal approximate static scheduler
- Suboptimal heuristic static scheduler
- Suboptimal approximate one-time centralized dynamic scheduler
- Suboptimal heuristic one-time centralized dynamic scheduler
- Suboptimal approximate adaptive centralized dynamic scheduler
- Suboptimal heuristic adaptive centralized dynamic scheduler
- Voluntary suboptimal approximate one-time distributed dynamic scheduler
- Mandatory suboptimal approximate one-time distributed dynamic scheduler
- Voluntary suboptimal heuristic one-time distributed dynamic scheduler
- Mandatory suboptimal heuristic one-time distributed dynamic scheduler
- Voluntary suboptimal approximate adaptive distributed dynamic scheduler
- Mandatory suboptimal approximate adaptive distributed dynamic scheduler
- Voluntary suboptimal heuristic adaptive distributed dynamic scheduler
- Mandatory suboptimal heuristic adaptive distributed dynamic scheduler

7.2 SCHEDULING ALGORITHM APPROACHES

In the last section, we learned about the various choices presented to a scheduling algorithm; in addition, we enumerated the various types based upon these choices. In this section, we examine a variety of approaches to scheduling algorithms. Each approach is first introduced and then an example scheduler utilizing the method is discussed in detail. The following is a list of the sample scheduler types presented and their corresponding sections.

♦ Section 7.2.1: load sharing, suboptimal, heuristic, one-time, centralized dynamic scheduler

♦ Section 7.2.2: load balancing, suboptimal, approximate, centralized, dynamic scheduler

♦ Section 7.2.3: load sharing, global, suboptimal, heuristic, static scheduler

♦ Section 7.2.4: load sharing, mandatory, suboptimal, heuristic, adaptive, distributed, dynamic scheduler

7.2.1 Usage Points

Usage points for each system may be maintained and utilized to ensure fair usage of the distributed system. This method generally involves a centralized server; thus, it is best employed with smaller distributed systems. The centralized server maintains a **usage table**, which contains an entry for each computer participating in the system. If a participant requests and utilizes a resource that is not local, such as utilizing a remote processor to schedule a process, it is charged **usage points**. If a participant allows another participant to utilize local resources, the location receives a reduction in usage points, as depicted in Figure 7.3. A generous location will have a lower number of usage points as compared to a location that has extensively utilized outside resources. The total number of usage points for a given location is utilized to determine scheduling. A location with lower usage points will always be scheduled for nonlocal service before a location with higher usage points.

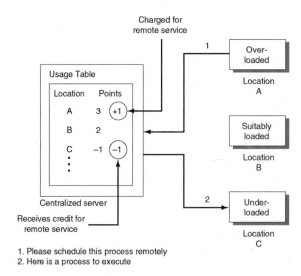

Figure 7.3 Usage Points.

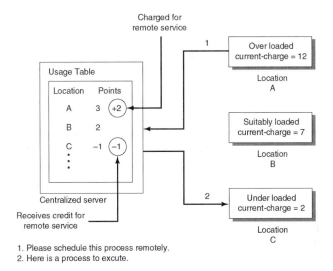

Figure 7.4 Economic Usage Points.

Usage points may be simple in that each action warrants one point whether it is a one-point charge for utilizing outside resources or a one-point credit for allowing an outside process to execute locally. In addition, a more complex economy-influenced scheme may be implemented. This approach is also referred to as **economic usage points**. In this variation to the usage points approach, the charge for utilizing an outside resource is based upon the load of that system. Utilizing outside resources on a more heavily loaded system would result in a greater charge than utilizing an outside resource that is lightly loaded. Allowing an outside process to execute locally would warrant a larger credit when your local system is more heavily loaded. In either case, the points charged to a location match the points credited to the system being utilized. Each location maintains a listing of its current charges as depicted in Figure 7.4. Establishing economic based points may be determined strictly on the load index of the utilized resource or it could be based on bidding. When bidding is incorporated into the algorithm, the points charged (still equal to the points credited) are negotiable. Thus, a system can shop around for the best deal. The idea of bidding was first introduced by Ferguson, Yemini, and Nikolaou [FYN88].

An example scheduling algorithm based on simple usage points is described in [MuLi87]. Their algorithm presents a suboptimal, heuristic, one-time, centralized dynamic scheduler referred to as Up-Down. In addition to receiving a reduction in usage points for allowing other participants to utilize resources, a participant also receives a temporary reduction for outstanding requests. A request to schedule a process may become outstanding if the centralized scheduler does not have any participants with available resources when a request is received. All locations also receive a reduction of usage points if the system has no requests pending and resources are available. This reduction may be a one-time event per occurrence or may allow multiple adjustments based upon a predetermined time frame in which this state exists. For example, all systems may receive a 1-point credit each time this state exists or all systems may receive a 1-point credit for each minute that this state exists. The Up-Down algorithm permits usage points to fall below zero, therefore allowing a generous location to accumulate credits for a time when it may require extensive assistance to execute processes in the future.

7.2.2 Graph Theory

The heart of this approach lies in graph theory; in particular, in obtaining the minimum **cutset** for a vertex of a graph or in calculating the maximum flow of a graph. We first examine the issue of a minimum cutset for a vertex, referred to as the **min-cut**. In this method, an assignment graph is utilized. In an **assignment graph**, the processes and their possible assignments are represented in an undirected graph, a graph with simple edges containing no arrows. A vertex of the graph represents a process if it is denoted by a p or a location if it is denoted by a l. No precedence relationships are represented. If two p vertices are connected via an edge, the represented processes communicate with each other and probably should be assigned together. If a p vertex is connected via an edge to a 'l' vertex, that process may be assigned to that location. The edges of the assignment graph contain some form of weightings that represent the goals of the particular scheduling algorithm. To make an assignment of processes to a given location, each location vertex must be cut from the graph. Cutting a graph is achieved by breaking the edges of a graph. To cut a vertex from a graph, a set of edges must be cut that leave the cut vertex separated from the rest of the graph. Thus, when a vertex is cut, there are no longer any edges connecting the subgraph containing the cut vertex to the rest of the graph as depicted in a two-processor example in Figure 7.5. The entire set of edges that have been cut to remove the vertex is referred to as a cutset. Each cutset must contain one l vertex, representing a location. When a p vertex is connected via an edge to an l vertex, the representative process is assigned to the given location. The cost of the cutset is the sum of the weight of all edges that were cut to remove the vertex. A minimum cutset represents the lowest cost possible for cutting a particular vertex. Any task that remains in the cut portion of the graph with the cut location is considered assigned to that location. The total cost of the processor assignment is the sum of the cost for every cutset necessary to cut each location vertex. Therefore, the goal is to minimize the total assignment cost. The lowest cost possible for cutting all location vertices for a given assignment graph, the min-cut, represents the optimal scheduling assignment.

We now examine the second graph theory variation based upon calculating the **maximum flow of a graph**. This approach utilizes a max-flow assignment graph. A vertex of the graph represents a process if it is denoted by a p or a location if it is denoted by a l. In this circumstance, the edges of the graph will be directed (indicated by an arrow) representing the possible assignment of a process to the pointed location vertex. Every edge contains a weight representing the flow of that edge. In this application, the larger weight represents a larger flow capacity between a given process and location. The object of a max-flow assignment graph is to sink processes into locations (by assignment) that consti-

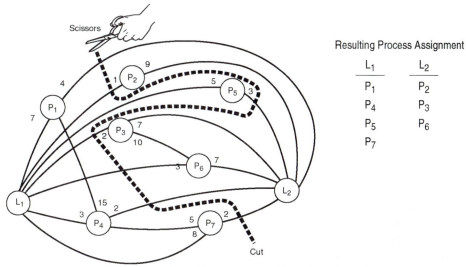

Figure 7.5 Two-Processor Min-Cut Example.

tute the largest flow for the entire graph. This is achieved by selecting the edges with the largest weight. Within the graph theory community, it is well known that the goal of obtaining the minimum cutset and the goal of obtaining the maximum flow are equivalent. There are many algorithms for evaluating a graph in terms of both approaches. Thus, the choice of which graph theory option is utilized in solving the scheduling problem is left to your discretion.

We now examine a scheduling algorithm example based on the minimum cutset of a graph. This example is a load balancing, global, suboptimal, approximate, centralized, dynamic scheduler and is described in [Lo88]. This algorithm may be utilized for one-time assignment or for adaptive scheduling. The following are the basis for evaluating performance.

♦ Minimize total execution and communications costs incurred by an assignment.

♦ Minimize total interference costs, thereby allowing an increase in concurrency.

The interference cost between two processes reflects their incompatibility. It is utilized to encourage processes with high interference costs to be scheduled at separate locations. An example of what warrants a high interference cost would be two processes that both require CPU-intensive operations. In contrast, a high input/output process and a CPU-intensive process would have a relatively low interference cost. This algorithm assumes that the compiler or system provides the execution and communication cost for all processes. In practice, these values would need to be approximations or the cost in the calculation would most likely interfere with system performance. This algorithm does not focus on or consider issues related to memory requirements, deadlines, and precedence relationships. Since this is an approximate algorithm, it utilizes intuition only in later steps of the algorithm. Disallowing or ignoring some information is allowable. In addition, it is quite common to ignore certain variables and assume that they are constant to study and evaluate a particular approach.

For this algorithm, the goal is to minimize the execution and communication costs related to the entire assignment throughout the distributed system. Utilizing an assignment graph, Lo's suboptimal heuristic algorithm proceeds with the following three phases.

1. *Grab*: For each location, a location grabs all processes that are strongly attracted to it as represented by a large weight. Since this weight is large, it represents an edge that we would most likely not want to cut. If this phase completes and the result is a complete cutset for each location, then we have obtained an optimal solution. Otherwise, we continue to the next phase.

2. *Lump*: Lump attempts to assign all remaining unassigned tasks to one location, thereby lumping them together. The cost of this possible assignment is computed and compared to a computed lower bound on relative communication costs. These communication costs can only be incurred if the processes are not lumped together. Thus, if the lower bound on communication cost is higher than the cost of lumping, the algorithm lumps accordingly, and the assignment is complete. Otherwise, lumping is not the least expensive nor is it the most efficient route; therefore, the algorithm proceeds to phase 3.

3. *Greedy*: The focus of greedy is to identify groups of processes whose communication cost among them is high, thereby demanding that these processes be scheduled together. However, each group of processes can be assigned to separate locations. This phase considers the cost associated for cutting in terms of the communication cost and the execution cost. Since every possibility is not examined, the result of this phase may be suboptimal.

In [Lo88], there are also several variations to this algorithm employing a more complex criterion in Phase 3, greedy; however, the simple version of greedy, as just presented, performed nearly as well as the more complex versions in simulation tests.

7.2.3 Probes

Messages may be sent out to members of a system to locate an appropriate processor to schedule a process. Such messages are referred to as probes. Schedulers utilizing probes may be optimal or suboptimal. Optimal implementations must probe every location and analyze the data. Suboptimal implementation may choose not to probe all locations and/or they may choose not to analyze completely the information received from the probes. If each location is responsible for sending out probes, it is considered a distributed scheduler. If a centralized server is the only distributed system participant sending probes and maintaining information, it is considered a centralized scheduler. In addition, the probes may be utilized to place a process or may be utilized to evaluate relocation possibilities, therefore performing in an adaptive manner. Finally, probes may also be utilized for an underloaded location that is looking for more work.

An example scheduler utilizing probes is described in [ELZ86]. In particular, it is a policy for a load sharing, global, suboptimal, heuristic, static scheduler. In this approach, location cost is considered more important than communication cost. A location cost is the cost associated with scheduling a process on a different type of system as compared to its original system. The justification for focusing on location cost as compared to communication cost is based on the involvement of heterogeneous systems and the related expenses to executing a process on a different type of system. Of course, a given location may not be an option at all if the code is not ported to a given host system at a specific location.

The scheduling algorithm policy involves the utilization of probes. When a given location needs to schedule or migrate a process remotely, it instantiates three to five probes (testing with more probes did not significantly increase performance). The probed locations must be homogeneous to the system sending the probe (thus the influence of the weighting upon location cost). Among the homogeneous locations available, the locations receiving a probe are randomly chosen. These probes test a location against probe limits. This limit represents what the load status state (as described in Chapter 2) would be if the process was migrated to that location. If the probed location limit reflects an overloaded state, the location is rejected. However, if the probed location's limit is in an underloaded state, we immediately schedule the transfer of the process to this location. Observe that the load status state of the chosen location may change between the time the probe is sent and the time when the process arrives. This will not and cannot affect the decision to migrate. In addition, no attempt to find or identify the best location is ever made; furthermore, the probe is only capable of determining the overall load status state but not a particular value or index within components in the calculation of the load status state.

7.2.4 Scheduling Queues

Centralized operating systems have long utilized scheduling queues, so it may be no wonder that it is possible to utilize this method in a distributed environment. When scheduling queues are utilized, a distributed scheduler generally maintains separate global and local queues. The local queue is the standard queue that exists in a centralized system that maintains a list of processes scheduled to run locally. The global queue is for processes not specifically scheduled locally but slated for possible execution in the larger distributed environment. Whether the global queue allows one to identify execution environment requirements such as preferred platforms or machines is dependent on the particular implementation. Generally, a centralized server is employed to maintain and update global queues although each participant may possess its own local copy of the global queue. One

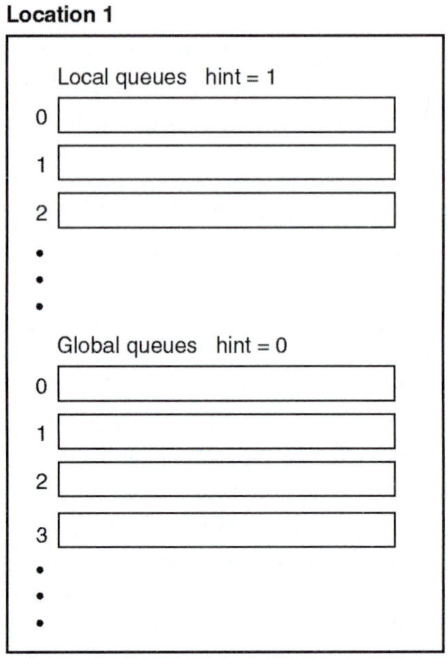

Location 1

Figure 7.6   A Station with Run Queues and Hints.

benefit is the ease with which scheduling algorithms utilizing queues can be incorporated on top of existing operating systems. The distributed scheduler can simply invoke a process to be scheduled. When this process is scheduled, it executes the distributed scheduling algorithm that may be utilized to bring a global process to the local processor for scheduling. Without a base operating system, scheduling queues can be used quite easily to implement distributed scheduling. How the global versus local scheduling queues are addressed by the system is dependent on the policy of the operating system.

An example scheduling algorithm utilizing scheduling queues is described in [Bla90]. In particular, the algorithm concerns the processor allocation scheduler utilized in Mach, a research distributed operating system developed at Carnegie Mellon University. It has since been taken over by the Open Software Foundation (OSF), and much of the operating system is incorporated into the OSF/1™ operating system. This algorithm is a mandatory, suboptimal, heuristic, adaptive, distributed, dynamic scheduler that can be utilized for load balancing or load sharing.

Scheduling is conducted at a thread level. Each location has a set of local run queues and a set of global run queues. Each individual run queue represents a different priority level. The probable location of the highest-priority thread that requires scheduling is maintained in a "hint" as depicted in Figure 7.6. Thus, if run queues 0 to 4 are empty, the hint would contain a 5, indicating that 5 is the highest-priority run queue containing a thread to be scheduled. For scheduling purposes, the highest-priority local thread is executed. A thread priority consists of a base priority and an offset that is representative of recent processor usage. The offset also reflects the current load on the system. There is also a mechanism to increase the priority based on the age of the thread. Each individual run queue contains a count for the number of threads maintained as well as a mutual exclusion lock. The global run queue is only examined if the local run queue is empty, as indicated by the queue's count. If there is no local thread, then the highest-priority global thread is executed. The local run queues are utilized for threads that are bound to a specific processor. A thread may be bound if it is designed for a particular architecture. In total, Mach utilizes 32 run queues. The run queue with the lowest number represent the highest priority.

Mach scheduling allows for scheduling hints from users. In particular, a user may indicate a discouragement hint or a handoff hint. Overall, discouragement hints allow the user to increase performance for concurrency control purposes. Discouragement hints have three levels: mild, strong, or absolute. Mild hints suggest not scheduling a thread or switching out a thread, while strong hints temporarily decrement the priority of a given thread. This increases performance for concurrency control by allowing the potential lock holder to execute in hopes that it will release the locked resource. Absolute hints prohibit a thread from being scheduled for a finite amount of time. This provides for the execution of a thread with a lower priority. If the lower-priority thread is holding a lock that the higher-priority thread requires, this provides a means to allow the lower-priority thread to execute and release the lock.

Handoff hints allow a thread to tell the scheduler to execute a particular thread instead of the thread providing the handoff hint. The new thread is then immediately given control of the processor, therefore bypassing the scheduling queue. This handoff can either be explicitly canceled by the original thread or will eventually timeout. The hand off technique can also be useful when a lower-priority thread controls a concurrency control lock required by a higher priority thread. In this situation, the higher-priority thread is allowed to handoff the processor to the lower priority thread. When the lock is released, the higher priority thread can explicitly cancel the handoff and resume computing with the formerly locked resource now available.

To allow gang scheduling, Mach provides an abstraction known as a processor set. If the user has a set of threads that require gang scheduling, they can be assigned to a particular processor set. Once a thread is assigned to a processor set, it must execute within a processor set. In addition, a processor set can only execute threads that are assigned to it. When the kernel attempts to schedule the threads assigned to a processor set, it utilizes this information in assigning particular processors to the processor set to guarantee the required simultaneous scheduling of all related threads.

7.2.5 Stochastic Learning

Stochastic learning is a heuristic that attempts to identify the best possible action based on previous actions, thereby learning from experience. All possible scheduling actions are associated with a probability. All probabilities are initialized to equivalent values when the distributed system is set up. The associated probabilities are utilized to select a location. After the choice has been made and the process has been sent to the location, the destination provides information back to the source. This information may be reward points or penalty points depending on the evaluation of the choice. If the destination is overloaded, it would send back penalty points. Likewise, if the destination is underloaded it would send back reward points. These points are then utilized to adjust the probability accordingly for the action just taken; therefore, the system is learning based upon the reward/penalty feedback.

This method may be further extended to allow the scheduler to record and act on the various states of the system. In particular, each possible state of the entire system is represented by an entry into an **automaton vector**. Each index represents a different workload for the distributed system. The contents of the vector are utilized with the probability associated with that participant when utilizing the scheduling algorithm. The utilization of the automaton vector requires participants periodically to report their load state to the various members of the distributed system. This information is utilized to calculate the system status state and thereby ensure that the correct automaton entry is referred to when making a scheduling decision. This method may employ a centralized server to maintain the automaton vectors as well as to collect the workload information but is also well suited to a distributed implementation.

We now examine an example scheduling algorithm utilizing a stochastic learning automaton, as described in [Kun91]. This provides for a mandatory, suboptimal, heuristic, one-time, distributed dynamic scheduler. This algorithm will not permit remote scheduling when the local processor is underloaded. In addition, remote scheduling is disallowed if all participants in the distributed system are overloaded. A system-wide status state is calculated based upon activity messages received from system participants. Activity messages are utilized to communicate an overloaded or underloaded state. The workload is based on processing time requirements of currently assigned processes as well as the input/output volume and memory requirements of the assigned processes. The algorithm has also been tested with the following workload indicators.

- One-minute workload averages
- Amount of free memory
- Amount of CPU idle time
- Frequency of context switches performed
- Frequency of system calls
- Length of the run queue

The workload descriptors are presented in increasing order of performance; thus, the one-minute load average performed the worst and the length of the run queue performed the best. In particular, Kuntz found a 32% difference in response time between the two descriptors. Additional tests were conducted utilizing a combination of workload descriptors, but results did not reveal any decrease in the response time of the system.

The status information based upon the workload is communicated to system participants every 8 seconds. The system status state is then calculated and mapped into a particular automaton state corresponding to a particular automaton vector entry. This entry is then utilized for scheduling decisions. When the scheduler is first initiated, all probabilities are equal, therefore providing an equal probability that a given remote location will be chosen to execute the remote process. The probability is adjusted for future actions based upon the reward or penalty notice from a selected location. This probability is then utilized to select at random a remote location for scheduling a process.

7.3 COORDINATOR ELECTIONS

Throughout every discussion related to centralized solutions to problems in distributed computing, there is a centralized server performing a critical role within the system. In this section, we examine the general method employed to determine what particular system within the distributed system functions as the centralized server for a given operation. In addition, this algorithm may be utilized to designate a new server should the primary server fail. The most cited reference for coordinator elections is by Garcia-Molina [Gar82]. This paper refers to the algorithm as the "Bully Algorithm". This algorithm, as all scheduling algorithms presented throughout the literature, relies on a participant's address number. When a location notices that there is no server, the participant sends a message to all members of the system requesting to become the coordinator. This message includes the participant's address number. If any member of the distributed system with a higher address number desires to become coordinator, the higher number participant can "bully" the lower numbered location and automatically become coordinator. Of course, the bully is subject to being bullied by another member of the distributed system with a higher address number, as depicted in Figure 7.7. Thus, when push comes to shove, the higher address number member is always able to bully its way into becoming coordinator, if the participant chooses. If no one chooses to bully a lower addressed participant out of the coordinator position, then this location becomes the coordinator. An example of bully coordinator algorithms is presented in Detail Box 7.3.

DETAIL BOX 7.3
A BULLY COORDINATOR ALGORITHMS

Respond to Coordinator Announcement

```
    IF receive(I_want_to_be_coordinator,recipient_address)
          & recipient_address < my_address
          & I_want_to_be_coordinator
    THEN announce_desire_to_be_coordinator
          & send(I_want_to_be_coordinator, my_address)
```

Announce Desire to Be Coordinator

```
    IF no_response_from_coordinator
    THEN forall(participant_address)
          send(I_want_to_be_coordinator, my_address)&
          settimer
```

Wait for Responses

```
    IF receive_message & recipient_address>my_address
    THEN cannot_be_coordinator
    ELSE   IF timer_expired
          THEN I_am_coordinator
```

This same process may take place not only when a coordinator fails but also when a new coordinator is being elected. One variation involves only sending messages to participants with higher addresses instead of all members since lower address participants cannot prevent a given member's right to become coordinator. The address of a participant is determined at network installation time and is generally unchangeable by the system thereby disallowing a system, from changing its address to "cut in line". In conclusion, seniority in terms of an address number can permit a particular distributed system participant to rule the system and become coordinator every time.

7.4 ORPHAN PROCESSES

One of the great concerns in a distributed environment is the handling of **orphan processes**. This problem was first addressed in [Nel81]. An orphan process is created when a parent process is prematurely terminated and is particularly a problem with remote procedure calls.

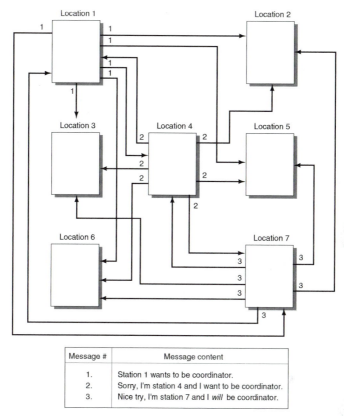

Message #	Message content
1.	Station 1 wants to be coordinator.
2.	Sorry, I'm station 4 and I want to be coordinator.
3.	Nice try, I'm station 7 and I *will* be coordinator.

Figure 7.7 The Bully Algorithm.

Any process created by the terminated process is a child process and will continue to execute unless some mechanism for dealing with orphan processes is incorporated within the distributed system process management. The orphan process will have no process to which it can return a value. In addition, even a child process, may create child processes thereby creating an even larger problem. When a process is executing without a parent process, it is wasting resources and can corrupt data. The most common resource wasted is CPU cycles but may also include network and memory resources. In addition, the orphan processes may be changing shared data in an irreversible manner. If the child process controls some type of concurrency control locking mechanism when it is told to terminate execution, it must release all locks. This, however, cannot guarantee that the data are irreversibly damaged. As we have learned when studying scheduling, a process may be scheduled anywhere throughout a distributed system; therefore, these orphan processes may be executing anywhere throughout the distributed system. We now examine three possible solutions for managing and handling orphan processes.

7.4.1 Orphan Cleanup

Orphan cleanup requires a process to clean up after itself when it comes back to life after a system or hardware crash. To accomplish this action, a process must keep a list of all processes it creates. The parent may require all processes to inform the parent when they create a child process or may require the child process to keep a list of its own children, as depicted in Figure 7.8. In either case, this family tree must be maintained in nonvolatile storage. Nonvolatile storage is necessary in case the process crashed due to a power outage. When the system is brought back up, it checks the family tree for all processes executing at the time of its crash. At this time, the cleanup must begin as all members of the family tree are notified of the death of their parent process and told to halt execution. If the child process is required to maintain its own family tree, it must notify all its child processes to cease execution.

One of the largest disadvantages of this approach includes the tremendous overhead to the system of the parent process. This overhead not only includes the amount of storage necessary for the family tree but also the inconvenience of constantly updating and maintaining the accuracy of the family tree. Example orphan cleanup algorithms are presented in Detail Box 7.4.

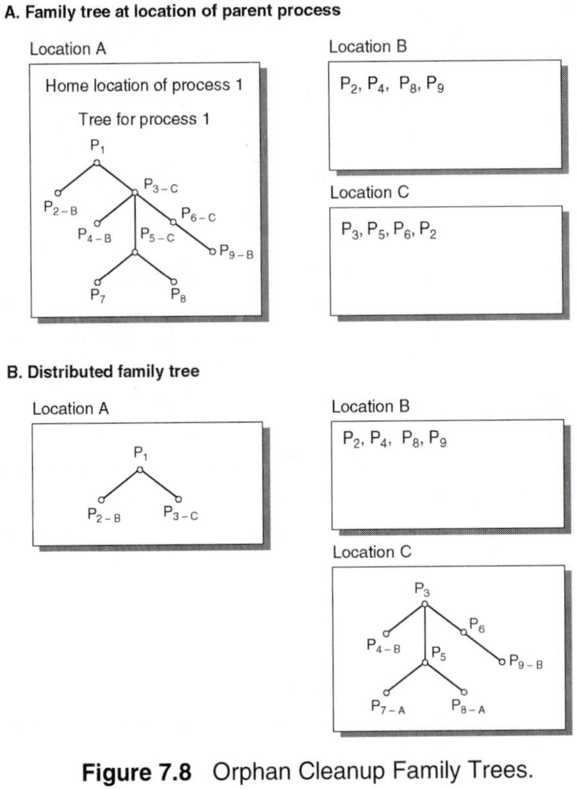

Figure 7.8   Orphan Cleanup Family Trees.

DETAIL BOX 7.4
ORPHAN CLEANUP ALGORITHMS

Recording Entries into Family Tree

```
    Repeat forever
    {
    Foreach process(PID)
                            // PID is process ID
                            // Must perform this operation for every process
            IF system created (PID)
                            // newly created process, system is the parent
            THEN
            {
                    Create family tree(PID);
                    Flush(family tree, stable storage)
                            // Must create new family tree and place in stable
storage
                    add(PID,process table);
                            // add this process to the list of processes that are
alive
            }
            ELSE
            {
                            // This is not a system-created process
                            // but a child process of another process
                    parent = look up parent(PID)
                    add to tree (parent, PID)
                            // add the new process to the family tree of its parent
            }
                            // end else, need to add to parent tree
    }
                            // end recording entries into tree
```

Recovery After a Crash

```
    Foreach process in process table
    {
            foreach process in tree(PID)
            send clean up message;
                            // notify all child processes to terminate
    }
```

7.4.2 Child Process Allowance

The second method for managing orphan processes requires that all child processes receive a time allowance, referred to as **child process allowance**. This allowance provides the child with a finite amount of time to execute. When the allowance has run out, the child must request an additional allowance from the parent. If the parent has died, the child cannot receive an allowance and therefore cannot continue to execute, as depicted in Figure 7.9. If the parent is still alive, the parent will issue an additional allowance to the child process. Once again, the child processes may still create their own child processes. These second and possible third- or fourth-generation child processes may receive their allowance from its parent or from the primary parent process. When a child process provides the allowance for its own children, it may not provide an allowance that exceeds its own remaining allowance plus a possible small amount. This small amount may be permitted to allow the immediate parent process to receive its own allowance prior to the request from its child. A child process that has not received an allowance cannot provide an allowance for its children. Therefore, when a parent process is prematurely terminated, all descendant processes will eventually die due to the lack of allowance.

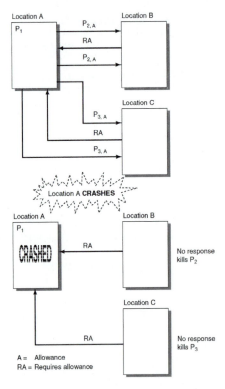

Figure 7.9   Child Process Allowance.

While this approach does not require a tremendous overhead to the system of the parent process, it does create extra network traffic. In addition, it can interfere with the execution of a child process, which may be inconveniently halted to ask for an allowance. Furthermore, when a system recovers from a crash, it cannot be allowed to begin processing immediately. If it were to begin immediately, a child process from before the crash may request an allowance. Therefore, a parent process would not be able to distinguish its child processes from processes that became orphaned before the crash. Thus, a system must wait one allowance period prior to commencing any processes following a crash.

7.4.3 Process Version Numbers

Process version numbers may be utilized to distinguish between a child of a process that crashed and a child of a process after a crash. This method requires each process to maintain a parent version number. When a system crashes, it announces a new version number to the entire distributed system. At this point, there are two implementation choices available to handle a child process created by that system.

1. The child may be forced to terminate execution since it originates from an out of date version number, as depicted in Figure 7.10.
2. It may attempt to locate its parent (who may have migrated since its creation). If the parent cannot be located, the child must terminate execution.

In either case, this method requires a large amount of communication each time a system fails. In addition, systems that may have no affiliation with the formerly crashed participant must receive and process the message announcing a new version number.

7.5 SUMMARY

In this chapter, we have taken an in-depth look at the various aspects of distributed process management. In particular, we examined issues involved in distributed process scheduling, election of coordinator process for centralized algorithms, and issues involved in handling orphan processes. There are many choices available when designing a distributed process scheduler, which controls process allocation to remote locations. Due to the numerous choices, there can be 42 different types of scheduler algorithms. Some algorithms can inherently serve for multiple scheduler types while others cannot. In particular, all algorithms that can function as a one-time scheduler can be utilized for adaptive scheduling, although optimal algorithms, which suffer from slowness, generally will not be employed in this manner. Some algorithms are not particular in terms of binding time. Others, such as the example probing algorithm, take advantage of the type of system to which a process is bound to lessen the search space when identifying possible remote locations for execution. All of the scheduler approaches may be utilized for load balancing or load sharing. In addition, one may utilize a combination of the approaches. Stochastic learning, for example, could be modified easily to work with probes instead of each location broadcasting its workload. One could employ the graph theory approach for initial scheduling information

A. Location A creates 2 processes.

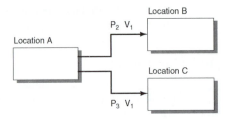

B. Location A crashes, location B and C have active processes with version number 1.

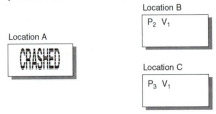

C. Location A is alive again. Locations B and C kill earlier version processes.

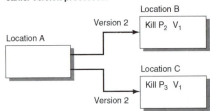

Figure 7.10   Process Version Numbers.

on the probabilities of stochastic learning. Usage points could be utilized to determine the priority of a process and used in conjunction with scheduling queues. Despite all the information available and research conducted regarding scheduling, it is still a very active research area. Some of the more difficult questions concern defining workload descriptors and their perspective threshold values as reflected in a location's status state. Additional research is focused on improving the efficiency of the schedulers.

Regarding coordinator elections, the general rule is that seniority rules. Seniority is established in terms of a station's address; a higher station address represents higher seniority. If a station has the highest address and wants to do the extra work, the algorithms typically allow that station to become coordinator. On the other hand, dealing with orphan processes is not quite as easy. Each method has some negatives but none of the negatives, are stronger than if no method of dealing with orphan processes is employed. While we examined the various possible methods for terminating processes, the issue of how this termination affects data has not been addressed. This issue can be answered with one word, *transactions* (the topic of discussion in Chapter 9).

Finally, one can never emphasize enough that this is still an active research area and great solutions simply do not exist yet! In addition to the topics discussed in this area, significant research in the following areas needs to occur.

♦ How to best handle processor congestion

♦ How to handle, identify, and prevent endemic system overload

♦ How to identify the ideal process level of granularity and address this issue in an efficient algorithm (large numbers of small processes may cause more problems than are solved by the distribution)

♦ How to identify the ideal level of processor granularity

With these areas relatively unsolved as well as the many topics introduced throughout the chapter, this is a difficult subject in practice but a great area for research, grants, and thesis topics! Perhaps the answers lie in adapting solutions from a different discipline such as business management (dividing and distributing (or delegating) workload is a common problem in the management discipline).

7.6 REFERENCES FOR FURTHER STUDY

The following references can provide more specific information on algorithm analysis for distributed scheduling algorithms [BGMR96] and real-time scheduling: [BuScSu97, Kop97, and SSRB98], respectively. Some appropriate traditional research papers concerning information in this chapter include [ArFi89, Bla90, CaKu88, EAL95, ELZ86, Esk89, Fer89, FeZh87, FYN88, Gar82, KrLi87, Kun91, LHWS96, Lo88, MuLi87, Nel81, Ous82, PaSh88, PTS88, SHK95 (a collection of classic papers), SKS92, VLL90, and WaMo85].

The general Internet search sites provided in Chapter 1 provide the best starting points for sources on the Internet concerning issues related to distributed process management.

EXERCISES

7.1   What are the disadvantages to designating your load distribution goal to be that of load balancing?

7.2   Is true load balancing possible in a distributed system? Is it necessary? Discuss the reasons behind your answer.

7.3   In Chapter 1, we introduced the concept of implementing a client/server environment in terms of a workstation model or a processor pool model. Which model is more conducive to a load balancing distribution goal? Why?

7.4   There is a common saying "be careful what you wish for because you just might get it." With this in mind, name three viable measures for scheduling efficiency along with at least one advantage and one disadvantage for each measure.

7.5   Describe an advantage of suboptimal approximate solutions over suboptimal heuristic solutions. Describe an advantage of suboptimal heuristic solutions over suboptimal approximate solutions.

7.6   What type of processor binding time would be more conducive in a distributed environment? Why?

7.7   Define and describe the relative advantages and disadvantages of the simple usage points versus the economic usage points approach to a distributed scheduler.

7.8   Write a simulation program for the simple usage points approach to distributed scheduling. If two processes belong to locations with equivalent usage points, utilize first come first served. Your program should read input from a file and expect input in the following form.

Time   Location   Process Number

Time indicates the time of the event. Location specifies the location creating the event. Process number is utilized to identify a particular process; if its value is 0, then the event indicates that the location is offering assistance. Any nonzero process number indicates a request for assistance. Your program output should include a message indicating when an event happens as well as when a process is scheduled at a location, including the location number. In addition, your program should indicate when a location receives a credit or charge. A final listing of the usage points for each location should also be included. You may assume that a centralized server maintains the usage table. In addition, you may assume that a location is given one usage point credit if it needs assistance and no locations are available for assistance. Test your program with at least four distinct test files. Be sure to indicate the focus/purpose of each test file.

7.9   The graph theory approach to scheduling presented is a centralized solution. What difficulties would one encounter in attempting to modify this approach to a distributed solution?

7.10   Lo's [Lo88] scheduling algorithm is an approximate solution. Why? Explain your answer.

7.11 What are the benefits of the example probe algorithm, as described in [ELZ86], in prioritizing location costs? What are some of the possible disadvantages?

7.12 When utilizing local and global scheduling queues in distributed scheduling, why are local queues serviced first? What are some of the advantages and disadvantages? What are the advantages to incorporating a "hint" in a distributed scheduler utilizing queues?

7.13 Describe the potential benefits of the Mach scheduler allowing user hints. Describe a possible alternative solution.

7.14 Describe the benefits of using an automaton vector with a stochastic learning scheduling algorithm. What are the disadvantages of not employing an automaton vector?

7.15 Designating a coordinator that is overloaded could have detrimental effects on a distributed system. How does the Bully Algorithm' accommodate the selection of an appropriate system for the coordinator position?

7.16 Define and describe the relative advantages and disadvantages to each of the three approaches for handling orphan processes. Be sure to identify what is affected by the advantages and disadvantages you list.

C H A P T E R **8**

Distributed File Systems

The **file system** is a very important subsystem of the operating system. This subsystem provides an abstract view of secondary storage and is responsible for global naming, file access, and overall file organization. These functions are handled by the name service (Section 8.1), the filer service (Section 8.2), and the directory service (Section 8.3), respectively. While an implementation must perform these services, they are not required to be implemented on different servers. In addition to the services required to be performed by a distributed file system, this chapter examines two popular distributed file system implementations. Specifically, Section 8.4 examines the Network File System implementation and Section 8.5 examines the X.500 specification.

8.1 DISTRIBUTED NAME SERVICE

A distributed **name service** focuses on the issues related to file names. There is a common expression, "What's in a name?" The distributed file systems may return with a question, "What would you like the name to communicate?" File names can communicate file types as well as file location. We address the issue of file types in Section 8.1.1, location transparency in Section 8.1.2, and a necessary requirement for location transparency, global naming and name transparency, in Section 8.1.3.

8.1.1 File Types

Various operating systems allow different types of files and support file types differently. Within the name, the type is generally communicated via an extension, the portion of the name following a period. The precise extension is generally considered more of a convention than a law although some applications do depend on them. The following is a partial list of file types and their possible extensions that are included in file names.

♦ *Library files:* Generally routines available for use within a user's program. Such files use extensions such as *lib* or *dll*.

♦ *Program files*: Programs written by users. Such files use extensions that indicate the particular programming language utilized through their extensions, such as *c, cpp, p,* or *pas*.

♦ *Object-code files*: Unlinked compiled programs generally in machine language. Such files use extensions such as *o* or *obj*.

♦ *Compressed files*: Files that have been compressed for storage. Such files use extensions such as Z, *zip,* or *gz*.

♦ *Archive files,*: Related files that have been grouped into a single file for storage. Such files use extensions such as *tar* or *arc*.

♦ *Graphic files*: Binary or ASCII files for printing or viewing. Such files use extensions such as *dvi, ps, gif,* or *jpeg*.

♦ *Sound files*: Binary files containing sound data. Such files use extensions such as *midi* or *wav*.

♦ *Index files:* Index files frequently contain indexing information for other mainframes. Such files use the extension *idx*.

♦ *Document files*: Files created by a word processor or to be translated by a typesetting program. Such files use extensions such as *doc, wp, tex*.

A name service must allow for all possible types of files. Some operating systems provide support for different file types. For example, some systems recognize binary files and do not allow a user to view said type. Other systems invoke an appropriate application for a given type. Some compilers will not compile programs that do not end in the proper extension. There are two additional file types in UNIX that are not distinguished by extensions: invisible files, whose name begins with a period, and directories. Support for file types can be useful when the system automatically invokes the application program but may hinder the flexibility the system and thereby hinder the flexibility of the user. In particular, if file types are inherently supported, then each new type must be reported to the operating system along with application information. Thus, full file type support can make it difficult for an operating system to support new types that may appear after the system has been developed.

8.1.2 Location Transparency

The second piece of information that can be communicated by the name of a file is the file's location. If the location of a file is communicated, then the name may include the location, machine, and file name, such as myuniversity.edu:/violet/u/galli/book/chapter8. If your distributed system wishes to provide location transparency, then you must provide name transparency through **global naming**, as described in Section 8.1.3. Location transparency is dependent on a name being location independent. This is not trivial to manage but is quite useful. Imagine if telephone numbers were location independent. If this were true, then there would be no area codes since area codes indicate the location of the telephone number holder. The advantage would be that if you relocated to another part of the country or world, your telephone number would not change. Everyone who knew your number prior to your move would still be able to contact you without knowledge of your move. That certainly would be convenient, particularly for a person that relocated often. Such numbers are referred to as **universal numbers**. An example of a universal number is an 800 or 888 number. Likewise, a file may be migrated to a new location or multiple copies of a file could exist throughout the system in a distributed file system. Without location transparency, users and/or their systems would need to constantly keep track of the locations of every copy of every file and explicitly state the location of a file to gain access. This would greatly hinder the basic idea behind a distributed operating system, whose primary goal is to provide a unified system view and thereby hide the fact that multiple systems at multiple locations are involved. Detail Box 8.1 describes an example of one disadvantage of location transparency: routing.

8.1.3 Global Naming and Name Transparency

For a distributed file system to support location transparency, it must support global naming. However, global naming does not itself imply location transparency. In particular, global naming assigns each file (or object) a globally unique name. If the globally unique name is location/machine_name/file_name, the system does not support location transparency! For a system to support location transparency, it must also support name transparency. Name transparency does require globally unique names but such names cannot contain any reference to the location of the file in any manner. It is sometimes incorrectly thought that a name can be related to a server and still provide name transparency. However, if the server name is contained in the file name, then the file is required to remain with that particular server. This inhibits overall system flexibility and interferes with location transparency since such an arrangement would prohibit a file from being relocated to a different server.

A global name space requires one or both of the following types of resolution.

♦ Name resolution

♦ Location resolution

DETAIL BOX 8.1
LOCATION TRANSPARENCY ROUTING PROBLEMS

One disadvantage of location transparency involves the routing of information. When the name includes location information, this information can be utilized to assist in routing. A complete master name to location translation table is not required. As an example of the difficulties involved in routing with location transparency, we examine Ipv4 (Internet Protocol version 4) and the use of IP addresses versus telephone numbers. IP addresses do not provide any indication of the location while telephone numbers do provide location information. It is important to take note that any naming system that utilizes a file name description AND an IP address does NOT provide location transparency. Such a file name is dependent on the IP address location and its name would require a change if it migrated to a different location as specified by the IP address. In addition, if a given location dictates or creates a location to number relationship within its IP scheme, the location has removed the location transparency feature of the routing. If a location changes, it will create exceptions or require a reassignment of a number. For this example, we are strictly examining IP addresses (without structure) versus nonuniversal telephone numbers.

We first examine how telephone numbers, which do provide location information, assist in routing. Telephone numbers provide the following three levels of location information: (1) Country code; (2) Area code; and (3) Local exchange.

The first two levels are optional and if not included are assumed to have the identical value as the originating source. Telephone routers examine the country code and area code to direct a call to the right general physical location. Once in the correct general location, the specific location is then narrowed down further based on the exchange. Once in the proper location for the said exchange, the exact location is based on the final digits. If a request is received for a location that is not local, the router simply passes the request to the appropriate location based on the following rules

1. If it is within my area code but for a different exchange, route to the appropriate exchange.
2. If it is not for my particular area code but is destined for an area within my country, route to the appropriate area code.
3. If it is not for my country, route to the appropriate country.

Upon the appropriate level receiving the request, it is then routed down to the appropriate area code and/or exchange as necessary, as depicted in Figure 8.1.

In contrast, Ipv4 routers have no such advantage. IP addresses are divided into various parts. Without complicating this example with unrelated details, one portion is the identifying address for the host and the rest indicates a particular machine related to that primary host. Once the location of the host is known, the message is sent to the host, which then proceeds to route the information to the particular machine; however, the address for the host itself reveals no location information. If the location is not known by a local router, a request for location information must be passed to a more all-knowing location generally referred to as a gateway. This gateway is (hopefully) a location with a larger address to location translation table that has knowledge of the location of the destination host. Once this information is obtained, a correct path for routing may be chosen. With the possibility of over 2 million hosts, such a complete table is very, very large! One assisting savior to IP addressing is the allowance of symbolic names with domain name specification, as discussed in Detail Box 8.2.

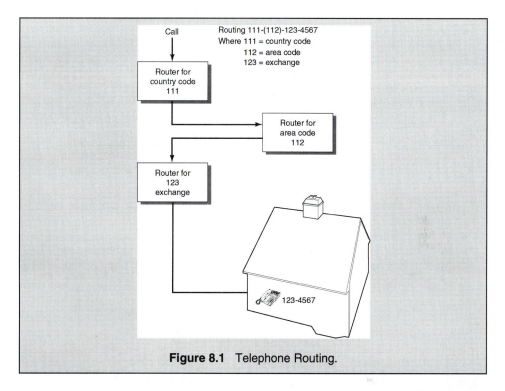

Figure 8.1 Telephone Routing.

Name resolution maps human-friendly, symbolic file names to computer file names. Symbolic file names customarily involve characters. Computer file names are frequently (not so human-friendly) numbers. While numbers may be easier to work with for computers, this approach is not popular with the human users[1]; therefore, each globally unique numeric name must be mapped to a globally unique character based name. In Chapter 6 we learned how Clouds and Amoeba implemented global naming. Specifically, both systems provided globally unique names that were (binary) numbers. These human-unfriendly names were mapped to human-friendly (ASCII) names automatically for users. While Ipv4 does not involve file name resolution, it does provide an excellent example of a global name resolution implementation and it is described in Detail Box 8.2.

Location resolution involves mapping global names to a location. This is a difficult task if name transparency and location transparency are both supported. Detail Box 8.1 focused on the routing difficulties surrounding location transparency. We now focus on various solutions to name-to-location mapping when said transparencies are supported. Location resolution may be solved by a centralized solution utilizing a centralized server

---

[1] The earliest version of IP only allowed numeric IP addressing. The inconvenience was quickly observed and symbolic names were instantiated.

DETAIL BOX 8.2
IPv4 NAME RESOLUTION

Ipv4 name resolution is carried out by the domain name server (DNS). This system is designed to provide IP address resolution to symbolic names. It is based on a hierarchical symbolic name space, as depicted in Figure 8.2. Each symbolic name includes a domain name. A sampling of domain names includes the following.

◆ EDU: for educational institutions
◆ ORG: for nonprofit organizations
◆ MIL: for military locations
◆ GOV: for government sites such as NSF (National Science Foundation)
◆ COM: for commercial locations
◆ NET: for internet service providers
◆ And country codes such as CA (Canada), DE (Germany), NE (Netherlands) and so on.

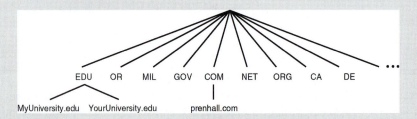

Figure 8.2   IP Hierarchical Name Space.

Notice that all U.S. domains do not require a country code for the same reason British stamps do not require the UK to be placed on their stamps: they started it. In other words, since the Internet as we know it started in the United States, all U.S. based domains do not specify the country but all other domains typically specify this domain under their two-letter country domain. The local site initially attempts name resolution. If information is not available locally for that specified location, the request is routed to an appropriate name resolution server for that given domain. The entire domain name server is organized as a tree, each domain representing a branch. Each node represents a complete domain name and specifies the exact IP address for the given symbolic name.

DETAIL BOX 8.3
DISTRIBUTED LOCATION RESOLUTION ALGORITHM

```
        location function location_resolution(name)
                                // returns location of a file
                                // takes name as input
                                // one possible implementation
        {
        IF local_request(name)
                                // determines if file is held locally
        THEN return_location(self)
                                // if local, return address of self as holder
        ELSE{
                address_code = distributed_addresses(name);
                                // perform mapping function to determine
                                // appropriate address code for the desired
                                // file name. This could be a hash function
                                // or some function based on the file type
                address_holder = location_holder(address_code);
                                // server_location is the table or tree that
                                // maintains a code-to-location
                                // translation. If multiple locations maintain
                                // information, it chooses a server and re-
turns
                                // the name of that server to the variable
                                // address_holder
                location =
                request_for_address(address_holder,name);
                                // request the particular file server
                                // to return the actual location of the file
                return_location(location);
                                // the function returns the address of the file
            }
                                // end ELSE not local
        }
                                // end function location_resolution
```

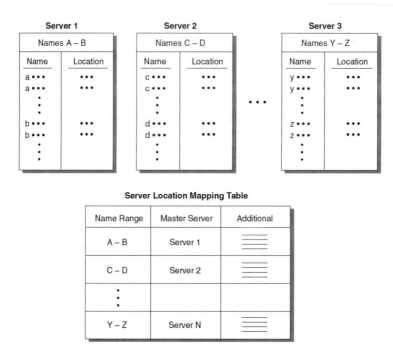

Figure 8.3   Distributed Solution for Name Resolution.

or may be solved by a distributed solution. Like all centralized solutions, utilizing a centralized server for location resolution creates a critical element and a system bottleneck. A distributed solution may involve all locations maintaining a complete location resolution table. This approach is not feasible if the size of the distributed system is significant. Therefore, any massive distributed system requires a distributed solution with multiple location resolution servers. Each server is responsible for a particular subset of names, as depicted in Figure 8.3. A server location mapping table is consulted to identify what server within the system is responsible for what set of names. There are two dominating approaches to segmenting names to the various servers. The first approach applies some type of hash function to the name. The result of this hash function dictates which server(s) is responsible for maintaining location information. The second approach divides the responsibility based on file types. Each type of file is serviced by a different server. In either case, when a file is relocated, the responsible server's information set is updated. This information set may be stored as a table or in a tree-structured manner. Detail Box 8.3 provides an example algorithm for location resolution. Distributed solutions commonly permit server replication; that is, there may be multiple servers responsible for the same subset of names. Issues related to replication are discussed in the next section.

8.2 DISTRIBUTED FILE SERVICE

A distributed **file service** is responsible for operations on a particular file. Section 8.2.1 discusses the varieties of files that may exist in a distributed system. Section 8.2.2 discusses issues related to file sharing, and Section 8.2.3 discusses the methods for implementing a file service. The topic of file services concludes in Section 8.2.4 with a discussion of issues related to file replication.

8.2.1 File Variations

In addition to file types discussed in Section 8.1, files may also vary in terms of how they are stored, the various attributes assigned to files, as well as the mode of protection utilized by the base operating system.

File Storage

Operating systems may store files in various manners. Some systems represent files as a continuous stream of bytes. This provides no inherent structure within a file. This method is utilized by a majority of modern operating systems. Such systems support unstructured files. In contrast, **structured files** represent data in terms of records as depicted in Figure 8.4. The file system may or may not provide indexing for individual records within a file. If indexing is supported, individual records may be accessed explicitly through the index. The record index is frequently stored in a data structure such as a B-tree or hash table. If no indexing is supported, individual records can only be accessed by specifying the exact position of the record within the file.

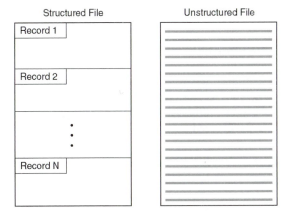

Figure 8.4 Structured versus Unstructured Files.

In addition, a file may be stored in binary form or ASCII form, both are always allowed. Binary files may be executables or encrypted files (see Chapter 11 for information on encryption). ASCII files include various data and source files that are readable by humans. Distinguishing between these two file types is most common in systems whose word lengths are not divisible by 8 bits, such as the PDP 10, a 36-bit system.

File Attributes

Files often have a set of attributes that provide additional information about the specific file. Different file systems provide support for different file attributes, and a distributed file system must be aware of and handle the various types of attributes. Some systems only allow a specific subset of attributes while others allow flexibility. The following is a list of commonly supported attributes.

- File name (including file type extension)
- File size
- Type of file ownership (individual or group)
- Name of file owner(s)
- Date of file creation
- Date of last file access
- Date of last modification
- Version number
- Relevant protection information (See below)

The directory service (discussed in Section 8.3) maintains these attributes and binds them to the file.

File Protection Modes

A distributed file system must be aware of the file protection modes employed by centralized systems. Centralized file protection modes are based on the types of file access permitted, the level of granularity defined for protection, and the type of file protection employed. A file may be accessed to:

- Read to the file,
- Write to the file,
- Truncate the file,
- Append to the file, or
- Execute the file.

Protection granularity may be in terms of individual users, a subset of users that can be individually listed, a group of users, all users from a particular organization, or all users in the world.

For centralized systems, there are two dominating types of file protection; **access lists,** also known as access control lists (ACLs), and **capabilities**. As an example depicting the differences between these two types of protection, consider yourself a member of high society. You have just been invited to the party of the decade. There are two methods the host may have utilized to ensure that only invited guests attend the said party. The first method would be to have a guest list available to security. When people arrive at the party, their name is checked against the guest list to see if it name appears. If their name appears, they are allowed into the party. The second method is to provide each guest with an invitation. This invitation must be produced to security upon the invitee's arrival. The guest list is analogous to the access list method of file protection in which each file maintains a list of what users are allowed to access the file and in what manner. The system maintains the access list. When one wishes to access a file, if the user and operation are listed as acceptable actions on the access list, the action is allowed. Likewise, capabilities parallel invitations. To access a file you must provide a capability that indicates the user is allowed to conduct said requested action.

The two methods have similar disadvantages to their analogies. In the same manner that a party host would encounter difficulties revoking an invitation, a file system cannot quickly or easily revoke a capability. While the party of the century may have a large guest list, access lists are also very large. They may be stored as a two-dimensional array (columns indicate file names, rows indicate users whether individual or groups, and entries represent access privileges granted) or as an actual list. When an access list is stored in a two-dimensional array, it is referred to as an **access matrix**, as depicted in Figure 8.5. Figure 8.6 depicts an access list for File 1. Both capabilities and access lists may also be utilized to protect and define access for any system resource.

	User 1	User 2	Group 1	Group 2
File 1	RWE	R	R	R
File 2	R			
File 3		RWE	RE	RE
File 4		RWE		RWE
R = Read access W = Write access E = Execute access				

Figure 8.5 Access Matrix.

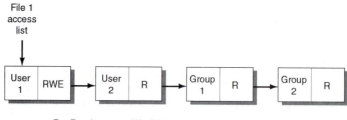

R = Read access   W = Write access   E = Execute access

Figure 8.6   Access List for File 1.

Access control may also involve a combination of capabilities and access lists. As an example, let's look at the security badges utilized at the 1996 Centennial Olympic Games. For extremely low-security areas, the mere presentation of the badge (dependent on the location and the type of badge) would provide access to a desired resource, such as riding the public transit. In contrast, for access to more security-sensitive areas, such as an Olympic venue or the computer labs, badges were scanned and the exact identification number was immediately verified against an access list. The access list cannot be checked without the presentation of the capability, the badge. Information on additional required security measures for distributed access control is presented in Chapter 11.

8.2.2 File Modification Notification

As we learned, basic file operations include reading, writing, and executing files. When multiple locations access shared files, every participant must agree upon a method for notifying other participants regarding modification to files also commonly referred to as **file access semantics**. There are two groups of notification methods. The first group regards all files as **immutable** (that is, modifications are not allowed). With no modifications allowed, no damage can occur to the data and no notification needs to take place. The second group of notification methods is for mutable or changeable files. The following are the three basic approaches for **modification notification** for mutable files and are depicted in Figure 8.7.

1. *Immediate notification*: With immediate notification, each and every operation to a file is instantaneously visible to every participant holding a copy of the file. This method is very difficult and impractical to implement in a distributed environment.

2. *Notification on close*: With notification on close, other participants are only notified of file modifications when a participant closes a file and thereby terminates their access to the file. Other members of the distributed system do not update their copies but continue working with their dirty copy. The final form of the file is determined by whatever system participant writes the file last.

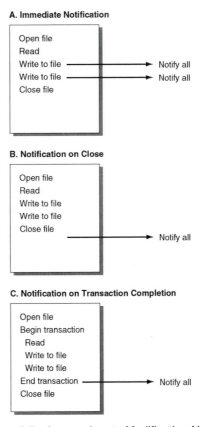

Figure 8.7 Approaches to Modification Notification.

3. *Notification on transaction completion*: A transaction is a fixed set of operations. When this fixed set of operations is completed, members of the
system are notified. The transaction approach is very successful in distributed systems and is the topic of Chapter 9.

8.2.3 File Service Implementations

File service implementations may be based on **remote access** or **remote copy** and may be
stateful or **stateless**. When remote access is utilized, the file server maintains the copy of
the file. The remote client must read, write, open, close, append, truncate, and handle
every operation it wishes to perform remotely by communicating over the network. The
client does not require any storage space for the file, but must deal with the constant network delays. The client does not receive an actual copy of the file and the server must
manage the possible numerous open copies of a given file. In contrast, if the file service is

implemented utilizing remote copy, a client receives a complete copy of the requested file. This implementation is also known as **whole file caching**. Implementations utilizing remote copy will generally only support read and write operations and require clients to have sufficient storage for the file. The only network delays encountered are upon initial and final file transfers. This approach is simple and quite successful when the entire file is going to be read by the client or changed. Generally, notification on close is the form of file modification employed. Observe that network resources and time may be wasted if only a small portion of the file is required by the client, generally in terms of blocks. This implementation is referred to as **block caching**. If remote copy was to allow access to portions of files such as block caching, the number of units a given server and the entire file system is responsible for managing would be greatly increased.

Stateful servers maintain information about all clients that are utilizing the server to access a file. In particular, the server maintains information regarding what file the client is utilizing as well as what operations have been performed. If a client is reading a file, a stateful server will maintain information regarding the current position at which the client is accessing the file. This greatly increases the efficiency of all information transfer operations following the initial contact with the server; however, it also increases the dependency of the client on a specific server for a given file. Thus, such a system cannot support failure transparency. In contrast, a stateless server maintains no client information. Each and every request from a client must include very specific request information, such as file name, operation, and exact position in the file. The client maintains the state information. While this method increases the overhead for each operation, it does provide the ability to support failure transparency.

8.2.4 File Replication

When file replication is supported by a distributed file system, the reliability and efficiency of the file service are greatly enhanced. Efficiency is improved in terms of response time, server load, and network traffic. In addition, if a given file server crashes the file service can still meet its obligations. Only if every server containing a replication of a given file is down will service be inhibited. Thus, file replication provides failure transparency since it allows a user to function without requiring user knowledge of a system failure. Early solutions involved explicit copy. That is, a user would issue a remote copy command and thereby receive a copy of the file. This approach was used in early network implementations using commands such as `rcp` (remote UNIX copy) or `ftp` (file transfer protocol associated with TCP/IP). An explicit approach may be satisfactory to a network operation system but is in direct conflict with the goals of a distributed operation system, which strives to present a unified view. Successful file replication in a distributed operating system must provide replication transparency. A user of the file system should not be aware that multiple copies exist within the system. In addition, any replication method must provide some form of data consistency, as discussed in Chapter 9.

Solutions to file replication in a distributed system may be centralized or distributed. A centralized solution involves the designation of one file server as the primary server for a set of files. All requests to update data are handled through this primary server. When the primary server is down, updates may not take place but the files are still available via the secondary servers for reading. The primary server may provide clients with a direct **file handle** for a copy on a secondary server or may provide all clients with an intermediate file handle. If an intermediate file handle is provided, the primary server must maintain a table mapping the intermediate file handles to actual file handles, as depicted in Figure 8.8. A file handle typically includes the location of the file and the necessary permissions to access the file. In addition, the handles may incorporate a sequencing number to assist in proper updating. Issues related to sequencing are discussed in Chapter 10.

There are two popular distributed solutions to file replication. The first solution utilizes group communication. Whenever a given participant changes the contents of a file, it communicates the write commands to all participants, as depicted in Figure 8.9. This communication may take place immediately, causing a short interruption to the writer, or may occur as a low-priority background process. Likewise, recipients may immediately update their copies or may update their copies on an "I'll do it when I get to it" basis. Immediate communication and immediate updates help minimize the chance that a file is changed again (locally or remotely) before the previous change order is processed.

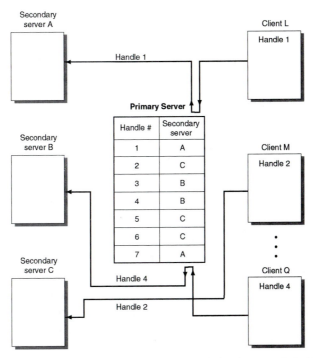

Figure 8.8 Employing a Mapping Table for Intermediate File Handles.

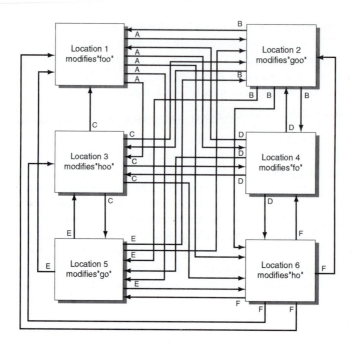

Source	Image
1	A = Here is a modification to file foo
2	B = Here is a modification to file goo
3	C = Here is a modification to file hoo
4	D = Here is a modification to file fo
5	E = Here is a modification to file go
6	F = Here is a modification to file ho

Figure 8.9 Distributed File Replication Employing Group Communication.

The second distributed approach involves voting and the association of version numbers. A client requests permission to modify a file from the various servers. Permission is achieved by a majority of the servers agreeing on the latest version along with the stipulation that no server has communicated the existence of any version number that is higher. A looser restriction is to receive simple permission from a majority of the participants (no agreement on version number is required) and consider the highest version number received as the current version number. In either approach, it is common to require a larger number of votes for write permission versus read permission. Upon receiving the file, the version number is incremented.

8.3 DISTRIBUTED DIRECTORY SERVICE

The distributed **directory service** of the distributed file system is responsible for the over-all file organization. It provides the interface for users of the distributed file system. We examine possible directory structures in Section 8.3.1. We then proceed with a discussion of directory management in Section 8.3.2 and conclude with a discussion on directory service operations in Section 8.3.3.

8.3.1 Directory Structures

The first directory structure is that of a **hierarchical directory structure**. This directory structure allows directories and subdirectories. A subdirectory may only have one parent directory. This allows users to organize their files easily but makes it difficult for multiple users to share files. In contrast, an **acyclic directory structure** allows an acyclic graph structure which lets a directory to have multiple parent directories. This provides for easy file sharing but complicates directory management. In particular, it is more difficult to identify and remove an orphan file, as we see in Section 8.3.2. An example of an acyclic graph structured directory service in a centralized system is UNIX. UNIX allows hard links (system administrator created if within the same file system) and soft symbolic links (user and cross-file system created) to files thereby creating multiple parents. In this cir-cumstance, UNIX allows the creation of a **cyclic directory structure,** where a node can be a parent and a child of another node. It is possible that this sort of structure can lead to a structure that is not unlike a tangled ball of yarn at best.

8.3.2 Directory Management

Directory management is concerned with maintaining a proper list of active directories and their respective files. In addition, it must be able to identify and remove unreferenced files. In a hierarchical structured directory system, a file only has one parent. When the parent is removed, it is either assumed or requested that all subdirectories and their re-spective files are also removed. Such files are no longer referenced, and their resources are released to the system. In contrast, if a directory structure is an acyclic graph, then a given file may have multiple parents. This raises the question of when a file is considered un-referenced. This is important to determine since it indicates when the directory service is allowed to reclaim the file's resources. This determination is made possible by the asso-ciation of a reference counter with each file. Each link added to a particular file increments the reference counter for that file. Each link removed from a file (due to file or directory removal) decrements the reference counter. Any resources associated with a file having a reference counter equal to 0 may be reclaimed by the directory service. In UNIX, hard links affect the reference counter but symbolic links do not. Therefore, if the primary owner of a file that has associated symbolic links decides to remove the file, the file is immediately removed. In contrast, all hard links must be removed before a file with hard links associated can be removed.

Directory management is also responsible for how the directory structure is stored. It may be stored at a centralized location or it may be distributed throughout the system. An example of a distributed directory service is the telephone directory service. If you wish to find a particular telephone number, you must contact the correct location for directory assistance. No single directory service maintains information on the entire system. Since the telephone system does not provide location transparency, the telephone directory service does not provide location transparency either; however, the information discussed relevant to file replication and distribution is also pertinent to directory replication and distribution. In particular, distribution can be based on some type of hash function or property, such as origination ownership.

8.3.3 Directory Operations

A directory service is responsible for supporting all or a subset of the following directory operations.

- ◆ Create a directory.
- ◆ Delete a directory.
- ◆ Rename a directory.
- ◆ List a directory's contents.
- ◆ Manage a directory's access permissions.
- ◆ Changing a directory's access permissions.
- ◆ Move a directory within the overall directory structure.
- ◆ Traverse the entire directory structure.

Any unsupported directory functions, which may be allowed by a possible underlying centralized operating system, should have some type of default mapping or equivalence. In addition, the directory server is responsible for the following file operations.

- ◆ Create a file.
- ◆ Delete a file.
- ◆ Rename a file.
- ◆ Move a file.
- ◆ Search for a file.
- ◆ Duplicate a file (to a new location with a new name).

As with directory functions, any unsupported file operations should have some type of default mapping or equivalence since they may be supported by an underlying base operating system.

8.4 NFS™

In this section, we examine the approach of SUN's Network File System (NFS) version 3. Section 8.4.1 describes the NFS file service, Section 8.4.2 describes the NFS directory service, and Section 8.4.3 describes the NFS Name Service.

8.4.1 NFS File Service

The NFS file service is a stateless file service and is based on block caching, as described in Section 8.2.3. NFS utilizes RPC mechanisms (as described in Chapter 3) that employ external data representation (as described in Chapter 2) to achieve transparent remote access for users of this distributed file system. Members of the distributed system can include anything from personal computers to high-performance parallel computers. File access control includes support for DES encryption keys utilizing Kerberos authentication, as described in Chapter 11. NFS encourages all servers to support all file attributes and file types. The actual size of file names is determined by mutual agreement of the client and the server. NFS version 3 extended version 2 to allow larger files; specifically, it can support 64-bit file sizes and file offsets. The RPC mechanisms along with all translation from the NFS file system to the local file system are handled by what is referred to as the virtual file system within NFS. This virtual file system resides on top of and interacts with a location's base file system.

When a client requests access to a given file, the entire disk is mounted and the initial block of the file is transferred to the client. In particular, the client receives a handle, including specific information on the system type and disk location, to retrieve the disk and the file contents on the mounted disk. This handle can be continuously used until the server utilizes its ability to revoke the handle given to a client. Giving a handle to a client is referred to as mounting. An overview of the mounting algorithm is presented in Detail Box 8.4. Mounting can be explicit, thereby allowing access to be conducted on an "as needed basis" or it may be automated. Automated mounting involves the use of an automated system program that automatically retrieves file blocks each time the system is booted or upon a client's attempt to access a remote file. In either case, upon invocation the automated retrieval utilizes the handle to send messages to all servers for all files on a given disk. The first server to respond is utilized as a source for the given disk. Thus, NFS can be utilized to support location, replication, and failure transparency; however, this feature is not intrinsic to NFS. It is also important to observe that no method for determining the most current and correct version of information is implemented or supported. Without the use of some form of locking, a race condition can occur.

Modification notification to the multiple file replications is handled as a background process. Thus, notification is not immediate; however, modification notifications are conducted prior to file closure. Portions of the file that have been modified by a client are marked as dirty. Only these dirty portions are communicated back to the servers.

DETAIL BOX 8.4
NFS MOUNTING

The following is an overview of the steps involved in NFS mounting and the utilization of the remote file handles.

1. NFS Mount is instantiated by the client. This instantiation must include information on the remote directory, identification of requester for security purposes, as well as the location on the client's file system to place the requested file.
2. Mount performs a NFS lookup operation to identify a server maintaining a copy of the desired disk.
3. An RPC is sent to an appropriate server requesting a handle for the desired disk.
4. The remote server performs appropriate security checks and if the client is permitted access to the contents of the disk, returns a handle.
5. The file handle is received by the client. The client's system records information regarding the file handle into the local file system table, including an indication that this file is a remote file (the same table is utilized to store information on local files).
6. This table is then utilized to access files. If access to a file that is flagged as a remote file is requested, the information in the table is utilized to initialize an NFS file request via a RPC. If the file is local, the base operating system handles the request.

8.4.2 NFS Directory Service

NFS assumes a hierarchical structured directory system but does support the creation of soft links to files as are common in UNIX. As described in Section 8.4.1, entire directories or subdirectories may also be transferred to a client. This is also referred to as mounting. A list of NFS-supported directory operations is contained in Detail Box 8.5.

DETAIL BOX 8.5
NFS DIRECTORY OPERATIONS

The following is a list of some of the directory operations supported by NFS as described in RFC 1813.

- *Lookup*: Returns information on a file along with its attributes.
- *Access*: Allows explicit verification of access permissions for a given file.
- *Read*: Utilized for reading files. Includes a boolean variable for end of file detection.
- *Write*: Utilized for writing to files (may specify if only a portion needs writing).
- *Create*: Utilized for creating files.
- *Remove*: Utilized for removing a file.
- *Rename*: Utilized for renaming a file or directory.
- *Rmdir*: Utilized for removing a directory.
- *Mkdir*: Utilized for creating a directory.
- *Mknod*: Utilized for creating special files.
- *Readdir*: Utilized for reading a directory and includes provisions for security validation.
- *Readdirplus*: Utilized for reading a directory and its attributes.
- *Fsinfo*: Provides information on a file system (max file size, availability of soft links).
- *Fsstat*: Provides file system statistics, including utilized and free space information.
- *Commit*: Forces dirty portions of a file to be written back to the server

8.4.3 NFS Name Service

NFS name service support is based on the mounting of a file or directory, as described in Section 8.4.1. NFS does not support (and cannot be made to support easily) one global name space. A client can share a remote name space through an explicit request to mount a file. When the file or directory is mounted, it appears to be part of the local directory structure to the client. Figure 8.10 depicts a file named "foo" mounted at two different locations. At this point, every aspect of the mounted information appears local, thereby providing location transparency. However, due to this implementation, each user of the NFS system has a unique global view and a file may have several "absolute" names within the system. This creates difficulties for distributed applications utilizing files based on NFS since a given file has several file names that are location dependent.

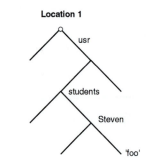

Location 1

Local name of foo = /usr/students/steven/foo

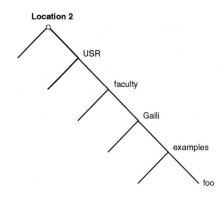

Location 2

Local name of foo = /usr/faculty/galli/examples/foo

Figure 8.10   Name Space and Mounting in NFS.

8.5 X.500

In this section, we provide a brief introduction of the X.500 directory service. It is also the basis for Lightweight Directory Access protocol (LDAP) employed in Windows 2000, as described in the Chapter 12 Case Study. The X.500 directory service is an international standard defined by the CCITT (International Telegraph & Telephone Consultative Committee) currently known as ITU-T (International Telecommunications Union-Telecommunication sector) and the International Standards Organization (ISO). This directory service is designed to provide the Internet equivalence of telephone companies white and yellow pages as well as mail and e-mail address lookup. The goals specified in RFC 309 for X.500 include the following.

◆ Decentralized maintenance: Each location is only responsible for maintaining local portions of the directory service. Thus, the information stored is considered to be immutable except locally.

◆ Support powerful and complex search queries.

◆ Provide a single global name space.

◆ Provide a structured information framework that allows local extensions.

◆ Design a standards based directory service so all applications can depend on a uniform interface to directory services.

We now examine X.500's file and name service (Section 8.5.1) and directory service (Section 8.5.2).

8.5.1 X.500 File and Name Service: The Information Model

X.500's file and name service is defined in terms of what it refers to as the information model. In particular, the information model is responsible for how the information is stored and arranged. This specification is not designed to function as an all-purpose distributed file system. The X.500 information model considers its primary construct an entry. Each entry holds information about the object that it represents. Each object has a set of mandatory attributes and optional attributes. Mandatory attributes are always inherited by objects. If an entry were to represent a person, then it might have the following collection of attributes.

◆ First name

◆ Surname

◆ Postal address

◆ Email address

◆ Work address

◆ Telephone number

◆ Fax number

In addition, each attribute has an associated syntax utilized to describe the type of data the attribute represents, such as text or picture. An example of attribute syntax is telephoneNumbern which permits the data to consist of numbers, parenthesis, and dashes.

The X.500 global name space is represented by the directory information tree (DIT), which is a strictly hierarchical structure. When one is referring to the name space along with all the data associated with the names, it is called the directory information base (DIB). Each entry in the DIB occupies a unique location within the DIT. If an entry has no children it is referred to as a leaf entry. Each DIT entry and its attributes make up the relative distinguished name (RDN) of that entry. Its complete distinguished name consists of its RDN along with the RDN of all its ancestors traced back to the root of the DIT. This approach alleviates duplicate names. To demonstrate, consider that a telephone book may have several S. Smiths listed. If S. Smith's telephone book entry included a complete list of mother's maiden names back 1000 years, the entry would be unique (assuming you could recognize your friend's name in this manner!). Thus, by including the heritage in the distinguished name, each entry has a globally unique name.

8.5.2 X.500's Directory Service: The Directory Model

X.500's directory service is defined in terms of what it refers to as the directory model, which is designed with the assumption that there will be significantly more queries versus updates. The two components to this model include the directory sser agent (DUA) and the directory system agent (DSA). The user agent accesses the system on behalf of a user while the system agent maintains a portion of the directory information base (DIB) and can provide an access point to the directory for the user agent. The entire DIB is maintained by DSAs. For the DSAs to support location and replication transparency, they use two techniques, referred to as chaining and referral. A particular portion of the DIB is maintained by one primary location referred to as a master. The secondary sites for this same portion of the DIB is maintained by its shadow DSAs. A shadow DSA can itself have shadow DSAs. However, only the master DSA can make changes. All changes reported to a shadow DSA must be passed to the master DSA for that portion of the DIB.

8.6 SUMMARY

A distributed file system has three primary responsibilities. First, it must provide a method for naming files and managing file names through a name service. This may be carried out in a manner that supports name transparency. Choices made in the global naming scheme also affect whether the entire file system is able to support location transparency. Second, a file system must manage files, including their various attributes, and properly authorize access. This is carried out by a file service. This service is also responsible for determining if files can be modified. If so, the service must determine how modifications to files will be carried out. In addition, it must determine if files will be utilized by clients while the files remain on the server or if clients will be able to copy the files locally. If file replication is to be allowed, it is the file service's responsibility to provide replication transparency to the system. Finally, a distributed file system includes a directory service. A directory service must provide a user interface and an overall structure to the files. Each of the three services within a distributed file system must be included; however, implementations of the services may be as individual units or they may be combined into one or two separate services. If the directory service is to meet the goals of a distributed operating system, it must support all forms of relevant transparencies.

In this chapter, we also examined two examples of distributed file systems. Both have very different approaches, yet each is well regarded as a groundbreaking implementation. NFS provides a full service file system while X.500 focuses primarily on functioning as a directory service. NFS provides global naming, but the name for the same file differs from location to location. In contrast, X.500 provides one global naming scheme. NFS does not inherently support replication, while X.500 supports full replication, taking advantage of globally immutable data.

To ensure an acceptable behavior in terms of information modification within the files, a distributed file system or the application utilizing it must also address the following issues. In particular, they must provide support for concurrency control (Chapter 5), decide on an appropriate consistency model (Chapter 9), and employ some form of sequencing (Chapter 10). Research regarding distributed file systems is continuously progressing. Currently, it appears as though LDAP might turn out to be the universal answer for UNIX and Windows-based systems. Regardless of the solution, transparent access to files must be solved. As the amount of information available and the types (particularly multimedia) of files that need to be supported increase continuously, providing efficient and secure access to information across the world will challenge researchers for years to come.

8.7 REFERENCES FOR FURTHER STUDY

The general references presented in Chapter 1 can provide some general information on distributed file systems. Some appropriate traditional research papers concerning information in this chapter include [BKT85, CAKLMS92, CBE95, DaBu85, Dio80, FrOl85, GNS88, HKMNSSW88, Kum91, LeSi90, LZCZ86, MiDi82, MSCHRS86, NWO88, San87, Sat90a, Sat90b, ScPu94, SMI80, and YSL97].

The following provide some great starting points for sources on the Internet concerning distributed file systems. The 1989 Request For Comments (RFC), which includes a detailed description of NFS can be found at http://www.cis.ohio-state.edu/htbin/rfc/rfc1094.html. The 1995 Request For Comments on version 3 of NFS can be found at http://www.cis.ohio-state.edu/htbin/rfc/rfc1813.html. A complete list of all RFCs related to NFS, can be found at http://www.cis.ohio-state.edu/cgi-bin/wais-rfc.pl?NFS. Additional information on NFS can be found by performing a search on NFS at SUN Microsystem's main Web page at http://www.sun.com. The following is a list of some of the request for comments that concern CCITT's X.500 directory service.

- ◆ http://www.cis.ohio-state.edu/htbin/rfc/rfc1308.html (an executive introduction)
- ◆ http://www.cis.ohio-state.edu/htbin/rfc/rfc1309.html (a technical overview)
- ◆ http://www.cis.ohio-state.edu/htbin/rfc/rfc1275.html (replication requirements)
  A complete list of RFCs for X.500 can be obtained at

♦ http://www.cis.ohio-state.edu/cgi-bin/wais-rfc.pl?X.500 (a complete list of all
  RFCs related to X.500)

AFS is another popular distributed file system that employs remote copy. AFS originally
stood for the Andrew File System, Andrew being the founder of Carnegie Mellon University
where the system originated. It is now commercialized and is a product of Transarc
Corporation. An overview of AFS can be found at http://www.alw.nih.gov/Docs/AFS/
AFS_toc.html. The home page for AFS at Transarc is located at http://www.transarc.com/
afs/transarc.com/public/www/Product/AFS. A list of frequently asked questions and answers on AFS can be found at http://www.transarc.com/afs/transarc.com/ public/www/
Product/ AFS/FAQ/faq.

The RFC for LDAP can be found at the following sites:

http://www.cis.ohio-state.edu/htbin/rfc/rfc2251.html,
http://www.cis.ohio-state.edu/htbin/rfc/rfc2252.html,
http://www.cis.ohio-state.edu/htbin/rfc/rfc2254.html,
http://www.cis.ohio-state.edu/htbin/rfc/rfc2255.html,
and
http://www.cis.ohio-state.edu/htbin/rfc/ rfc2307.html.

An online version of the LDAP users manual can be found at
http://www.umich.edu/~dirsvcs/ ldap/doc/man/. In addition, a page with multiple links for
LDAP documentation, including the FAQ site can be found at http://www.umich.edu/
~dirsvcs/ldap/doc/.

EXERCISES

8.1   What are the primary functions of a distributed name service? Is a name service necessary for
      a centralized operating system? If no, explain why. If yes, explain any additional features re-
      quired of a distributed name service.

8.2   If file types are supported, what problems can be created in a distributed operating system
      when participants utilize different base operating systems? Name and describe two possible
      solutions to supporting/handling files of locally unknown types.

8.3   Name and describe two advantages and two disadvantages (or complications) associated with
      supporting location transparency.

8.4   Early operating systems sometimes provided a flat name space and a flat directory structure.
      In particular, treelike structures were not allowed. All files were at the same level. What are
      some of the possible complications associated with a flat name space and directory structure

for a multiuser environment? Would this be a practical approach for a distributed environment?

8.5   What are the disadvantages of a distributed system that requires each participant to maintain a complete name-to-location mapping table?

8.6   Name and describe three advantages of utilizing replication in a distributed file system.

8.7   What type of application would benefit from using structured files? Name and describe a disadvantage of supporting structured files.

8.8   Evaluate capabilities and access rights according to the following possible types of access rights revocation. In particular, can that method support the respective type of revocation? If it can be supported, indicate why. If it cannot be supported, indicate a possible solution to allow its support. State any assumptions you are making.

A. Immediate revocation
B. Revocation of rights applying only to an individual
C. Partial revocation of rights to an individual (e.g., lose write but keep read access)
D. Temporary revocation of rights

8.9   Define and describe the advantages and disadvantages of a distributed file system only supporting immutable files.

8.10   Compare and contrast stateful and stateless file servers in terms of the following.

A.   Support for failure transparency
B.   Support for location transparency
C.   Support for replication transparency
D.   Efficiency

8.11   Compare and contrast file servers based on remote access versus remote copy in terms of the following.

A.   Support for failure transparency
B.   Support for location transparency
C.   Support for replication transparency
D.   Modification notification
E.   Managing file modifications
F.   Demands placed on the servers
G.   Demands placed on clients
H.   Efficiency

8.12   What are the advantages of utilizing intermediate file handles in a distributed file versus system utilizing direct file handles?

8.13   Define and describe the difficulties one would encounter supporting an acyclic directory structure in a distributed system. What implications could such a structure impose on the global naming scheme? What are the implications of allowing soft links?

8.14   Does NFS support location transparency? Why or why not? Explain your answer in detail.

8.15   Why is it difficult for NFS to support a global name space? Describe a possible solution for NFS to support a global name space.

8.16   Discuss the implications of the X.500 assumption that queries are frequent and changes are rare. What issues does this allow X.500 to avoid that NFS could not avoid?

8.17   What are the advantages of a distributed file system in providing decentralized maintenance as is provided in X.500?

8.18   What are some of the possible advantages of allowing an X.500 shadow DSA to have shadow DSAs itself?

8.19   Why must applications utilizing a distributed file system be sure that some form of concurrency control mechanism is employed at some level?

8.20   Compare and contrast NFS and X.500 with AFS (pointers to information in Section 8.7) relevant to the three services supported by a distributed file system.

CHAPTER 9

Transaction Management and Consistency Models

*I*n several of the topics discussed in previous chapters, we frequently needed to allow multiple participants in a distributed system to access and change shared data. In this chapter, we focus on the issues related to ensuring proper data manipulation. In Chapter 5, we learned several methods for concurrency control. In this chapter, we focus on issues related to one of the most successful approaches for manipulating shared data in a distributed system, transaction management. Transaction management may be incorporated with a DSM or a distributed file system and may be implemented utilizing some of the concurrency control mechanisms we studied. In Section 9.1, we look at some examples of incorporating transaction management in a distributed system. In Section 9.2, we examine the definition of a transaction and the ACID properties essential for transactions. Section 9.3 presents the various forms of consistency that may be provided by a transaction management system as well as by a DSM. A popular protocol for implementing transaction management is discussed in Section 9.4. Section 9.5 presents the concept of nested transactions while, Section 9.6 discusses various issues related to implementing a transaction management system.

9.1 TRANSACTION MANAGEMENT MOTIVATION

A **transaction** is a set of operations on shared data that are grouped together and treated as a single action. **Transaction management** is the service employed to ensure proper transaction handling. One may recall that a **race condition** results when the output of a function or the value of a variable is dependent on the timing of the inputs; specifically, the two inputs may be racing to ensure that their result is the new result. Transactions handle the distributed variation of the race condition problem.

There are many ways to motivate people and to elicit one's interest. One common way is to discuss money; perhaps that is where the expression "Money talks" originates. Thus, this section demonstrates two potential problems that could occur without proper transaction management, the lost update and retrieval disparity. We utilize a bank account as an example. Just think, without transaction management, the example account could be yours!

9.1.1 The Lost Update

In this section, we introduce one classic problem motivating transaction management, the lost update. The **lost update** is the term used throughout the literature to refer to a data manipulation that is not properly handled and the results of a specific action are lost. To demonstrate the lost update problem, we consider the following two actions.

Action 1

Lynn has a "cash card" that automatically accesses her shared bank account. She approaches the automatic teller and requests to withdraw $200.

Action 2

Steven also has a cash card that automatically accesses his bank account, which he shares with Lynn. He approaches the automatic teller and requests to withdraw $300.

Now suppose both Lynn and Steven approach a different automatic teller at precisely the same moment. The current balance of the account is $2500. If the automatic teller system was not set up to function properly in a distributed environment, any of the following scenarios might result. Pseudocode examples are presented in Detail Box 9.1.

Scenario 1

Both automatic teller machines retrieve the account balance of $2500. Lynn's action is completed first. Thus, a $2300 balance is written back to the account. Moments later, Steven completes his action and a $2200 balance is written back to the account, as depicted in Figure 9.1. Observe that the correct balance should be $2000.

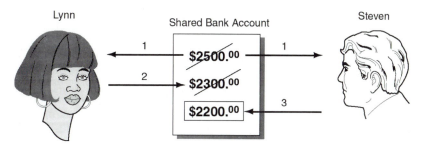

1. Retrieve balance
2. Lynn's action is recorded
3. Steven's action is recorded

Figure 9.1 The Lost Update.

Scenario 2

Both automatic teller machines retrieve the account balance of $2500. Steven's action is completed first. Thus, a $2200 balance is written back to the account. Moments later, Lynn completes her action and a $2300 balance is written back to the account. Observe that the correct balance should be $2000.

You might be thinking, "Hey, that is great! Lynn and Steven made some money!" but what if they had been making deposits or what if you were the bank? Neither scenario is correct or acceptable. Data manipulation in a distributed environment must be handled in a manner that would not only have allowed both actions to occur but provided a means to ensure an accurate balance, in this case $2000.

9.1.2 Retrieval Disparity

One would like to believe that when a data value is returned, it is accurate. While this is definitely a desirable property, without transaction management to ensure proper manipulation for *all* copies of your data, this may not be true. **Retrieval disparity** is one problem that can occur if either the first or both of the following conditions exist.

♦ Changing of shared data is not atomic.

♦ Multiple copies of data exist.

DETAIL BOX 9.1
THE LOST UPDATE

```
Action 1
Get Balance;
Balance=Balance-200;
Return Balance;


Action 2
Get Balance;
Balance=Balance-300;
Return Balance;


Scenario 1
ACTION1: Get Balance;
                              // Balance=$2500
ACTION2: Get Balance;
                              // Balance=$2500
ACTION1: Balance=Balance-200;
ACTION2: Balance=Balance-300;
ACTION1: Return Balance;
ACTION2: Return Balance;
RESULT: Balance=2200


Scenario 2 (Figure 9.1)
ACTION1: Get Balance;
                              // Balance=$2500
ACTION2: GET Balance;
                              // Balance=$2500
ACTION1: Balance=Balance-200;
ACTION2: Balance=Balance-300;
ACTION2: Return Balance;
ACTION1: Return Balance;
RESULT: Balance=2300
```

In particular, retrieval disparity involves the retrieval of data that do not reflect the latest transaction. When the changing of shared data is not atomic, not only can the lost update problem occur, but retrieval disparity may also occur. This problem is even more likely to occur if multiple copies of the data exist and these copies are not atomically updated. The primary difference between the lost update problem and retrieval disparity can be summarized in one word: timing. In the lost update, both actions commenced at the same time. Retrieval disparity can occur anytime a transaction has occurred but copies of the data are not updated prior to another transaction retrieving the data. We now look at an example of retrieval disparity that displays the timing element. We again utilize *Action1* and *Action 2* from Section 9.1.1.

Action 1

Lynn has a cash card that automatically accesses her shared bank account. She approaches the automatic teller and requests to withdraw $200.

Action 2

Steven also has a cash card that automatically accesses his bank account, which he shares with Lynn. He approaches the automatic teller and requests to withdraw $300.

Now suppose both Lynn and Steven approach a different automatic teller machine, this time at approximately the same moment, albeit one person slightly behind the other. The current balance of the account is $2500. Suppose the automatic teller system was not set up to function properly in a distributed environment. Then any of the following scenarios might result. These examples are presented in a pseudocode form in Detail Box 9.2.

Scenario 1

Lynn reached the automatic teller first. She retrieves a balance of $2500. From this balance, $200 is withdrawn, leaving a $2300 balance. Before this correct balance is propagated through the system, Steven reached the automatic teller. He retrieves an incorrect balance of $2500 that does not reflect Lynn's actions. From this balance, $300 is withdrawn, recording a $2200 balance. Observe that Lynn's action was recorded but retrieval disparity caused an incorrect manipulation of the shared data, as depicted in Figure 9.2.

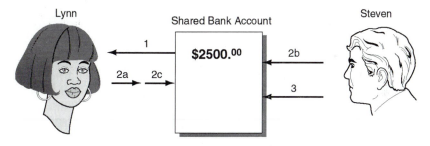

1. Lynn retrieves balance and withdraws $200.00
2a. Lynn's transaction results begin traveling to the bank account records
2b. Steven retrieves balance and withdraws $300.00 [Retrieval Disparity Occurred!]
2c. Lynn's results propagate to the bank records
3. Steven's results travel to the bank records

Figure 9.2 Retrieval Disparity.

DETAIL BOX 9.2
RETRIEVAL DISPARITY

Action 1
```
Get Balance;
Balance=Balance-200;
Return Balance;
```

Action 2
```
Get Balance;
Balance=Balance-300;
Return Balance;
```

Scenario 1
```
ACTION1: Get Balance;
```
                              // Balance=$2500
```
ACTION1: Balance=Balance-200;
ACTION1: Return Balance;
ACTION2: Get Balance;
```
                              // Balance=$2500 -- an incorrect value!
```
ACTION2: Balance=Balance-300;
ACTION2: Return Balance;
RESULT:  Balance=2200
```

Scenario 2

```
ACTION2: GET Balance;
```
                              // Balance=$2500
```
ACTION2: Balance=Balance-300;
ACTION2: Return Balance;
ACTION1: Get Balance;
```
                              // Balance=$2500   -- an   incorrect
value!
```
ACTION1: Balance=Balance-200;
ACTION1: Return Balance;
RESULT:  Balance=2300
```

Scenario 2

Steven reached the automatic teller first. He retrieves a balance of $2500. From this balance, $300 is withdrawn, leaving a $2200 balance. Before this correct balance is propagated through the system, Lynn reached the automatic teller. She retrieves an incorrect balance of $2500. From this balance, $200 is withdrawn, recording a $2300 balance. Observe that this time Steven's action was recorded but again retrieval disparity caused an incorrect manipulation of the shared data.

9.2 ACID PROPERTIES OF A TRANSACTION

The lost update and retrieval disparity problems are just two examples of problems that can occur when manipulating shared data in distributed systems. Another problem involves a server that crashes in the middle of data manipulation. In all scenarios, the identification of a set of actions as a transaction and the use of transaction management ensure proper data manipulation, even if a system crashes. Recall that a transaction is a set of related actions and transaction management is the term that describes appropriate handling of all transactions throughout a distributed system. Harder and Reuter, in [HaRe83], have suggested the use of the mnemonic **ACID** to remember the essential properties of a transaction. The properties are as follows.

♦ *Atomicity*: A transaction must ensure that either the entire transaction occurs or none of the transaction occurs. Even in the presence of failures, the transaction must be all or nothing.

♦ *Consistency*: A transaction must begin in a consistent state and leave the system in a consistent state. The various types of consistency are discussed in Section 9.3.

♦ *Isolation*: In addition to requiring transactions to be performed in an all or nothing manner, other participants are not allowed access to intermediate results. All intermediate operations are performed in isolation. Outside participants are only allowed access once the consistent state has been reached.

♦ *Durability*: Once a server has committed to a transaction, it completes the transaction even if it suffers a system failure. Furthermore, these results will be permanent results.

Now let's examine why a proper transaction would not suffer from the lost update problem. First, transactions must be atomic. Therefore, multiple participants in a distributed system would not be able to retrieve the same balance concurrently for the purpose of changing said balance. According to the consistency property, neither of the aforementioned scenarios could result since both results left the system in an incorrect and inconsistent state. Third, according to the isolation property, one action could not see the results or interfere with the other action. In all actuality, one action would be forced to wait until the other action has completed. According to the durability principle, actions must persist. In contrast, if in the lost update example Lynn completed first, her actions were not permanent and did not persist.

We now examine if these ACID properties could prevent the retrieval disparity problem that the Steven and Lynn example presented earlier in this chapter. First, if the actions were atomic, then the reading of the balance, the changing of the balance, and the writing back of the balance would occur as one single action. Therefore, the second action couldn't hop in between this single action. This is further strengthened by the isolation requirement; however, the most important property may be the consistency property. By not ensuring that the actions were atomic, the system was left in an inconsistent state. Specifically, if it were in a consistent state and abided by the durability property, retrieval disparity could not have occurred. Therefore, if proper transactions are utilized, only the following two scenarios could result. The pseudocode presentations are given in Detail Box 9.3.

Transaction 1

Lynn has a cash card that automatically accesses her shared bank account. She requests to withdraw $200.

Transaction 2

Steven also has a cash card that automatically accesses his bank account, which he shares with Lynn. He requests to withdraw $300.

Scenario 1

Lynn's transaction is handled first, and the resulting balance of $2300 is permanently recorded. Steven's transaction is then handled and a new balance of $2000 is permanently recorded, as depicted in Figure 9.3.

Scenario 2

Steven's transaction is handled first and the resulting balance of $2200 is permanently recorded. Lynn's transaction is now handled and a new balance of $2000 is permanently recorded.

In either scenario, the use of transactions that function according to the ACID properties ensured proper results.

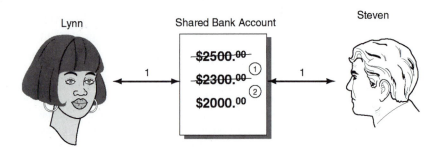

1. Lynn's atomic transaction occurs. The $2500 balance is retrieved, $200 is withdrawn, and the new $2300 balance is permanently is recorded.
2. Steven's atomic transaction occurs. The $2300 balance is retrieved, $300 is withdrawn, and the new $2000 balance is permanently recorded.

Figure 9.3   Proper Transaction Management.

DETAIL BOX 9.3
TRANSACTIONS

Transaction 1
```
Get Balance;
Balance=Balance-200;
Return Balance;
```

Transaction 2
```
Get Balance;
Balance=Balance-300;
Return Balance;
```

Scenario 1
```
Begin TRANSACTION1
TRANSACTION1: Get Balance;
```
                              // Balance=$2500
```
TRANSACTION1: Balance=Balance-200;
TRANSACTION1: Return Balance;
```
                              // Balance=$2300
```
End TRANSACTION1

Begin TRANSACTION2
TRANSACTION2: Get Balance;
```
                              // Balance=$2300
```
TRANSACTION2: Balance=Balance-300;
TRANSACTION2: Return Balance;
End TRANSACTION2

RESULT: Balance=2000
```

Scenario 2
```
Begin TRANSACTION2
TRANSACTION2: GET Balance;
```
                              // Balance=$2500
```
TRANSACTION2: Balance=Balance-300;
TRANSACTION2: Return Balance;
```
                              // Balance=$2200
```
End TRANSACTION2

Begin TRANSACTION1
TRANSACTION1: Get Balance;
```
                              // Balance=$2200
```
TRANSACTION1: Balance=Balance-200;
TRANSACTION1: Return Balance;
End TRANSACTION1

RESULT: Balance=2000
```

9.3 CONSISTENCY MODELS

As we have learned, consistency is one of the desired properties of a transaction. We have also seen this term when discussing various forms of manipulation of shared data in Chapter 4. In this section, we examine the various types of consistency models. Each consistency model has its own level of complexity. The more complex models tend to affect system performance negatively. Once a **consistency model** is chosen, all participants in the distributed system, including the programs, the DSM, and the directory service, must adhere to the model. We address the models beginning with the strictest and most complex model and concluding with models utilizing looser constraints.

9.3.1 Strict Consistency Model

The **strict consistency model** requires the strongest form of memory coherence to be guaranteed by the transaction management system. Specifically, the value returned by a read operation must always be the latest and most up-to-date value. That is, it must return the value of the latest write operation regardless of who conducted the write operation and where they are located within the distributed system. To identify the latest value of a particular set of data, there must be a concept of global time. Therefore, to implement the strict consistency model you must employ one of the global time methods discussed in Chapter 10.

Even with the methods for creating a global time, it is not generally considered wise to require or promise strict consistency in a distributed system. In particular, even if the system believes it found the most up-to-date value, a new value may be written for that data a nanosecond before this value is returned to the client. Perhaps this value is being written as the now 'out-of-date' value begins to be transmitted over the network to the destination. Therefore, the value returned to the destination is no longer the most recent value and strict consistency was not provided. Thus, a consistency model that would be easy to take for granted in a centralized environment is practically unachievable in a distributed environment.

9.3.2 Sequential Consistency Model

A slightly weaker but more realistic consistency model is the **sequential consistency model**, which was first proposed by Lamport [Lam79]. The sequential consistency model requires that all participants and their processes in the distributed system share a common view regarding the order of the memory access operations on shared memory. It does not guarantee that a value received is the latest and most up-to-date copy. Therefore, it is possible to receive different outputs from two different executions of the same exact program.

To understand sequential consistency, let us reexamine the example presented in Section 9.2. Both scenarios are legal scenarios in sequential consistency; however, it would not be permissible for some participants to see Scenario 1 and others to see Scenario

2. If one participant sees that Lynn's transaction happened first, then all participants must share that view under the sequential consistency model.

The primary difference between sequential consistency and strict consistency is the reliance on a global time. Sequential consistency does not rely on a global time, but rather a global ordering of events. This method, though intuitive for programming applications, does suffer from an important performance issue. In particular, read and write performances are inversely related. Any steps to improve read performance degrade write performance, and any steps to improve write performance degrade read performance [LiSa88]. Of course, if it is used in an application that predominantly uses only read operations, this relationship could be a beneficial feature.

9.3.3 Casual Consistency Model

The **casual consistency model** was first proposed by Hutto and Ahamad [HuAh90]. This model further relaxes the requirements of sequential consistency. Specifically, not all events need to be seen by all members of the distributed system in the same order, only those that are **casually related**. If events are casually related, then they must be seen in the same and correct order. This leaves us to define casually related events. A casually related event affects the events to which it is casually related. Events are casually related if they change the same set of shared data.

For example, if you read the balance and then write a new balance, this read and write are casually related. Thus, this read and write must not only be seen in the same order by everyone, but the read must be seen first followed by the write. Utilizing the example in Section 9.2, Lynn's read and write are casually related to each other. Steven's read and write are casually related to each other. Lynn and Steven's transactions are casually related since whose transaction occurs second reflects the results of both transactions occurring together. If Susan maintains a (different) bank account at the same bank and performs a transaction on her account, her transaction is not at all related to those of Lynn and Steven, as depicted in Figure 9.4. Susan's transaction is not casually related to Steven's or Lynn's. Thus, casual consistency only places ordering constraints on related events. This consistency model generally employs some type of relationship graph. This relationship graph, sometimes referred to as a dependency graph, must record which process has seen which write operations, thereby recording casual relationships. Unrelated events are denoted by an absence of a casual relationship in the relationship graph and do not have restrictions under this consistency model. These unrelated events are viewed as concurrent operations. Concurrent operations may be seen as occurring in a different order at a different location.

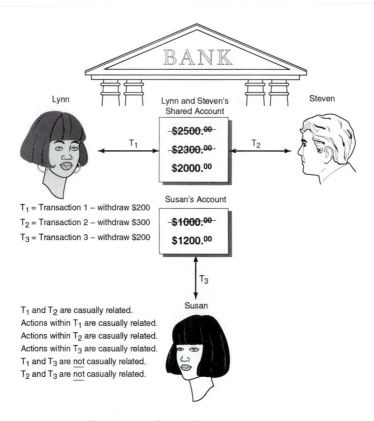

Figure 9.4   Casual Consistency Example.

9.3.4 PRAM Consistency Model

The **pipelined random access memory (PRAM) consistency model** was first proposed by Lipton and Sandberg [LiSa88]. This model is a weaker model than casual consistency. Specifically, only write operations performed by a single process are required to be viewed by other processes in the order that they were performed, as depicted in Figure 9.5. Each process can be thought of placing its operations in a first-in-first-out queue or pipeline. Observe that there is no mention of the order with regards to other participants. Each participant may view operations from multiple locations in any order; but the order for operations coming from a single

INCORRECT* PRAM CONSISTENCY

Process 1	
Local Actions	Global View
read foo	(P_1, W_1)
write foo (P_1, W_1)	(P_1, W_2)
write foo (P_1, W_2)	$(P_2, W_2)^*$
	$(P_2, W_1)^*$

Process 2	
Local Actions	Global View
read goo	$(P_1, W_2)^*$
write goo (P_2, W_1)	$(P_1, W_1)^*$
write goo (P_2, W_2)	(P_2, W_1)
	(P_2, W_2)

All Processes must see writes in same order

CORRECT PRAM CONSISTENCY

Process 1	
Local Actions	Global View
read foo	(P_1, W_1)
write foo (P_1, W_1)	(P_2, W_1)
write foo (P_1, W_2)	(P_1, W_2)
	(P_2, W_2)

Process 2	
Local Actions	Global View
read goo	(P_2, W_1)
write goo (P_2, W_1)	(P_2, W_2)
write goo (P_2, W_2)	(P_1, W_1)
	(P_1, W_2)

All Processes see writes in same order

Figure 9.5   PRAM Consistency Model Examples.

location must be preserved. That is, while each location views the transactions from a single site in the same order, how these transactions are ordered with regard to other transactions throughout the system may differ from location to location. In conclusion, each location is allowed to be viewed as operating concurrently.

9.3.5 Processor Consistency Model

The **processor consistency model** proposed by Goodman [Goo89] is very similar to PRAM consistency and is sometimes confused with PRAM consistency, although it actually has tighter restrictions. Its requirements are the same as PRAM consistency plus an additional requirement of memory coherence. Thus, not only must all operations for a given location be pipelined, but for any particular memory location, the entire system must agree on the order of all write operations at that location, as depicted in Figure 9.6. While Goodman did not specify the ordering of read access for the processor consistency model, Ghorechorloo et al. provided the following two conditions [GLLGGH90].

INCORRECT EXAMPLE

Process 1			Process 2	
Local Actions	**Global View**		**Local Actions**	**Global View**
read foo	(P_1, W_1)		read foo	(P_2, W_1)
write foo (P_1, W_1)	(P_2, W_1)		write foo (P_2, W_1)	(P_1, W_1)
write foo (P_1, W_2)	(P_1, W_2)		write foo (P_2, W_2)	(P_2, W_2)
	(P_2, W_2)			(P_1, W_2)

Since all write operations are to the same location,
all must view the write operations in the same order!

CORRECT EXAMPLE

Process 1			Process 2	
Local Actions	**Global View**		**Local Actions**	**Global View**
read foo	(P_2, W_1)		read foo	(P_2, W_1)
write foo (P_1, W_1)	(P_2, W_2)		write foo (P_2, W_1)	(P_2, W_2)
write foo (P_1, W_2)	(P_1, W_1)		write foo (P_2, W_2)	(P_1, W_1)
	(P_1, W_2)			(P_1, W_2)

Same global view for access
to same memory location.

Figure 9.6   Processor Consistency Example.

1. All previous read accesses must be performed before a read operation is allowed at any other location.

2. Before a write operation is allowed at a location, all previous read and write operations must be performed.

These conditions allow reads that follow a write operation to bypass the write. Ghorechorloo et al. warn that to prevent a deadlock, an implementation using the processor consistency model with these rules should guarantee that all writes are eventually performed.

9.3.6 Weak Consistency Model

The **weak consistency model** was proposed by Dubois et al. [DSB86, DSB88]. The definition of this model depends on the use of a new type of variable, a **synchronization variable** used for synchronizing memory. A synchronization variable is used to propagate all writes to other machines and to perform local updates with regard to changes to global data that occurred elsewhere in the distributed system, as depicted in Figure 9.7. Thus, the synchronization variables can be used to group memory references. Using these synchronization variables, we can now define the three requirements for weak consistency.

1. Access to synchronization variables must obey the sequential consistency model.
2. Access to a synchronization variable is not allowed until all previous write operations are completed everywhere throughout the distributed system.
3. Access to nonsynchronization variables is not allowed (not even read only) until all previous accesses to synchronization variables have been completed.

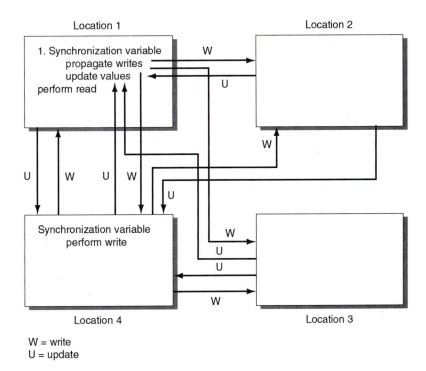

Figure 9.7   The Use of a Synchronization Variable in Weak Consistency.

Thus, Point 1 states that all processes in the distributed system share a common view regarding the order of the memory access operations to the synchronization variables. Recall that the sequential consistency model does not guarantee that a value received is the latest and most up-to-date copy. However, Point 2 requires all locations to complete all write operations that are in progress or that have been completed but not written. Therefore, by performing a synchronization prior to a read, a program can ensure that it is receiving the most up-to-date copy from memory. If a synchronization is performed after modifying shared data, a programmer can communicate the new value throughout the system. Since Point 3 prevents access to nonsynchronization variables when utilizing a synchronization variable, one may also ensure the most up-to-date value by performing a synchronization prior to accessing any shared data.

This model is able to achieve better performance than the other models. In particular, it recognizes that many applications can take advantage of the following characteristics.

- Many (frequently most) participants in the distributed system do not need to see every write operation.

- Many (frequently most) participants in the distributed system do not need to see intermediate write operations. In fact, if these intermediate results occur due to an operation in the middle of a critical region, they should not be seen at all.

In conclusion, weak consistency utilizes sequentially consistent synchronization variables to group memory references. Due to the overhead of performing synchronizations, best performance is achieved when access to shared data is bursty with each burst performing many memory operations versus a program with regular, singularly isolated memory operations. If a program contains singularly isolated memory operations, it is not able to take advantage of the memory reference grouping provided by weak consistency. While weak consistency is able to increase performance, it does place some burden on the developers, designers, and programmers for applications utilizing this model, where performing local and global synchronizations involves updating *all* shared variables. The system is not able to distinguish a synchronization performed by accessing a synchronization variable for the purpose of reading data versus distributing a recent write value throughout the system. In both circumstances, weak consistency will distribute all writes and update all local copies of data.

9.3.7 Release Consistency Model

The **release consistency model** was proposed by Gharachorloo et al. [GLLGGH90] and is similar to weak consistency but provides the ability to distinguish between synchronization actions prior to entering critical regions and synchronization actions upon completion of a critical region. In particular, the release consistency model provides **acquire access** and **release access**. Acquire access is employed to notify the system that a process is about to enter a critical region. In this circumstance, all changes made by other participants should be propagated to and updated by the local processor. Release access is employed to notify the system that the process is exiting a critical region and that the local changes to shared memory should be propagated to the

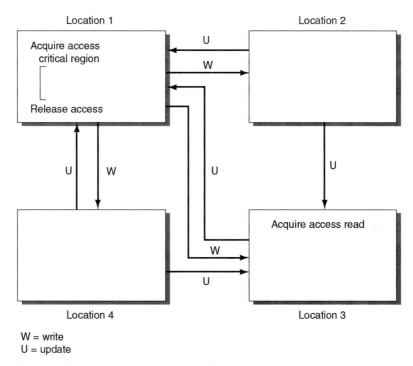

Location 1

Acquire access
critical region

Release access

Location 2

U

W

U   W

U

U

Location 4

W

U

Acquire access read

Location 3

W = write
U = update

Figure 9.8 The Use of Acquire and Release Access in Release Consistency.

other participants. This enables release consistency to increase the performance of weak consistency by only performing the appropriate actions for each particular type of synchronization, as depicted in Figure 9.8.

If critical regions are not utilized, release consistency provides for **barriers**. A barrier provides synchronization by distinguishing different phases of execution. A barrier utilized in phase *n* prevents any process from entering phase *n+1* until all processes have completed phase *n*. The utilization of acquire and release access with barriers parallels the critical region implementation if you consider an entire phase a critical region. Specifically, when a process begins a new phase, it performs an acquire access. When it reaches a barrier, a process performs a release access. Generally, a centralized server is employed to ensure that all related processes have completed a given phase. Once the server has determined that a phase is complete, it notifies the processes that they may proceed to the next phase.

Release consistency enables one to designate what variables should be kept consistent. In particular, it does not require all variables to be kept consistent, only those designated as **protected**. These variables or portions of memory that are designated as protected must obey the following rules to be considered in compliance with the release consistency model.

1. All previous acquires by a process must have successfully completed before that process may access a shared variable.
2. All reads and writes must complete prior to performing a release access.
3. All acquire and release accesses must comply with the processor consistency model.

Release consistency does allow unrelated acquires, releases, and barriers to function independently. A DSM system employing release consistency is able to obtain the same results as a DSM system employing the sequential consistency model. Gharachorloo et al. [GLLGGH90] showed that these results hold if the three rules associated with the release consistency model are followed and the acquire and release access synchronization tools are properly employed.

9.3.8 Lazy Release Consistency

The **lazy release consistency** model was purposed in 1992 by Keleher et al. [KCZ92]. While the basic release consistency model does attempt to increase performance as compared to weak consistency, one further step may be taken. Recall that in the release consistency model, a release access is employed to notify the system that the process is exiting a critical region and that the local changes to shared memory should be propagated to the other participants. In the lazy release consistency model, these changes are not immediately propagated; they are only transmitted over the network on demand. Specifically, changes to shared data are only communicated when an acquire access is performed by the other location. All other aspects of release consistency remain unchanged. This one change allows for an improvement in performance, especially in terms of network traffic. If a location does not access a shared variable, it never needs to be notified of changes, as depicted in Figure 9.9 and compared with Figure 9.8.

9.3.9 Entry Consistency Model

The **entry release consistency** model was purposed by Bershad et al. [BeZe91, BZS93]. This model is similar to the basic release consistency model. In addition to the utilization of acquire and release access, the entry consistency model requires each variable to be associated with some type of synchronization variable, such as a lock or a barrier. The necessity to associate variables with a synchronization variable places an additional burden on the programmer but yields greater performance. If this method is employed correctly (that is, utilizing appropriate synchronization techniques) then access to shared memory will appear to be sequentially consistent.

9.4 TWO-PHASE COMMIT PROTOCOL

Most transactions rely on the **two-phase commit protocol** first proposed by Gray [Gra78]. The purpose is to ensure that all transactions appear to occur atomically throughout the distributed system. The goal is for data to be held in a permanent state. This protocol involves the following two phases.

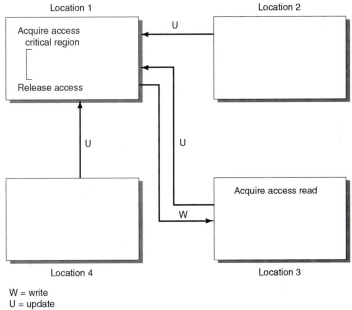

W = write
U = update

Figure 9.9 Lazy Release Consistency.

1. Prepare to commit phase
2. Commit phase

In general terms, the first phase is a negotiation and set-up phase for the completion of a transaction while the second phase is the contracted execution of the transaction. We now examine each of these phases, which are depicted in Figure 9.10.

9.4.1 Prepare to Commit Phase

The two-phase commit protocol involves a coordinator for each transaction, generally the originating location. The coordinator is responsible for enlisting and receiving the commitment of the servers necessary to perform the transaction. The following is the list of steps to be performed.

♦ Identify what resources are necessary and what locations should be contacted.

♦ Contact the desired locations and ask them to commit to completing the action.

♦ Record the answers from each of the servers contacted.

♦ If a server does not respond or responds negatively, attempt to enlist the commitment of another server.

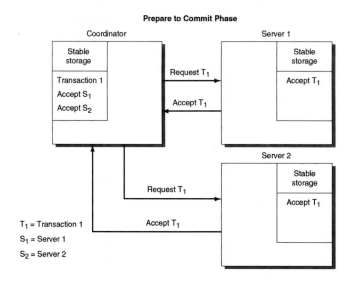

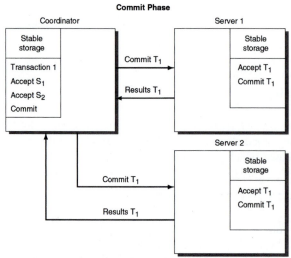

Figure 9.10   Two-Phase Commit Protocol.

When a server receives a request, it must decide if it is able to complete the request. Once a server commits to a transaction, it must complete the transaction no matter what may happen. A commit response to the transaction request is like a binding contract. However, it is important to note that a server receiving a request and accepts by responding with a commit response does not mean that the transaction will occur. In particular, until the commit phase is entered, the transaction is only a proposed transaction. A location may decide to begin on the transaction when it receives the request; however, it must be prepared to roll back should the transaction be canceled prior to reaching the commit phase. A roll back involves returning all data to the original state, prior to executing any portion of the transaction. Thus, the original state must be recorded prior to completing any portion of a transaction. The final result upon the data is that it appears that no part of the transaction was ever attempted and the data are in their safe original, permanent state.

The question that remains regards entering the commit phase. To enter the commit phase, the transaction coordinator must receive a commit message for all aspects of the transaction. At this point and only at this point, the transaction coordinator sends out a commit message to each committed location and the transaction proceeds to the second phase, the commit phase. If the transaction coordinator is not able to receive a commitment on all aspects of the transaction (possibly due to the lack of a response), it cannot enter the second phase. The transaction coordinator must notify the servers and the servers must roll back any actions they may have taken to complete their portion of the transaction. Thus, the system's state is not and cannot be affected by the failed attempt to complete a transaction. Observe that only the coordinator may call off the transaction. Once a server returns a commit message, it cannot change or alter its decision.

9.4.2 Commit Phase

Once the commit message is received, the servers may return their results and consider the changes permanent. When all the servers complete their actions, the transaction is completed. Sounds simple; but what if one of the committed servers crashes?

For the two-phase commit protocol to function properly, it must be able to withstand a system failure. To accomplish this, each server receiving a request to commit records this request on nonvolatile storage. This notation must be made prior to returning the message to the coordinator to eliminate chaos should the server crash immediately after sending the commit message and prior to recording its intent. In addition, the commit message from the transaction coordinator as well as the status of the transaction by the coordinator is also recorded on nonvolatile storage. Thus, all participants, even the coordinator, have a stable copy of their responsibility regarding the status of the transaction. When any participant (including the coordinator) recovers from a crash, it checks these nonvolatile and thereby crash-resistant records. If there is a commit to transaction notation, it immediately proceeds to complete its portion of the transaction. If the participant is not the coordinator and has a notation that it would commit but not confirmation back from the coordinator, it must contact the coordinator to determine if the commit phase has been entered.

9.5 NESTED TRANSACTIONS

A transaction may be a simple transaction or a **compound transaction**. A compound transaction contains a set of **nested transactions** while a simple transaction does not. Each of the nested transactions within a compound transaction may also be a compound transaction consisting of a set of nested transactions. Compound transactions may be pictorially represented as a tree, the original transaction being the parent node and the first layer of nested transactions representing the next layer in the tree. The transactions contained in a parent are sometimes referred to as subtransactions. Designing and organizing transactions with nested sub-transactions has several benefits.

♦ Increase in concurrency

♦ Increase in performance

♦ Increase in fault tolerance

With the utilization of concurrency control, subtransactions at the same level may execute simultaneously. This simultaneous execution increases the ability for concurrent execution and, therefore, an increase in performance. Each subtransaction is individually committed or aborted. All sub-transactions must be committed before the parent transaction may enter the commit phase. If a subtransaction aborts, the parent has several options to accomplish the subtransaction, including the enlistment of a different client. The overall hierarchical design is conducive to easy transaction management, with each subtransaction representing a subgoal and checkpoint for the parent. Furthermore, each subtransaction maintains and adheres to all of the ACID properties. Therefore, the results of a sub-transaction are only visible to the parent upon completion; each sub-transaction is viewed as an atomic operation. Finally, if the parent transaction determines that it cannot enter the commit phase, then this transaction and all related nested transactions must perform a roll-back. Detail Boxes 9.4 and 9.5 present the algorithms for the prepare to commit and the commit phase, respectively, for nested transactions.

DETAIL BOX 9.4
PREPARE TO COMMIT PROTOCOL FOR NESTED TRANSACTIONS

```
        Commit flag=1
                                    // Initiate commit flag to equal 1 for true.
        flag PREPARE-TO-COMMIT {transaction a)
                                    // Function returns flag value indicating
                                    // status of commit and takes as input
                                    // a transaction. The transaction structure is
                                    // responsible for maintaining information
                                    // on sub-transactions.
        {
        IF childless(transaction a)
                                    // This transaction contains no nested
                                    // transactions and is not a compound
                                    // transaction.
        THEN
                flag=flag & Request commitment(transaction a)
                                    // By 'anding' the return value of the request
                                    // to commit and the current value, the
value
                                    // will only remain 1 if all agree to commit.
                                    // Some implementations may wish to add
                                    // complexity here to identify exactly
                                    // who cannot commit in order to allow
                                    // further attempts.
        ELSE
                                    // This transactions contains subtransac-
tions.
                                    // Prepare to commit is not for compound
                                    // transactions so we must recurse.
                {
                FORALL children(transaction a)DO
                                    // We will recurse on each child or
                                    // sub-transaction until we reach our base
case,
                                    // a simple transaction.
                PREPARE-TO-COMMIT(transaction a(current child));
                                    // Recursive function call for all subtrans-
actions.
                }
        }
```

DETAIL BOX 9.5
COMMIT PHASE PROTOCOL FOR NESTED TRANSACTIONS

```
COMMIT-PHASE
IF (flag=1)
                          // Prepare to commit phase was successful so we
                          // may enter the commit phase.
THEN    IF childless(transaction a)
                          // Take advantages of the nested structure and
                          // recurse until a childless transaction.
        THEN    {
                record in stable storage
                        (commit, transaction a)
                          // Must record in a nonvolatile location that
                          // the transaction is officially in the commit phase
                          // and messages are being sent to clients.
                notify commitment(transaction a);
                          // Notify client that the commit phase has begun.
                }
        ELSE
                          // The current transaction is a compound transaction.
        {
        FORALL children(transaction a)DO
                          // Perform recursion until the base case, a simple
                          // transaction, is obtained.
        COMMIT PHASE(transaction a(current child));
        }
    }
                          // end if entered. Prepare to commit phase. May add
an
                          // else condition regarding actions to be taken if
                          // the commit phase cannot be entered or to attempt
                          // to rectify barriers to entering the commit phase.
```

9.6 IMPLEMENTATION ISSUES FOR TRANSACTIONS

While transaction systems may seem simple enough to implement, this section presents some difficulties and implementation issues that might occur when implementing transaction systems.

To ensure proper transactions, these issues must be avoided and the ACID properties must be observed.

9.6.1 Premature Reads and Writes

In Section 9.1, we looked at two problems that can occur without transactions. Unfortunately, they may also occur if one utilizes improperly implemented transactions. Other related problems that can occur include premature reads and premature writes. A premature read occurs when one transaction performs a read operation on a piece of data that is being manipulated by another transaction that is later aborted. Premature writes can occur if a transaction performs a write operation on a piece of data that is being manipulated by another transaction. Both problems involving the interaction of separate transactions can be prevented if the transaction management service is implemented utilizing delayed execution. Delayed execution prevents reads and writes to data that are involved in a transaction until the first transaction either has entered the commit phase or has been aborted. The minor delay encountered may hinder performance slightly, but it ensures that the isolation property of the transactions is maintained and enforced.

9.6.2 The Domino Effect of Aborts

If a transaction is unable to enter the commit phase, it will be necessary to abort the transaction. The abortion of this transaction may suffer from the **domino effect** if other transactions have seen the results related to the aborted transaction. The domino effect is particularly likely if the transaction management system suffers from premature writes. Any transaction that has acted based upon data from a premature write originating from a now aborted transaction must also abort. Likewise, any transaction that has utilized data from the second-generation aborted transaction must also abort. The effect of such aborts can be quite significant.

9.6.3 Ensuring Recoverability

The following two steps can greatly increase the recoverability of a transaction management system. Our primary purpose is to ensure that the ACID properties are upheld.

- ♦ Delay a commit if there is another outstanding request to commit involving the same data. This also assists in preventing the domino affect of aborts.
- ♦ Utilize local temporary copies of the data until the commit phase is officially entered. The temporary copies may be maintained locally in volatile storage. If the commit phase is never entered, delete the temporary copies. If the commit phase is entered, copy the temporary copies to permanent, nonvolatile storage. This step may also assist in minimizing or eliminating premature read and write operations since the temporary copies are maintained locally.

9.7 SUMMARY

In this chapter, we studied a very important topic in a distributed operating system, transaction management. Transaction management is responsible for ensuring proper data manipulation within the DSM and the directory service. For transaction management to be successful, it must be resilient and able to survive despite system failures; that is, it must be fault tolerant. In the discussion of the two-phase commit protocol, we have seen that it is possible to implement a fault-tolerant transaction management system.

Consistency Model	Requirements
Strict Consistency	Must always read latest and most up-to-date value. Relies on global time.
Sequential Consistency	All share common global view. Relies on global ordering.
Casual Consistency	Casually related events must be viewed as occurring in same order.
PRAM Consistency	All write operations performed by a single process must be viewed as occurring in the same order on all systems.
Processor Consistency	PRAM consistency plus memory consistency. Specifically, all operations performed on a given memory location must have an agreed-upon order throughout the system.
Weak Consistency	Uses synchronization variable that is used to perform all writes and conduct all updates. Access to the synchronization variable must follow sequential consistency. All reads and writes must complete prior to performing a release access. Finally, all acquire and release accesses must comply with the processor consistency model. Synchronization variables for unrelated data may act independently and concurrently.
Release Consistency Model	Same as weak consistency but divides synchronization actions into acquire access and release access. A release is access is performed when entering a critical region and brings in all updates. A release access occurs at the end of a critical region and distributes all modifications. This model also supports a concept known as barriers.
Lazy Release Consistency Model	Same as release consistency except changes only propagate on demand.
Entry Consistency Model	Same as release consistency except all synchronization variables are associated synchronization variables such as lock.

Table 9.1 Summary of Consistency Models and Their Requirements

Any operating system or transaction management service within an operating system that does not ensure consistent data would be greatly failing in its duties. In this chapter, we studied the exact meaning of data consistency and surveyed the most popular models. Table 9.1 presents a summary of the models and their relative requirements. Data consistency is a topic that is probably more complex then most would think at the onset. Developer is not familiar with a distributed system may mistakenly take data consistency for granted. Just as it is important for a centralized programmer to understand the types of parameter-passing methods being employed by a language, it is imperative that any developer in a distributed environment have a thorough and complete grasp of the consistency model being employed. Understanding this model will help ensure proper development, execution, and interpretation of the environment. While there are several models varying in degree of strictness, many researchers have found that the looser consistency models are not only adequate but also efficient, an important consideration when one already needs to consider network delays. Discovering sufficient and efficient consistency models and incorporating these models into the transaction management service will continue to be an active research area for the near future.

9.7 REFERENCES FOR FURTHER STUDY

The general references presented in Chapter 1 can provide some general information on transaction management. The Tuxedo On-Line Transaction Processing system is described in [Prim95]. In addition, the following books can provide some additional helpful information: [GrRe93, Jal94, PTM98, and RaCh96]. Some appropriate traditional research papers concerning information in this chapter include [AdHi90, BeZe91, BZS93, DSB86, DSB88, GGH91, Goo89, GLLGGH90, Gra78, HaRe83, HuAh90, ISL96, KCZ92, Lam79, Lam81, LiHu89, LiSa88, ShSn88, Wei91, and Wei93].

The following is a starting point for information on Transarc Corporation and its commercial transaction management product Encina™: www.transarc.com. You may also find information by searching the general Web sites presented in Chapter 1.

EXERCISES

9.1   Describe three everyday applications that can utilize transaction management. For each application, discuss the consequences if it were to suffer from the lost update problem as well as the retrieval disparity problem.

9.2   For each of the ACID properties of a transaction, describe a scenario that could result in an improper transaction if that property was not observed.

9.3   What are some of the dangers and potential problems that can occur if the isolation property of a transaction is not observed?

9.4   Name four major areas that are impacted by a distributed operating system's choice for a consistency model. For each area, describe how the consistency model choice affects it.

9.5   Describe an example for each of the following.

    a.   A set of actions that follow sequential consistency but not casual consistency
    b.   A set of actions that follow casual consistency but not PRAM consistency
    c.   A set of actions that follow processor consistency but not PRAM consistency

9.6   Describe an advantage and disadvantage of each of the following consistency models.

    a.   Weak consistency
    b.   Release consistency
    c.   Lazy release consistency
    d.   Entry consistency

9.7   In what manner can a transaction management service contribute to the fault tolerance of the entire distributed operating system? Provide examples.

9.8   In what circumstances could a client, who has accepted a request for a transaction, be forced to perform a roll back? Describe a possible approach that a file service may utilize to ensure its ability to perform a roll back.

9.9   In the two-phase commit protocol, why would it be unacceptable for a client to change its mind with regard to accepting a transaction request?

9.10   Describe three advantages and three complications that arise from allowing a transaction to consist of nested transactions.

Distributed Synchronization

Synchronization requires either global time or global ordering. The concept of time in a centralized system is actually quite simple: All processes reside on the same system utilizing the same clock. In contrast, time in a distributed system is a lot like synchronizing everyone's watch in the classroom on the first day of class. How synchronized will they be during the final exam? In this chapter, we explore issues involved in the concept of global time and an alternative approach, global ordering. Section 10.1 provides a general introduction to the concept of global time. Section 10.2 discusses issues and algorithms relevant to physical time. Section 10.3 describes the Internet standard for physical time, the Network Time Protocol (NTP). Section 10.4 discusses issues and algorithms relevant to logical time and logical ordering.

10.1 INTRODUCTION TO GLOBAL TIME

A distributed system involves many participating locations and individual computer systems. Each location and each system maintains its own local clock. Even if it is possible to synchronize all the clocks at a moment in time, system clocks are subjected to **drifting**, not unlike the watches around our wrists. Drifting is the gradual misalignment of once synchronized clocks caused by the slight inaccuracies of the time-keeping mechanisms.

Throughout our study of advanced systems, we have seen many protocols requiring a sense of global time or, alternatively, global ordering. **Global time** is utilized to provide time-stamps for processes and data. If one participant's clock is running slow (for example the clock says it is 9:15 when it is really 9:25), all processes at that location would have an unfair benefit throughout the system. In particular, every process or action on the system resulting from the inaccurate clock would appear older than it really is in actuality.

One important concept to identify when discussing synchronization involves relativity. Computer systems do not really care what time it is in the same manner as people care. In contrast, systems are only concerned with time for the sake of determining the relative ordering of events. Thus, when discussing time, it is important to realize that there are two fundamentally different types of clocks. Clocks that are concerned with "people" time are referred to as **physical clocks**. Clocks that are only concerned with relative time and maintaining logical consistency are referred to as **logical clocks**. We now examine the issues involved with each type of clock.

10.2 PHYSICAL CLOCKS

Physical clocks are utilized to convey a sense of "people" time throughout the distributed system; they are the computer system's wristwatch. The "wristwatch" service is a time service and may be implemented in a centralized manner or a distributed manner. It is responsible for providing a sense of global synchronized time to be utilized by all processes and services throughout the system. There are two aspects to be considered when implementing a physical time service. The first aspect involves obtaining an accurate value for physical time and is discussed in Section 10.2.1. The second aspect involves synchronizing the concept of physical time throughout the distributed system and is discussed in Section 10.2.2. A physical time service may be implemented utilizing centralized algorithms, as described in Section 10.2.3, or distributed algorithms, as described in Section 10.2.4. Detail Box 10.1 describes how typical computer clocks on each individual system are implemented.

10.2.1 Obtaining an Accurate Physical Time

To obtain an accurate value for physical time, a physical time server is required to access the current time from a universal time coordinator (UTC). The UTC is an international standard for the current time employed as a basis for all clocks today. Two sources for UTC include the WWV[1] shortwave radio station in Ft. Collins, Colorado and the Geostationary Operational Environmental Satellites (GEOS). Before the UTC time can be synchronized, a time service must first adjust the value to accommodate the delays incurred in communicating the time. Once the time is reported from a UTC server, it is immediately outdated as time passes while communicating the time to the client, including the time necessary to travel, as depicted in Figure 10.1. This necessary correction is not

---
[1] WWV is the stations call letters and is not an acronym

constant as network conditions or atmospheric conditions can vary, thereby varying the amount of the exact delay and complicating the process to obtain a truly accurate time. It is possible to equip computers with a **time provider**, a commercial device that is capable of directly receiving information from a UTC server and making appropriate adjustments due to communication delays. Systems are also starting to use UTC's Russian's "cousin", known as the global system for mobile communications (GSM). Like most things in life, the quality and therefore the accuracy of the time provider vary according to the price of the time provider. Generally, time providers cost thousands of dollars for the "cheaper" models and tens of thousands for the most accurate models.

10.2.2 Synchronizing Physical Time

The second aspect of a physical time service involves the synchronization of time throughout the distributed system. Before examining how the clocks in the distributed system may become synchronized and maintain synchronization, it is important first to define what is meant by synchronization. Previously, we have learned that clocks inherently suffer from drifting. This is inevitable and unavoidable; therefore, assuming all clocks are always precisely synchronized throughout the distributed system is unrealistic. Thus, we must allow and define an acceptable range for clock drift. The difference in time between two clocks due to drifting is defined as **clock skew**. A distributed system physical clock service defines a value for the maximum clock skew allowed throughout the system. As long as any and every two clocks differ by a value less than the maximum skew value, the time service is considered to be maintaining synchronization.

The question then arises of how to identify if all clocks differ by less than this maximum skew value. To analyze the difference between any two individual clock values within the distributed system, each participant must be able to read another participant's clock value. Consider that location A is reading location's B clock. To obtain the value, the following steps occur.

1. The information necessary to read the value must be communicated across the network to location B.
2. B's clock value must be read.
3. B's clock value is communicated back to location A.
4. B's clock value is adjusted to reflect the time necessary to travel across the network.
5. B's clock value is compared to A's clock value.

Step 4 is difficult to implement accurately. The amount of time to transmit any message over a network continually varies according to system and network loads as well as the particular path the message traveled along the network. In addition, the message may be transmitted multiple times if a network error occurs, thereby increasing the delay by a factor of the number of attempts.

DETAIL BOX 10.1   IMPLEMENTATION OF COMPUTER CLOCKS

The following are six relevant components to a computer clock.

1.   A quartz crystal
2.   A counter register
3.   A constant register
4.   A fixed starting date
5.   A fixed starting time
6.   Tick counter

We first examine the use of the first three components. The quartz crystal, much like the crystal in a quartz watch, oscillates at a predefined constant frequency. These oscillations are recorded in the counter register. As the name implies, the constant register stores a constant value that is dependent on and determined by the frequency of the oscillations of the quartz crystal. With each oscillation of the quartz crystal, the counter register is decremented by a value of 1. When the counter register reaches the value of 0, an interrupt is generated and the value returns to its initial value. The initial value chosen for the counter register is based upon the quartz oscillations so that each interrupt is as close to $1/60_{th}$ of a second as possible. Therefore, each interrupt generated by the counter register is equivalent to a clock tick.

The last three components are utilized to calculate the actual "'people" time. Each system clock's functionality is determined by the fixed starting date and time. In a UNIX system, the fixed starting date is January 1, 1970 and the fixed starting time is 0000. If a system does not have any form of battery backup for onboard memory, whenever the system is rebooted the system administrator must enter the current time and date. At this time, the system calculates the number of ticks that have occurred since the fixed starting date and time and places this value in the tick counter. For each interrupt generated by the counter register, the tick counter is incremented by a value of 1. Based on the tick counter as well as the fixed starting date and time, the system is able to calculate the actual 'people' time. Realizing that all quartz are not exactly the same and the initial value chosen may not be as precise as one might like, computer clocks are periodically required to be resynchronized to maintain maximum accuracy. In particular, computer clocks based on an oscillating quartz may suffer from a drift of more than 1 second in less than a two-week period of time.

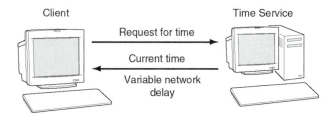

Figure 10.1 Network Delays when Communicating Time.

10.2.3 Centralized Physical Time Services

A centralized physical time service in a distributed operating system may be designed to function in one of two manners: It may be broadcast based or it may be request driven. As with all centralized approaches we have studied, a centralized time server is a critical point of failure within the distributed system. In addition, traffic around the server will increase. Scalability is also hindered when utilizing a centralized approach; however, for smaller scale distributed systems a centralized solution can be quite successful. We now examine the two approaches and their respective issues.

Broadcast Based

In broadcast-based implementations for a centralized approach to a physical time service, the time service periodically broadcasts the current time to members of the distributed system. There are two approaches that may be taken upon receiving this broadcast time. In the first approach, the participants evaluate their clock in comparison to the broadcast time received while accommodating the delay due to network travel time. Participants then adjust their local clocks accordingly, but they may not set their clocks to an earlier time. Specifically, the following two scenarios may result.

- ♦ If a given participant's clock is ahead of the time server's clock, the participant slows down its clock so that it will continually move closer to the accurate time. A clock cannot be turned back since events have already been generated reflecting the current time.
- ♦ If a participant's clock is behind the time server's clock, the participant moves its clock forward, as depicted in Figure 10.2. Alternatives do include gradually speeding up the clock.

In this approach, fault tolerance is not built into the algorithm. If a time server's message experienced longer than normal network delay or was retransmitted several times, the participant would not be aware. In contrast, the participant would assume that the message's transmission was a standard one-time transmission experiencing normal network delays and adjust its clock accordingly.

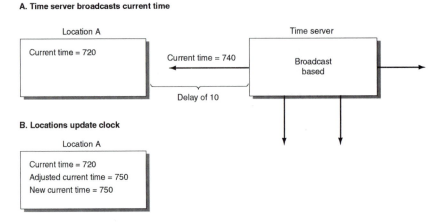

Figure 10.2   Forward Adjustment of a Clock.

The second approach for a broadcast based implementation of a centralized physical time service is known as the Berkeley algorithm. The Berkeley algorithm was proposed by Gusella and Zatti [GuZa89]. It is referred to as the Berkeley Algorithm because it was utilized for the synchronization of clocks on systems running Berkeley UNIX 4.3. It does not require the time server to have access to the UTC source. Much like the first approach, the centralized time server broadcasts the current time periodically. The algorithm then involves the following steps, as depicted in Figure 10.3.

1. Each participant sends its current clock value to the centralized time server upon receiving the broadcast time.

2. The time server adjusts the time messages received from system participants according to an individually predefined constant that reflects the average network delay for each participant.

3. Any adjusted times that differ from the other times by more than a predefined constant are disregarded. The disregarded times are considered to be the result of some type of fault within the system and therefore deemed inaccurate.

4. The remaining times along with the value of the clock for the time server are averaged. This average time is now considered to be the current time.

5. The time server calculates the amount of adjustment required of each individual participant. This required adjustment value is sent to each participant.

6. Each participant adjusts its clock. Again, fast clocks cannot be turned back in time; therefore, such locations are required to slow down their clocks.

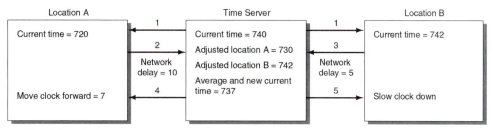

1. Current time = 740
2. My current time is 720
3. My current time is 742
4. Adjust forward 7
5. Adjust slowdown to accommodate 5

Figure 10.3 The Berkeley Algorithm for Physical Clock Synchronization.

Request Driven

The request driven approach was first proposed by Cristian [Cri89]. In a request-driven implementation for a centralized physical time service, each participant sends a request to the time service for the current time. Specifically, the algorithm then involves the following steps, as depicted in Figure 10.4.

1. A participant sends a request for the current time to the time service.
2. The time service then returns its value of the current time.
3. The participant then calculates the difference between the participant's own clock and the time returned from the time service. This difference is the adjustment time. Observe that this implementation will experience network delays as well as an interrupt delay. This interrupt delay is encountered at the time service and incorporates two values. The first value reflects the average time that is required for the time service to generate an interrupt, indicating that a message has arrived. The second value is the required time for the server to respond to the request.
4. If this adjustment time is larger than a predefined threshold value, it is considered inaccurate, possibly due to extensive network delays. Inaccurate values are discarded.
5. If the value is considered accurate, the participant adjusts its clock accordingly. Again, fast clocks cannot be turned back in time; therefore, such locations are required to slow down their clocks.

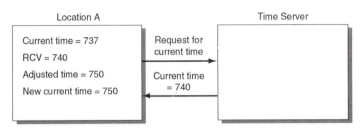

Figure 10.4   Request-Driven Physical Clock Synchronization.

10.2.4 Distributed Physical Time Services

The distributed approach for implementing a physical time service requires each location to broadcast its current time at predefined set intervals. Since clocks are subject to drifting, it is not assumed that the broadcast messages will occur at precisely the same time. Once a location has broadcast its time, it starts a timer. It then collects time messages that it receives. Each time message that arrives is stamped with the local current time. This process continues until the timer expires. Upon the expiration of the timer, each message is adjusted to reflect the network delay time estimated for the message source. At this stage, the participant calculates the average time according to one of the following approaches.

- Calculate the average of all messages. This average is considered the current time. This approach could cause erroneous results since some messages might be inaccurate due to extensive network delays or retransmission.

- Compare each value according to a fault-estimate threshold value. The fault-estimate threshold value reflects the maximum network delay that could occur for a single transmission. Any values exceeding the fault-estimate threshold value are discarded and considered faulty. The remaining values are averaged. This average is considered to represent the current time, as depicted in Figure 10.5.

- Discard the highest x values and the lowest x values and then average. This final approach resembles the approach taken when judging gymnastics or figure skating. In particular, the highest m values and the lowest m values are considered erroneous and are discarded. The remaining values are averaged and the result is considered the current time, as depicted in Figure 10.6.

The clocks are then updated in the same manner as previously discussed. In the interest of efficiency, some implementations limit the extent of the broadcast. Requiring all participants to broadcast to all other participants generates an extensive amount of traffic. Thus, one modification involves requiring participants only to broadcast to other participants in their neighborhood. The neighborhoods of the system are designed to overlap to provide a global service. This variation greatly decreases the amount of traffic as well as the number of values each participant must receive to calculate a new current time.

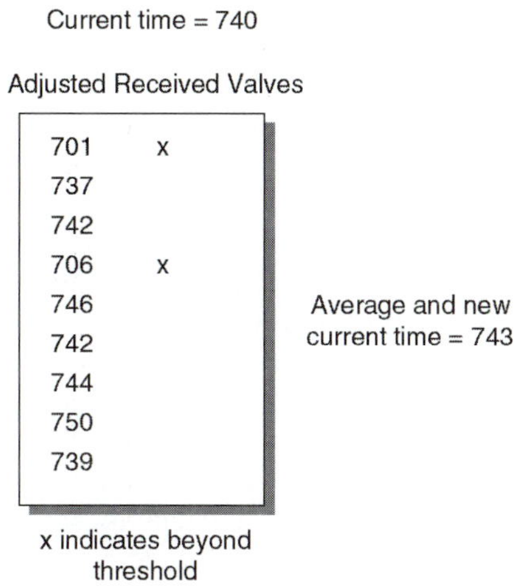

Current time = 740

Adjusted Received Valves

701   x
737
742
706   x
746   Average and new
742   current time = 743
744
750
739

x indicates beyond
threshold

Figure 10.5   Fault-Tolerant Threshold Method.

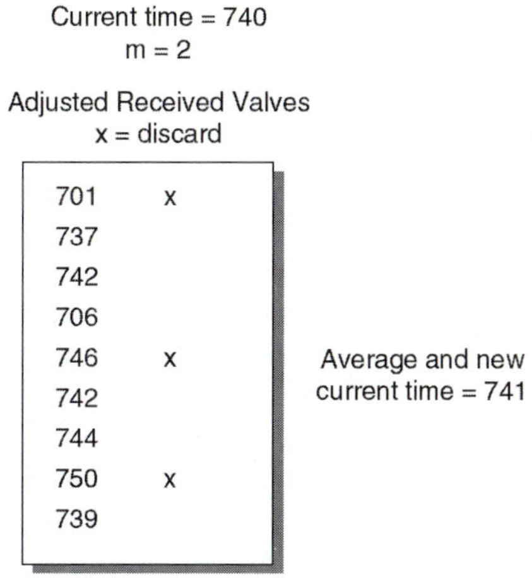

Current time = 740
m = 2

Adjusted Received Valves
x = discard

701   x
737
742
706
746   x   Average and new
742   current time = 741
744
750   x
739

Figure 10.6   Discard *m* Highest and Lowest Values.

10.3 NETWORK TIME PROTOCOL (NTP)

Information on the Network Time Protocol (NTP) version 3 can be found in RFC 1305 [Mil92]. NTP is designed to operate in a large distributed system and can accommodate systems connected via slow modem links to the fastest connections possible. It has been widely adopted on the Internet. As early as 1991, there were already approximately 30 primary NTP servers and over 2000 secondary NTP servers on the Internet across North America, the UK, and Norway [Mil91a]. Version 3 came into existence to better accommodate the high-speed networks in use on the Internet today. It is backwardly compatible with older NTP versions, but updating is highly recommended due to the increased accuracy provided. It is able to achieve accuracy within 1 to 50 microseconds. While designed to execute on top of the Internet's IP and UDP, it is so easily adopted for other network transport protocols that it is generally considered protocol independent. Section 10.3.1 defines the NTP architecture. Section 10.3.2 defines the goals of NTP. NTP service modes are described in Section 10.3.3. Finally, the Simple Network Time Protocol (SNTP) is described in Section 10.3.4.

10.3.1 NTP Architecture

To accommodate a large number of systems on the Internet, the NTP architecture is organized into a hierarchical tree structure. This structure must be a tree and never form a loop. The entire architecture consists of multiple trees; each tree parent is a primary server. Primary servers are directly connected to UTC time sources. The purpose of NTP is to communicate the time from these primary servers to secondary participants throughout the distributed system. The particular primary server that a secondary server utilizes to obtain time information is the referenced primary server. Primary servers may have a back-up server that utilizes a less reliable method for obtaining UTC time. The back-up servers are only provided in the interest of fault tolerance and are only utilized should the primary server fail. The secondary participants are arranged by levels. NTP utilizes the terminology established in the telephone industry for identifying the various levels. Specifically, each level is referred to as a **stratum,** as depicted in Figure 10.7. The parent nodes that represent the primary servers are at stratum 1. Secondary participants can be found in stratums 2 through n. Participants in stratum 2 are directly connected with primary servers. Stratum 3 participants are synchronized with stratum 2 participants, and so on. The lower the stratum number of a participant, the more accurate the time is maintained since the participant is closer to the primary source. The extent to which accuracy degrades is highly dependent on the network path and the stability of the local clock. The entire hierarchy is referred to as a synchronization subnet.

10.3.2 NTP Design Goals

The following are the four primary design goals of NTP.

1. Allow accurate UTC synchronization.

2. Enable survival despite significant losses of connectivity.

3. Allow frequent resynchronization.

4. Protect against malicious or accidental interference.

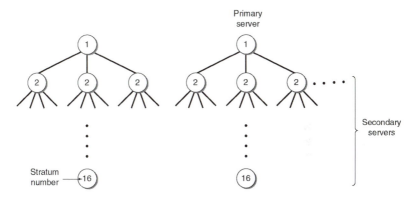

Figure 10.7 Stratas in the NTP Architecture.

To achieve the first goal, NTP must be able to service all clients and provide accurate times despite constant variance in network delays. This is accomplished through statistical techniques for filtering data. To describe the filtering techniques, we must first identify what information NTP communicates. NTP is designed to provide the following three pieces of information relative to the primary server. The format of the data is presented in Detail Box 10.2.

1. Clock offset

2. Round-trip delay

3. Dispersion

The clock offset is defined as the difference between two clocks. In particular, it is the value that the participant's clock must be adjusted to become synchronized with the reference primary clock. Round-trip delay allows a participant to launch a message destined to arrive at the reference primary clock at a specified time. **Dispersion** reflects the maximum error for a local clock relative to the primary reference clock. Only positive values are allowed when specifying dispersion. Together, this information is provided to obtain the time as well as indicate the quality and accuracy of the time. The higher the dispersion factor, the less reliable the data and, therefore, lower accuracy is attained. In conclusion, NTP is able to discriminate between the various qualities of sources for clock information.

The statistical technique employed requires multiple comparisons of timing information. Multiple exchanges are necessary to synchronize the clock within a few seconds.

Numerous exchanges over several hours are necessary to identify relative clock skew and maintain time within a millisecond. Therefore, the statistical based accuracy is directly related to and dependent on the time taken to achieve synchronization. It is important to note that each exchange is relatively nonintrusive to system and network performance.

DETAIL BOX 10.2
NTP DATA FORMAT

NTP timestamps are represented as 64-bit unsigned fixed-point numbers. All timestamps are relative to time 0 on January 1, 1900. The integer portion of the timestamp is the first 32 bits. The fraction portion of the timestamp is the last 32 bits. The 64 bit field is sufficient to represent time until the year 2036.The precision of this representation is 300 picoseconds. The format was chosen to allow for convenient multiple-precision arithmetic conversion to time protocol representation (seconds) as well as easy conversion to other time protocols.

All data in the protocol is specified in twos compliment, fixed-point arithmetic. Data may be specified as an integer or fixed-point representation. When fixed-point representation is utilized, the precision and decimal location is not specified. All data bits are numbered in big-endian, starting from the left or high-order position.

The second goal requires NTP to enable survival despite significant losses of connectivity. To achieve this goal, NTP incorporates the use of redundant time-servers and redundant paths between servers. In addition, it allows easy reconfiguration in the event that a server is unreachable for an extended period. Reconfiguration involves a network routing detour around inoperable or faulty portions of the network. The new primary server chosen must be the closest primary available. Closeness is determined by the network delay between the secondary and primary server, referred to as the synchronization distance. In the event of a tie, the new primary server is chosen randomly from among the servers involved in the tie. If all primary servers in a particular subnet should fail, the back-up servers are employed.

The third goal allows frequent resynchronization. This resynchronization is necessary to offset the drift rates found in computers. While allowing frequent updates, NTP is also able to scale its service to accommodate the number of potential clients and servers in a massively distributed system.

The final goal involves protection against malicious or accidental interference and is crucial in a massively distributed system. The more participants in a system, the greater the probability that a time service within the system may accidentally go awry and distribute incorrect information. In addition, it is also possible for the system to contain a purposefully malicious time service. Accommodating the potential of malfeasance, all time services employ authentication (discussed in Chapter 11) and return address verification. In addition, 64-bit DES keys (discussed in Chapter 11) may be employed. Whenever authentication or encryption is utilized, there is an additional delay encountered due to the time necessary for the security procedures. This security time delay in addition to the network delay must be factored in when adjusting time. Like the network delay, the security delay is not a precise measurement; therefore, the adjusted clock values will not be as accurate.

10.3.3 NTP Synchronization Modes

NTP servers may synchronize in any of three modes: multicast, client/server and symmetric mode. Multicast synchronization mode is intended for use on high-speed LANs. It is not the most accurate mode of operation but proves to be sufficient for many applications. A **multicast** is a network message intended for a subset of all users. When operating in multicast mode, a time-server will periodically broadcast the current time. The recipients then utilize this time to adjust their clocks, taking into consideration a small network delay time, as described in Section 10.2.3. This algorithm parallels the first approach presented for broadcast-based centralized physical clock synchronization. When multicast is not supported by the network, most utilize the client/server mode of operation.

The client/server mode is similar to the request-driven approach described in Section 10.2.3. One server accepts requests from participants in the system. Each request receives a response consisting of the current time. Requests from clients are sent at each reboot and at periodic intervals thereafter. These intervals are based upon and determined by the needs of the client. The server maintains no state information on clients. The overall mechanism employed represents a simplified remote procedure call.

The final mode of operation is the symmetric mode. This mode is utilized whenever the highest levels of accuracy are desired. The operation consists of a pair of servers exchanging time information. This message exchange is employed to obtain information on the current latency between the two servers and to improve accuracy. This method works best when the stratum numbers vary by at most 1. This mode of operation is more reflective of a peer-to-peer model of computing versus the client/server model.

All modes of operation assume that the underlying transport protocol (IP or UDP) handles error control involving error detection and retransmission. Detail Box 10.3 presents the frame format employed for NTP. All modes of operation perform eight validation tests on the data before the data are passed to the clock update procedure. Four tests are executed to validate that the data and four tests are executed to validate the message header that accompanied the data. Detail Box 10.4 provides a list of the eight tests performed.

10.3.4 Simple Network Time Protocol (SNTP)

SNTP is an adaptation of NTP and is employed when ultimate performance is not required. SNTP can operate in all modes available and specified in NTP. This protocol is not actually a new protocol but a clarification of how to simplify access to an NTP server. Despite the simplifications, it is still possible to obtain accuracy in the order of microseconds. Information on the Simple Network Time Protocol (SNTP) can be found in RFC 1769 [Mil95].

The operation of the protocol involves stateless remote procedure calls. It is highly recommended that locations functioning as SNTP clients only be located at the highest stratum number in a subnet. SNTP clients should not be utilized to synchronize other NTP or SNTP clients. While the modes of operation and the format of the data are the same as those for NTP, SNTP servers do not implement the capabilities to provide for fault tolerance

---

DETAIL BOX 10.3
NTP FRAME FORMAT

The NTP frame format complies with the UDP frame format as described in [Mil95]. Since UDP is a client of IP, this frame format is also in compliance with the IP protocol. The frame format consists of the following fields.

♦   LI
♦   VN
♦   MODE
♦   Stratum
♦   Poll
♦   Precision
♦   Root Delay
♦   Root Dispersion
♦   Reference Identifier
♦   Reference Timestamp
♦   Originate Timestamp
♦   Receive Timestamp
♦   Transmit Timestamp
♦   Authenticator

The field LI, leap indicator, is a two-bit field that communicates if a **leap second** has occurred. Leap seconds occasionally occur to keep UTC, an atomic-based time, accurate with astrological time. This field may have the following values and meanings.
♦   00: no warning
♦   01: last minute contained 61 seconds
♦   10: last minute contained 59 seconds
♦   11: alarm state: system not synchronized

The field VN, version number, is a three-bit integer utilized for indicating the version of NTP that is employed. As previously stated, the current version number is 3.

The mode field is a three-bit field used to communicate the current mode of operation for NTP. There are eight values in all. Modes 0, 6, and 7 are reserved. Mode 1 and 2 are used to designate the symmetric mode of operation. Mode 1 is for broadcast based, also referred to as active symmetric mode. Mode 2 is for request driven also known as passive symmetric mode. Mode 3 designates client mode while Mode 4 designates server mode. Finally, Mode 5 designates multicast mode.

The stratum field is an eight-bit field used to communicate the stratum number of the local clock. The value of 0 is unspecified. If the stratum number is 1, the local clock is a primary reference such as a radio UTC clock. IF the stratum number is in the range 2 to 15, the local clock is a secondary reference such as an NTP server. Network clocks sources are generally stratum 1 or 2. Values 16 to 255 are reserved.

The poll field is an eight-bit signed integer employed to communicate the maximum allowable time between successive messages. All values are in seconds to the nearest power of two. Most applications use the value 6 or 10 representing 64 or 1024 seconds, respectively.

Precision is also an eight-bit signed integer. It is used to communicate the precision of the local clock in seconds to the nearest power of two. The values are generally in the range of -6 to -20 (workstations).

Root delay is a 32-bit signed fixed-point number. It is employed to communicate the total round-trip delay to the primary reference. Time is once again in seconds with the fraction point placement between bits 15 and 16. Values may be positive or negative and generally range from a few negative milliseconds to positive values upward of several hundred milliseconds.

Root dispersion is a 32-bit unsigned fixed-point number utilized to represent the normal error in relationship to the primary reference. The value provided is in seconds with the fraction point placement between bits 15 and 16. Values frequently range from 0 to several hundred milliseconds.

The reference clock identifier is a 32-bit field. This field is employed to identify the source of information. The contents may indicate anything from an NTP secondary source IP address, to a generic radio service such as WWV, discussed earlier, to a satellite service such as GEOS, also discussed earlier.

All timestamps are 64-bit fields. The reference timestamp communicates the last timestamp at which the local clock was corrected. The originate timestamp communicates the time of the request. The receive timestamp is the time the request was received by the server. The transmit timestamp is the time when the reply departed from the server.

The authenticator field is an optional 96-bit field used when the authentication option is being utilized. Authentication is discussed in Chapter 11.

DETAIL BOX 10.4
NTP'S EIGHT VALIDATION TESTS

The following are the eight tests performed by NTP prior to entering the update clock procedure. The first four tests ensure valid data. Valid data are necessary to calculate offset, delay, and dispersion. The last four tests ensure valid header information. These tests determine if a peer can be selected for synchronization.

1. Requires that the timestamp provided is not the same as the last timestamp received. This ensures the message is not a duplicate message.
2. Requires that the originate timestamp to be equal to the last timestamp received. This test ensures the timestamp messages are processed in order and the message is from the proper primary server.
3. Requires that the originate and receive timestamps be nonzero. A zero timestamp indicates that the time server is unreachable or synchronization has never been attained.
4. Requires that the calculated network delay be within an acceptable range.
5. Requires that the authentication mechanism be disabled or that the message has passed the authentication test.
6. Requires that the peer clock be synchronized.
7. Ensures that the clock will not be synchronized with a clock of a higher stratum number.
8. Requires reasonable values for packet delay and dispersion.

and redundancy. Due to the lack of redundancy, it is highly recommended that SNTP servers operate in conjunction with a source of external synchronization, such as a reliable radio UTC clock. In this circumstance, SNTP servers would be located at stratum 1. Since SNTP does not allow for authentication, the server should be known by the client.

10.4 LOGICAL CLOCKS

Since it is difficult to align clocks precisely, it is difficult to utilize physical clocks to order events uniquely in distributed systems. With this in mind, the question arises if there is another approach that can be used to order events. In this section, we study the use of logical clocks for obtaining a unique ordering of events in a distributed system. The essence of logical clocks is based on the happened-before relationship presented by Lamport [Lam78]. In Section 10.4.1, we explore this relationship. Section 10.4.2 examines the use of this relationship for logical ordering. Section 10.4.3 presents an algorithm for obtaining total ordering through the employment of logical clocks.

10.4.1 Happen-Before Relationship

The **happen-before relationship** was first described by Lamport [Lam78]. If event *a* happens before event *b*, the relationship is denoted by a > b. In this classic paper, the following significant observations regarding event ordering were made.

- ◆ If two events, *a* and *b*, occurred at the same process, they occurred in the order of which they were observed. That is, *a* > *b*.

- ◆ If *a* sends a message to *b*, then *a* > *b*. That is, you cannot receive something before it is sent. This relationship holds regardless of where events *a* and *b* occur. This is similar to the casual relationship described in Chapter 9.

- ◆ The happen-before relationship is transitive. If *a* happens before *b* and *b* happens before *c*, then *a* happens before *c*. That is, if *a* > *b* and *b* > *c*, then *a* > *c*.

It is important to observe that this relationship is not reflexive, an event cannot happen before itself. Any two events that are not in a happen-before relationship are concurrent; nothing can be said relative to the ordering of concurrent events. Detail Box 10.5 presents an example of the happen-before relationship.

10.4.2 Logical Ordering

Logical ordering does not rely on a common clock, which cannot exist in a distributed system; nor does it rely on synchronized physical clocks, which are difficult to achieve and maintain. The benefit of the happen-before relationship is its lack of dependence on physical clocks. To obtain logical ordering, timestamps that are independent of physical clocks are employed. Timestamps may be implemented with a simple counter as long as they obey the happen-before relationship. Each event receives a timestamp. Each system's clock is considered accurate if all happen-before relationships are observed. If one considered $T(a)$ to be the timestamp for event *a*, the following relationships must hold in a distributed system utilizing logical ordering.

- ◆ If two events, *a* and *b*, occurred at the same process, they occurred in the order of which they were observed. That is $T(a) > T(b)$. A clock for a given process can never go backwards.

- ◆ If *a* sends a message to *b*, then $T(a) > T(b)$. That is to say, you cannot receive something before it is sent.

- ◆ If *a* happens before *b* and *b* happens before *c*, $T(a) > T(b)$, $T(b) > T(c)$, and $T(a) > T(c)$.

DETAIL BOX 10.5
HAPPEN-BEFORE RELATIONSHIP EXAMPLE

As an example, let us consider the events a, b, c, and d as depicted in Figure 10.8a. Events a and b occur at the same location. Therefore, according to the happen-before relationship, $a > b$. Event b involves sending a message to another location. The receiving of this message is event c. According to the happen-before relationship, $b > c$. One may also conclude that by the transitive property that $a > c$. Finally, the event d occurs at some point in time at another location. Since events a, b, and c occur at a different location and are not related to event d, the event d is considered concurrent with the other three events. Nothing can be said relative to the ordering of d in relationship to a, b, and c.

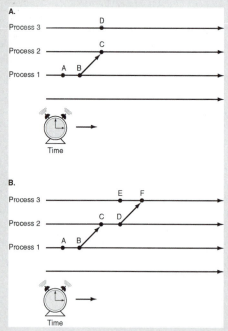

Figure 10.8   *Happen-Before Relationship Examples.*

    To further clarify, let us examine Figure 10.8b. In this situation, events a, b, and c maintain the same relationship as in the first example. However, events c and d are now in a happen-before relationship as are events d and e. Since $c > d$ and $d > f$, $c > f$ due to the transitive property. Finally, since events e and f belong to the same process, $e > f$. It is important to note that events a, b, c, and d are considered concurrent to the event e.

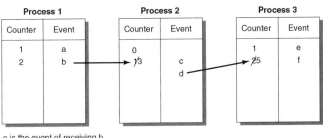

c is the event of receiving b
f is the event of receiving d

Each requires a counter adjustment to preserve the happens-before relationship.

Figure 10.9 Logical Ordering of Events Using Counters.

The algorithm presented by Lamport [Lam78] incorporates the happen-before relationship and implements logical ordering with the following two rules.

1. Each process increments its clock counter between every two consecutive events. The timestamps reflect the current value of the clock.

2. If a sends a message to b, then the message must include $T(a)$. Upon receiving a and $T(a)$, the receiving process must set its clock to the greater of $[T(a) + 1,$ Current Clock]. That is, if the recipient's clock is behind, it must be advanced to preserve the happen-before relationship.

The example depicted in Figure 10.9 utilizes the same example described in Detail Box 10.4. In this circumstance, counters are employed to obtain logical ordering. The happen-before relationships are as follows: $a > b$, $b > c$, $c > d$, $d > f$, and $e > f$. Event b carried a timestamp equal to 2. Therefore, due to rule 2 the clock for process 2 had to be adjusted when event c occurred. Likewise, the clock for process 3 had to be adjusted when event f occurred to preserve the happen-before relationship. Event e is considered concurrent to events a, b, c, and d.

It is also possible to implement logical ordering while utilizing physical clocks. Obeying the first rule for logical ordering is generally not a problem. It is quite common for a computer clock to tick several times in between events. Accommodating the second rule is also quite straightforward. If a message arrives with a timestamp less than the recipient's current physical time, the physical time is advanced to one unit ahead of the timestamp. One must keep in mind that if a participant's clock is inaccurate by being significantly ahead of the correct time, it may negatively affect the accuracy of the physical time throughout the distributed system. Despite this potential drawback, this implementation is quite effective for obtaining a logical ordering of events using physical time.

An example depicting the use of physical clocks to obtain logical ordering is presented in Figure 10.10. The happen-before relationships are once again: $a > b$, $b > c$, $c > d$

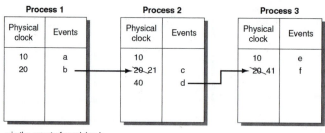

c is the event of receiving b
f is the event of receiving d

Each required a clock adjustment to preserve the happens-before relationship.

Figure 10.10   Logical Ordering of Events Using Physical Clocks.

$d > f$, and $e > f$. Event b carried a physical timestamp equal to 20. Therefore, due to rule 2 the physical clock for process 2 had to be adjusted to 21 when event c occurred. Likewise, the physical clock for process 3 had to be adjusted to 41 when event f occurred to preserve the happen-before relationship. Event e is considered concurrent to events a, b, c, and d.

10.4.3 Total Ordering with Logical Clocks

As we have seen by the examples in Section 10.4.2, the happen-before relationship is only able to achieve partial ordering. This relationship was not able to order concurrent events. To obtain **total ordering**, no two events can be allowed to occur at precisely the same time. One straightforward solution, first proposed by Lamport [Lam78], is to utilize process identification numbers in the low-order bits of timestamps. Since each process has a unique process number, even if two events occur at the same time at separate participants in the distributed system, they will possess unique timestamps. For example, if both process 001 and process 002 have an event that occurs exactly at time 32, the event belonging to the first process will be given the timestamp 32.001. The event belonging to the second process will be given the timestamp 32.002. It is now possible for each event to have a unique timestamp and for the system to obtain a unique total ordering.

10.5 SUMMARY

In this chapter, we have focused on issues and solutions to obtaining system-wide synchronization. There are two bases for synchronization: the use of physical clocks reflecting "people" time and the use of logical clocks. As we have seen, synchronizing physical clocks can be quite difficult. Each location's clock is subjected to drifting, thereby causing a clock skew between it and other clocks throughout the system. Utilizing messages, whether one is taking a centralized or distributed approach to synchronization, involves many complications. One must accommodate an unknown and unpredictable network delay. In addition, if the solution is request driven, there is also the unknown interrupt delay to take into consideration. Without precise knowledge of how much time has passed since a time value was read from the server's clock, it is difficult to adjust the clock properly. Many approaches involve averaging results. The best approaches utilize a 'fault-tolerant' average and attempt to disregard timestamps that seem to be unreasonable. We have also examined a widely used protocol for synchronizing physical clocks, NTP. This protocol also allows one to authenticate the time server. While this is a definite advantage, it adds the possibility of another unknown time factor, the time to authenticate the message. With so many variables, it is amazing that NTP is able to synchronize physical clocks to within 300 picoseconds. This accuracy level is generally sufficient for even the most sophisticated applications. To achieve this accuracy level, several hours of messages and replies must be exchanged. The best method for a quick accurate time is directly utilizing a UTC server, but that comes at a great financial expense.

Despite the success of synchronizing physical clocks, the use of such clocks may still provide undesirable results in a distributed system, where many applications require total ordering. The best and most widely cited method for obtaining total ordering is based upon Lamport's happen-before relationship and derived logical clocks that take advantage of casual relationships. Employing this method along with timestamps derived from physical clocks and process IDs allows one to obtain total ordering in a distributed system.

10.6 REFERENCES FOR FURTHER STUDY

The general references presented in Chapter 1 can provide some general information on distributed synchronization. Some appropriate traditional research papers concerning information in this chapter include [Bra80, Cri89, GuZa89, HSSD84, KoOc87, LaMe85, LiKa80, LuLy84, MaOw85, Mil88, Mil90, Mil91a, Mil 91b, Mil92, Mil95, Mit80, and Ric88].

The following provide some great starting points for sources on the Internet concerning synchronization. In particular, the RFC for NTP can be located at http://www.cis.ohio-state.edu/rfc/rfc1769.txt. The RFC for SNTP that also includes clarification information on NTP can be located at http://www.cis.ohio-state.edu/rfc/rfc1769.txt All RFCs related to NTP can be found at http://www.cis.ohio-state.edu/cgi-bin/wais-rfc.pl?NTP.

EXERCISES

10.1   Name and discuss three common difficulties that one encounters while attempting to synchronize physical clocks in a distributed operating system.

10.2   Name three algorithms in a distributed operating system that require the use of global time or global ordering.

10.3 Describe three events that could occur that make it difficult to obtain and calculate an accurate value for a physical clock.

10.4 Calculate the maximum skew per minute on a distributed system where most participants' clocks tick 1200 times per millisecond but one clock ticks at 1100 times per millisecond and another at 1230 times per millisecond.

10.5 Calculate the necessary adjustment for a computer clock that reads 11:07:34 (where the time format is hours:minutes:seconds) that is informed that the current time is 11:07:26. Consider that the adjustments must be made to become synchronized within the next 4 seconds. Describe one adjustment that cannot be made along with a motivating reason.

10.6 Name and describe three fault-tolerant features that can be incorporated into distributed clock synchronization algorithms.

10.7 What are the advantages of utilizing network neighborhoods when employing a distributed time service? What cautions must be taken when using this approach?

10.8 Why are participants at higher stratum numbers in NTP considered less accurate?

10.9 Why are multiple time-message exchanges between a secondary participant and a reference primary server required to synchronize clocks employing NTP?

10.10 Describe three scenarios that motivate the use of authentication in a system employing NTP for its time service. Describe a disadvantage of employing the authentication mechanism.

10.11 For each of the following NTP timestamps, describe the use and advantage of each timestamp within a distributed system.

A. Reference timestamp
B. Originate timestamp
C. Receive timestamp
D. Transmit timestamp

10.12 Why is it not advisable to employ an SNTP client to synchronize another SNTP client?

10.13 Fill in each of the corrected time (when necessary) in the following tables, employing the happen-before relationship for logical clocks. Identify all happen-before relationships as well as all concurrent events.

Process 1

Time	Corrected Time	Event
2		A
4		B (send message to process 2)
6		C (receive message F from process 2)
8		D (send message to process 3)

Process 2

Time	Corrected Time	Event
3		E (receive message B from process 1)
6		F (send message to process 1)
9		G (receive message J from process 3)
12		H (send message to process 3)

Process 3

Time	Corrected Time	Event
4		I
8		J (send message to process 2)
12		K (receive message H from process 2)
16		L (receive message D from process 1)

10.14 Write a program to implement the happen-before relationship for logical ordering. Use Exercise 10.13 as one of your sample input files. Your program should be able to calculate corrected times for each of the processes, and identify all happen-before relationships as well as all concurrent events.

Distributed Security

Whenever someone discusses distributed computing, one of the first questions raised is, "Can it be secure?" Computer security frequently consists of two parts: authentication and access control. **Authentication** involves the verification and identification of a valid user. **Access control** strives to prevent unwanted tampering with data files and system resources. In an isolated, centralized, single-user system such as a PC, security is accomplished by locking up the room where the computer is stored and locking up the disks. Thus, only the user with the key to the room and disks may access the system resources and files. This accomplishes both authentication and access control. The security is only as good as the keys that lock the computer and the room.

In isolated centralized systems with multiple users, security is a bit more complex. In this scenario, authentication involves the verification and identification of a valid user and is usually managed by some type of password and user identification combination. Control of access to the files, data, and resources to prevent unwanted tampering is generally accomplished through capabilities or access lists and is managed as part of the operating system.

In this chapter, we see that like the previous scenarios, authentication and access control are once again our primary concerns when we connect our system to a network of other systems. While authentication and access control are thought of as tasks to be taken care of by the operating system, distributed access control may be handled by the routers and application software. Furthermore, since we are communicating using an outside shared resource (the network), we also need to secure the content and verify the originator's identity of the information that we are sending across this network by employing cryptography and digital signatures respectively.

While distributed security continues to be a very active research area, there is enough current technology to understand the basis of the security problem and various solutions available to a distributed operating system. In Section 11.1 we examine the various types of cryptography, including their use for digital signatures. Section 11.2 presents two common approaches to authentication, and Section 11.3 presents various methods of access control in distributed systems. The methods discussed in this chapter are used in addition to the necessary authentication and access control techniques usually employed for centralized systems, some of which were presented in Chapter 8.

11.1 CRYPTOGRAPHY AND DIGITAL SIGNATURES

While computer users may occasionally wish to secure information by means of encryption on isolated computer systems, many users desire and require encryption for communication across networks. **Encryption** involves encoding data using a key in such a manner that an eavesdropper cannot easily read the data. This encrypted data is referred to as **ciphertext** while the original data is referred to as **plaintext**. The process of going from ciphertext to plaintext is referred to as **decryption**. Figure 11.1 depicts the classic cryptography couple, Alice and Bob, communicating by means of the Caesar Cipher. The Caesar Cipher is a simple cryptosystem that rotates the data; in this case, two letters forward. Obviously, this is not a very secure encryption algorithm and could be decoded with a cereal box decoder ring. The most popular means for measuring the security of a encryption algorithm is that is **computationally secure.** An encryption algorithm is computationally secure if the system cannot be broken by systematic analysis with available resources. There are two general categories of encryption: private-key and pubic-key encryption. In addition to encrypting an entire message, both types of encryption can be employed to sign a document digitally. Section 11.1.1 examines symmetric encryption and uses DES as an example. Section 11.1.2 examines asymmetric encryption and uses RSA as an example. Both examples presented are computationally secure when using a significantly long key.

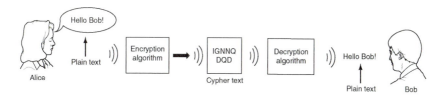

Figure 11.1 Alice and Bob Use Cryptography.

11.1.1 Symmetric Encryption

Symmetric encryption refers to encryption algorithms where the encryption and the decryption algorithm utilize the same key. Specifically:

```
E(p,k)=C & D(C,k)=p
where
E = encryption algorithm,
D = decryption algorithm,
p = plaintext (original data),
k = encryption key and
C = ciphertext.
```

Since the same key is utilized to encrypt and decrypt the data, this key must be kept private. This type of encryption is also referred to as secret-key encryption as well as conventional encryption. One of the difficulties in using such a system is, of course, communicating the key! One simple way to overcome the key exchange problem is first to use public-key encryption to exchange keys and then employ private-key encryption. Detail Box 11.4 describes one public-key encryption method for exchanging keys; specifically, the Diffie-Hellman key exchange algorithm. This is also very practical since DES encryption typically operates at approximately 45,000 kbps and public-key cryptography typically operates at 20 kbps. We now examine the most popular private-key encryption algorithm, DES (pronounced DEZ), which was declared the U.S. standard by the National Institute of Standards and Technology (NIST)[1] in 1977 [NIST77]. Other private-key encryption algorithms include IDEA [Lai92] and Skipjack (used in the clipper chips) [NIST94a].

Data Encryption Standard

DES was implemented as a standard in 1977 and is reaffirmed every five years, typically in December. All U.S. federal agencies and other organizations that process information on their behalf must utilize DES (for nonclassified documents). Its use is also common among

---

[1] Formerly known as the National Bureau of Standards (NBS).

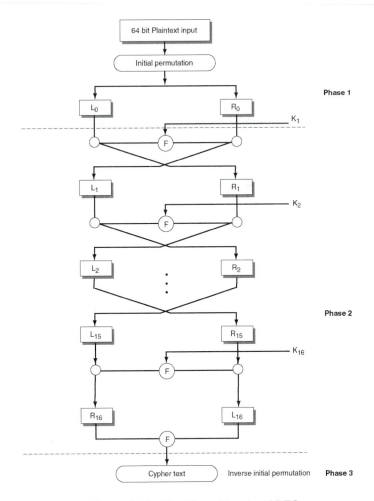

Figure 11.2   The Three Phases of DES.

nongovernment corporations. It was based on IBM's LUCIFER system, which employs a 128-bit key. Generally, the larger the key, the more secure the system. DES utilizes a 64-bit key; however, 8 bits are for error detection thereby effectively making DES a 56-bit key system for security purposes. It is referred to as a block cipher since it encrypts data in blocks of 64 bits of binary data. The security of DES is based on the secrecy of the key, not the secrecy of the algorithm. The security is further enhanced by the size of the key since there are seventy quadrillion (70,000,000,000,000,000) possible keys; thus, the chances of deriving the key are low enough to be secure for most distributed environments. Of course, with the power of the average PC continually increasing, the ability to search sequentially for a key and break a code is proportionately increasing as well. There are three phases to the encryption algorithm, which are depicted in Figure 11.2. Decryption is accomplished by performing these three phases in reverse order including using the key blocks described in phase 2 in reverse order (K_{16} to K_1).

DES Phase 1: Initial Permutation

The first phase of DES involves a permutation of the 64-bit block that changes the order of the bits within each block. The term **permutation** is used in the strict mathematical sense; only the order is changed. The exact permutation is specified by a table (see Detail Box 11.1). The 64 bits of data are now broken up into two halves: L_0 (left half) and R_0 (right half). The zero subscripts indicate the original halves. These subscripts are incremented after each iteration in phase 2 of the DES algorithm.

DETAIL BOX 11.1
THE DES PERMUTATION

The exact table used by the DES standard for the initial permutation is depicted in Table 11.1 [NIST77]. Thus, the first bit after the permutations was the 58_{th} bit prior to the permutation. The second bit after the permutation was the 50_{th} bit prior to the permutation. The last bit of the permuted data was originally the 7_{th} data bit of the plaintext.

58	50	42	34	26	18	10	2
60	52	44	36	28	20	12	4
62	54	46	38	30	22	14	6
64	56	48	40	32	24	16	8
57	49	41	33	25	17	9	1
59	51	43	35	27	19	11	3
61	53	45	37	29	21	13	5
63	55	47	39	31	23	15	7

Table 11.1 DES Initial Permutation [NIST77].

DES Phase 2: Shifting (Repeated 16 Times)

The second phase involves a table-dependent algorithm that utilizes the key. This action is generally referred to as shifting the data. The algorithm is repeated 16 times, each time the shifting behaves differently since it utilizes a different subblock of the key. The subblock of the key is determined by another set of tables and its own shifting algorithm. After each iteration, the subindexes of L (left half) and R (right half) are incremented to represent each stage, as represented in Figure 11.2. The result after the 16_{th} iteration is referred to as the pre-output and is passed into phase 3. The exact tables and various algorithms are presented in [NIST77].

DES Phase 3: Inverse Permutation

The final phase of DES involves a permutation of the 64-bit block that changes the order of the bits within each block just like phase 1 but utilizes a different table. The exact permutation is specified by a table (see Detail Box 11.2). The output of this permutation is the ciphertext.

DETAIL BOX 11.2
THE DES INVERSE PERMUTATION

The exact table used by the DES standard for the final inverse permutation is depicted in Table 11.2 [NIST77]. Thus, the first bit after the permutations was the 40_{th} bit of the preoutput. The second bit after the permutation was the 8_{th} bit prior to the preoutput. Finally, the last bit of the ciphertext was the 25_{th} data bit of the preoutput.

40	8	48	16	56	24	64	32
39	7	47	15	55	23	63	31
38	6	46	14	54	22	62	30
37	5	45	13	53	21	61	29
36	4	44	12	52	20	60	28
35	3	43	11	51	19	59	27
34	2	42	10	50	18	58	26
33	1	41	9	49	17	57	25

Table 11.2 DES Inverse Permutation [NIST77].

TRIPLE DES

One can further enhance the security of DES by utilizing Triple DES. Triple DES utilizes three 64-bit keys. The data is sent through the three phases of DES with the first key to produce C1. C1 is then sent through the three phases of DES with the second key to produce C2. This second ciphertext is then sent through DES a final time with the third key as described here and depicted in Figure 11.3.

```
E (p, k₁) = C₁
E (C₁, k₂) = C₂
E (C₂, k₃) = C₃
```

where E is the DES encryption algorithm,

```
kᵢ is the iᵗʰ key,
p is the original plaintext and
and C₃ is the final ciphertext.
```

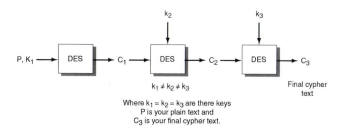

Figure 11.3 Triple DES.

Digital Signatures with Symetric Key Encryption

When sending data over a network, there are two basic methods to sign a document digitally. We now examine the first method that utilizes private-key encryption. A digital signature is also referred to as a **message digest** and employs a secure hash function as described in [NIST93B]. This hash function is referred to as a **digest function** and is typically 128 bits long. The deterministic digest function is applied to the entire document and produces a value that is dependent on every bit of information in the message. There are two methods for computing the digest utilizing a shared private key. The easiest and quickest method calculates a hash value for the message that is then encrypted by the private key. The message is then sent with the encrypted digest. The recipient may then calculate the message digest, encrypt it, and compare values. If they match, the document contents have not been altered. The second method prepends the private key to the message and then calculates the hash value. The result of this method is as follows.

```
Compute D(M,K) where
D is a digest function
M is the message and
K is a shared private-key
```

The document can then be published or distributed. This message digest has the additional benefit of preventing forgery of the digest value itself since third parties do not have knowledge of the private key that is necessary to compute the correct digest value. In both cases, only those with knowledge of the secret key can verify its integrity, and all fraudulent documents are readily detected.

11.1.2 Asymmetric Encryption

Asymmetric encryption involves two keys—a pubic key and a private key—and is also known as public key encryption. If a piece of information is encrypted with a public key, the corresponding private key can decrypt the information as follows.

```
E(p,k_u)=C & D(C,k_r)=p
```

```
where
E = encryption algorithm,
D = decryption algorithm,
p = plaintext (original data),
k  = public-key,
 u
k  = private-key, and
 r
C = ciphertext.
```

If a piece of information is encrypted with a private key, the corresponding public key can decrypt the information as follows.

```
E(p,k )=C & D(C,k )=p
     r           u
where
E = encryption algorithm,
D = decryption algorithm,
p = plaintext (original data),
k  = private-key,
 r
k  = public-key, and
 u
C = ciphertext.
```

You cannot decrypt a message with the same key that encrypted it, as depicted in Figure 11.4. Furthermore, it is mathematically difficult to obtain one key from the other. The private key is to be kept a secret by the user and thus its name. Of course, if everyone knew the private key, it wouldn't be so private! The public key is not kept a secret and may be made publicly available through a public listing service, usually implemented using X.509 (which is described in Section 11.2.2). The idea of public-key encryption was first proposed by Diffie and Hellman in 1976 [DH76] in the context of a method for key exchange and is presented in Detail Box 11.4. The most popular form of public-key cryptography is RSA [RSA78], which we now examine in detail.

RSA

RSA is a patent-protected, public-key encryption algorithm developed by Rivest, Shamir, and Adleman in 1978. To utilize RSA, there are three phases. Phase 1 involves the determination of your public and private keys. Phase 2 involves encrypting a message. Finally, Phase 3 involves decrypting a message. The three phases are described next and illustrated in Detail Box 11.3.

RSA Phase 1: Determining your public and private keys.
To determine the public and private keys, each user must do the following six steps.

1. Choose two large primes, P and Q.

2. Compute $N = P * Q$.

3. Compute $F(n) = (P - 1)(Q - 1)$.

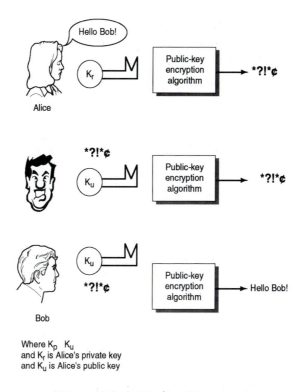

Figure 11.4 Public-Key Cryptography.

4. Choose e, where 1 <= e <= n-1 and GCD (e, F(n)) = 1.

5. Compute *d*, where *ed = 1 (mod f(n))* (using the Extended Euclidean Algorithm).

6. Make *d and n* public; these values constitute the public key.

RSA Phase 2: Encrypting a message.
To encrypt the message *M* using RSA, where *1 <= M <= N - 1* you must compute the following.

```
C=Mᵉ (Mod N) where C is your ciphertext.
Send C.
```

RSA Phase 3: Decrypting the ciphertext.
To decrypt the ciphertext *C* using RSA, you must compute the following.
```
Cᵈ (Mod N)=M where M is your original plaintext.
```

DETAIL BOX 11.3
AN EXAMPLE OF THE THREE PHASES OF RSA

Phase1:
1. Let Alice choose P = 5, Q = 11.
2. Thus, N = P * Q = 55.
3. F(N) = (P - 1)(Q - 1) = 40.
4. Choose e = 7
(verify GCD (40 , 7) = 1 using the Euclidean Algorithm
$40 = 5 * 7 + 5$
$7 = 1 * 5 + 2$
$5 = 2 * 2 + 1$
$2 = 2 * 1 + 0$).
5. Use the Extended Euclidean Algorithm to determine D expressed as a linear combination of e and f(N).
$1 = 5 - 2 * 2$
$= 5 - 2 (7 - 1 * 5)$
$= -2 * 7 + 3 * 5$
$= -2 * 7 + 3 * (40 - 5 * 7)$
$= 3 * 40 - 17 * 7$
Hence 1 = - 17 * 7 (Mod 40) = 23 (Mod 40) and
D = 23.

Phase 2.
Send message *M = 25* to Alice.
Compute $C = M^e$ *(Mod N)* = 25^7 *(Mod 55) = 20.*

Phase 3.
Decrypt ciphertext *C = 20* received from Alice, whose public key is (*D = 23, N = 55*).
Compute C^d *(Mod N) = M* = 20^{23} *(Mod 55) = 25 = M.*

DETAIL BOX 11.4
DIFFIE-HELLMAN KEY EXCHANGE

Alice and Bob would like to exchange keys using this method; they have to follow the next five steps for employing the Diffie-Hellman key exchange. Figure 11.5 depicts Alice and Bob going through this example.

1. Alice and Bob agree on a prime number that is openly communicated, p and an integer a.
2. *Alice* generates a random value $x: 2<=x<=p-1$.
3. Alice computes a^x (Mod p)=A and sends A to Bob.
4. Bob generates a random value $y: 2<=y<=p-1$.

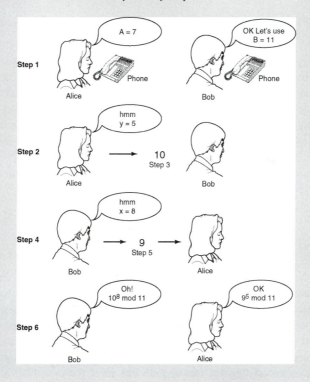

Figure 11.5 Diffie-Hellman Key exchange.

5. Bob computes a^y *(Mod p)=B* and sends B to Alice.
6. Bob computes $(A)^y$ *(Mod p)=$(a^x)^y$ (Mod p)*.
7. Alice computes $(B)^x$ *(Mod p)=$(a^y)^x$ (Mod p)= $(a^x)^y$ (Mod p)!*

Thus, $(a^x)^y$ *(Mod p)* is their common shared key!
For example.

1. Alice and Bob agree to let *p=11, a=7.*
2. Alice generates *x=5* where *2<=5<=11-1.*
3. Alice computes a^x *(Mod p)* or 7^5 *(Mod 11)=10* and sends the *10* to Bob.
4. Bob generates *y=8: 2<=8<=11.*
5. Bob computes a^y *(Mod p)=* 7^8 *(Mod 11)=9* and sends *9* to Alice.
6. Bob computes $(A)^y$ *(Mod p)=*$(7^5)^8$ *(Mod 11)* $= 7^{8*5}$*(Mod 11.)*
7. Alice computes $(B)^x$ *(Mod p)=*$(7^8)^5$ *(Mod 11)=* 7^{5*8}*(Mod 11)!*
   Thus, 7^{5*8}*(Mod 11)* is their common shared key.

Digital Signatures with Public-Key Encryption

The public-key encryption method for digital signatures employs RSA. In this method the origi-nator utilizes its private key to encrypt either the entire data file (expensive) or its signature to the file by using a digest function. The primary benefit over the private-key counterpart is that there are no key distribution problems. This method does assume that you can trust the source that publishes the public key (see Section 11.3.1). A recipient may then utilize the public key to decrypt the signature or file and verify its origin and/or contents. Recall that due to the intrica-cies of public-key cryptography (Figure 11.4), only the proper public key will decrypt the message or the digest. Finally, if you are sending a message to someone with a known public key, you may encrypt the message or the digest with the recipient's public key so that only the recipient can verify the contents by utilizing their own private-key.

11.2 AUTHENTICATION

There are several steps necessary in providing authentication in a distributed environment. The first step is authenticating or verifying the identity of a user. There are three basic methods for accomplishing this [Sha77, WL92]. First, one may verify a user by something that is known by the user such as a password, the most popular method although not necessarily the most secure. The second method involves something that is possessed by a user, such as a key. The third method involves something the user is, such as the user's fingerprints or retina patterns, the most secure and expensive method. Observe that up until this point, these methods are all possible to use on a centralized system as well. A distributed operating system must also accommodate the following concerns.

1. *Eavesdropping*: How do we prevent someone from eavesdropping on the communication line?

2. *Multiple password management*: If we are accessing multiple systems, does every system keep a copy of the user ID and password? Every database storing authentication information is a target for a system security loophole. Furthermore, do we need to present our password everytime we want to accomplish something?

3. *Replay*: Someone could copy authentication information while it is transmitted on the network, even if it is encrypted, and replay it at a later time, thus allowing inappropriate access.

4. *Trust*: Should authentication be unilateral or should the user be able to verify and have confidence that the service being utilized is legitimate as well. A centralized system trusts itself; a distributed system has to find a way to trust others.

A common solution to these concerns is using one of the certificate management systems. A certificate is a computer-generated, frequently time-valid, authenticated packet of information utilized in distributed systems to allow easy access to the various resources. The time-valid feature helps prevent replay at a later time. This may be accomplished with a timestamp or with a nonce. A **nonce** is a random value unique for each communication. Thus, no two communications share a nonce and replays are easy to detect. There are two basic approaches to certificate management. The first approach, presented in Section 11.2.1, involves utilizing certificate lists that contain a list of certificates from a trusted certificate authority and is exemplified by X.509. Any service wishing to verify an identity must examine a list to verify the authenticity of the client. The second approach, presented in Section 11.2.2, involves a centralized certificate distribution center where clients obtain a certificate for each service that the user they wish to use. The client then presents this service certificate when utilizing a service.

11.2.1 Certificate Lists

Certificate lists are based on pubic-key cryptography, as presented in Section 11.1.2. The identifying information of the users is referred to as a **certificate** and may be contained in a **certificate list**. The authentication authorities verifying the identities of the users are referred to as certificate authorities and verify the user's public-keys. Figure 11.6 depicts how a service such as RPC may utilize a certificate list.

The certificates are authenticated by the certificate authority's digital signature as described in Section 11.1. There may be several certificate authorities. We now examine how certificate lists function by looking at X.509 as an example.

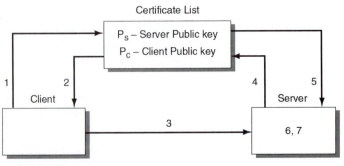

1. Request P_s
2. Receive P_s
3. Send $P_s (R_c (RPC\ MSG))$
   Where Rc is the client's private key
4. Request P_c
5. Receive P_c
6. Apply R_s to $P_s (Rc (RPC\ MSG))$ where
   R_s is the server's private key
   resulting in $R_c (RPC\ MSG)$
7. Apply P_c to $R_c (RPC\ MSG)$ resulting in RPC MSG

Figure 11.6   Certificate List Utilized in Secure RPC.

X.509

X.509 is the authentication portion of the X.500 directory service discussed in Chapter 7. The directory service provides the location for the certificate lists but assumes that a trusted certificate authority exists to create these certificates. The certificates are signed by the issuer (encrypted with the issuer's private key) to bind the certificate holder's name with the issuer's public-key. The following is a list of the elements contained in an X.509 certificate (version 1).

V: Version; the version differentiates among successive versions of X.509. The default is the 1988 version.

SN: Serial number; the serial number is an integer value that is unique within the issuing certificate authority. The serial number is unambiguously associated with a certificate the same way that a Social Security number is unambiguously associated with a U.S. Citizen or immigrant.

AI: Algorithm identifier; the algorithm identifier identifies the algorithm used to sign certificate's by the certificate authority. The certificate authority signs each certificate with its private key.

CA: Issuer or certificate authority; the certificate authority is the one that created this certificate.

T$_{A}$: Period of validity; provides the first and last date it is valid, similar to a credit card's date.

A: Subject; whose identity the certificate verifies.

Ap: Public-key information; provides the public-key and algorithm identifier for the subject identified by the certificate.

Signature: The certificate signature covers all other fields of the certificate. The signature is a hash code of other fields and is encrypted with the certificate authority's private key to ensure the integrity of the information in the entire certificate. If one uses the certificate authority's public key to decrypt the hash code and computes the hash code for the certificate and they do not match, a portion of the certificate has been illegitimately altered.

Any user with the certificate authority's public key can recover and verify the authenticity of each certificate in the certificate list. X.509 provides three procedures for authentication using these certificate lists: one-way authentication, two-way authentication, and three-way authentication.

One-Way Authentication

One-way authentication protects the integrity and originality of a message. This is accomplished when someone signs a timestamp, nonce value, and identity of the destination with the usesr's signature (private-key). The receiver may then verify the information by "unsigning" the information with the originator's public key as verified in the certificate list. Since only the destination is authenticating, this is referred to as one-way authentication.

Two-Way Authentication

Two-way authentication allows the receiver or destination also to be verified by the originator or sender. In addition to going through one-way authentication, the destination sends a reply to the originator. This reply includes a new timestamp, the original nonce, and a new nonce. This reply is then signed with the originator's public-key. Recall that in public-key cryptography only the corresponding private key, or the originator's private key can decrypt the reply. Furthermore, the nonce must be the original nonce or the message is not authentic.

Three-Way Authentication

Three-way authentication is employed when the destination and originator do not have synchronized clocks or do not wish to trust the clocks. In addition to going through two-way authentication, the originator then sends a reply to the reply of the destination including the new nonce contained in the original reply, as shown in Figure 11.7. Upon verifying the matching nonce values, there is no longer a need to verify timestamps.

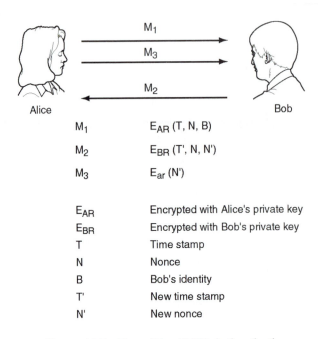

M₁	E_{AR} (T, N, B)
M₂	E_{BR} (T', N, N')
M₃	E_{ar} (N')

E_{AR}	Encrypted with Alice's private key
E_{BR}	Encrypted with Bob's private key
T	Time stamp
N	Nonce
B	Bob's identity
T'	New time stamp
N'	New nonce

Figure 11.7 Three-Way X.509 Authentication.

Revoking Certificates

One potential problem with certificate lists involves revoking a certificate prior to the expiration time of the certificate. This is accomplished by maintaining a revocation list. This list is kept along with the certificate list and must be consulted to ensure that the certificate is still valid. This is similar to the old-fashioned credit card books that maintained a list of credit cards that were invalid prior to their expiration date. The revocation list does contain a message digest that is digitally signed with the certificate authority's private key to maintain and ensure the integrity of this list.

Using Multiple Certificate Authorities in X.509

Another potential problem is the existence of multiple certificate authorities. However, you may verify the identity of someone who uses a different certificate authority if the appropriate certificate authority is listed with your authority. To do this, you must verify the other authority's identity with your authority. Once this is accomplished, you have the other authority's public key and you may verify the identity of anyone listed with the other authority as displayed in Figure 11.8. This is referred to as chaining certificate authorities and may be compared to the mathematical transitive principle. If Alice knows Certificate Authority 1 and Certificate Authority 1 knows Certificate Authority 2 who knows Certificate Authority N, who knows Steven, Alice knows Steven.

How Alice verifies Steven's public key

1. Alice knows certificate authority 1
2. Certificate authority 1 knows certificate authority 2
3. Certificate authority 2 knows certificate authority N
4. Certificate authority N knows Steven
5. Conclusion: Alice can trust and knows Steven public key

Figure 11.8 Chaining Certificate Authorities in X.509.

Classes of Certificates

Finally, X.509 provides for different classes of certificates. Each class has passed a different degree of verification and thus reflects the level of reliability of the authentication information in the certificate lists.

The lowest level is Class 1. For a Class 1 certificate, the identity was verified by the subject providing an Email address and the authority sending a reply to this Email address. At the other end of the spectrum is Class 4, which requires physical presentation of the subject and the certificate authority must perform a background check. X.509 certificates may be employed within the protocol known as secure socket layer (SSL) as described in Detail Box 11.5.

11.2.2 Centralized Certificate Distribution Center

A centralized certificate distribution center relies on one site to manage the distribution of all of the certificates. Thus, the certificate distribution center becomes a critical element in the distributed system. If the certificate distribution center crashes or is compromised, the entire distributed system suffers. This site maintains a copy of the private keys for all valid users and services of the system in the certificate database manager. The certificate distribution center uses these private keys to distribute system and service certificates to the users for each service they wish to utilize. These service certificates must be presented by the client to use a service. There is a unique service certificate for each user and for each service. These service certificates parallel the capability security concept in centralized systems. Thus, a single user may have several service certificates, and these service certificates must be presented to use a service. Service certificates are only valid for a limited time and a particular service. If a user's service certificate has expired, the user must obtain a new service certificate from the certificate distribution center using the user's system certificate. We now examine how a centralized certificate distribution center functions by examining Kerberos version 5.

DETAIL BOX 11.5
SECURE SOCKET LAYER

SSL began at Netscape for secure communication through Web pages and is supported by most browsers. Most recently, WinSock now includes SSL. The Internet Engineering Task Force (IETF) formally developed the SSL standard. Its goals are to ensure privacy, integrity, as well as authenticity. Applications may range from the original domain within browsers to developing secure transmissions among corporations collaborating on a project and wishing secure communication. The use of SSL allows two entities to communicate over a public network in a somewhat (depending on the key length) secure manner and without much reworking of code that may already exist. This option is most likely more cost effective and more efficient than purchasing and utilizing a dedicated line connection.

SSL consist of three phases. The first phase is the authentication handshake and accomplishes the following tasks.

1. It establishes the protocol the two will employ to communicate.
2. Define the encryption algorithm.
3. They determine if data compression will be utilized.
4. They exchange keys.
5. They may verify the identity of each using X.509 certificates including the ability to chain X.509 certificates.

The second phase the actual communication of the data takes place. This data is transmitted in an encrypted manner, as determined in phase 1. In addition, each block of data is digitally signed generally employing DES. The final phase simply consists of performing an additional handshake to ensure both are aware the connection is closing and, finally, closing the connection. Generally, SSL is employed using a 40-bit key as current U.S. trade restrictions prohibit larger keys for export.

Kerberos v.5

Kerberos was the first distributed authentication protocol in widespread use and influenced many of the later protocols, such as SESAME and KryptoKnight. It is available free from ftp://athena-dis.mit.edu/pub/kerberos and is described in [NeTs94]. Its purpose is to provide a trusted third-party authentication system. By using a third party, every location involved in the distributed system was relieved of keeping a complex database of user ids and passwords. Instead, Kerberos kept a single master database of authentication information referred to as the Kerberos database management system (KDBM). The KDBM was assisted by several possible Kerberos key distribution services, which contained read-only copies of the master database and helped avoid a bottleneck at the KDBM. The Kerberos key distribution services also allowed the system to function if the KDBM was temporarily unreachable. The Kerberos system involves the following four phases, which are further described in Detail Box 11.6.

Phase 0: Registering with Kerberos

Before any user may establish a session, the identify of the user must first be established off-line to the Kerberos key distribution center. Once this is accomplished, user's ID and password are stored in an encrypted manner in the Kerberos database manager. At this point, the user is considered registered and is prepared to utilize the network services through the Kerberos protocol.

Phase 1: Obtaining a System Ticket

Kerberos certificates for authentication are referred to as tickets. Phase 1 involves obtaining a system ticket, which may be used to obtain service tickets from the ticket granting service (TGS) in Phase 2. To obtain a system certificate, one must be registered with Kerberos (Phase 0). The Kerberos system ticket obtained is encrypted with TGS's special private key. This system ticket contains identification information for the client, including the following.

- A temporary session key for use between the TGS and client
- The client identity
- The identity of the TGS
- Expiration time of the ticket
- The network address of the client

The ticket is encrypted by Kerberos so that only the TGS can verify that the system ticket is valid. An invalid ticket would not be encrypted with TGS's private key, which only Kerberos and the TGS know. The system ticket is sent to the client along with the identity of the TGS, a session key created by Kerberos for the TGS and client to use, and returns the nonce value that the client sent to Kerberos. If the nonce value matches the value sent to Kerberos, the client knows the system ticket is legitimate and new.

Phase 2: Obtaining a Service Ticket

To obtain a service ticket, a client sends a packet to the TGS encrypted with the session key that the client shares with the TGS. This packet includes the client's name, network address, a nonce value, and the name of the service the client wishes to use. In addition, the system ticket is sent unencrypted.

When the TGS decrypts the system ticket with its key, it verifies that the information in the system certificate matches the information in the packet received. If they match, the TGS can be sure that this is a valid request. Given that the request is valid, the TGS prepares a packet for the client. This packet includes a service ticket encrypted with the private-key of the service (thus, only the service can verify the ticket), the name of the service, an expiration time, and the nonce. This packet is encrypted with the client's and the serverice's shared session key. If the nonce values match, the client knows this is the appropriate reply. We now have a key to use a specific service listed with Kerberos.

DETAIL BOX 11.6
KERBEROS AUTHENTICATION SERVICE V.5

Let

ID_T = Ticket Granting Service's ID
ID_c = Client's ID
ID_s = Server's ID
N_i = Nonce value
K_c = Client's private-key
K_s = Application Server's ID
K_T = Ticket Granting Server's private-key
K_1 = System Ticket
K_2 = Service Ticket
T_s = Starting time stamp
T_e = Ending time stamp
$E(a,K)$ = Applications of encryption algorithm to a with key K.

Phase 1 is depicted in Figure 11.9, Phase 2 in Figure 11.10, and Phase 3 in Figure 11.11.

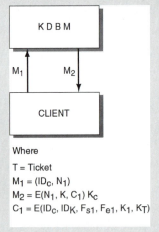

Where
T = Ticket
$M_1 = (ID_c, N_1)$
$M_2 = E(N_1, K, C_1) K_c$
$C_1 = E(ID_c, ID_K, F_{s1}, F_{e1}, K_1, K_T)$

Figure 11.9   Kerberos Phase 1 Details.

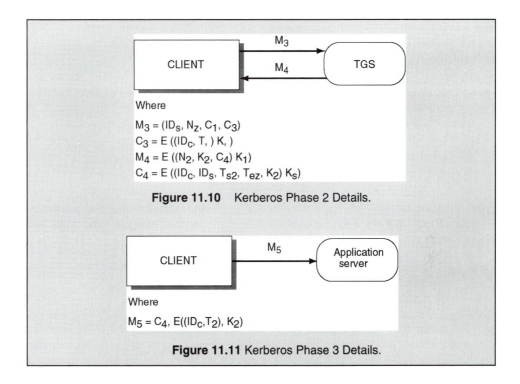

Where

$M_3 = (ID_S, N_z, C_1, C_3)$
$C_3 = E ((ID_C, T,) K,)$
$M_4 = E ((N_2, K_2, C_4) K_1)$
$C_4 = E ((ID_C, ID_S, T_{s2}, T_{ez}, K_2) K_s)$

Figure 11.10   Kerberos Phase 2 Details.

Where

$M_5 = C_4, E((ID_C, T_2), K_2)$

Figure 11.11 Kerberos Phase 3 Details.

Phase 3: Employing Mediated Services

Now the client has a service ticket and is ready to use a service. This service ticket allows the service to authenticate or verify the identity of the client. To use a service, a client sends a packet to a service, including the service ticket and the client's identity. Recall that the service ticket is encrypted with the service's private-key and contains the client's identity and timestamp. If the timestamp has not expired and the identity matches, the client is authenticated and free to employ the service.

11.3 ACCESS CONTROL (FIREWALLS)

While open distributed systems are designed to allow the free flow of information between all the systems attached to the network, a distributed operating system must provide access control so that only the information we intend on sharing is, in fact, shared. Furthermore, the needs of one system may not be the needs of another system. A corporation may follow a security policy stating "anything not explicitly allowed is not allowed" and a university or private site might follow the other extreme. Specifically, "anything not explicitly disallowed is okay." Frequently, while access control is an operating system concept, the distributed operating systems of today must rely on hardware assistance. In either case, access control in current distributed systems is generally accomplished by what is known as a **firewall**.

A firewall should be immune to security threats and prevent all security threats from passing through the wall and to the system(s) it protects. Firewalls should not prevent activities that conform to the security policy of the organization.

Firewalls generally fit into one of the following two categories.

1. Packet-filtering gateways

2. Proxy services

Frequently, a location may employ both types of firewalls to realize the desired access control. We examine each of the two basic categories of firewalls and then examine some of the basic firewall architectures incorporating both types.

11.3.1 Packet Filtering Gateways

A packet-filtering gateway firewall involves a security engineer who must explicitly state what may pass through the wall. This includes what internal information may go out of the firewall as well as what outside locations are allowed through the firewall. Furthermore, the security engineer may configure the firewall to specify what internal computer services may be shared with the outside world.

Packet-filtering gateway firewalls are generally implemented on the router that connects the internal system to the outside world. While general routers can perform packet-filtering functions, firewall routers tend to provide a better user interface and are generally easier to configure for security-based filtering. Just as the postal services around the world require addresses on envelopes, networks require messages to have addresses. It is these addresses that this type of firewall checks against its list before allowing a message to pass through in either direction. Since all messages must pass through the router that functions as a firewall, all messages are checked by the firewall.

The rules of a packet filter gateway might be as depicted in Table 11.3.

Action	Destination Address	Destination Port	Source Address	Source Port
Deny	us.net		Enemy.net	
Allow	us.net		Friend.net	

Table 11.3 Packet Filter Gateway Rules.

These rules deny anything to us.net coming in from enemy.net on any of our ports or connections to the network. Furthermore, they allow anything to us.net coming from friend.net on any port. The exact syntax varies and depends on the particular router and its manufacturer. Regardless of the manufacturer, the security engineer setting up the system must explicitly state everything that is allowed or disallowed. This is not always easy to decide or specify. Some services, such as the UNIX X11 window manager, are desirable to the internal users; however, if someone internally can use X11, external usage cannot be prohibited. An unauthorized X11 user may conduct screen dumps and record keystrokes of internal users, which is a very serious security threat. Finally, any loopholes left in the firewall may be penetrated and defeat the security and protection of your system.

11.3.2 Proxy Services

A proxy service represents an internal client's service to the outside world. While it is representing this service, it may act a little differently to increase security. There are two basic types of proxy services.

1. Application-level gateway proxy services, and
2. Circuit-level gateway proxy services

An application-level gateway firewall provides access control by rewriting all major applications. The new applications reside on centralized hosts that everyone must utilize. These hosts are referred to as **bastion hosts,** named after highly fortified medieval castles and are considered the critical security points. These hosts are frequently **dual-homed hosts** or hosts that reside on more than one network. The applications seem to function in the same manner as their original applications except that the security loopholes are removed. Specifically, the new applications involve one small but important added feature: authentication by one of the methods discussed previously in this chapter. Application gateway firewalls are excellent complements to packet filter gateways and could be used to rewrite applications such as X11.

Circuit-level gateways are similar to application-level gateways in that they are designed for an individual application. Unlike application-level gateways, they are transparent to the users. Specifically, an outsider may connect to a network through TCP ports. In circuit-level gateways, the firewall provides the TCP port and relays the bytes back and forth, acting like a wire and thus completing the circuit without ever interpreting the application protocol.

Since they operate at a lower level, circuit-level gateways need to modify the client to obtain the destination address, which is otherwise readily available for application-level gateways. Frequently, the modified clients are used only for external connections. All filtering is conducted based solely on source and destination without additional information on the specific commands.

In addition to relaying the bytes, the modified client and, thus, the circuit-level gateway keeps a log of the number of bytes relayed as well as the TCP destination. If there is a known site that has had a security problem, the system administrator could use this log to notify anyone on the system who has unfortunately connected to the corrupted site.

11.3.3 Firewall Architectures

We now examine three basic firewall architectures incorporating packet-filtering firewalls and proxy-service firewalls.

Bastion Host Architecture

The simplest architecture is that of a bastion host. This design exclusively utilizes a bastion host to provide proxy-services. While the host is capable of routing information from one network to another, this feature of the host is not recommended for it may be abused and ultimately used to circumvent your firewall. All local systems are considered internal systems. All nonlocal systems are considered external systems. The bastion host is a dual-homed host that resides between the internal and external systems. It is not directly on either network but operates as a gateway between the networks. All internal systems can communicate with the bastion host and all external systems can communicate with the same bastion host. The internal and external systems may not communicate directly with each other but communicate by having the host proxy the services on each other's behalf, as depicted in Figure 11.12. If the host receives a packet of information on its external connection with an internal address, that packet must be fraudulent. This architecture exhibits all the weaknesses of proxy-service firewalls, including the limitations of what services they may provide.

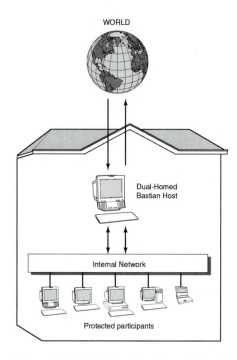

Figure 11.12   Bastion Host Firewall Architecture.

Filtering Host Architecture

The filtering host architecture utilizes a bastion host with proxy services and a router acting as a screen and providing packet-filtering capabilities. Unlike the previous architecture, the bastion host resides on the internal network, as depicted in Figure 11.13.

The packet-filtering capabilities on the filtering router route all permissible external traffic with internal destinations to the bastion host. Furthermore, the packet-filter may be configured to allow only the bastion host external access. If internal hosts other than the bastion host are denied access to the packet-filtering router, the internal hosts are forced to use the proxy services of the bastion host to reach external hosts. Thus, a site with strong security requirements would likely disallow internal hosts access to external network directly through the packet-filtering firewall.

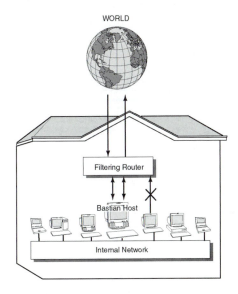

Figure 11.13   Filtering Host Firewall Architecture.

Filtering Subnet Architecture

The most secure of the three firewall architectures is the filtering subnet architecture. This architecture involves two packet-filtering firewalls and a proxy-service firewall. The proxy-service firewall or bastion host is connected to its own network situated between the two packet-filtering firewalls. One packet-filtering firewall connects the bastion host's subnet to the external network. The other packet-filtering firewall connects the bastion host's subnet to the internal network, as depicted in Figure 11.14.

The subnet with access to the external network is referred to as a filtering subnet. Since it is possible on most local area networks for any host on the network to 'snoop' or see all traffic on the network, the major benefit of this architecture is the lack of internal-only information on the filtering

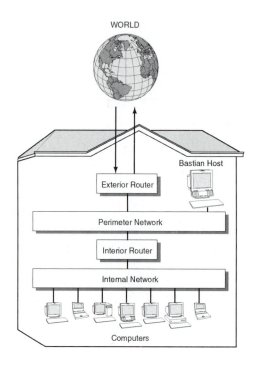

Figure 11.14   Filtering Subnet Firewall Architecture.

subnet. Thus, an intruder would have to bypass the external packet-filtering router, compromise the bastion host, and bypass the internal packet-filtering router to compromise the access control.

11.4 SUMMARY

This chapter discussed security methods added on to an already secure isolated system when attached to a network. Like centralized systems, distributed security involves both authentication and access control. In addition, distributed systems need to consider the use of encryption and digital signatures. One must always keep in mind the value of what is being protected when determining what methods to employ. Furthermore, one must consider the time frame of the information. For example, Microsoft™ assumably no longer worries if someone knows they *were* planning on releasing Windows95™ since it has already been released. However, when this product was first conceived and during its planning and development, this information was obviously important and had to remain very secure. With this in mind, a given system on a network may choose only to employ a packet-filtering gateway while others *also* choose to utilize a proxy server. Likewise, not all systems maintain information worthy of the complexity and expense to utilize a Class 4 certificate authority. However, a company such as Equifax, which maintains extensive credit databases on U.S. citizens, chooses to utilize isolated networks and considers any risk of connection to outside networks too great despite all available technology in distributed security. In summary, just like standard operating systems on isolated computers, it is possible to achieve a high level of security; however, there are no 100% guarantees.

11.5 REFERENCES FOR FURTHER STUDY

The following references can provide more general information on distributed security: [Bra95, Car95, ChBe94, ChZw95, KPS95, McC98, Pfl97, Pow95, Sta95, and Wil94]. Some appropriate traditional research papers concerning information in this chapter include [ABCLMN98, AbPo86, ADFS98, AGS83, AJP95, And94, BAN90, BBF83, BFMV84, ClHo94, DH76, DESA81, DoMc98, Erick93a, Hel78, Klu94, LABW94, Lai92, Nes83, NeTs94, NIST77, NIST93B, NIST94a, NIST94b, Opp97, Opp98, PaSh98, RSA78, RuGe98, Schn98, Sim92, Sha77, THPSW98, and WoLa92].

The following provide some great starting points for sources on the Internet concerning security issues. An extensive list of security related links can be found at http://www.semper.org/sirene/outsideworld/security.html. This site includes links to standards and protocols, and alert sites among many other resources. By sending Email to rsaref@rsa.com, one can receive information on how to obtain RSAREF. RSAREF is a free (only available to U.S. and Canadian Citizens) educational tool, written in C, which handles RSA encryption and key generation, DES, Diffie-Hellman key agreement, and Triple DES among other features. The Kerberos Request for Comments: 1510 document can be found online at ftp://ftp.isi.edu/in-notes/rfc1510.txt. Information on how to retrieve (the free) Kerberos software can be found at http://web.mit.edu/kerberos/www/krb5-1.0/announce.html. A list of Kerberos Papers and Documentation can be found at http://nii.isi.edu/info/kerberos/ documentation.html. The source code and information about obtaining Sesame, a distributed access control program that builds upon and expands Kerberos, can be found at http://www.esat.kuleuven.ac.be/~vdwauver/sesame.html. A free version of SSL along with pointers to references on SSL can be found at http://psych.psy.uq.oz.au/~ftp/Crypto/. A set of links to algorithms and standards for cryptography-related information can be found at http://www.ssh.fi/tech/crypto/.

EXERCISES

11.1   What are some of the additional security concerns presented to a distributed system? Is it possible to provide the same level of security as compared to an isolated centralized system?

11.2   Discuss the advantages and disadvantages of symmetric encryption and asymmetric key encryption.

11.3   Using the RSA public-key encryption algorithm presented in Section 11.1, let P = 7, Q = 11 and e = 4.

    a.   Compute the value of D.
    b.   What is the public key?
    c.   If the message is M = 17, what is the encrypted message that is sent?
    d.   Verify the message by decrypting it using the public key.
    e.   Calculate the shared key in Detail Box 11.4.

11.5   Write a program that implements the Diffie-Hellman key exchange algorithm described in Detail Box 11.4.

Option 1: Allow both Alice and Bob to use the same terminal and exchange keys. Allow the program to choose your random numbers.

Option 2: Have the user be Alice and the program be Bob. Allow Alice and Bob to exchange numeric messages.

Option 3: Use an IPC mechanism studied in Chapter 4 to allow two users on different computers to exchange keys and numeric messages.

Option 4: Allow the user to select any of the preceding three mode options.

11.6   Discuss the relative advantages of one-way, two-way, and three-way authentication in X.509.

11.7   Discuss a potential use for each of the following X.509 authentication procedures.

    a.   One-way authentication
    b.   Two-way authentication
    c.   Three-way authentication

11.8   Describe one viable algorithm for exchanging messages to accomplish phase 1 of SSL using four keys and allowing each to validate the other's identity (a public key of a given user is counted separately from the private key of the same user).

11.9   Discuss the relative advantages and disadvantages of using a certificate list versus a certificate distribution center for distributed authentication.

11.10 What are the advantages of having several key distribution services in Kerberos?

11.11 In a centralized system, it is common to utilize an access matrix whose rows represent the users (or collection of users) and the columns represent the resources (also defined in varying degrees of granularity). The information within the matrix defines if and to what extent a user has the privilege to utilize a resource. Describe some of the complications that might occur when implementing an access matrix for a distributed system for each of the following options.

a. Implemented on a single centralized server.
b. Implemented with multiple copies of the matrix throughout the distributed system (Hint: Think Chapter 7).

11.12 Some locations prefer to utilize multiple bastion hosts. Discuss some of the advantages of this approach.

11.13 Of the three firewall architectures presented in this chapter, which is the most secure and why?

11.14 While it is generally considered OK to utilize multiple exterior routers in the screened subnet firewall architecture, it is considered a serious security risk to utilize several interior routers. Why?

11.15 Inherent in the use of cable modems for home access is the cable modem architecture, which involves a single cable going in and out of each home in a neighborhood (much like a pearl necklace) and turning the neighborhood into a virtual LAN.

a. What basic security problems could this implementation present and why?
b. Give an example of how corporate security could be compromised due to cable modem Internet access in the home.

11.16 Password cards, known by many proprietary names, are credit card like password token generators. The exact token is dependent on the current time and the identify of the card. The token generated and the identity of the appropriate owner together constitute proper authority. Such a card may be used for authentication in terms of access to a system or a building. Based on the material you have learned about synchronization as well as the information you have learned in this chapter, name two advantages and two disadvantages (or complications) that could be associated with the implementation of a password cards security system. Why is this type of technology crucial in an environment when data are transported insecurely over networks?

11.17 Distributed security frequently is faced with a tradeoff between being effective and being easy to use. Discuss four examples that show this dichotomy might exist.

CASE STUDY: Windows 2000™

Windows 2000 is built on Windows NT technology and was referred to as Windows NT 5.0 in its early development stages. A significant focus point of the popular Windows product's mission statement is to support distributed computing, therefore making it a likely and wise choice to evaluate as an example of a distributed operating system. In 1989, Microsoft's NT's Subsystem Design Rationale declared that Windows NT would be a portable operating system that would be flexible, robust, secure (over time), and easy to maintain. One of Windows 2000's contributions is its incorporation and adoption of more standards conducive to interoperability with other systems, thereby increasing its ability to function as a distributed operating system. Some of these features which will be explored within this case study, include the following.

- Microkernel design
- Hardware abstraction layer
- Plug and play
- NT file System
- Active directory and the use of LDAP and DNS
- Change journal
- Index server and its compatibility with HTTP

◆ Microsoft management console

◆ Cluster service

◆ Security configuration editor

◆ Encrypted file system

◆ Microsoft security support provider interface and its ability to work with DES and RSA

◆ Incorporation of DCOM

While there are many different components to Windows 2000, few people realize that there are actually four Windows 2000 operating systems.

1. Windows 2000 Professional, which is a replacement to NT workstation.

2. Windows 2000 Server, which functions as a replacement to NT Server that offers a slight superset. This version is meant to support applications such as web servers.

3. Windows 2000 Advanced Server, which provides substantial support for network and distributed computing, including cluster technology and load-balancing support.

4. Windows 2000 Datacenter server, the largest superset, which supports up to 64 GB of physical memory.

In this case study, we examine the entire superset of Windows 2000 technology, Windows 2000 advanced server and datacenter server. The information in this case study is abstracted from Microsoft's white paper series on Windows NT, including Windows 2000 and related technologies [Micr98]. At the time this book went to print, the full production version of Windows 2000 was not available to evaluate fully. The second Beta version and, thus, the upcoming production release incorporates some significant changes including the incorporation of plug and play, active directory, Microsoft management console, and distributed security extensions. Some reference to previous releases is included in this study for historical context. Section 12.1 expands on the design goals of Windows 2000 base technology while Section 12.2 presents an overview of the Windows 2000 microkernel, including information on Windows 2000's address space. Section 12.3 presents Windows 2000's implementation of plug and play. The Windows 2000 files system is presented in Section 12.4 and the Active Directory is presented in Section 12.5. The Microsoft management console is the subject of Section 12.6. Windows 2000's cluster technology, available in Windows 2000 advanced server, is presented in Section 12.7, while Section 12.8 focuses on Windows 2000's security-based features. Section 12.9 presents a brief overview of the thin client, code named Hydra.

12.1 OVERVIEW: WINDOWS 2000 DESIGN

There are five primary design goals for Microsoft Windows 2000 operating system inherited from its base technology, Windows NT. In this section, we present these goals
and discuss how these goals are addressed within the design. The first goal is robustness. Most would agree, relative to other Windows operating systems, the Windows NT
family of operating systems is more robust. The specific concerns relative to a robust
system involved the system's ability to protect against internal malfunctions as well as
accidental and deliberate external malfunctions relative to the operating system. This is
beneficial to a system intended to be distributed and therefore connected to a network
and possibly subjected to external events. For a system to be robust, it must act in a
predictable manner and be based upon well-specified interfaces and system behavior.
The following are five decisions made by Microsoft to help ensure the goal of robustness.

1. The kernel mode exports well-defined application programming interfaces
   (APIs) that attempt to minimize the need for parameters and "magic
   flags" when programming. This decision was made to increase the ease
   of which applications may be implemented, tested, and documented.

2. The entire system was formally designed, and that design was documented *prior* to coding.

3. Major components, such as Win32, OS/2, and POSIX, were partitioned
   into separate subsystems. This simple yet elegant design allowed each
   subsystem to focus on implementing only those features required by its
   API set.

4. Windows NT and its subsystem employed frame-based exception han-
   dlers, thereby allowing efficient identification of programming errors and
   bad/ inaccessible parameters in a reliable yet efficient manner.

5. Perhaps one of the most noticeable decisions is that of dividing the operating system into kernel mode systems services and subsystems. The
   result of this decision is that a poorly behaved application should not be
   able to crash the operating system.

The second design goal of Windows NT-based technology involves extensibility
and maintainability. It is hoped that the design of this system will be able to accommodate the needs of computers, computer-related manufacturers including Microsoft itself,
and original equipment manufacture (OEM) applications and users for the foreseeable
future. With this in mind, perhaps it is no coincidence that Windows 2000 is designed
to support distributed computing. The following are five decisions made to help ensure
the second goal.

1. The design of the system is simple and well documented. The system was developed utilizing a common coding standard. Thus, the common need to depend on "folklore" to maintain the system has been removed.

2. Each major portion of the system is implemented as a subsystem, thereby increasing the ability of Windows 2000 to isolate and control dependencies. As a result, if there were changes to POSIX, only the POSIX subsystem would require changes. A new subsystem could be added to increase the portability of the system and allow additional component types within a distributed environment without affecting existing participants who deployed earlier versions without the subsystem.

3. The subsystem design allows an additional subsystem. This addition does not require any changes to the base subsystem or the executive. This type of design should eliminate or at least greatly reduce the ability of future modifications to create unwanted system side effects in previously functioning applications, thereby adversely impacting the system. This is also helpful when operating in a distributed environment where not all components are guaranteed to be updated simultaneously if updated at all.

4. Every subsystem can be coded to take advantage of the security features of Windows 2000, as described in Section 12.8.

5. Each subsystem must validate or ensure the correctness of all arguments on which it operates. This is accomplished by capturing its values and examining the argument at appropriate points. Generally, this probing should be conducted at the outset, particularly where pointers are concerned. The practice of validating arguments in this manner ensures that the caller or one of its threads is prevented from dynamically altering or deleting the argument's value following a read. While the benefits are apparent, explicit capture is not as common as it may appear as arguments are frequently passed in registers. If an argument is passed in memory, it is probed and captured by the system service dispatcher.

The third goal is portability, an important goal for a distributed system that may operate on numerous types of heterogeneous platforms. Specifically, it is hoped that the system architecture allows its operation on a number of different hardware platforms with minimal re-coding. This benefits not only the users but also Microsoft, which may then utilize its resources in going forward and adding features or developing new products versus reworking the system for new platforms after its initial release.

The fourth design goal is that of performance. The primary focus to achieve a high level of performance was that of the choice of algorithms and related data structures. In addition, choices made to achieve high-level performance must not interfere with the system's ability to remain flexible.

The fifth and final goal of Windows NT-based technology involves two parts. First, it is desired to utilize a POSIX-compliant API. POSIX compliance allows applications to be easily ported from one platform such as Windows 2000, to another such as UNIX or, possibly even more important for Microsoft, port from UNIX to Windows 2000. The decision to make Windows 2000 POSIX-compliant, which involves UNIX-style interfaces, will probably be considered a landmark decision due to the widespread implications for the entire industry. In particular, while a distributed application attempting to execute in non-POSIX compliant system must handle various APIs, the same application in a POSIX-compliant environment is not faced with such heterogeniality and can be greatly simplified. Of course, one would generally assume that this simplification would also reduce the likelihood of errors. In addition, some government contracts require POSIX compliance. The actual subsystem design implements both an OS/2 and POSIX API as protected subsystems in a client/server architecture outside of the actual Windows NT executive. The subsystem design employed for Windows NT-based technology, unlike preliminary draft NT designs that included the APIs within the executive, is able to support each of Windows 2000's design goals.

The second portion of the final goal concerns government C2 certification. This certification requires a system to include security features, such as an auditing capability, access detection, resource quotas on a per-user basis, as well as resource protection. Without these features and C2 certification, Windows 2000 could not be used in all government operations. Of course, while some business applications may not be involved with the government and therefore are not required to employ a C2 certifiable systems, businesses may still desire such certification.

12.2 KERNEL MODE OVERVIEW

As indicated in Chapter 2, Windows 2000 is implemented with a microkernel design. Chapter 2 focused on issues related to kernel designs, while many features of Windows NT related to this design were presented in Section 12.1. An overview of this information is presented in Table 12.1. Figure 12.1 depicts the organization of these services in Windows NT version 3.51 and earlier. Likewise, Figure 12.2 depicts the organization of these services as of Windows NT 4.0. The primary modifications to this architecture involve the implementation of plug and play as a user mode service. The architecture for Windows 2000 is presented in Figure 12.3. As depicted, Windows 2000 has a kernel that is logically divided into two parts. The Executive, further described in Section 12.2.4, utilizes kernel objects and builds upon the Hardware Abstraction Layer and the device drivers, as described in Sections 12.2.1 through 12.2.3, respectively.

Table 12.1 Windows NT Micro-Kernel

Common to Microkernels	Windows NT-based technology Implementation
Modular design	Modular design
Known for ease of maintenance	Desired easy maintenance
Separate all architecture-dependent features	Use of separate subsystems
Limited device management	Decided to take plug and play approach
Known to be easy to extend	Desired to create a system that is easy to extend.

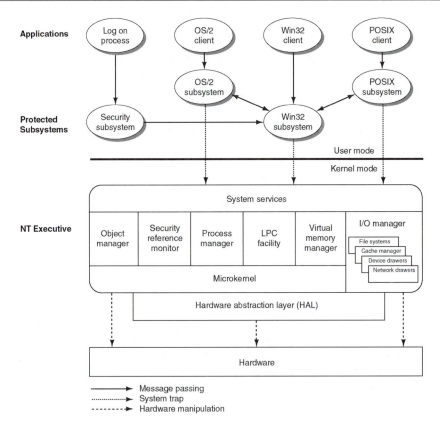

Figure 12.1   Windows NT 3.51(and earlier) Basic Architecture.

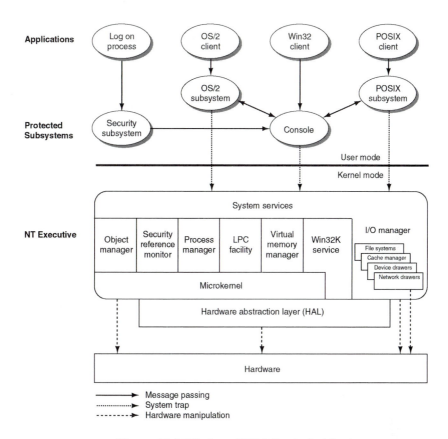

Figure 12.2 Windows NT4.0 Basic Architecture.

12.2.1 Kernel Objects

Kernel objects are a set of simple objects that support the creation of executive-level objects. Kernel objects are divided into groups depending on their functionality. Objects in the control objects group include the following.

♦ Kernel process object

♦ Deferred procedure call object (DPC)

♦ Interrupt object

Another group of objects is known as the dispatcher objects and can alter or affect thread handling. Such objects include the following.

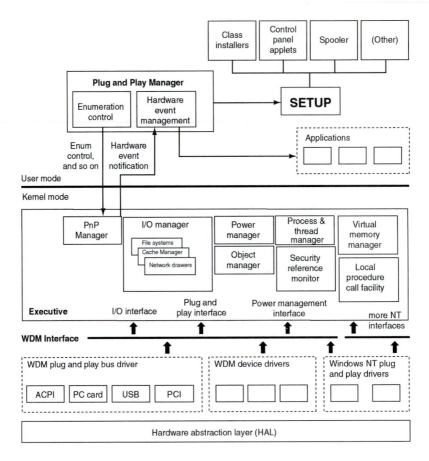

Figure 12.3   Windows 2000 Plug and Play Architecture.

- Kernel thread object
- Mutant (mutex) object
- Event object
- Kernel event pair object
- Semaphore object
- Timer object
- Waitable timer object

These objects provide well-defined, predictable primitives and mechanisms. When used in combination with the executive, more advanced mechanisms can be created. The only policies implemented at this level involve thread scheduling and dispatching.

All other policies are left to the executive, thereby allowing maximum flexibility in the design.

12.2.2 Hardware Abstraction Layer (HAL)

The hardware abstraction layer (HAL) is a loadable kernel mode module. This layer provides the interface to the actual physical hardware on which Windows 2000 is executing. Functions that are architecture specific, such as thread context switching, are implemented within the HAL of Windows 2000. All hardware-dependent details, such as I/O interfaces and interrupt controllers, are implemented in this layer. All other Windows 2000 internal components as well as all applications interface with the HAL for platform-dependent information and functionality. This design allows every aspect of the system above the HAL to operate independent of the hardware and maintain the portability necessary for a heterogeneous distributed environment.

12.2.3 Device Drivers

Device drivers are loadable kernel mode modules. Most device drivers are stored in files with the extension 'SYS'. These drivers provide an interface between the I/O system within the executive and the HAL. If implemented correctly, these device drivers will always employ HAL routines and therefore maintain the portability of the entire system. The entire manner in which devices are managed and abstracted within Windows 2000 is one area of substantial improvement over NT 4.0 due to the incorporation and support of plug and play. Due to its importance for Windows 2000, more detailed information on device drivers as well as plug and play is contained in Section 12.3.

12.2.4 The Executive

The **executive** implements the system services for Windows 2000 and requires all system services to ensure the validity of its arguments. Generally, all arguments are captured and probed at appropriate points. This always holds true for arguments that are pointers and must be probed for accessibility. These actions can prevent a caller or a caller's thread from dynamically altering an argument after its value has been verified. While this may seem like a burden to the system, most arguments are passed in registers and therefore do not require explicit capturing. An algorithm of the System Service operation is contained in Detail Box 12.1.

DETAIL BOX 12.1
SYSTEM SERVICE OPERATION

The following are the steps taken when a system service is called.

1. Trap handler gains control
2. Saves state
3. Transfers control to system service dispatcher
4. System service dispatcher obtains the address of appropriate system service
5. System service determines number of in-memory arguments (from dispatch table).
6. If the previous mode was kernel, the kernel invoked the service, and the arguments will not be bad. If the previous mode was user, the addresses are probed to ensure that references are within that user's space. If an access violation occurs, an exception is raised.

All executive objects consist of a collection of kernel objects. The following is a list of kernel-mode system services for Windows 2000.

1. *Object Manager*: The object manager creates, manages, and deletes Windows 2000 executive objects. Additional semantics and functions are available through the executive as compared to the related kernel objects.

2. *Process and Thread Manager*: The process and thread managers create and terminate all processes and threads. The process and thread managers are sometimes considered a type of object manager. Threads were a topic of discussion in Chapter 2.

3. *Security reference monitor*: This monitor is responsible for enforcing all security policies on the local computer. This responsibility extends to resources as well as performing runtime object protection and audits.

4. *Local procedure call (LPC) Facility*: The LPC facility is responsible for passing messages between client and server processes. It is a flexible and optimized version of the standard RPC discussed in Chapter 4.

5. *Virtual memory manager*: The virtual memory manager not only implements virtual memory but is also responsible for the memory management scheme in terms of private address space, protections of said space, as well as support for the underlying cache. The address space layout for Windows 2000 is described in Detail Box 12.2.

6. *I/O Manager*: The I/O manager implements all device-independent I/O requests to the appropriate device drivers. The I/O manager works with the file systems, cache manager, device drivers, and network drivers.

DETAIL BOX 12.2
ADDRESS SPACE LAYOUT

As part of the kernel design, the address space layout was designed to ensure separation of user address space from system address space. There is a 64K memory barrier between the two sections that is inaccessible to both the kernel and all users. This memory barrier allows a simple comparison against the boundary to determine a valid address. The kernel and the kernel mode own any pages in the system portion. Users own the pages in the user address space. The executive never creates a page owned by the kernel and places it in the user address space; in contrast, if a page is double mapped to a user and the kernel, it is kept in the kernel address space.

Another substantial improvement and change in Windows 2000 over NT 4.0 is the support of **very large memory** (VLM). VLM is capable of supporting 28 gigabytes of memory and allows for a 64-bit version of NT. All x86 family of processors will not be able to support VLM; however, there is a new family of architectures forthcoming from Intel in partnership with Hewlett Packard (known under the code name Merced) that allow true 64-bit Windows 2000. A true 64-bit system implies that each 64-bit process will have a single, large flat address space at least 512 gigabytes in size. This allows the accommodation of the ever-increasing storage and processing requirements of data by today and tomorrow's Microsoft-based applications. The small set of new Win32 APIs allows applications to execute through a Win32 or Win64 binary. Only VLM-enabled Win32 applications can take advantage of the full support of 64-bit pointers. Any address accessed through the 64-bit pointers must be backed by locked physical memory. Virtual memory cannot be committed to an application that is not physically available. Page faults are never taken on VLM unless those addresses are being used to map data to an actual physical file. Despite this restriction, the current implementation is still considered a significant step in the correct direction for the future and will be beneficial for data-intensive applications such as database management.

12.3 PLUG AND PLAY

Plug and play is combination of hardware and software support to provide the (semi) automated ability of Microsoft Windows 2000 to recognize and adapt to hardware configuration changes thereby permitting dynamic device changes. Furthermore, these changes do not require manual configuration or knowledge of a device's particulars but do receive automatic resource allocation from the plug and play manager. Not only should plug and play allow these dynamically changing collection of devices to work together, this feat is accomplished without significant user intervention. This feature can be beneficial for a distributed system for many reasons. One practical benefit is the workload on the system administrator. Since there are numerous devices and systems connected to the distributed system, the administrator's attention can be placed on details other than reconfiguring each system whenever a new component is added to a participant's system. In addition, plug-and-play allows the scenario for a laptop to be connected via a LAN at one moment and then shutdown and connected through a modem the next without the user's intervention of the system configuration. While not new to Windows, plug and play is new to Windows 2000 and the product line based on NT technology. An overview of plug and play's history is presented in Detail Box 12.3.

DETAIL BOX 12.3
HISTORY OF PLUG AND PLAY

Plug and play was first introduced as part of Microsoft's Windows 95. Its purpose is to simplify personal computers for end users. The Windows 95 version of plug and play relied on an advanced power management (APM) BIOS or plug and play BIOS. Both BIOS versions not only supported plug and play but also supported power management. Since that time, APM has been replaced by the advanced configuration and power interface (ACPI), which allows the operating system to control power management and new configuration capabilities. Windows 98 still supports APM for the purpose of backward compatibility.

The plug and play design consists of a layered architecture composed of drivers and their corresponding objects. We now examine each of the major components of this architecture.

The kernel mode plug and play manager is in charge of maintaining central control. Specifically, it directs bus drivers to perform enumeration and configuration of devices attached to them while directing device drivers to either add a device, start a device, or perform any other appropriate action. This manager coordinates with the user mode plug and play counterparts to pause, remove, or synchronize devices that are available for such actions when deemed necessary and appropriate by the system.

Within the kernel mode component, the power manager works in combination with the policy manager to handle the power management APIs, coordinate power events as well as generate I/O request packets (IRPs) related to power management. As an example, when the system receives several simultaneous requests to be turned off, it is the power manager that collects the requests. Upon receipt, it determines if any of the requests must be serialized or ordered and then generates the appropriate IRPs. The Policy Manager monitors system activity. Information gathered regarding the status of users, applications, and device drivers is integrated into the power policy. Upon request or under specified circumstances, the policy manager can also generate IRPs to change device power states.

The I/O manager provides the core service to the device drivers. Specifically, it is the kernel mode component that translates user mode read and writes to read or write IRPs. In addition, it manages all main system IRPs. The interfaces for the I/O manager in Windows 2000 are the same as those in Windows NT 4.0. Therefore, it is possible to install a plug and play driver in Windows NT 4.0 even though 4.0 did not support plug and play.

The Microsoft Win32 Driver Model (WDM) Interface for plug and play provides a layered architecture for drivers. This interface allows for different types of WDM drivers, driver layers, and device objects. Within the plug and play architecture, there are three basic types of drivers.

1. *Bus drivers*: Drive I/O buses as well as any device-independent per-slot functionality. A plug and play bus is any device that has other physical, logical, or vitual devices attached and may include traditional buses such as SCSI or PCI or a bus may be a parallel or RS232 port.

2. *Function drivers*: Drive individual devices.

3. *Filter drivers*: Segregate I/O requests for a device by filtering them as requests for a device, class of devices, or a bus.

Each device can have two or more driver layers: a bus driver for the related underlying I/O bus or perspective plug and play manager as well as a function driver for the device. Alternatively, a given device may utilize one or more filter drivers for the bus and/or device.

Each of the plug and play drivers create the following device objects for each device they control.

1. *Physical device objects (PDOs)*: Represent individual devices on a bus to a bus driver.

2. *Functional device objects (FDOs):* Represent individual devices to a functional driver.

3. *Filter device objects (filter DOs)*: Represent individual devices to a filter driver.

The WDM bus drivers control the bus power management as well as plug and play. WDM bus drivers are standard WDM drivers that are utilized to expose the bus capabilities. Recall that within Windows 2000, any device from which other devices are enumerated is referred to as a bus. The following is a list of the primary responsibilities of the WDM bus driver.

♦ Enumerating devices on its bus, which includes identifying devices and creating device objects for the devices

♦ Reporting the dynamic events on its bus to the system

♦ Responding to IRPs

♦ Multiplexing access to the bus when appropriate

♦ Performing any other miscellaneous duties necessary to administrate the devices on its bus

While a bus driver does perform certain operations on behalf of the devices on its bus, it does not handle the reads and writes to the devices (these are handled by the related function driver). The only exceptions relate to certain circumstances when the bus driver is incorporated into a driver that performs the duties of the bus driver as well as a function driver. Examples of such multifaceted drivers include the bus drivers for the bus controller, adapter, bridge, or an ACPI driver. For more information on ACPI, see Detail Box 12.4.

The user-mode plug and play components provide user-mode APIs for controlling and configuring devices that are 32-bit extended versions of Windows 95-based configuration manager APIs. Functionally, these APIs are a superset of the Windows 95 `SetupxDi` routines and are exclusively user mode APIs that applications can use for customized hardware event management as well the for the creation of new hardware events.

Having described the architecture, we now examine the implementation of plug and play for RS232 serial devices in Windows 2000. While previous versions of Windows required each hardware vendor to implement the detection protocol and provide a bus driver, `Serenum.sys` (for Serial enumeration) in Windows 2000 provides this functionality. When `Serenum.sys` finds hardware, it creates a PDO for the found device. Serenum.sys functions as both the bus driver and the filter driver for RS-232 devices. Since Windows 2000 implements the protocol and the driver, this design is able to enjoy all of the traditional advantages of code reuse. Traditional serial devices handled by `Serenum.sys` include mice, pointing devices, modems, digital cameras, and graphics tables. Any non-plug and play serial devices that do not utilize `Serenum.sys` require manual installation. These legacy devices with their legacy drivers function in the plug and play environment in the same manner as a legacy environment. Actually, some plug and play device installations choose not to utilize plug and play drivers; therefore, they do not enjoy optimal plug and play support. For more information on Microsoft Windows NT 4.0 handling of serial devices, see Detail Box 12.5.

DETAIL BOX 12.4
ADVANCED CONFIGURATION AND POWER INTERFACE

ACPI results from the OneNow design initiative, which seeks to define a comprehensive, system-wide approach to controlling system and device configuration and power management [Micr98]. ACPI Version 1.0 defines a new system board and BIOS. The purpose of this design is to extend plug and play data to include power management as well as additional configuration capabilities, all of which are under the complete control of the operating system

Windows 2000 is optimized for computers that include ACPI system boards. One of the primary benefits of ACPI is providing the operating system the ability to learn about devices that either cannot be enumerated in a standard manner to the bus driver or a device that is simply new (such as an embedded controller). In addition, ACPI is able to install upper-level filter drivers. This ability is useful for devices that have functionality beyond the standard for their bus, thereby providing access to this functionality. For example, if one installed a graphics controller that had power controls, not supported by the PCI bus, the ACPI driver would be able to install the upper-level filter to access this added functionality. In this manner, the ACPI can provide added flexibility to a system. This design provides advantages not only to laptops that require advanced power management but also are visible to desktop users, who will no longer be required to wait and wait upon start-up of the operating system.

DETAIL BOX 12.5
WINDOWS NT 4.0 SERIAL DEVICE DRIVERS

To allow independent hardware vendors to utilize the serial bus driver on NT 4.0, a specific order for loading all serial device drivers was required. The serial bus driver was called Serial.sys and allowed the connection of hardware on the computer to NT 4.0. Drivers designed for 4.0 that depend on the Serial.sys load order would require modification to operate in Windows 2000.

12.4 NT FILES SYSTEM IN WINDOWS 2000 (NTFS)

Windows NTFS is described in [CAPK98, Micr98]. It supports several file systems, including NT files system (NTFS), file allocation table (FAT — used in 3.5 diskettes),

FAT 32 (used in Windows 98 volumes), CD Files System (CDFS for data stored on CDs), and Universal Disk Format (UDF, for data stored using the DVD format). File systems are considered compatible if they provide a means to interchange files among different types of media. All of the aforementioned file systems are compatible except NTFS; however, calls in the Win32 file system operate regardless of the underlying file system type. A given volume may utilize any file system. The default file system type is determined at the time the volume is formatted. As of NTFS version 5, the underlying on-disk data format has changed and requires all NT 4.0 and systems employing a combination of Windows 2000 and NT 4.0 to utilize a service pack to enable interoperability. The new NTFS 5.0 has features that can be labeled as volume oriented or directory oriented. A new NTFS 5.0 volume-oriented feature is the ACL check accelerator, as described in Section 12.4.1. The new NTFS in Windows 2000 file-oriented features include reparse points, as described in Section 12.4.2, and optimizing storage management, as described in Section 12.4.3. Additional features, such as the change journal and replication support, are also relevant to directory services and are discussed in Section 12.5.

12.4.1 Access Control Lists (ACLs)

NT 4.0 employs access control lists (ACLs) as part of its security measures to protect access. File ACLs are administered at each physical share and cannot be administered system-wide. In addition, ACLs do not maintain consistency between different volumes. This last fact may be surprising, but this decision is necessary since ACLs cannot be kept consistent between alternate volumes for the following reasons.

  ◆ For ACLs to guarantee a consistent state between alternate volumes, it would be necessary to employ a centralized database. This database can "Net Use" or use through the network the physical resource and thereby bypass the ACL system.

  ◆ Since logical distributed file systems can cross between FAT and NTFS volumes, there is no practical method to set an inherited DENY ACL from NTFS passing through FAT through NTFS and terminating on a NetWare volume (a very possible required situation that would mandate proper functionality).

  ◆ To create a tool to "walk" the logical name space and appropriately set ACLs, a complicated combined messaging/transaction engine would be required to queue and update unreliable networks. The thought alone can provoke nightmares in many terms, including required resources to execute.

  ◆ Since Windows 2000 supports storage quotas, support of ACLs across volumes would require storage and calculation of quotas among all possible volumes.

Supporting all the foregoing should be an all-or-nothing choice. The "all choice" would produce a very slow system, thereby making it not feasible with today's technology. Perhaps as technology continues to improve, the technology may someday be viable in a Window's environment.

With Windows 2000, optimization, referred to as ACL check accelerator, has been added to make ACLs more efficient. Specifically, each ACL is only physically present in a given volume once. A hash function is employed and all ACLs are stored in a common area. Microsoft [Micr98] points out two benefits associated with this choice. First, the total storage space required for the maintenance of ACL is substantially reduced. Second, the total time necessary to validate and allow a user to access a file appropriately is substantially decreased due to the reduced overhead; however, there are currently no comparative benchmarks.

12.4.2 Reparse Points

To allow arbitrary behavior to a file or a directory, Windows 2000 employs **reparse points**, that enable layered file system filters. This is very beneficial for handling files that are passed from system to system or for files that incorporate several different file types within one file. This technology allows the issue of how a file is handled to be determined at handling time, thereby creating a sort of dynamic file-handling capability as compared to a static handling determined strictly by standard methods (described in Chapter 8). In effect, it prevents the system from "judging the book by its cover" and provides the capability to reparse or reevaluate how the file should be handled through the use of filters. The reparse points alter standard open file processes through forcing the file name to be reparsed. Whenever a reparse point is encountered, NTFS places the reparsed data in the appropriate buffer. This buffer is acceptable to the file system filters. The reparse point is a system-controlled attributed called $REPARSE. This greatly enhances the ability of a system to handle various file types, some of which may be nonnative due to the system's existence in a distributed environment. Any file or empty directory may set this attribute. Reparse tags are 32 bits long and are grouped as follows.

- *Bits 0–15*: Tag value. This field is used to determine the specific reparse tag if this file requires reparsing.
- *Bits 16–28*: Reserved bits. This field is used in conjunction with the tag value.
- *Bits 29*: N. The third bit is the name surrogate indicator. If set to 1, the name surrogate bit communicates that the reparse point is representative of another named entity in the system.
- *Bit 30*: L. The second bit is the latency bit. If set to 1, the latency bit indicates a substantial delay to retrieve the first byte and will therefore cause the user interface to display this entity with an icon such as an hourglass.

♦   *Bit 31*: M. The highest-order bit is the Microsoft bit. If the reparse tag is a
     Microsoft tag, it is set to 1; otherwise, it is set to 0.

If a reparse point is encountered, the user-controlled data are placed in a buffer and
made available to the file system. Through information contained in the reserved bits
and the tag value, file filters that are installed handle the request. Each filter has two
opportunities to inspect each I/O request as the request passes up and down the stack of
filters. NTFS itself is placed in this stack, below the other filters. The primary advantage of the reparse points is that they allow Windows 2000 to operate with third party
file system filters, thereby allowing the possibility of customized and advanced storage
management features.

12.4.3 Storage Management

Efficient management of storage for server-based as well as remote-storage environments is provided through two services within Windows 2000. The first storage
management service is a single-instance storage scheme. This scheme identifies data
streams that are duplicated within a volume and replaces them with references to a single instance. Information that is frequently inadvertently duplicated may include font
files, shared libraries, or shared application executables. If these shared data are modified, references are modified in a copy-on-write or notification on transaction
completition manner as described in Chapter 8. As one might assume, benefits of the
single-instance storage scheme include reduced storage space as well as a simplified
administration mechanism.

   The second scheme is that of remote storage. This mechanism allows remote storage to be recalled to local storage when updating is required. Generally, remote storage
is employed for data that may have been active data but have since become relatively
inactive. The logic for remote storage is much like the logic behind storing a winter
coat. In winter, the coat is active and used regularly, but when spring rolls around, this
piece of clothing becomes utilized with decreasing frequency and is moved to secondary storage, such as a cedar chest. Imagine that a sudden cold front appears (of course,
the week after the coat was moved to the cedar chest). Wouldn't it be great if you
could open up the closet and the coat was magically moved from the cedar chest back
to the closet without your physical intervention — even if you were required to open
the closet door and wait for just a bit? This example demonstrates the behavior of the
remote storage scheme. The data will still appear local when they are moved to remote
storage but the latency to retrieve the data may be slightly increased. The primary
benefit is that the action of the user did not have to change and the user do not have to
be aware that the data have been relocated from primary to secondary storage or vice
versa; the action is transparent to the user.

12.5 ACTIVE DIRECTORY

One of the significant changes to the Windows 2000 server is the incorporation of the newly designed directory service known as the active directory, which is meant to take advantage of the best features of DNS and X.500 as described in Chapter 8. This service substantially enhances the former distributed file system (DFS) service of previous releases of Microsoft Windows NT-based technology but provides a mechanism for an easy upgrade for current Windows NT 4.0 operating system users. Microsoft describes active directory as a secure, distributed, partitioned and replicated directory service. Its purpose is to facilitate easy navigation and management of information in a distributed environment. The active directory provides straightforward APIs and supports a wide range of well-defined protocols and formats. The Active Directory's relationship to X.500 is described in Detail Box 12.6. Microsoft's approach is designed to provide a transparent yet tightly integrated directory system to assist in the management and maintenance of the massive amounts of files and resources on today's networked computing environments (which, if history continues to repeat itself, is probably minuscule relative to tomorrow's storage requirements). The active directory was created to meet the challenge of unifying and bringing order to the diverse server hierarchies and name spaces in a distributed environment. Time will tell if the active directory truly meets this challenge. The planned features and benefits of the Active Directory include the following.

- APIs designed to be easy to use for programmers using a scripting language as well as C/C++
- Use of drag-and-drop administration and hierarchical domain structure aimed to be simple and intuitive for the administrator
- Directory object extensibility via an extensible scheme
- Fast lookup and Internet publishing via a global catalog
- Efficient and convenient updates due to the utilization of multimaster replication
- Support for short life span services such as chat, IP telephony, and conferencing services
- Backward compatibility
- Interoperability with NetWare environments

The active directory can be viewed as a service provider, and its functions are summarized in Figure 12.4. The architecture is designed to be flexible in terms of the size of the enterprise that utilizes the system; therefore, it should be able to satisfy the directory needs of the smallest companies to the largest international corporations. Of

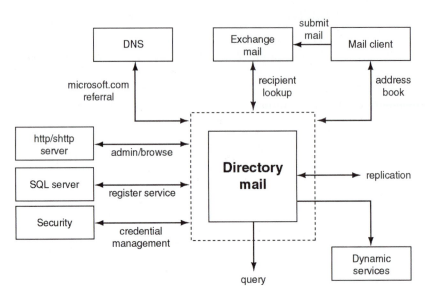

Figure 12.4   Active Directory Functionality.

course, the largest challenge may be proving that the entire system is stable enough to warrant the attention of such audiences. In any event, Microsoft promises that this directory system will interoperate not only with previous releases of Windows NT server but also with large portions of Novel NetWare 3.x and 4.x.

12.5.1 Name Space

The Internet concept of name space is integrated into Windows 2000's concept of directory service through the use of DNS as a location service. This location service is employed to translate a name into an IP address. The intention of this integration is to create a scalable, unified, manageable environment. The following are the intended benefits of this name space.

- ◆ Support for open standards, including domain name system (DNS) as well as standard protocols such as LDAP and HTTP. More information on issues related to the name space is provided in Section 12.4.1.
- ◆ Support for standard name formats for ease of migration and use.

Windows 2000 allows multiple domains to be connected into a tree structure. An example of relative object names when viewed locally and via the Internet is depicted in Figure 12.5. Windows 2000 does not utilize primary or back-up domain controllers but rather considers all domain controllers to be peers; therefore, any and all updates to any

DETAIL BOX 12.6
ACTIVE DIRECTORY AND X.500

While not requiring systems to host the entire X.500 directory system as described in Chapter 8, Windows 2000 supports the X.500 information model through its use of the lightweight directory access protocol (LDAP) as described in RFC2251, RFC2252, RFC2255, and RFC2256. In addition, the active directory supports X.500's directory access protocol (DAP), directory system protocol (DSP), and the directory information shadowing protocol (DISP). Microsoft Windows 2000 operating system's approach does differ from X.500 in the following ways.

1. Windows 2000 is TCP/IP based and does not focus on OSI, for which X.500 was originally intended.
2. X.500 requires some defined authority to manage the top of the tree internationally in each country for its global directory structure. Windows 2000 does not assume such a global structure.
3. While X.500 names are a series of touples as demonstrated in Chapter 8, Windows 2000 uses Internet form names such as galli@companyname.com.
4. Windows 2000 defines actual APIs to allow tools to interface with its directory service; X.500 never defined APIs.

domain controller will be replicated on all other domain controllers. In terms of resolving unrecognized names, Windows 2000 operating system employs the Windows Internet naming service. The integration of Windows Internet naming service with DNS is an intermediate solution until the Internet standards for DNS are updated to support dynamic DNS. Dynamic DNS would allow clients with dynamically assigned addresses to register and update DNS tables on the fly.

The organization of multiple domains into a domain tree is the principle factor providing scalability for Microsoft's Windows 2000. Specifically, this name space structure utilizes a "bottom-up" method for building a tree versus the more complex and time consuming "top-down" partitioning process. The entire name space is organized as a tree of trees; each subtree is considered a Windows 2000 domain that publishes its existence in DNS. This tree structure is possible due to the active directory. Each domain is a complete partition of the directory. This domain can then be further subdivided into organizational Units (OUs), as seen in Figure 12.6. These OUs are utilized for administrative purposes and are exceptionally helpful for creating structure among the tens of millions of objects within a domain tree.

12.5.2 Change Journal for Replication and Scalability

We now examine the approach taken to maximize efficiency of Microsoft's peer-to-peer Multimaster replication mechanism. In any massive system that is charted with administrating a large collection of machines that share files, a simple and appropriate file-sharing replication service is required, as discussed in Chapter 8. In this section, we describe the file replication services provided for in Windows 2000. As we have learned in the context of memory management in Chapter 4, if the files are replicated strictly for read purposes, replication may be implemented with ease. If a majority of the file access requests are read-only requests, the efficiency of the system overhead is kept to a minimum. The key to the active directory approach is based on the observation that 99% of all directory service requests involve queries as opposed to 1% update requests. This multimaster replication approach allows multiple replications, each considered to be a master as compared to the more common master/slave approach; therefore, it is considered a more advanced peer-to-peer solution. This peer-to-peer approach is substantially more scalable.

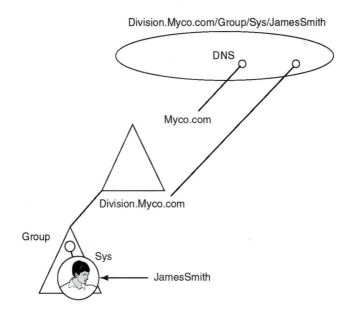

Figure 12.5   Two Views Due to Windows 2000 DNS-Based Locator Service.

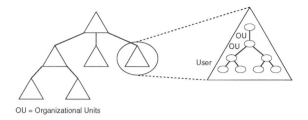

OU = Organizational Units

Figure 12.6   The Division of Domains into Organizational Units.

Hopefully, one question that comes to your mind is that of maintaining consistency of the data while employing multiple master copies, as discussed in Chapter 9. To achieve a sense of ordering for changes to data, Windows 2000 uses a change journal. The change journal implements revision control on volumes. Revision control is the general concept of tracking changes through the logging of notes for each change and enumerating each change. The change journal enables the system administrator to administer the large number of files and directories and track changes to these entities. Each new change is accompanied by a change reason. This change reason accompanies each open/close session. Microsoft chose to use logical ordering through the employment of **update sequence numbers** (USNs) and alleviate all the known problems associated with physical timestamps for ordering (discussed in Chapter 10). Thus, each record contains a 64-bit USN identity. The USN is monotonically incremented with each modification. While no records are kept for read-only access, there are 21 actions that generate a change record. These actions include the following.

- Creating a directory
- Deleting a directory
- Modifying data in file
- Appending data in a file
- Changing file attributes including ACLs
- Renaming a file

Each of these change records is generally smaller than 128 bytes. Within these 128 bytes, the USN record allows a reference to the parent file, the source, and the identity of the change as well as a field to indicate the reason for the change. Through the use of the change journal, Windows 2000 allows multiple stores for information while allowing each store to hold more then 10 million objects. Anytime a user writes to an object in a directory, the object receives a USN. This USN is held per computer and incremented each time a change is made to an object. This incremented value is then written into the object along with a unique signature of the computer that wrote the change. In addition to utilizing USNs for object content, a USN is associated with each directory object property. As with object USNs, object property USNs are incremented with each change to a property. The replication service works with the change journal to record changes to a file and uniquely identify each change. This provides the ability to identify each and every change to a given file should a problem arise.

Recall that a USN record is created only when a change is forced to the disk. Therefore, the USN records only track durable changes. These changes are recorded at the file level and not the volume level through a field to record the actual file name, file name length, file name offset, as well as the file name attributes. The advantage of this approach is that the number of records is directly proportional to the number of changes and not the number of entries in a volume. Old change records are freed from storage in 4-Kbyte units. Each change journal contains a three-part identity field that must be unique from previous change journal identities for that entity. The first identity field typically stores the major version number and the second part records the minor version. Using an example change record for version 2.01, the major version number would be 2 and the minor version number would be 01. This two-part identity allows each change to be identified uniquely. The third and final identify field is a security identify field. USN records also include a timestamp value as well as source information. Source information may fall into one of three categories: normal changes from applications, storage changes resulting from storage functions such as file replication, and auxiliary application changes produced by applications such as the production of thumbnail links resulting from an application functioning on a complete full-scale image.

To synchronize changes between master copies, a replication partner asks a source partner computer for all its changes greater than the last USN received to become updated. The source computer then examines its directory and identies each object with a USN greater than the presented USN. Property changes are reconciled individually. In the event of a collision or multiple changes to the same property, the victor is determined by timestamp therefore allowing the latest change to win. Since the timestamp is only employed as a tie-breaker (since no coins are available to toss), synchronization is not considered important.

One final note: the aforementioned approach is based on data that are queried 99% of the time. Data subject to frequent changes are considered volatile. Volatile information is generally not stored in a directory but connected via a transparent link mechanism that enables alternate information stores within the directory structure. Specifically, volatile objects are stored in separate storage employing different replication characteristics but maintaining the common user view.

12.5.3 Microsoft Index Server and HTTP Support

Hypertext transfer protocol (HTTP) is the standard on the Internet's World Wide Web (WWW). Windows 2000's Microsoft Internet information server (IIS) translates requests for directory objects into HTML pages for viewing in any HTML client. Therefore, any and all queries and objects can be conducted utilizing the familiar Web-browsing model. Furthermore, the line between local and remote resources is minimized as access to both types is presented to the user in the same manner. As we have mentioned many times, this is an important feature to a distributed operating system. Part of the IIS is the Microsoft index server which is responsible for implementing Web-type browsing on corporate intranets and Internet sites. This index server employs the services of the change journal described in Section 12.4.1. In this section, we take a closer look at the index server and its relationship to the Windows 2000's directory.

The Microsoft index server allows a database type of access to the objects within one's directory. In particular, it allows full-text indexing. This text-based indexing supports the following types of searches.

- Searches for words or phrases
- Searches utilizing boolean operators such as AND, OR, and AND NOT
- Searches utilizing wild cards such as *, ?, and regular expressions
- Searches utilizing relative qualifiers (<, <=, >, =>) against constants such as dates and file size
- Searches based on proximity to other words
- Searches within a specific document type
- Searches within a specific section of a specific document type
- Searches based on properties such as authorship and creation dates
- Ranking by quality of the match

Perhaps one of the more impressive aspects of the Microsoft index server is the fact that this system requires zero maintenance; it is automatically updated and includes automatic corruption detection and recovery. In addition, its searching capabilities are integrated into the system security; therefore, searches will only provide information and documents to which the user instantiating the query has permission to access. Admittedly, any avid UNIX user can accomplish any and all of these above tasks but not while using such an easy interface. To provide these services with the lowest possible overhead, indexing is controlled on a per-virtual root basis and supports incremental refreshing of the index. Finally, support for the following seven languages is included for international environments.

1. English
2. French
3. German
4. Spanish
5. Italian
6. Dutch
7. Swedish

If additional language support is required, other languages can easily be incorporated utilizing the open specification. It is not clear how adaptable this specification is in terms of support for other types of languages. Detail Box 12.7 conducts a walkthrough of the indexing process.

12.6 MICROSOFT MANAGEMENT CONSOLE (MMC)

Once known under the code name Slate, the Microsoft management console (MMC) was designed to provide a common framework for management applications for Windows NT 4.0 and up. While not actually providing any management applications, the MMC provides a common environment and stable interface to 'snap-in' management applications and permit their seamless integration into the system. It is part of the Windows software developer's kit (SDK). With MMC, each management tool can be created by a collection of smaller tools; each is known as a snap-in, thereby allowing easy extension and hierarchical organization. The resulting tool is what is generally utilized to manage a resource such as a network. Of course, each tool created can be saved for future use and reference. While multiple tool creation is allowed, an administrator only needs to load the particular tools needed at a given moment and may unload any individual tool when it is no longer necessary. It is also possible to mail a tool definition to another administrator. When the second administrator receives the tool, all necessary snap-ins are automatically downloaded and installed.

The following four benefits for administrators using MMC have been identified.

1. *Task Orientation*: The tools defined within MMC are task oriented. Administrators can use pieces of tools from various vendors to create their own tool, which is designed to focus on as well as present the information in a task-oriented manner. The information is not presented as raw objects.

2. *Integration*: A single console is utilized to collect all tasks that must be performed by an administrator. The user interface will integrate any new additional applications into the existing console.

3. *Delegation*: The ability of MMC to allow existing tools to be modified to create new tools with reduced functionality and less complex views. These simpler tools can then be given to other individuals. Therefore, the receiving individuals can complete their chores utilizing the simpler, more manageable view of their assigned task.

4. *Interface Simplification*: All tools built for MMC will have a similar look and feel regardless of which vendor developed the tool. Statistically, this should reduce the learning curve of any new MMC tools acquired. In addition, this should enable the user to choose and combine MMC tools from various vendors with consistent functionality. The latter is a common advantage when uniform APIs are established and employed.

DETAIL BOX 12.7
INDEXING PROCESS

The index server does not burden system resources through constant polling for changes; instead, this server is registered with the file system for change notification and updates the indexes when appropriate. The indexing process is a four-step process. Steps 2 through 4 are depicted in Figure 12.7.

1. *Collecting change notifications*: This is a lazy process that occurs in the background and only when resources are available. When a document on a volume is modified, the file system notifies the index server. When resources can be utilized that will not interfere with system performance, the index server opens the document and starts the indexing process. Using the operating system for collecting change notifications is substantially more scalable than the more traditional polling approaches.

2. *Filtering*: Content filters are produced using the open standard IFilter Interface by those most familiar with the particular data type since documents tend to use private file formats. Thus Microsoft would produce the filter for all Word documents. The filtering system opens the file and then selects and employs the appropriate content filter. Chunks of text are extracted and passed to the next phase. Index filters are also capable of handling embedded objects, such as figures and spreadsheets and the text contained in them. Finally, the filtering process is capable of tagging text to communicate information such as the language of the chunk of text.

3. *Word breaking*: The streams of characters emitted from the filtering process must now be broken into words, a much more difficult task for a computer as compared to a human. While many languages, such as English, utilize blank spaces to delimitate words, other languages, such as Japanese, do not. Regardless of differences in languages, the word breaker accepts a stream of characters and emits words. These words are presented in and stored in Unicode.

4. *Normalization*: The normalization process is employed to clean the words. Normalizing will handle capitalization, punctuation and noise issues, thereby allowing a uniform representation of words once placed into the index. Common noise issues includes "useless" or content-less words such as the, of, and and. Noise removal assists in reducing the total size of the index and the process allows for customization. Once normalized, words are put into the content index.

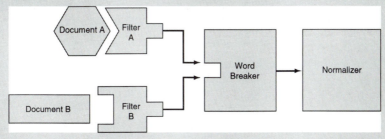

Figure 12.7   Indexing Process.

Although transparent to administrators, all MMC snap-ins support one or both of the following two possible modes.

1. *Stand-alone snap-in*: This type of snap-in can function alone and does not require any type of supporting snap-ins. It does not rely on the presence of any other snap-in.

2. *Extension Snap-in*: This type of snap-in can only provide functionality when invoked by its parent snap-in. It is declared a subordinate of a specific type of snap-in and for each and every occurrence of that type.

If a snap-in supports both modes, it contains some functionality that is independent and therefore stand-alone and some optional functionality that extends an existent snap-in. If the existent snap-in is not present in a given environment, the subset (and only that subset) of extended functionality is not available. For example, a printer log snap-in may exist in both modes. If the system contains a list of defined printers, the printer log snap-in will function on the defined printers and operate in an extension mode. However, if no printers are defined, the snap-in functions in the stand-alone mode and will require administrator input to define the set of printers on which the snap-in should focus. Detail Box 12.8 describes some examples of various types of snap-in extensions that may be utilized.

DETAIL BOX 12.8
MMC EXTENSION TYPES

The following is a sampling of types of MMC extensions that are available.

1. *Name space enumeration*: This type of extension would operate within a node. A node is defined as a manageable task or object, such as a computer or collection of Web pages. A name space is an ordered listing of all of the nodes available in the current tool. A name space is formatted as a tree.

2. *Toolbar and toolbar button*: These types of extensions would operate within a view. A view is defined as a visual representation of a snap-in. These extensions can add an entire toolbar within a window or add a button to a toolbar in an existent toolbar.

3. *Create new*: This type of extension is used to add items to the 'create new menu' structure for a given node or object. Multiple '"create new" snap-ins are allowed for a given node.

While Microsoft encourages all developers to create all management tools using MMC, it does provide a means to integrate non-MMC tools with MMC tools. In particular, shortcuts to non-MMC tools can be crated and saved to an .MSC file. An administrator can then create shortcuts to any executable program of this non-MMC tool using the .MSC file within MMC.

12.7 CLUSTER SERVICE

A cluster is often referred to as a collection of independent systems that take advantage of resource synergy thereby working together to provide better services than any single system could provide alone. To be useful, a cluster must be easy to implement, program, and manage. Ideally, all client applications should be able to interact with a cluster as though it was a simple, single server. Advantages include increased reliability and fault tolerance. Sometimes the individual systems in a cluster are substantially cheaper than their nonclustered counterparts; thus, the entire cost of a cluster is not as much as one might think. The exact cost, of course, depends on what one chooses to put into the cluster. Section 12.7.1 presents an overview of the Microsoft Windows 2000 Operating System cluster service that is part of Windows 2000 Server. Section 12.7.2 presents the various cluster abstractions while Section 12.7.3 focuses on the cluster service architectures. Application deployment is the subject of Section 12.7.4.

12.7.1 Cluster Service Overview

The first appearance of the Microsoft's **cluster** service appeared in Windows NT 4.0 operating system. It is described in Microsoft's White Paper Series [Micr98] and in [GaShMa98]. The implementation in Windows 2000 includes a "wizard" to assist in the creation of clusters as well as several features to provide substantially improved integration with existing services or application environments based on COM and DCOM, as described in Chapter 6.

The cluster service is designed to provide an easy interface to a fault tolerant scalable environment. The cluster service relies heavily on RPC mechanisms, Windows 2000 name management, network interface management, security, resource controls, and the file system. To provide a simplified interface, Windows 2000 cluster service employs abstractions, as described in Section 12.7.2. The scalable, fault-tolerant architecture is described in Section 12.7.3. The manner in which application services can be deployed to take advantage of the cluster service is described in Section 12.7.4. Some traditional features of clusters that are currently absent in the Windows 2000 cluster service include support for fault-tolerant application support, state recovery, and constant migration. It is promised [GaShMa98] (and hoped) that support for these abilities will appear in the near future.

12.7.2 Cluster Abstractions

The cluster service abstractions within Windows 2000 operating system are designed to be beneficial to system administration, to the user, and to the cluster service itself. As described by [GaShMa98], the Windows 2000 cluster service employs several abstractions, including resources, resource dependencies, resource group, and virtual Windows 2000 server abstractions. The resource abstraction is the basic unit of management within a cluster. There are two basic predefined resource types: physical resources and logical resources. An example of a physical resource is a small computer systems interface (SCSI – pronounced scuzzy) disk, while an example of a logical resource is an IP address. Additional resource types and their related control libraries (such as DLL) can be added to a cluster by application developers, thereby allowing a cluster's capabilities to become extended. Regardless of the precise resource type, the purpose of typing resources is to enable existing applications to utilize the cluster service to its fullest extent. The interface for each resource is (and must be) identical, therefore enabling all resources to be monitored and managed easily.

The resource dependency abstraction utilizes a dependency tree to describe and define the initiation sequence of services within the cluster, often referred to as starting services. As an example, a resource implementing an object broker such as those employed in a CORBA environment must be started prior to starting any services requiring the object broker to communicate and accomplish a task. This dependency follows the same logic as the following telephony example. Specifically, the connection between the parties wishing to communicate must be established prior to communication. Thus, the conversation is dependent on the communication link being established. The dependency tree is also employed to describe and define the sequence in which services must be shut down, commonly referred to as the termination or shutdown sequence. This dependency tree also contains information necessary to determine what subgrouping of resources must be kept together when migrating a resource to another location within the cluster. An example of a common location dependency is a database and the disks employed to store the database.

The resource group abstraction enables the combination of resources into larger logical units. This abstraction is beneficial for the management of resources. Generally, related resources that together can perform the entire function of an application are organized into a resource group. This group is managed as a single unit in every manner. If a single entity within the group fails, the entire team fails. For another group to be identified as the fail-over group, the new group must be capable of supporting each and every resource in the failed group. The precise set of resources and resource dependency trees are assigned by the cluster administrator on a per-group basis. In addition, this administrator is responsible for setting the fail-over policies, including the time delay between rebooting a group and when the service applications may return (referred to as the fail-back window), the list of preferred owner nodes for a group, and so on.

The final abstraction is the virtual Windows 2000 server abstraction. This abstraction encapsulates the services and all required resources providing the given service. Popular services that are deployed utilizing a cluster service include file servers, databases, Web servers, e-mail servers, and other servers that are essential to standard daily business operations. For each virtual server, a network name and IP address is visible to all clients. This information does not change based on changes within the cluster, thereby providing the illusion of a single, stable environment to all clients, applications, and administrators.

12.7.3 Cluster Service Architectures

Physically, a cluster may consist of a large collection of personal computers connected via an Ethernet or it may be a high-performance supercomputer. In either case, the cluster provides fault tolerance, reliability, and the illusion of a single server or single system image. Through fault tolerance, the cluster service can detect and restart failed hardware or software components. If a failed component is unable to recover, the functionality of that component is migrated to another member of that cluster. The availability of back-up components for fail-over groups provides reliability. Workload disbursement, whether due to the demands on the cluster or due to fail-over operations, is generally transparent to the cluster, thereby further assisting in the illusion of a single server.

There are two software models generally employed for cluster technology: the common resource model and the independent resource model. Both models can be supported within a single Windows 2000 cluster. Generally, applications desiring maximum scalability should employ the independent resource model. If workloads are difficult to partition, the common resource model is frequently employed. Now let's examine both models.

The common resource model allows systems within a resource to access any resource connected to any system within that cluster; therefore, all resources are commonly accessible within the cluster. An example of a common resource of a cluster is one system's disk that is accessed by others within the cluster. To prevent potential conflicts and ensure the integrity of the data and operations, shared memory (as described in Chapter 4) along with some sort concurrency control (as described in Chapter 5) and/or transaction management (as described in Chapter 9) is employed.

The independent resource model only allows one system to own and access a given resource at a time unless the owner fails. In the case of owner failure, another system within the cluster may dynamically take ownership. All requests to the cluster for a particular service are automatically routed to the current owner of the necessary resource. If a client requests the cluster server to perform a task requiring access to multiple resources, one component of the cluster is chosen to host the request. This host then divides the request into subrequests and distributes them accordingly. The host collects the local responses and assembles the response of the cluster.

As mentioned, Windows 2000 allows each cluster to use either model or a combination of both models. The basic configuration information is generally maintained in the registry, a local database. In the case of a clustered system, a cluster-wide registry is employed to allow each cluster service as well as the applications to obtain a unified global view in terms of the state of the resources and the current cluster configuration.

All updates to this registry are completed in an atomic manner employing an atomic update protocol.

12.7.4 Cluster Service Deployment to Applications

There are two methods available for applications to employ a cluster-based service. The first method is for applications aware that the service is a cluster-based service, and the second is for those unaware of the cluster. Applications aware that they are utilizing a cluster-based service are often referred to as custom applications [GaShMa98]. Customization does not require a modification to the application but the development of a cluster interface layer. This layer is then employed to manage and respond to failure. Therefore, a custom application may explicitly take advantage of the automatic failover feature of the cluster through the failures detected by the custom resource DLL. In addition, these interfaces provide the ability to start and stop specific resources within the cluster as well as monitor each resource to determine if it is still operational. Thus, the level of granularity of control is substantially increased for custom applications.

Not all applications are required to be custom applications but may be generic applications. These generic applications have not undergone any modifications to operate with a cluster service. The level of granularity for the control and monitoring is not substantial in custom applications; therefore, the reliability and failure detection are primitive in comparison. Failure detection cannot be conducted on an individual service within the cluster but is generally implemented by checking the status of the process. A hung application may not always be detected, and a custom resource DLL should be implemented if a more sophisticated failure detection mechanism is required for generic applications.

12.8 WINDOWS 2000 SECURITY

As discussed in Chapter 11, all modern operating systems must address security on many levels. Windows 2000 provides full support for the following industry-standard, security protocols.

1. Diffie-Hellman key exchange
2. Digital Signatures, specifically hash message authentication codes such as MD5, SHA and CBC
3. Kerberos authentication protocol
4. SSL
5. Private-key encryption, specifically DES

In addition to these industry standards, Windows 2000 provides three other key security features. In this section we examine these features; specifically, we examine the security configuration editor in Section 12.8.1, the encrypting file system in Section 12.8.2 and the Microsoft security support provider interface in Section 12.8.3.

12.8.1 Security Configuration Editor

The Microsoft security configuration editor is a MMC snap-in tool. This single tool is designed to assist in defining, managing, and verifying the security configuration of a Windows 2000-based system in a cost-effective manner. This tool is particularly useful in a Windows 2000 environment since the complexity of administrating security configurations is greatly increased with the increased support for distributed computing at the enterprise-level. This tool is not meant to replace the user manager, server manager, and the access control list editor but rather should function as a complement to these tools. Regularly required operations can be automatically performed in the background. The security features listed in Table 12.2 can be configured and analyzed through the security configuration editor.

One helpful feature of the security configuration editor is its ability to allow the definition and utilization of security configuration templates. These templates may include settings for security attributes and can be employed on any aspect of security. Furthermore, the administrator may perform analysis of the enterprise system based on a set of base templates. Of course, these base templates may either be the default set that is included with Windows 2000 or may be a set of templates defined by the administrator as recommended templates for that enterprise. These templates are standard text-based .inf files. Once a template is installed, the security configuration editor's configuration engine parses the template and makes the appropriate changes to the system. Through the editor, the administrator can also create a template from an existing system.

Table 12.2 Security Features Configurable by the SCE.

Security Feature	Description
System Security Policy	This editor allows access to the policy, including how and when users are able to log onto the system, the password policy, overall system objects security, audit settings, and domain policy.
User Accounts	This editor assists in the assignment of group memberships, privileges, as well as user rights.
System Services	This editor enables the configuration of different services that are installed, including networks, file sharing, and printing.
System Registry	This editor can be employed to set the security values in the system registry.
System Store	This editor can set the security for local system file volumes and directory trees.
Directory Security	This editor can be employed to manage the security of objects within Windows 2000 active directory.

There are five basic security areas Microsoft identified.

1. *Security policies.* These policies apply to various local and domain security policy attributes, including machine-level settings. Windows 2000 domains are defined to be a physical security boundary. A policy may include types of passwords that are acceptable, lifetime of a Kerberos ticket, account lockout, and so on.

2. *Restricted group management.* This functionality is employed to groups with membership identified as sensitive by the system administrator. Common restricted groups include printer operators, server operators, power users, and so on. This group is analyzed not only in terms of simple membership but also in terms of recursive membership.

3. *Rights and privilege management.* This area pertains to the management of users and groups that are granted specific rights and privileges on the system. This area includes the capability to specify trusted domains and groups who may also enjoy rights and privileges on local machines.

4. *Object trees.* This area includes directory objects, registry keys, and the local file system. The security editor enables the configuration of object ownership, the access control list as well as auditing information. For directory objects, the administrator may utilize the security descriptor definition language (SDDL), which allows the complete specification of a list of qualifying LDAP names and security descriptors for each name. Registry objects can be controlled in terms of fully qualified registry key path and security descriptor also in SDDL format. The file system security employs the dynamic inheritance model, a model that is also supported by NTFS. All volumes of a given system are treated as a single tree.

5. *System services.* This area includes all local and network system services. This area is designed to be extendable and may include services such as file and print services; telephony and fax services; and Internet/intranet services. The most important restriction to adhere to in this category is that it requires the name of the service utilized in the security configuration editor to be the same as the one used by the service control manager.

Additional areas can be added through MMC snap-ins without breaking backward compatibility with existing templates. For each of these areas, the system administrator can define, configure, analyze, and view the security data through a graphical user interface (GUI). There is also a limited command-line utility that is capable of configuration and analysis. The GUI interface is quite easy to use and is recommended. For example, when performing an analysis, the current setting is displayed next to the template recommended setting. The use of colors, fonts, and icons is designed to assist in the identification of potential problem areas, and corrections can be made with a click of the mouse. In addition, previous settings are recorded in the event that one wishes to revert to previous settings.

With the security configuration editor, there are two modes of security analysis for Windows 2000-based systems. The first mode is referred to as configured system analysis. This mode of operations refers to the analysis of a system that has first been configured with a configuration template prior to the performance of the first analysis of the system. The analysis utilizes the database created as a result of these templates. The second mode of security analysis is referred to as unconfigured system analysis. This mode of operation refers to the analysis of a system as compared to a base template. This base template is used for comparisons throughout the analysis and is stored along with the database output for future analysis. The administrator may update the system settings by changing this base template and employing the reconfiguration option within the security configuration editor.

12.8.2 Encrypting File System

The encrypting file system (EFS) is included with Windows 2000 operating system as part of the kernel. Since components of a distributed system are connected to a network, possibly the Internet, it is very beneficial to store all files in an encrypted format in the event that a breach of security occurs. Windows 2000's EFS employs asymmetric as well as symmetric encryption. The specific steps for EFS are as follows.

1. The user's plaintext file is encrypted using a randomly generated file encryption key (FEK). FEK employs symmetric encryption. Currently, the private-key technology chosen for 2000 is DES, but future releases of EFS allow for alternate encryption schemes.

2. This FEK key is stored along with the file as an attribute; specifically, it is stored in the data decryption field using the user's public key as well as in the data recovery field using a recovery key, as depicted in Figure 12.8. If the file belongs to multiple users, the data decryption field contains an encrypted FEK for each file owner.

3. To decrypt the file by the user, the user's private key is employed to retrieve the FEK. The FEK is then employed to retrieve the contents of the file. The use of the data recovery field is discussed in more details later. Decryption may be performed on a block-per-block basis; only the specific blocks physically accessed are decrypted.

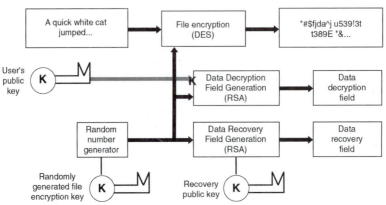

Figure 12.8 EFS Encryption Process.

EFS capabilities are available through a GUI environment, through the Windows 2000 Explorer context menu, as well as from a command prompt. There is no administrative effort required to start encrypting files. If a user does not have a public-key pair, EFS automatically generates one for the user. If a directory is marked for encryption, all files and subdirectories are automatically encrypted. Each file has a unique encryption key to assist and ensure proper rename operations. Once a file is encrypted, it remains encrypted even if it is renamed and moved to a directory not marked for encryption.

If that user does not possess and present the appropriate private key for a particular file, access to that file is denied. Without Windows 2000 operating system, the entire mechanism to access the files is dysfunctional; therefore, this approach prohibits security attacks that attempt to by-pass a system's security through booting as a different operating system.

EFS runs as an integrated system service to make it easy to manage yet difficult to attack. EFS is tightly integrated with NTFS. All temporary copies of an encrypted file are also encrypted. This capability can extend to remote file servers; however, EFS only addresses encrypting data on a disk. Network protocols supported by Windows 2000 operating system such as SSL/PCT, as described in Chapter 11, can be employed to encrypt data that are going to be transferred over a network.

In a business environment where employees may cease to be with a company with little or no notice, a company requires a security system that can grant access to the former employee's information on its resources. Windows 2000 operating system with EFS provides a built-in data recovery support through the inclusion of the Data Recovery Field. The recovery capability is considered to be under the control of domain administrators but can be delegated to a designated data security administrator to provide better control and flexibility. Actual recovery capability is provided through the recovery key that is defined at the domain controller for each domain. A given system can be configured for multiple recovery keys all of which are stored in the data recovery field. During the recovery process, only the system's private key needs to be employed to recover the FEK; therefore, no other private information, such as a user's private key, is revealed.

12.8.3 Microsoft Security Support Provider Interface

The Microsoft security support provider interface (SSPI) is a well-defined API for obtaining access to anything from authentication, to message integrity, to message privacy, and to security quality of services for distributed applications. SSPI may be employed in one of two manners. First, SSPI may be directly employed through application interfaces to services such as DCOM (Chapter 6), secure RPC, WinSock 2.0, and WinInet. We first examine the APIs of SSPI followed by the capabilities of the package.

SSPI consists of four basic groups of APIs. The first group of APIs is the credential management APIs. Interfaces of this group provide access to credentials such as passwords, security tickets, and so on. The specific credential management APIs are contained in Table 12.3.

API Name	Description
AcquireCredentialsHandle	This acquires a handle to the reference credentials.
FreeCredenialsHandle	This method releases the credential and related resources.
QueryCredentialAttributes	This method allows queries on credential attributes such as associated name and domain name.

Table 12.3 Credential Management APIs.

The second group of SSPI APIs is the context management APIs. Context management provides methods for creating and using the various security contexts whether created on the server side or the client side. The context management APIs are presented in Table 12.4.

The third group of SSPI APIs is the message support APIs. These APIs provide communication integrity and privacy services. The message support APIs are presented in Table 12.5.

The fourth and final group of SSPI APIs is the package management APIs. These APIs provide for access to different security packages that a given security provider supports. The package management APIs are presented in Table 12.6.

Future expansion of SSPI APIs is scheduled to provide message support routines for encryption technology. In general, SSPI allows usage of various security packages without changing the interface to security services. Through the SSPI management functions, an application may list and select a security package to support its needs. A security provider that is a dynamic-link library implements SSPI. SSPI makes one or more security packages available to applications and maps the SSPI functions to a specific implementation of a security protocol for that package, such as Kerberos or SSL. The actual name of the package is employed during the initialization process to identify the specific package.

API Name	Description
InitializeSecurityContext:	This API initiates a security context by generating a security token referred to as an opaque message that can be passed to the server.
AcceptSecurityContext	This API uses the opaque message received from the client to create a security context.
DeleteSecurityContext	This API frees a security context and all associated resources.
QueryContextAttributes	This API allows queries on various context attributes.
ApplyControlToken	This API applies a supplemental security message to an existing security context.
CompleteAuthToken	Completes an authentication token for protocols, such as DCE RPC, that require revisions to the security information once the transport has updated some message fields.
ImpersonateSecurityContext	This API attaches the client's security context as an impersonation token to the calling thread.
RevertSecurityContext	This API ceases security context impersonation and defaults the calling thread to its primary security token.

Table 12.4   Context Management APIs.

API Name	Description
MakeSignature	This API generates a secure signature. This signature is based on a message and a security context.
VerifySignature	This API verifies that a received signature matches the required signature.

Table 12.5   Message Support APIs.

API Name	Description
EnumerateSecurityPackages	This API lists all available security packages along with their capabilities.
QuerySecurityPackageInfo	This API is able to query a single security package for its capabilities.

Table 12.6   Package Management APIs.

The various capabilities of a security package determine exactly what services are available to an application through the package. The capabilities are broken into three groups. The first group of capabilities are the authentication-related capabilities including client-only authentication, authentication chaining (referred to by Microsoft as Multileg authentication), as well as Windows 2000 impersonation. The second group of capabilities is the transport-layer (as discussed in Chapter 1)related capabilities, including datagram-style transports, connection-oriented transports as well as data stream connection semantics. The final group of capabilities is the Message-related capabilities including support for message integrity and message privacy.

12.9 HYDRA — A THIN CLIENT

Hydra is the code name for the version of Windows 2000's thin client. This thin client provides a Windows-based terminal support for the Windows 2000 server operating system and a super thin client for the entire Windows operating system family. The aim is to provide the benefits of a managed Window-based environment in a low-cost terminal. Through the terminal, the user will be able remotely to access and conduct business through Windows 2000 server, but the actual terminal will only be responsible for allowing logins and for communicating with the server. It will not have full functionality such as saving files to a removable disk locally available at the terminal, but will strictly allow access to the entire network environment. With a thin client, only local resources on the terminal allow connection and functionality with the server. For those who may be familiar with the UNIX world, the thin client is equivalent to X terminals.

12.10 SUMMARY

In summary, Windows 2000 promises and is designed to provide great advances over NT 4.0 operating system, particularly in terms of support for distributed computing. Almost every major aspect of the base NT technology has been redesigned to address the needs of today's applications, which demand every operating system to provide the functionality of a distributed operating system. Hopefully, lessons from earlier systems and the experimental systems provided enough of a knowledge base so that the design decisions within Windows 2000 will truly advance computing to the fully distributed level, but this is something that only time will tell. Time will also tell how efficient and practical these solutions are for the needs of our applications. To be sure, future releases of this and other operating systems will improve on the technology based on what is learned once Windows 2000 operating system becomes widely deployed. No matter what platform you grew up on, it is hard to believe that Widows 2000 will not have a significant impact on the future of computing—particularly distributed computing.

As a closing thought, remember that many once thought that computing would never be realizable at the desktop level and that the Internet was only for scientists. Distributed computing knowledge was thought to be necessary only for the specialists, not for all computer scientists. I believe this last thought will soon become a myth we soon look back upon and chuckle about—very soon.

12.11 REFERENCES FOR FURTHER STUDY

The following white paper references can provide more detailed information on Windows 2000 and related protocols of the base technology at Microsoft's NT server white paper site, www.microsoft.com/ntserver/nts/techdetails [Micr98]. In addition, there are some papers in traditional research journals regarding Windows 2000 including [CAPK98, GaShMa98, Micr98, and Sol98].

The Microsoft NT and Windows 2000 operating system white paper series provides some of the best technical information on the Internet concerning Microsoft's Windows 2000 operating system. Information regarding some of the protocols employed also can be found on the Internet. The RFCs for LDAP are located at the following URLs.

- http://www.cis.ohio-state.edu/htbin/rfc/rfc2251.html
- http://www.cis.ohio-state.edu/htbin/rfc/rfc2252.html
- http://www.cis.ohio-state.edu/htbin/rfc/rfc2254.html
- http://www.cis.ohio-state.edu/htbin/rfc/rfc2255.html
- http://www.cis.ohio-state.edu/htbin/rfc/rfc2307.html

An online version of the LDAP user's manual can be found at http://www.umich.edu/~dirsvcs/ldap/doc/man/. In addition, a page with multiple links for LDAP documentation: including the FAQ site, can be found at http://www.umich.edu /~dirsvcs/ldap/doc/.

EXERCISES

12.1   Throughout the entire design of Windows 2000, there is a strong emphasis on providing APIs. What are the advantages of providing actual, specific APIs?

12.2   Discuss two advantages of incorporating subsystems into the Windows 2000 architecture.

12.3 Name three significant design elements for Windows 2000 that exist in order to increase interoperability and hardware independence. Describe why each design element provides this benefit.

12.4 What are three major benefits of the change journal? Why?

12.5 Discuss the benefits of a peer-to-peer replication strategy for a massive, scalable, distributed system.

12.6 What is different about a distributed environment that allows it to benefit from the use of USNs?

12.7 What are three advantages of the use and incorporation of plug and play in an operating system?

12.8 What can one accomplish easily on a system with reparse points that would be difficult to accomplish without this technology?

12.9 Why are the services of the index server so beneficial in Windows 2000 as compared to an old single-user DOS system with floppy drives? Name and describe three reasons.

12.10 Name and describe three advantages of active directory over X.500.

12.11 How many forms of transparency are supported by cluster abstraction? Name and describe why each of the forms you listed is inherent to clusters.

12.12 Discuss the advantages of embedding EFS technology in a distributed operating system.

12.13 Discuss your favorite new feature found in Windows 2000 and describe why it is beneficial to distributed computing.

12.14 Why were changes required for Windows 2000 to run processes in a 64-bit address space?

Surgical Scheduling Program

The surgical scheduling program provides a practical example to supplement the information presented in Part I of this book. Specifically, this program demonstrates the utilization of pthreads (Chapter 2), INET sockets (Chapter 3), and mutex for synchronization (Chapter 4). This program is implemented in a client/server environment, the client being a surgeon system requesting a surgical suite, the server being the hospital system which maintains scheduling of the surgical suites. The surgeon places a request and sends it to the hospital. The hospital responds with available times to schedule the suite. The surgeon selects a time and sends the request back to the hospital. The hospital responds with confirmation or denial.

The documentation for the program is presented in Sections A.1-A.5. Specifically, A.1 presents a documenation overview, Section A.2 presents the design documentation, Section A.3 presents the functional descriptions and function interfaces, Section A.4 contains the data dictionary and Section A.5 presents the user documenatation including installation and execution instructions. Sections A.6-A.8 contain the source code for the client, server and the common source code respectively. In all written documentation within this appendix, excluding source code, all **variables** are identified in bold type, all `functions()` with open and close parenthesis and in `courier` font, and all "enumerated types" are presented with open and closed double quotes.

It is important to note that this code is meant to clearly demonstrate the distributed programming features. It is not written as nor is it meant to be an industrial strength program. As such, some design decisions such as using constants for the names of surgeons would not be recommended or encouraged outside of this realm. Decisions such as these were meant to keep the code as simple as possible outside of the distributed features.

A.1 DOCUMENTATION OVERVIEW

Each source code listing is placed in the order that the function appears in the main() file. Next, the makefile for that program is presented followed by the header file, and remaining source code files. Each source code file lists the functions housed in that file in preceding comments. One additional program that is required but only referenced in the server and client documentation is the Initialization File program. Its operation is described in the Section A.5 while functional description is provided Section A.3 and its source code is presented in Section A.8. It is a simple program used to build a file of structs. It needs to be run once for each server and should be executed at the time of installation.

The Data Flow diagrams are broken down to point where a bubble is a function, at which time the reader may reference Functional Descriptions in Section A.3 to get an understanding of each function's operation. The data flow diagrams are presented in Figure A.1-A.11 with the client data flow diagrams in A.2-A.4 and the server in Figures A.5-A.11. Figure A.1 depicts the overview of the data flow for the entire program. An overview of the surgeon program data flow is presented in Figure A.2. Figure A.3 focuses on the actual surgeon system with Figure A.4 focusing on the make selection data flow portion of the client.

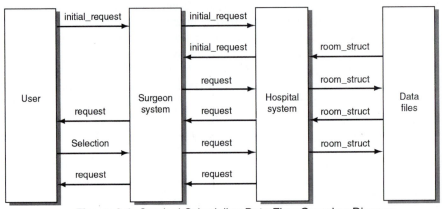

Figure A.1 Surgical Scheduling Data Flow Overview Diagram.

• in
  Selection
  request
  initial_request

• out
  initial_request
  request

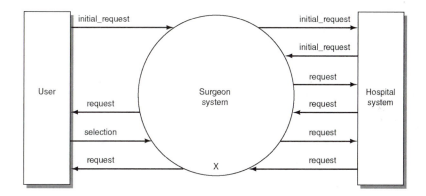

Figure A.2 Surgeon Data Flow Overview Diagram.

• in
  Selection
  request
  initial_request

• out
  initial_request
  request

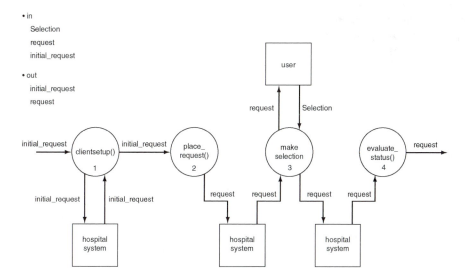

Figure A.3 Surgeon System Data Flow Diagram.

• in

   Selection

   request

• out

   request

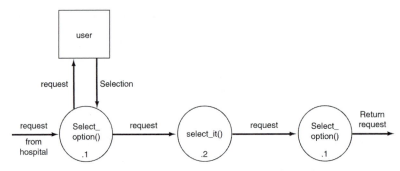

Figure A.4 Surgeon Make Selection Data Flow Diagram.

• in

   Request

   initial_request

   menu_option

   room_struct

• out

   initial_request

   room_struct

   request

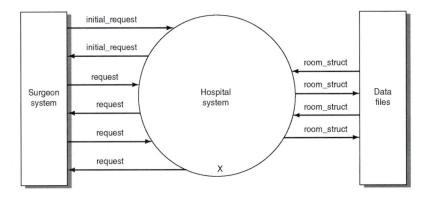

Figure A.5 Hospital Data Flow Overview Diagram.

An overview of the hospital data flow is presented in Figure A.5. The hospital system data flow diagram is presented in Figure A.6 while Figure A.7 focuses on the data flow of processing the initial request. The data flow for establishing/confirming availability is presented in Figure A.8. Figure A.9 presents the data flow for reviewing a file status and Figure A.10 presents the data flow for evaluating a room selection. Figure A.11 presents the data flow diagram for the shutting down the server.

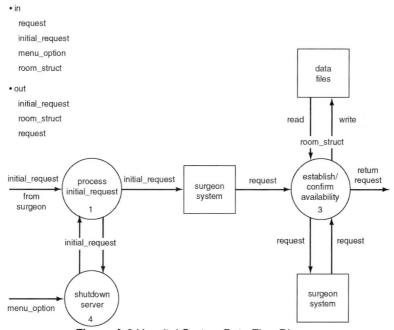

Figure A.6 Hospital System Data Flow Diagram.

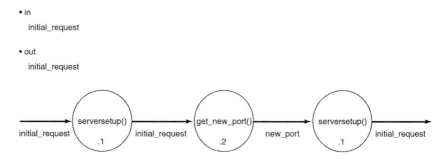

Figure A.7 Hospital System Process Initial Request Data Flow Diagram.

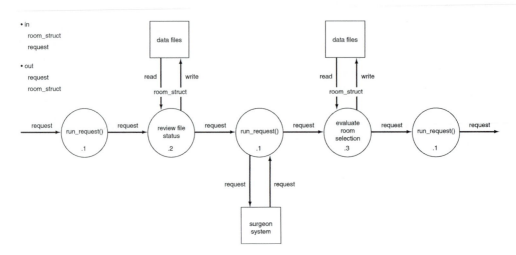

Figure A.8 Hospital System Establish/Confirm Availability Data Flow Diagram.

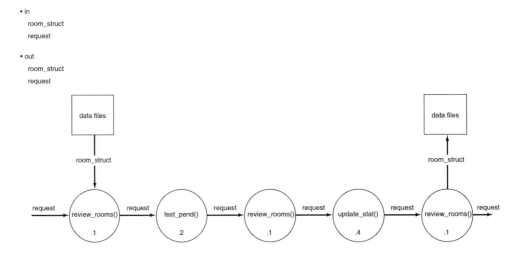

Figure A.9 Hospital System Review File Status Data Flow Diagram.

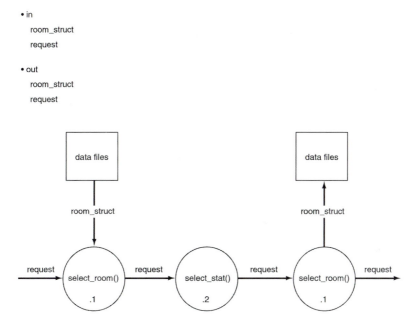

Figure A.10 Hospital System Evaluate Room Selection Data Flow Diagram.

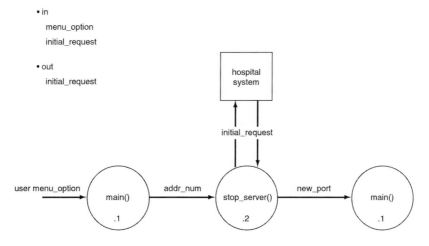

Figure A.11 Shutdown Server Data Flow Diagram.

A.2 DESIGN DOCUMENTATION

The Surgical Scheduling Program actually consists of 2 programs, the client program (surgeon), and the server program (hospital). Both programs were implemented in the UNIX environment in ANSI C programming language. The sockets are implemented using INET datagrams, threads are implemented using the POSIX standard pthread library, and synchronization is realized through pthread mutex locks. The program did not attempt to compensate for leap year, or for Monday through Friday scheduling. The assumption is made that surgery may be scheduled 7 days a week, in hourly slots, from 0800 - 1600.

This design overview does not reference all functions used in the program; functions used primarily for simplicity and improved programming style were not mentioned because they add confusion to the general flow of the program. All functions are listed in the Functional Descriptions in Section A.3.

Prior to the initial run of the server, the program named File Initialization must be run. This program is added in the documentation under its own heading since it is not a user option, and must be run separately from the client/server programs.

Initialization is accomplished for server and client programs by use of each programs respective "makefile". This file contains construction commands indicating appropriate dependencies. Following initialization, the server program must be started first since program interaction is initiated by a request for service from the client.

The server is started by use of the command "hospitalrun". When this command is entered, the server program begins at `main()` which creates a thread to accept requests from a client. Server `main()` then awaits user input inside a while loop, allowing the user 1 valid option, to shutdown the server. `serversetup()`, called during thread creation, initializes a known socket port, enters a while loop, and sits in receive mode awaiting a client request. **main_thread** will sit in receive mode until a client makes a request, or the user requests shutdown of the server.

Client operation is started by use of the command "surgeonrun". When this command is entered, client `main()` enters a do-while loop awaiting user input. The user has the option to place a request or shut down the client program. If the user selects option "R" to make a request, `clientsetup()` is called. This function initializes a client socket port and sends **initial_request** to the server on the known port. **initial_request** is of struct type initial_connect, which includes enumerated type "dr_id", and integer **new_port**. Each client has a fixed "dr_id" set in the code for that specific client, so the user is not required to know this information.

When **initial_request** is received by **main_thread** running in `serversetup()`, the request is passed to server function `get_new_port()`. This function returns a port number which can be dedicated to the client for connection until the request is complete. Server function `serversetup()` then returns **initial_request** to the client through the INET socket, indicating the port number which can be used by the client for connection to complete the request. `serversetup()` then spawns **surgeon_thread** to handle the request which will be sent by the client. When this thread is spawned, server function run_request() is called, which initializes a socket waiting on the port returned by get_new_port(). The thread then waits in receive mode for connection by the client. Since **main_thread** running serversetup() has resolved the initial request, it now returns to receive mode on the well known port, by use of the while loop.

When the new port value sent by the server is received by client function client-setup(), this function returns the port value to main(), which calls client function place_request(). This function initializes a socket with the new port value, and interfaces with the user to obtain a Julian date of the request and the type of surgery required. place_request() then passes **request** to the server. **request** is struct type day_request, and includes the enum type "dr_id", int **julian_date**, enum type surgery_type, and enum type room_status from **status0800 - status1600**.

request is then received by **surgeon_thread** running server function run_request(). A pointer to **request** is then passed to server function review_rooms() to identify which rooms are available for the day and surgery type requested. review_rooms() sets a mutex lock for the file type to be opened, opens the correct file, and builds array **init_room**[366]. This array is of type struct room_struct, which includes int **julian_date**, enum room_status from **status0800 - status1600**, long int **ptime0800 - ptime1600**, and enum "dr_id" **dr0800 - dr1600**. **request** is then updated based on the current status of the respective room file. **request** may be updated with three possible room status' at this time; "busy", "open", or "pending". If the time is already committed, **request** is updated with "busy" status in the status field. Example: "status0800 = busy". If the time has already been sent to another surgeon as "open" in the past ten minutes, **request** is updated in that status field as "pending". If the room is available, then **request** is updated with "open" for that time slot, and the array is updated with current server time and the "dr_id" of the surgeon which just made the request. The array is also updated with "pending" status, which indicates that the time slot is now on hold for ten minutes and cannot be shown as available to another surgeon unless ten minutes has passed. The array is then written to file, the mutex lock unlocked, and control is returned to server function run_request() with **request** updated with available times. run_request() then passes **request** back to the client, which has been sitting in receive mode waiting for a reply.

When the client function place_request() receives **request** from the server, client function Select_option() is called, and is passed the address of **request**. Select_option() interfaces with the user to allow the user to select one of the times returned by the server in "open" status. The selections are displayed on the screen, and the user is required to input a valid time which is in "open" status. Time "0000" is used to exit with none of the valid options selected. **request** is then updated by client function Select_option(), and control is returned to client function place_request(). **request** is then passed back to the server thread waiting for a response from this client.

surgeon_thread receives **request** while running function run_request(), and calls server function select_room() as soon as **request** is received. select_room() is passed the address of request. select_room(), sets a mutex lock for the file type to be opened, opens the correct file, and builds array **init_room**[366] (this data structure has been previously defined). The function then traverses **request** to find a value of **Select** in a time status slot. This indicates which time slot the surgeon has requested. The function compares this **room_status** for the selected time with the array room_status for the same time. If the "dr_id" is the same for both the array and struct **request**, then **request** is updated with status "confirm" in that room_status slot, and the array is updated with "busy" status for that time slot. The array is written to file, the file is closed, mutex lock is unlocked, and control is returned to server function `run_request()`. `run_request()` sends the updated **request** to the client, closes this socket, and exits **surgeon_thread**.

Client function `place_request()` now receives **request** through the socket. **request** is printed for the user, and an evaluation of status is made. The program identifies to the user if the request was confirmed or denied. If denied, possible reasons are listed. Control now returns to function `main()` in the client which allows the user to place another request or shut down the client program.

The server is still sitting in receive status on **main_thread** and may or may not have requests running by other clients. The only option the user has is to stop the server. If the user selects this option, `main()` calls `stop_server()` with a parameter of the known port number. `stop_server()` establishes a socket and passes **initial_request** with "dr_id" of "master" through the INET connection to function `serversetup()`. This "dr_id" is passed to function `get_new_port()`, which returns value "99999". This value interrupts the while loop in `serversetup()`. `serversetup()` then mutex locks all files (so no file can be left open), returns **initial_request** to `stop_server()` which indicates that all files are locked. `serversetup()` then closes its socket and exits **main_thread**. Control is then returned to `stop_server()` which returns to `main()`. Since all files have been locked, `main()` now calls the function `pthread_kill_other_threads_np()`, which kills any threads which may have been left running. At this time the program enters an if statement and the user is given the option to print a days schedule from any room type. If the user selects 'R' for reports, function `print_files()` is called.

If the user selects any character other than 'R', the program ends. If 'R' is selected, `print_files()` enters a do-while loop allowing the user to print any day of any room type. When the user enters 'Z', `print_files()` returns to `main()`. The server program now ends and may be restarted with "hospitalrun".

A.3 Functional Descriptions

In this section, the functional descriptions as well as the interfaces to the functions are presented. Section A.3.1 presents the main client functions and Section A.3.2 presents the main server functions. Functions common to both are presented in Section A.3.3.

A.3.1 Client Functions functional Descriptions

This section presents the functional descriptions for `clientsetup()`, `evaluate_status()`, `main()`, `place_request()`, `place_request()`, `select_it()`, and `select_option()`. Figure A.12 depicts the state diagram of these functions.

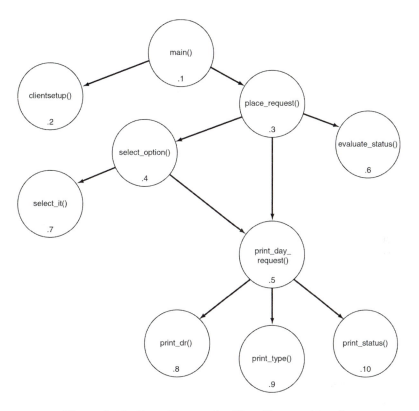

Figure A.12   State Diagram for Client/Surgeon Functions.

`int clientsetup(int addr_num)`
This function is used to initialize the client. The function is passed the well known port value **addr_num** used for binding with the server socket. The function first declares struct type initial_connect **initial_request**. Enumerated type "dr_id" of this client is then stored in **initial_request.** This value is constant for each client. **initial_request new_port** is initialized to 0 to give it any int value. A socket is then created of INET datagram type and **initial_request** is sent by datagram to the server. `clientsetup()` then waits in receive mode for the server to return **initial_request**, which carries the integer **new_port** value. When this value is returned from the server, **new_port** is returned to the calling program.

`int evaluate_status(struct day_request *request)`
This function evaluates the status of struct day_request **request** advising user of what transpired. `evaluate_status()` is passed a pointer to the current **request.** The function then enters an if statement, which evaluates **request->status0800 - request_status1600**. If any of the values = "confirm", then "Your request has been confirmed" is printed to the user. If

none of the values = "confirm", then an explanation of possible reasons is printed to the user. The function returns the value 0.

void main()

Client `main()` declares char **user_select** and int **new_port**. The function prints a welcome greeting to the user and then enters a do-while loop, waiting for user input **user_select** with `scanf()`. The user has 2 valid options, 'R' to place a request, or 'Q' to quit the program. All other options cause re-entry to the do-while loop. Inside the do-while loop is a switch statement, using **user_select** as the test expression. If 'R' is selected to place a request, `clientsetup()` is called, passing **KNOWN_PORT,** which was defined in commonh.h as the server common port for all initial requests. `clientsetup()` will create a socket and pass datagrams to the server, and returns int value of the port to be used for completion of the request. The returned value is stored in **new_port**. When clientsetup() returns this value, `place_request()` is called, and is passed the value of **new_port.** The request is then handled by `place_request()`. When `place_request()` completes, the do-while loop is re-entered giving the user the option to place another request or quit the program. If 'R' is selected, the client re-enters the previous scenario. If 'Q' is selected, the function `main()` ends and can only be restarted with the command "surgeonrun".

int place_request(int new_port)

This function is used to complete communication with the server on a port dedicated to the client for this request. `place_request()` is passed **new_port** which is the value of the dedicated port. The function first declares struct type day_request **request**, which is the data type used to pass the request from client to server, and for the server to return status. Int **my_sock** is declared, which is used to identify the socket used for the connection. Int **julian_date** and **Selection** are declared, **julian_date** being used to read the requested date from user, and **Selection** used to store the menu selection. A socket is built and bound. `place_request()` then enters a do-while loop, accepting user input for the date requested, **julian_date.** The do-while loop ensures that the date submitted by the user is between 1 and 365. The function then enters another do-while loop, requesting input to indicate the type of surgery requested. do-while is used to ensure that **Selection** is within bounds. Selection is then used as a test expression to store the appropriate enum type surgery_type in **request.surgery_name**. "open" status is then stored into **request.status0800 - request.status1600**. "open" status is required since the server depends on the request originating in this state. If not initialized to "open" status, the server will not update **request** with all available times. **request** is then sent to the server in a datagram. `place_request()` now waits in receive mode for a response. When a datagram is received from the server, **request** has been updated with available times for this surgery type and date. `place_request()` now calls `Select_option()` and passes the address of **request**. `Select_option()` interfaces with the user and updates **request** with the selection the user chooses. When `Select_option()` returns, `place_request()` sends **request** in a datagram to the server, and again waits in receive mode. When the datagram is received from the server, `print_day_request()` is called and passed a copy of **request. request** is printed for the user to see. When `print_day_request()` returns, `evaluate_status()` is called, and is passed a pointer to **request**. `evaluate_status()` prints to the user whether the request was confirmed by the server, or suggestions as to why it was not. When evaluate_status returns, the socket is closed, and function returns 0.

`int select_it (enum room_status *this_room_status,int time_Select)`
This function evaluates the status of **this_room_status**, and determines if the selection is valid. The function evaluates **this_room_status** with an if statement. If the value of **this_room_status** is "open", then the value of **this_room_status** is updated to "select" status, indicating it is a valid selection. The function then returns 0. If `this_room_status` is not in "open" status, a prompt message is printed indicating that the selected time is not valid, prints the selection **time_Select** and returns 1.

`int Select_option (struct day_request *request)`
This function allows the user to select what time they would like to schedule surgery of the times available. The function is passed the address of the current **request** after being returned by server(hospital). Int **time_Select** is declared which is used to store the user's selection. Int **valid_Selection** is declared and used as a flag to identify when a valid Selection has been input by the user. Int value 1(false) is stored in **valid_Selection,** and the function enters a while loop dependent on the **valid_selection** being changed to 0(true). The while loop continues until a time is chosen by the user which is in "open" status, indicating that the time is not "busy" or "pending". `print_day_request()` is called and passed a pointer to **request**. This prints a list of times available to the user. When `print_day_request()` returns, the user is prompted to input the time they would like to select, **time_select**. The value in **time_select** is then used as the test expression in a switch statement. If **time_select** value equates to the respective **request->status0800** - **request->status1600** being in "open" status, then **request->statusXXXX** is updated to "Select" status and **valid_selection** is updated with a value of 0, exiting the while loop. If **time_select** value DOES NOT equate to the respective **request->status0800** - **request->status1600** being in "open" status, a prompt message is printed indicating that the selected time is not valid, and the while loop is re-entered. A value of 0 entered by the user will exit the while loop with no selection made. When **valid_selection** is set to 0, the while loop exits, and the function returns 0.

A.3.2 Server Functions functional Descriptions

This section presents the functional descriptions for `get_new_port()`, `main()`, `print_files()`, `review_rooms()`, `run_request()`, `select_room()`, `select_stat()`, `serversetup()`, `stop_server()`, `test_pend()`, and `update_stat()`. Figure A.13 depicts the state diagram of these functions.

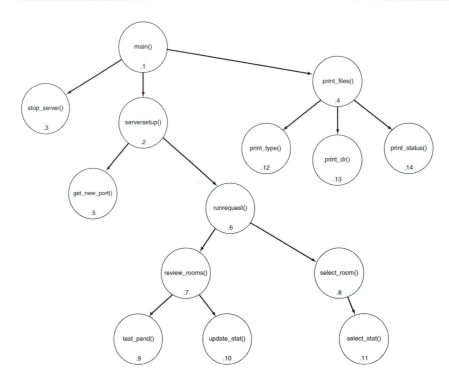

Figure A.13   State Diagram for Server Functions.

int get_new_port(struct initial_connect update_port)
This function is used to maintain list of valid "dr_id"'s and returns the port reserved for them on the server. The function is passed struct type initial_connect which holds the enumerated type "dr_id". The function evalutes this value by use of a switch statement. The "dr_id" is used as the test expression. The function returns the integer value of the assigned port for that "dr_id" value.

void main()
The server main() first declares a pthread called **main_thread**. It then declares and allocates memory for a pointer to int value **addr_num**, which stores the value of **KNOWN_PORT**, the known port address for the server. Type char **menu_option** is also declared. **main_thread** is created with pthread_create(), and serversetup() is called during pthread creation. The thread created is **main_thread** which will spawn other threads to handle surgeon requests. main() then enters a do-while loop, waiting for user input **menu_option**. The server sits at scanf(), waiting for the user to input the only valid option at this time, shutdown the server. Char value of '&' was chosen as the value required for input because it is physically difficult to select in error. The do-while loop continues to request input from the user until the value '&' is selected. During this time, **main_thread** is

handing all initial requests to the server and spawning child threads to handle requests to completion. When '&' is selected, `main()` calls `stop_server()`, and passes a pointer to the value of **KNOWN_PORT,addr_num**. `stop_server()` will cause the server to mutex lock all critical sections (files), exit **main_thread**, and allow safe shutdown of the server. As soon as `stop_server()` completes, `main()` kills all threads by calling `pthread_kill_other_threads_np()`. **main_thread** and any child threads of **main_thread** are now killed. `main()` now allows the user to print files by use of an if statement. If the user selects 'R' for reports, `print_files()` is called, which allows printing of any day and any file status. If the user does not select to `print_files()`, or `print_files()` completes, the program ends and can only be restarted with "hospitalrun" command.

int print_files()

This function is used to print files at the server site. Struct room_struct **init_room[366]** is declared to build an array of room structs from file. The function enters a do-while loop which loops until the user requests to exit. Inside the first do-while loop, another do-while loop is entered, which loops until the user inputs a valid selection. The function then prints a selection of files for the user to open and print from. When the user inputs a valid selection, the appropriate file is opened, and **init_room** is loaded with the file data. The user is prompted to input the day to be printed. Another do_while loop is entered, again to ensure a valid selection between 1 and 365. When a valid user selection is made, that day is printed to output, using `print_type()`, `print_status()`, `print_dr()`, and `printf()` functions. The file is closed. The user is again returned to the main selection do-while loop, given the option to select another type of room and day to print. When the user selects 'Z', the while loops exit, the function ends, and returns the value 0.

int review_rooms(struct day_request *request)

This function identifies which hospital rooms are available for the day a client requests to schedule surgery. The function is passed a pointer to the current request with all hours previously assigned open status. Char type array **roomtype** is declared to identify which file needs to build an array from file. Var type struct room_struct **init_room[366]** is declared as the array which will hold the values contained in the selected file. The function then enters a switch statement using **request->surgery_name** as the test expression. This switch statement will identify which room type the surgeon requires. Base on the room type, `strcpy()` is used to assign **roomtype** the proper string values of the file to use. `pthread_mutex_lock()` is called to set a lock of the appropriate file process through the switch statement. The required file is then opened, and array **init_room** is loaded with room_struct values from the file. The function then calls `test_pend()` multiple times passing the address of individual values of **init_room[i].status0800** - **init_room[i].status1600** and **init_room.ptime0800** - **init_room[i].ptime1600.** Function `test_pend()` will evaluate if "pending" status has expired and update **init_room** accordingly. `review_rooms()` then calls `update_stat()` multiple times passing the address of individual values of **init_room[i].status0800** - **init_room[i].status1600,**

init_room.ptime0800 - **init_room[i].ptime1600,** **request->status0800** - **request->status1600,** and **request->"dr_id".** Function `update_stat()` will review each room_status for "open" status, update **request** and **init_room** accordingly. Read file is then closed, and the file is reopened in write status. **init_room** is then written back to file, a switch statement is used to identify which mutex lock to unlock with **request->surgery_name** as the test expression. The write file is closed, mutex is unlocked, and the value 0 is returned.

```
void run_request(int  *new_addr)
```
This function is called following creation of **surgeon_thread** and is used to process a request from a client on the port value passed to it. The port value is used as a dedicated port to completion of the incoming client request.

       The function first creates a socket using the value of the **new_addr**. The socket is created, bound, and waits in receive mode for an incoming request from the client that is assigned to this port. When the datagram is received from the client, it contains struct type day_request, **request**. The function passes the address of **request** to function `review_rooms()`, which updates **request** with available times that the client may choose based on the date reflected in **request**. When `review_rooms()` completes, **request** is sent back to the client through a datagram, and `run_request()` sits again in receive mode waiting for a response from the client. When **request** is received from the client through a datagram, the client has updated it with a selected time, and `run_request()` calls function `select_room()`, passing the address of **request**. `select_room()` updates the appropriate files, and performs required checking. When `select_room()` completes, `run_request()` sends the now completed **request** back to the client with confirmation information. The socket is closed, and **surgeon_thread** is exited.

```
int select_room(struct day_request *request)
```
This function will update the appropriate room file and confirm a request for the day and time a client requests a room. The function is passed a pointer to struct day_request with one time in "Select" status. char type array **roomtype** is declared to identify which file needs to be used to build an array from file. Struct type room_struct **init_room[366]** is declared as the array which will hold the values contained in the selected file. The function then enters a switch statement using **request->surgery_name** as the test expression. This switch statement will identify which room type the surgeon requires. Based on the room type, `strcpy()` is used to assign **roomtype** the proper string values of the file to use. `pthread_mutex_lock()` is also set for the appropriate file process through the switch statement. The appropriate file is then opened, and array **init_room** is loaded with room_struct values from the file. The function then enters multiple if-else statements comparing **request->status0800** - **request->status1600** for "Select" status. If the value of the request for this time is "Select", then `select_stat()` is called, passing the addresses of **request.statusXXXX** (XXXX = the appropriate value 0800-1600), **init_room[i].statusXXXX,** **request->dr_name,** and **init_room[i].drXXXX.** `select_stat()` will confirm or deny the request in select status based on the values of the

parameters passed, and update them accordingly. When `select_stat()` returns, readfile is closed, and the file is reopened in write status. **init_room** is then written back to file, a switch statement is used to identify which mutex lock to unlock with **request->surgery_name** as the test expression. The write file is closed, mutex is unlocked, and the value 0 is returned.

`int select_stat(enum room_status *request_room_status, enum`
`room_status *file_room_status, enum "dr_id" *request_dr, enum`
`"dr_id" *file_dr);`
This function will confirm or deny a request from a client based on the values of the passed parameters. The function is passed **request_room_status* with status of "Select". The function first enters an if statement testing the value of **request_dr.** If **request_dr = file_dr** then file_room_status is updated with "busy" status and **file_dr** is left as is and thus unchanged. **request_room_status** is updated with "confirm" status. If **request_dr != file_dr**, then **request_room_status** is updated with "busy" status since the room has since been selected by another client. Note: regardless of the status, if this client's ID is on file_room_status, it is safe to assign the room. No client has requested it since this client or the "dr_id" would change. Also, a room should never be in "open" status once it has been selected the first time. Only the "dr_id" should change on pending status. This function returns the value 0.

`void serversetup(int *addr_num)`
This function is called during `pthread_create()` and is run by **main_thread** of the server program. The function is passed a pointer to the known port value, **addr_num**, used for binding with server socket. The function first declares a thread to spawn child threads used for completion of client requests on a dedicated port. The thread declared is **surgeon_thread**. Int * **new_addr** var is also declared. The function then creates a socket, binds it, and initializes mutexes to be used by child threads. The function then enters a while loop which causes the function to continue running until the user requests the server be shutdown (shutdown operation will be explained later in this functional description). Once the while loop is entered, the function causes the thread to sit in receive mode waiting for a client to send a datagram which includes type struct initial_connect, **initial_request**. When the datagram is received, `serversetup()` calls `get_new_port()` and passes **initial_request**. `get_new_port()` returns the integer value which is assigned to that client. **initial_request.new_port** is updated with the new port value returned by `get_new_port()`. A datagram is then sent to the client which includes the new port value. **surgeon_thread** is then created, calling `runrequest()`. `runrequest()` will create a socket to handle the remainder of this client's request. `serversetup()` then returns to the while loop in receive mode waiting for another client datagram with an **initial_request.** The previous scenario will continue for all requests until `stop_server()` sends a datagram to `serverinit()` with an **initial_request."dr_id"** of "master". When this datagram is received, `serverinit()` calls `get_new_port()`. A "dr_id" of "master" causes `get_new_port()` to return the value "99999". This value causes the while loop to exit. When the while loop exits,

`pthread_mutex_lock()` is called for all mutex locks. This will ensure data integrity. `serverinit()` then sends a datagram back to `stop_server()` with **initial_ request.new_port** set to 99999. This indicates to `stop_server()` that all mutex's are now locked. The socket is then closed, and `pthread_exit()` is called to exit **main_thread**.

int stop_server(int addr_num)

This function is used to stop the server. The function is passed the well known port value **addr_num** used for binding with server socket. The function first declares a struct of type initial_connect, **initial_request**. This struct is then loaded with the "dr_id" of "master" which indicates to the server to shutdown when it has access to all critical sections. The **initial_request.new_port** is initialized to 0 to give it any int value. A socket is then created of INET datagram type and **initial_request** is passed to the server. The function then waits in a receive mode for any return value which indicates that server has shut down. The socket is closed and value of '99999' is returned to the calling program.

int test_pend(enum room_status *this_room_status long int *this_time)

This function will review status of the room passed, and update if pending status has expired. The function first declares type struct timeval, **current_time,** used to timestamp the request. The current time of day is established through function `gettimeofday()`. The function then enters an if statement evaluating **this_room_status** to identify if the value is enumerated type "pending" status. If the value for the requested room is "pending", the function enters another if statement. The second if statement compares **this_time** to the current time of day timestamp. If the request is over ten minutes old, **this_room_status** is updated with "open", since time has expired for the request which put the timeslot in pending status. If not "pending", or the pending status is less than 10 minutes old, then **this_room-status** is left with the same value as was passed to the function. This function returns the value 0.

int update_stat(enum room_status *request_room_status, enum room_status *file_room_status, long int *this_time, enum "dr_id" *request_dr, enum "dr_id" *file_dr);

This function is used to update the status of the requested room_status and "dr_id", based on the data file status. `update_stat()` first declares type struct timeval **current_time,** used to timestamp the request. The current time of day is established through function `gettimeof-day()`. The function then enters an if-else statement to review **file_room_status** for "open" status 08:00 - 16:00. If the file does not reflect a timeslot as being available ("open" status), then the status in the array is assigned to **request_room_status** and nothing is changed in **file_room_status**. If the value of **file_room_status** is "open", "pending" is written to **file_room_status, current_time** is written to **this_time** and "open" is left in **request_room_status**. The surgeon will be advised that this timeslot is available. The client(surgeon) now has ten minutes to respond to the request or may lose it. **file_dr** is updated with the "dr_id" of the surgeon for whom the slot is being held. if - else exits, and function returns the value 0.

A.3.3 Common Functions functional Descriptions

This section presents the functional descriptions for `print_day_request()`, `print_dr()`, `print_status()`, `print_type()`, and `run_request()`.

int print_day_request(struct day_request request)

This function is used to print a request from either the server or the client. The function is passed a var of type struct day_request **request**. Surgeon name, request date, surgery name, and status of the time slots from 08:00 - 16:00 are printed. Printing of the surgeon name is done via a call to `print_dr()`, and passing **request.dr_name**. Printing of the surgery type is done by a call to `print_type()` and passing **request.surgery_name.** Surgery date is printed directly, as the date is type int. Room status for the various times is printed via calling function `print_status()` and passing **request.status0800 - request.status1600**. This function returns the value 0.

int print_dr(enum "dr_id" this_dr)

This function prints a doctor name. The function is passed a variable of enum type "dr_id". The function uses a switch statement with **this_dr** as the tested expression. Based on the expression value, the appropriate name is printed. This function returns the value 0.

int print_status(enum room_status this_room_status)

This function prints status of a room. The function is passed a variable of enum type room_status. The function uses a switch statement with **this_room_status** as the tested expression. Based on the expression value, a representation of the appropriate status is printed. This function returns the value 0.

int print_type(enum surgery_type this_type)

This function prints a surgery name. The function is passed a variable of enum type surgery_type. The function uses a switch statement with **this_type** as the tested expression. Based on the expression value, a representation of the appropriate surgery_type is printed. This function returns the value 0.

A.3.4 File Initialization

void main()

File initialization `main()` is used to initialize files for the server to use in the Surgical Scheduling Program. The program should only need to be used once for the server, as all updates to the files should be made through the server program. It also may be used to initialize the data files if they become irrevocably corrupted. **Warning**: This program will erase all previously scheduled values.

The function declares struct room_struct **init_room[366]** , struct timeval **current_time**, char **user_select,** char **this_file[],** and int **I.** The value of 366 was chosen to reflect 365 days of the year. Julian day 1 = **init_room**[1], Julian day 2 = **init_room**[2] etc. The function enters a do-while loop (while user does not request to exit), and enters another do-while loop inside the first. The second do-while is used to ensure that the user selects a valid option. main() prints a message to the user, asking for a selection of the various files to initialize. The user is allowed 'A' - 'D' (valid files options), or 'Z' to exit. The function waits for user input **user_select** with scanf(). When the user selects one of 'A' - 'D', strcpy() is used to the appropriate file name to **this_file**. Gettimeofday() is called to get the correct time of day and is loaded in **current_time**. The function then enters a for loop, for i= 1 to 366. Array **init_room** is built using the following default values.

♦ init_room[i].statusXXXX = "open",

♦ init_room[i].ptimeXXXX = current_time.tv_sec,

♦ init_room[i].drXXXX = "none".

♦ (XXXX = 0800 - 1600)

The function then writes the array to the appropriate file based on the user selection. The file is closed, and user is returned to the previous while loop for further selection. This continues until the user selects 'Z', at which time the function exits and program ends.

A.4 DATA DICTIONARY

Asssumptions:

```
        alphanumeric =    {A...|Z|a...|z|0...|9}
        char =      {A...|Z|a...|z}
        numeric =      {0...|9}

        FILE =

                *defined in man pages*

        pthread_mutex_t =

                *defined in pthread library man pages*

        pthread_t =

                *defined in pthread library man pages*

        sockaddr_in =
```

defined in socket library man pages

Dictionary:
addr_num = [numeric]
cardio_room mutex = [pthread_mutex_t]
client = [sockaddr_in]
client_len = [numeric]
current_time = [timeval]
day_request = [dr_name + surgery_name + julian_date +
                 status0800 + status0900 + status1000 +
                 status1100 + status1200 + status1300 +
                 status1400 + status1500 + status1600]

dr0800 = ["dr_id"]
dr0900 = ["dr_id"]
dr1000 = ["dr_id"]
dr1100 = ["dr_id"]
dr1200 = ["dr_id"]
dr1300 = ["dr_id"]
dr1400 = ["dr_id"]
dr1500 = ["dr_id"]
dr1600 = ["dr_id"]

"dr_id" =
     ["johnson"|"smith"|"williams"|"jones"|"master"|"none"]

dr_name = ["dr_id"]
DRNAME = ["dr_id"]
error_num = [numeric]
file_room_status = [room_status]
i = [numeric]
initial_connect = [dr_name + new_port]
initial_request = [initial_connect]
init_room[] = [room_struct]
julian_date = [numeric]
KNOWN_PORT = [numeric]
known_sock = [numeric]
main_thread = [pthread_t]
menu_option = [alphanumeric]
my_sock = [numeric]
neuro_room_mutex = [pthread_mutex_t]

```
new_add = [numeric]
new_addr = [numeric]
new_port = [numeric]
ortho_room_mutex = [pthread_mutex_t]
plastic_room_mutex = [pthread_mutex_t]
ptime0800 = [numeric]
ptime0900 = [numeric]
ptime1000 = [numeric]
ptime1100 = [numeric]
ptime1200 = [numeric]
ptime1300 = [numeric]
ptime1400 = [numeric]
ptime1500 = [numeric]
ptime1600 = [numeric]
request = [day_request]
room_file = [FILE]
room_status = ["busy"|"open"|"pending"|"Select"|"confirm"]
room_struct = [julian_date
                + status0800 + ptime0800 + dr0800
                + status0900 + ptime0900 + dr0900
                + status1000 + ptime1000 + dr1000
                + status1100 + ptime1100 + dr1100
                + status1200 + ptime1200 + dr1200
                + status1300 + ptime1300 + dr1300
                + status1400 + ptime1400 + dr1400
                + status1500 + ptime1500 + dr1500
                + status1600 + ptime1600 + dr1600]
roomtype = [alphanumeric]
Selection = [alphanumeric]
server = [sockaddr_in]
SERVER_HOST = [numeric + "." + numeric + "." + numeric
                + "." + numeric ]
server_len = [numeric]
status0900 = [room_status]
status1000 = [room_status]
status1100 = [room_status]
status1200 = [room_status]
status1300 = [room_status]
status1400 = [room_status]
status1500 = [room_status]
status1600 = [room_status]
stop_request = [initial_connect]
surgeon_thread = [pthread_t]
```

```
surgery_name = [surgery_type]
surgery_type = ["neuro"|"cardio"|"plastic"|"ortho"]
surg_type = [surgery_type]
this_dr = ["dr_id"]
this_file[] = [alphanumeric]
this_room_status = [room_status]
this_time = [numeric]
this_type = [surgery_type]
thread_sock = [numeric]
time_Select = [numeric]
update_port = [initial_connect]
user_select = [alphanumeric]
valid_Selection = [(0|1)] };
```

A.5 USER DOCUMENTATION

This section includes documentation necessary to run the program. Section A.5.1 presents installation instructions. Section A.5.2 presents information on how to run the program.

A.5.1 Installation Instructions

Installation of the server requires setting two definitions prior to compiling. KNOWN_PORT and SERVER_HOST. KNOWN_PORT is the value assigned as a common port for clients to call, and SERVER_HOST is the IP address of the server. Both definitions are found in file "commonh.h". The server also requires program Initialize Files to be run. The source code for this program is provided in file "write_ca.c" . To run this program, the installer compiles the program by typing "cc write_ca.c". When the program completes compiling, type "a.out". The File Initialization program is self prompting from this point on. It will build 4 separate files each for a different type of surgical room. The program also initializes the files with default values.

During installation, the server program also needs to have correct enumerated type dr-id's reflected in the commonh.h file and various switch statements need to be updated with all valid "dr_id" values. The associated switch statements can be found in function get_new_port() and prnt_dr().

Client installation requires setting two definitions prior to compiling, KNOWN_PORT and DRNAME. KNOWN_PORT is defined as explained in the server. DRNAME is the "dr_id" assigned for this client. No further action is required for the client.

A.5.2 How to run the program

NOTE: Ensure installation is complete prior to attempting to run this program!! See previous **Installation** section.

      The only requirements for running the program are to ensure all files are available in the same UNIX directory, and a current level of C compiler is available on the UNIX system. The client was run on Redhat Linux level 4.2, C compiler GNU level 2.7. The server was also run on Redhat Linux level 4.2, C compiler GNU 2.7. Server files required are: commonc.c, hospital.c, inethosp.c, serverinit.c, write_ca.c (program init_files used to build and initialize data files), commonh.h, hospital.h, and makefile (made specifically for the server). The files required for the client are: commonc.c, surgeon.c, inetsurg.c, clientinit.c, commonh.h, surgeon.h, and makefile (made specifically for the client).

      Once the files are available, the user must ensure that the directory holding the files is the working directory. The user must type "makefile" to compile, link, and bind. When this process completes, the user should enter "hospitalrun" if at the server, and "surgeonrun" if at the client. From this point, both programs are self-prompting and menu driven.

      NOTE: When room_structs are printed at the server, the output will indicate "pending" status for any time that day has been previously requested by a client and the time was not selected. When a request is displayed for the client, "Open" will be displayed for a request in "open" status every time.

A.6 CLIENT SOURCE CODE

A.6.1 inetsurg.c

```
/*
    "inetsurg.c"  file used for server function main() in the
    Surgical Scheduling Program
    Functions included: main().
    Written by John A. Fritz under direction of Dr. D. L. Galli.
*/


    #include "commonh.h"
                    /* .h files and definitions required for both
                        client and server */
    #include "surgeon.h"
                    /* .h files and definitions needed exclusively
                        for surgeon. */


/******************* main ********************/
```

```
void main()
 {
    enum "dr_id" this_doc;
                /* declare a var to be able to print welcome */
    char user_select[1];
                /* for user to select option */
    int new_port;
                /* port for client to hook up with */
    this_doc = DRNAME;
                /* assign this_doc the name of the the defined id */
    printf("\n\n\n Welcome to the Surgeon Scheduling
            Program Dr. ");
    print_dr(this_doc);
                /* print the surgeons name. make it friendly */
   do
                /* continue allowing user to place requests until
                    selection 'Q' to exit */
    {
     printf("Enter 'R' to make a request, 'Q' to quit \n");
     scanf("%s", user_select);
     user_select[0] = toupper(user_select[0]);
     switch (user_select[0])
        {
          case 'R':
                     new_port = clientsetup(KNOWN_PORT);
                     place_request(new_port);
                 break;
          case 'Q':
                     printf("Shutting down system.\n");
                     printf("Please Enter 'surgeonrun'
                            to begin again \n");
                 break;
          default:
                     printf("You have chosen an invalid
                            option.\n");
                 break;
       } /* end switch */
     } /* end do while */
    while(user_select[0] != 'Q');
    } /* end main */
```

A.6.2 Client Makefile

Surgical Scheduling Program makefile for the client.

```
surgeonrun:inetsurg.o clientinit.o surgeon.o commonc.o
    cc -o surgeonrun inetsurg.o clientinit.o surgeon.o commonc.o
inetsurg.o:commonh.h surgeon.h
clientinit.o: commonh.h surgeon.h
surgeon.o: commonh.h surgeon.h
commonc.o: commonh.h hospital.h
```

A.6.3 Surgeon.h

```
/* "surgeon.h" file used to maintain include files and
   definitions used exclusively for the client. Surgical
   Scheduling Program
*/
```

```
#define DRNAME smith;
                /* establish the "dr_id" of the dr making request from
                   this client program. Each client program should
                   have this field set for the proper surgeon. */
int clientsetup(int addr_num);
                /* function used to initialize client.
                   pre - function is passed well known port value
                        used for binding with server socket.
                   post - function waits in receive mode for value
                        of new port. When this value is
                        returned from the server, the new port value
                        is returned to the calling program. */
int place_request(int new_port);
                /* function used to initialize new port dedicated to
                   this request.
                   pre - function is passed new port value which will
                        be dedicated to this request until completed.
                   post - function will complete request for surgical
                        scheduling of a room. */
int select_option (struct day_request *request);
                /* function allows the user to select a surgery
                   time based on the slots available.
                   pre - function is passed pointer to struct
                        day_request.
```

post -function updates request with the selection
made by the user. */

```
int evaluate_status(struct day_request *request);
```
/* function evaluates status of struct day_request
advising user of what transpired.
pre - function is passed address of the current
struct after being returned by server(hospital).
post - function prints to user what the status of the
request is, based on values in the struct. */

```
int select_it(enum room_status *this_room_status, int
time_Select);
```
/* This function will evaluate *this_room_status
to identify if it is in "open" status.
pre - function is passed enum type room_status.
post - if *this_room_status = open, return 0.
else notify user and return 1. */

A.6.4 Clientinit.c

/* "clientinit.c" file used for function clientsetup() in the
Surgical Scheduling Program
Functions included:
   clientsetup().
*/

```
   #include "commonh.h"
```
/* local file kept for all common include files */
```
   #include "surgeon.h"
```
/* local file kept of all include files specific
to the client (surgeon). */
```
struct initial_connect initial_request;
```
/* struct passed to server requesting connection
on dedicated port */

/***************** clientsetup *********************/
```
   int clientsetup(int addr_num)
```
/* function used to initialize client.
pre - function is passed well known port value
used for binding with server socket.
post - function waits in receive mode for value
of new port. When this value is returned
from the server, the new port value is

```
                          returned to the calling program */
{
    int known_sock,      /* used to identify this particular socket */
               server_len;
                          /* used to identify length of server information */
    struct sockaddr_in server,
                          /* used to produce internet version of port
                            for both server*/
               client;
                          /* and client */
    struct msghdr msg;
                          /* declare struct to be used in sendmsg */
    struct iovec iov[1];
                          /* declare struct to be used to hold values
                            for data and length of data for sendmsg */
    initial_request.dr_name = DRNAME;
                          /* store the value previously defined for this
                            client into initial request. */
    initial_request.new_port = 0;
                          /* initialize request for new_port to 0 prior
                            to sending request to server. */
    server.sin_family = AF_INET;
                          /* establish this connection as internet type */
    server.sin_port = htons(addr_num);
                          /* assign port number passed to function */
    server.sin_addr.s_addr = inet_addr(SERVER_HOST);
                          /* lookup inet adress, actual value for this
                            host was given in the commonh.h file */
    if ((known_sock = socket(AF_INET, SOCK_DGRAM, 0)) < 0)
                          /* create a handle for this connection.
                            domain of connection is AF_INET used for
                            connection between different machines.
                            SOCK_DGRAM is the style of communication,
                            using datagrams versus stream. Connection is
                            "connectionless". The third parameter is the
                            protocol to be used, 0 indicates default value */
        {
          perror("Client Socket Error ");
          exit(1);
        } /* end if */
    client.sin_family = AF_INET;
                          /* establish this connection as internet type */
    client.sin_addr.s_addr = htonl(INADDR_ANY);
```

```
                    /* address is set to INADDR_ANY, to allow
                        default assignment. */
    client.sin_port = htons(0);
                    /* default value 0 allows connection to any port. */
    if (bind(known_sock, (struct sockaddr *) &client,
                sizeof(client)) <0)
                    /* bind the socket values to this socket.
                        known_sock is the value of this socket,
                        &client is the client information, family
                        name and protocol. third parameter is the
                        number of bytes in the address. */
      {
        perror("Client Bind Error");
        exit(1);
      } /* end if */
    server_len = sizeof(server);
    msg.msg_name = (char *) &server;
    msg.msg_namelen = server_len;
    msg.msg_iov = iov;
    msg.msg_iovlen = 1;
    msg.msg_control = NULL;
    msg.msg_controllen = 0;
                    /* assign values for msg struct and iov for sendmsg.
                        msg_name is optional, carries address of the
                          receiver. (not required on connection  protocol.
                        msg_namelen = length of name.
                        msg_iov = array of input/output buffer.
                        msg_iovlen = number of elements in msg_iov.
                        msg_control = ancillary data, set to NULL.
                        msg_controllen = value result arg for recvmsg. */

    iov[0].iov_base = &initial_request;
                    /* assign address of the initial_request to be sent */
    iov[0].iov_len = sizeof(initial_request);
    if (sendmsg(known_sock,&msg,0) < 0)
                    /* send message to server, requesting
                        new port value to reconnect with in
                        msghdr iovec. Also pass struct
                        client for return message.
                        1st parm is socket file descriptor,
                        2nd parm is pointer to msghdr,
                        3rd value is flags */

      {
```

```
            perror("Sendmsg");
            exit(1);
            } /* end if */
    if (recvmsg(known_sock, &msg ,0) < 0)
                    /* receive message sent from server.
                       This message holds port value to reconnect
                       with to complete request.
                       1st parm is socket file descriptor,
                       2nd parm is pointer to msghdr,
                       3rd value is flags */

        {
          perror ("Client Recvmsg Error");
          close(known_sock);
          exit(1);
          } /* end if */
      close(known_sock);
                    /* close socket, no longer used for this client
                       transaction */
      return(initial_request.new_port);
                    /* return value of port which will be dedicated to
                       complete the request from this client */
      } /* end function clientsetup */
```

A.6.5 Surgeon.c

```
/* "surgeon.c" maintains functions used exclusively in the
   client for the Surgical Scheduling Program.
   Functions included:
    place_request(),
    Select_option(),
    evaluate_status(),
    select_it().
*/

    #include "commonh.h"
                    /* local file kept for all common include files
                       and definitions. */
    #include "surgeon.h"
                    /* local file kept for all include files and
                       definitions exclusive to the client (surgeon)*/
    struct day_request request;
                    /* struct format used to pass request from client
```

to server and return */

```
/**************** place_request *******************/
   int place_request(int new_port)
                /* function used to complete request on port dedicated
                to this request.
                pre - function is passed new port value which will
                    be dedicated to this request until completed.
                post - function will complete request for surgical
                    scheduling of a room. */
   {
     int my_sock,        /* used to identify this particular socket */
                server_len,
                /* used to identify length of server information */
                julian_date;
                /* used to read requested date from user */
     char Selection[1];
                /* used to read Selection of options from user */
     struct sockaddr_in server,
                /* used to produce internet version of port
                for both server*/
                client;
                        /* and client */
   struct msghdr msg;
                        /* declare struct to be used in sendmsg
*/
     struct iovec iov[1];
                /* declare struct to be used to hold values
                for data and length of data for sendmsg */
     request.dr_name = DRNAME;
                /* assign this request the #define value in
                surgeon.h. This value must be set for each
                client and doesn't change. */
     server.sin_family = AF_INET;
                /* establish this connection as internet type */

     server.sin_port = htons(new_port);
                /* assign port number passed to function */
     server.sin_addr.s_addr = inet_addr(SERVER_HOST);
                /* lookup inet address, actual value for this
                host was given in the commonh.h file,
                #define SERVER_HOST */
     if ((my_sock = socket(AF_INET, SOCK_DGRAM, 0)) < 0)
```

```
                   /* create a handle for this connection.
                      domain of connection is AF_INET used for
                      connection between different machines.
                      SOCK_DGRAM is the style of communication,
                      using datagrams versus stream. Connection is
                      "connectionless". The third parameter is the
                      protocol to be used, 0 indicates default value */
        {
           perror("Client Socket");
           exit(1);
        } /* end if */
client.sin_family = AF_INET;
                   /* see previous descriptions for server */
client.sin_addr.s_addr = htonl(INADDR_ANY);
                   /* address is set to INADDR_ANY, to allow
                      default assignment. */
client.sin_port = htons(0);
                   /* default value 0 allows connection to any port. */
if (bind(my_sock, (struct sockaddr *) &client,
           sizeof(client)) <0)
                   /* bind the socket values to this socket.
                      my_sock is the value of this socket,
                      &client is the client information, family
                      name and protocol. third parameter is the
                      number of bytes in the address. */
  {
      perror("Client Bind");
      exit(1);
  } /* end if */
server_len = sizeof(server);
                   /* request information from user for date of requested
                      service and what type of surgery. load into the
                      struct to be sent to hospital */
do
{
                   /* continue requesting julian date until valid
                      day is input */
     printf("What Julian Date are you requesting surgery for ? \n");
     scanf("%d", &julian_date);
   } /* end do-while */
while((julian_date<1) || (julian_date >365));
request.julian_date = julian_date;
                   /* store value user would like to request into
```

struct request to be passed to client.
Then print options to user and request type of
room. */

```c
do
{
  printf("\n\n\n What type of surgery would you like to schedule?
\n");
  printf("Please make Selection out of the following choices: \n");
  printf(" A = neuro surgery \n");
  printf(" B = cardio-vascular surgery \n");
  printf(" C = plastic surgery \n");
  printf(" D = orthopedic surgery \n");
  scanf("%s", Selection);
  Selection[0] = toupper(Selection[0]);
  switch (Selection[0])
              /* based on user selection, load request with what
                 type of surgery to be passed to server */
  {
    case 'A':
      request.surgery_name = neuro;
      break;
    case 'B':
      request.surgery_name = cardio;
      break;
    case 'C':
      request.surgery_name = plastic;
      break;
    case 'D':
      request.surgery_name = ortho;
      break;
    default:
      printf("Invalid Selection \n");
  } /* end switch */
              /* set open status into each room status of the request.
                 Server depends on this being done. The server operates
                 by changing a request status if a room is NOT
                 available. Therefore, it doesn't change the request to
                 status "open", it just leaves that value untouched
                 if the room is available. */
} /* do-while */
              /* continue to loop giving user options until valid
                 option is selected */
while    ((Selection[0] != 'A')
```

```
              && (Selection[0] != 'B')
              && (Selection[0] != 'C')
              && (Selection[0] != 'D'));
   request.status0800 = open;
   request.status0900 = open;
   request.status1000 = open;
   request.status1100 = open;
   request.status1200 = open;
   request.status1300 = open;
   request.status1400 = open;
   request.status1500 = open;
   request.status1600 = open;
   server_len = sizeof(server);
   msg.msg_name = (char *) &server;
   msg.msg_namelen = server_len;
   msg.msg_iov = iov;
   msg.msg_iovlen = 1;
   msg.msg_control = NULL;
   msg.msg_controllen = 0;
                /* assign values for msg struct and iov for sendmsg.
                   msg_name is optional, carries address of the
                      receiver. (not required on connection  protocol.
                   msg_namelen = length of name.
                   msg_iov = array of input/output buffer.
                   msg_iovlen = number of elements in msg_iov.
                   msg_control = ancillary data, set to NULL.
                   msg_controllen = value result arg for recvmsg. */
   iov[0].iov_base = &request;
                /* assign address of the initial_request to be sent */
   iov[0].iov_len = sizeof(request);
   if (sendmsg(my_sock,&msg,0) < 0)
                /* send the request to the server to obtain a
                   list of hours available for the requested
                   day and type of surgery.
                   1st parm is socket file descriptor,
                   2nd parm is pointer to msghdr,
                   3rd value is flags */
     {
       perror("Sendmsg");
       close(my_sock);
       exit(1);
     } /* end if */
   if (recvmsg(my_sock, &msg ,0) < 0)
```

```
                    /* receive message sent from server.
                       This message holds times available
                       to complete request.
                       1st parm is socket file descriptor,
                       2nd parm is pointer to msghdr,
                       3rd value is flags */
       {
        perror ("Client Recvmsg Error");
        close(my_sock);
        exit(1);
       } /* end if */
   Select_option(&request);
                    /* send the request to function Select_option
                       to view what times the server indicates is
                       available, and allow the user to select a
                       slot out of those available. */
   if (sendmsg(my_sock,&msg,0) < 0)
                    /* send the request to the server with option
                       Selected out of the choices given.
                       see previous "sendmsg". */
      {
       perror("Sendmsg");
       close(my_sock);
       exit(1);
      } /* end if */
   if (recvmsg(my_sock, &msg ,0) < 0)
                    /* receive response from the server.
                       struct request should either confirm our
                       request or notify us of need to resend
                       request. Either way, program ends. */
      {
       perror ("Client Recvmsg Error");
       close(my_sock);
       exit(1);
      } /* end if */

   print_day_request(request);
                    /* display struct request to user to show status
                       as returned by server (hospital) */

   evaluate_status(&request);
                    /* evaluate status and explain to user whether
                       the request was confirmed or they must resubmit
```

```
                    */
        close(my_sock);
                        /* close socket, no longer used for this client
                            transaction */
        return(0);
        } /* end function place_request */


/*************** Select_option ********************/
    int Select_option (struct day_request *request)
                    /* function allows user to select what time frame
                        they would like to schedule surgery of the
                        times available.
                        pre - function is passed address of the current
                            struct after being returned by server(hospital).
                        post - function updates struct with the users request.
                        */
    {
        int time_Select,
                        /* used to read user Selection of time Selected for
                            surgery out of the options given */
                valid_Selection;
                        /* used to identify when a valid Selection has
                            input by the user. */
        time_Select = 0;
                        /* initialize to any value other than a valid value */
        printf("Following is the status of times
                of your request \n");
        valid_Selection = 1;
                        /* set var to invalid variable to check for
                            valid Selection status being set. */
        while (valid_Selection != 0 )
                        /* continue until a valid time is chosen which is in
                            open status, saying that the time is not
                            already comitted or in pending status */
        {
            print_day_request(*request);
                        /* print the struct of times available which was
                            passed to the function */
            printf("Please type in the numeric time
                            you would like to Select in the \n");
            printf("following format : XX00, where XX
                    is the hour. Example: 0800 \n");
            printf("If you would like to return with
```

```
            no option ", "selected, please enter 0000 \n");
scanf("%d", &time_Select);
        /* get user option, then enter switch statement
        to process user selection.*/
switch (time_Select)
 {
   case 800:
            valid_Selection =
                select_it(&request->status0800,
                time_Select);
        /* select_it will identify if the selection is valid
           ("open" status) or already selected (other than
           "open" status). If the selection was valid, select_it
           returns 0 and while loop is exited. If selection is not
           valid, then 1 is returned, and user must select again.
        */
            break;
   case 900:
            valid_Selection =
                select_it(&request->status0900,
                time_Select);
            break;
   case 1000:
            valid_Selection =
                select_it(&request->status1000,
                time_Select);
            break;
   case 1100:
            valid_Selection =
                select_it(&request->status1100,
                time_Select);
            break;
   case 1200:
            valid_Selection =
                select_it(&request->status1200,
                time_Select);
            break;
   case 1300:
            valid_Selection =
                select_it(&request->status1300,
                time_Select);
            break;
   case 1400:
```

```
                    valid_Selection =
                        select_it(&request->status1400,
                        time_Select);
                break;
        case 1500:
                    valid_Selection =
                        select_it(&request->status1500,
                        time_Select);
                break;
        case 1600:
                    valid_Selection =
                        select_it(&request->status1600,
                        time_Select);
                break;
        case 0:
                    valid_Selection = 0;
                break;
```
            /* return struct with no selection made */
```
            default:
                    printf("Time Selection %d
                is not valid or is not in open status. \n",
                time_Select);
                        printf("Please choose again.\n");
```
    } /* end switch */
  } /* end while */
} /* end function Select_option*/

/*************** evaluate_status *******************/
```
    int evaluate_status(struct day_request *request)
```
                /* function evaluates status of struct day_request
                advising user of what transpired.
                pre - function is passed address of the current
                    struct after being returned by server(hospital).
                post - function prints to user what the status of the
                    request is, based on values in the struct. */

    {

                /* if any status was confirmed, notify the user.*/
```
    if ((request->status0800 == confirm)
        || (request->status0900 == confirm)
        || (request->status1000 == confirm)
        || (request->status1100 == confirm)
        || (request->status1200 == confirm)
        || (request->status1300 == confirm)
```

```
            || (request->status1400 == confirm)
            || (request->status1500 == confirm)
            || (request->status1600 == confirm))
    {
     printf("Your request has been confirmed. \n");
    } /* end if */
    else
```
            /* else explain to the user why it may not have been */
```
    {
     printf("Your request has been denied. \n
               Possible reasons: \n
                 1) Your ten minute response window
                    had expired. \n
                 2) You chose to not make a selection. \n
                 3) System error.\n");
    } /* end else */
} /* end function evaluate_status */

  /***************** select_it ********************/
int select_it(enum room_status *this_room_status, int time_Select)
```
            /* This function will evaluate *this_room_status
               to identify if it is in "open" status.
               pre - function is passed enum type room_status.
               post - if *this_room_status = open, return 0.
                   else notify user and return 1. */
```
  {
                if (*this_room_status == open)
```
            /* if the status is open, it is a valid selection, so
               update the status with selected */
```
                    {
                       *this_room_status = Select;
                       return(0);
                    } /* end if */
                   else
```
            /* else, it is an invalid selection, so advise the
               user and return 1 */
```
                    {
                       printf("Time Selection %d
                       is not valid or is not
                       in open status. \n", time_Select);
                       printf("Please choose again. \n");
                       return(1);
                    } /* end else */
```

```
}  /* end function select_it */
```

A.7 SERVER SOURCE CODE

A.7.1 Inethosp.c

```
/*
   "inethosp.c"  file used for server function main() in the
   Surgical Scheduling Program.
   Functions included:
     main().
   Written by John A. Fritz under direction of Dr. D. L. Galli.
*/
```

```
    #include "commonh.h"
                    /* .h files and definitions required for both client and
                       server */
    #include "hospital.h"
                    /* .h files and definitions for the server only */
    pthread_t main_thread;
                    /* declare main thread used to spawn threads to
                       handle scheduling requests. */

/******************** main ***********************/
    void main()
    {
     int error_num;        /* used for return of error messages */
     int * addr_num;       /* used to identify main port address */
     char menu_option[1];
                    /* used for user input of menu option */
     if ((addr_num = (int*) malloc (sizeof(int))) == NULL)
                    /* allocate space for main port value */
      {
        perror ("malloc");
        exit(1);
      }  /* end if */
     *addr_num = KNOWN_PORT;
                    /* assign value of main port for clients to
                       call for initial connection. Then create
                       main thread to start the server */
```

```
    error_num =
      (pthread_create(&main_thread,NULL,(void
*)serversetup,addr_num));
      if(error_num != 0)
```
                /* create a thread to execute function serversetup.
                    The 1st parameter is a pointer to the thread ID.
                    The 2nd parameter is a pointer to thread
                        attributes, in this case default values are
                        are used with "NULL".
                    The 3rd parameter indicates the function to
                        to be called immediately following thread creation.
                    The 4th parameter contains a pointer to arguments. */
```
      {
        printf("pthread create failed error: %d \n ", error_num);
        exit(1);
      }
```
 /* end if */
```
      else
      {
        printf("\n\n\n Server Has Started \n");
      }
```
 /* end else */
```
    do
```
                /* display and accept user options */
```
      {
        printf("Please input '&' to shutdown the server \n
            & = Server Shutdown\n");
        scanf("%s", menu_option);
```
                /* get user selection */
```
        switch (menu_option[0])
        {
          case '&':
                    printf("\n\n\n Beginning Server
                            Shutdown \n");
                    stop_server (KNOWN_PORT);
                    pthread_kill_other_threads_np();
                    printf("Server Shutdown is
                            Complete \n");
            break;
          default:
              printf("\n\n\n You selected an invalid option:
                            %c \n",
                    menu_option[0]);
            break;
        }
```
 /* end switch */
```
```

```
} /* end do while */
while (menu_option[0] != '&');
            /* continue loop until user selects the only valid
                option, to stop server. option = '&' */
printf("Enter 'R' if you would like to print
        reports \n");
printf("Any other character to quit the
        program \n");
scanf("%s", menu_option);
menu_option[0] = toupper(menu_option[0]);
if (menu_option[0] == 'R')
  {
    print_files();
  } /* end if */
printf("Program has exited - Enter 'hospitalrun'
        to begin again \n");
} /* end function main */
```

A.7.2 Makefile for Server

Surgical Scheduling Program makefile for the server.

```
hospitalrun: inethosp.o serverinit.o hospital.o commonc.o
    cc -o hospitalrun inethosp.o serverinit.o hospital.o commonc.c
-lpthread
inethosp.o:commonh.h hospital.h
serverinit.o: commonh.h hospital.h
hospital.o: commonh.h hospital.h
commonc.o: commonh.h hospital.h
```

A.7.3 Hospital.h

```
/* "hospital.h" file used to maintain include files and
    definitions used exclusively in the server for the
    Surgical Scheduling Program .
*/
```

```
#include <sys/times.h>
pthread_mutex_t neuro_room_mutex,
                cardio_room_mutex,
                plastic_room_mutex,
                ortho_room_mutex;
```

```
                    /* declare pthread mutex, one for each type of
                    room. This will allow only one thread at a time
                    access to each data file). */
struct room_struct
                    /* struct format used to save room availability
                    status. */
  {
  int julian_date;
                    /* date requested for the surgery */
  enum room_status status0800;
                    /* status of availability at a specific time */
  long int ptime0800;
                    /* timestamp of when room was put into "pending
                    status. If time stamp is > than 10 minutes,
                    will reset value with next request for
                    availability at that time. */
  enum "dr_id" dr0800;
                    /* id of the client selecting this room for
                    "busy" or "pending"status. This is needed for
                    the server to be able to keep track of which
                    client has a room scheduled. */
  enum room_status status0900;
  long int ptime0900;
  enum "dr_id" dr0900;
  enum room_status status1000;
  long int ptime1000;
  enum "dr_id" dr1000;
  enum room_status status1100;
  long int ptime1100;
  enum "dr_id" dr1100;
  enum room_status status1200;
  long int ptime1200;
  enum "dr_id" dr1200;
  enum room_status status1300;
  long int ptime1300;
  enum "dr_id" dr1300;
  enum room_status status1400;
  long int ptime1400;
  enum "dr_id" dr1400;
  enum room_status status1500;
  long int ptime1500;
  enum "dr_id" dr1500;
  enum room_status status1600;
```

```
    long int ptime1600;
    enum "dr_id" dr1600;
};
```

```
void serversetup(int *addr_num);
```
                    /* function used to initialize server and socket.
                        pre - function is passed port value used for
                            common server socket.
                        post - server is bound to well known port and
                            runs continuously waiting in receive mode for
                            client to send a datagram. When a datagram
                            is received, this function spawns a thread
                            to handle the request.   */

```
int get_new_port(struct initial_connect update_port);
```
                    /* function used to maintain list of valid surgeons
                        and return the port reserved for them on the system.
                        pre - function is passed struct initial connect
                            which lists the enumerated type of "dr_id".
                        post - function returns the port number which
                            is identified for this client. */

```
void run_request(int *new_add);
```
                    /* function handles client request to completion.
                        pre - function is passed port value to dedicate to
                            this request used for binding with
                            server socket.
                        post -struct day_request is passed back and forth
                            between client and server. available rooms
                            are passed to the client, client selects,
                            updates are made to files, confirmation is
                            returned to client. */

```
int review_rooms(struct day_request *request);
```
                    /* function will identify which hospital rooms are
                        available for the day client requests to
                        schedule surgery
                        pre - function is passed pointer to the current
                            request with all hours to be reviewed in
                            open status.
                        post - function will update the current request
                            with those times which are not available,
                            leaving available times in open status. */

```
int select_room(struct day_request *request);
```
/* function will update room_file for day
and time client requests the room.
pre - function is passed pointer to
struct day request with one time
time selected.
post - function will verify that this
request is authorized for selected time
and will update struct day_request with
time reserved.   */

```
int stop_server(int addr_num);
```
/* function used to stop the server.
pre - function is passed well known port value
used for binding with server socket.
post -function passes "master" as "dr_id"
which indicates to the server to
shutdown when it has access to all
critical sections. All files are closed.
function waits in receive mode for
return value which indicates that server
has shut down. */

```
int print_files();
```
/* this function is used to print files from
the server site.
pre - function is called and files are built.
post - user is given selection of which room type
and day they would like printed. Respective
information is printed to screen. */

```
int test_pend (enum room_status *this_room_status,
                long int *this_time);
```
/* This function will review status of the room passed,
and update if pending status has expired.
pre - function is passed a pointer to enum room
status and a pointer to the time room was put in
that status.
post - Time is check to identify if the request is over
ten minutes old. If so, then update the
file with status "open", since time expired for
the request which put the timeslot in pending
status.

If not pending, or pending status is less than
ten minutes old, leave status as is. */

```
int update_stat(enum room_status *request_room_status,
                enum room_status *file_room_status,
                long int *this_time,
                enum "dr_id" *request_dr,
                enum "dr_id" *file_dr);
```

/* Function will update status of request room status
and request "dr_id" based on data file status.
pre - function is passed a pointer to request
room status, request "dr_id", and file
timestamp, file room_status.
post - function updates these values based
on the value of the file_room_status. */

```
int select_stat(enum room_status *request_room_status,
                enum room_status *file_room_status,
                enum "dr_id" *request_dr,
                enum "dr_id" *file_dr);
```
/* Function will update the values if status when
sent info regarding a room which is in "select"
status.
pre- function is passed pointers to
the pertinant parameters
of a room_status which is "select" status.
post- function updates the parameters based on
the following:
if the value of the request for this time is
selected, then check for status of the array.
If this "dr_id" is the last ID for this time,
then update this time to busy status leaving
this "dr_id". */

A.7.3 Serverinit.c

/* "serverinit.c" initialize main port of server acting
as hospital for Surgical Scheduling Program.
Functions included:

```
        serversetup().
*/

    #include "commonh.h"
                    /* local file kept for all common include files
                        and definitions. */
    #include "hospital.h"
                    /* local file kept for all include files and
                        definitions exclusive to the hospital */
    pthread_t surgeon_thread;
                    /* declare thread id for connection to port
                        for dedicated connection. */
    struct initial_connect initial_request;
                    /* struct passed to server requesting connection
                        on dedicated port */
/************** serversetup ******************/
    void serversetup(int *addr_num)
                    /* function is passed well known port value
                            used for binding  with server socket.
                        pre - function waits in receive mode for client
                            to pass request for dedicated socket.
                        post - function spawns a thread to handle request,
                            returns value of dedicated port to the
                            client requesting service, and returns
                            to receive mode for another request. */
    {
      int known_sock,      /* used to identify this particular socket */
          server_len,
                            /* used to identify length of server and
                                client information */
          client_len,
              error_num;
                    /* used to identify errors on pthread create.
                        errno not supported */
        int * new_addr;
                    /* declare var used to pass the new port value
                        in pthread_create.*/
    struct sockaddr_in server,
                    /* used to produce internet version of port for
                        both server, */
                        client;
                    /* and client */
      struct msghdr msg;
```

```
                    /* declare struct to be used in sendmsg */
        struct iovec iov[1];
                    /* declare struct to be used to hold values
                     for data and length of data for sendmsg */
        if ((known_sock = socket(AF_INET, SOCK_DGRAM, 0)) < 0)
                    /* create a handle for this connection.
                        domain of connection is AF_INET used for
                        connection between different machines.
                        SOCK_DGRAM is the style of communication,
                        using datagrams versus stream. Connection is
                        "connectionless". The third parameter is the
                        protocol to be used, 0 indicates default value */
            {
              perror("Server Socket ");
              exit(1);
            } /* end if */
        server.sin_family = AF_INET;
                    /* establish this connection as internet type */
        server.sin_port = htons(*addr_num);
                    /* assign port number passed to function */
        server.sin_addr.s_addr = inet_addr(SERVER_HOST);
                    /* lookup inet address, actual value for this
                        host was given in the commonh.h file */
        if (bind(known_sock, (struct sockaddr *) &server,
                sizeof(server)) <0)
                    /* bind the socket values to this socket.
                        known_sock is the value of this socket,
                        &server is the server information, family
                        name and protocol. third parameter is the number
                        of bytes in the address. */
          {
            perror("Server Bind");
            exit(1);
          } /* end if */
    pthread_mutex_init(&neuro_room_mutex,NULL);
    pthread_mutex_init(&cardio_room_mutex,NULL);
    pthread_mutex_init(&plastic_room_mutex,NULL);
    pthread_mutex_init(&ortho_room_mutex,NULL);
                    /* initialize all pthread mutex, one for each type of
                        room. Initializing here will ensure all threads created
                        by the server will have required threads initialized */
        msg.msg_name = (char *) &client;
        msg.msg_namelen = sizeof(client);
```

```
    msg.msg_iov = iov;
    msg.msg_iovlen = 1 ;
    msg.msg_control = NULL;
    msg.msg_controllen = 0;
```
/* assign values for msg struct and iov for sendmsg.
    msg_name is optional, carries address of the
        receiver. (not required on connection protocol.
    msg_namelen = length of name.
    msg_iov = array of input/output buffer.
    msg_iovlen = number of elements in msg_iov.
    msg_control = ancillary data, set to NULL.
    msg_controllen = value result arg for recvmsg. */
```
    iov[0].iov_base = &initial_request;
```
/* assign address of the initial_request to be
sent */
```
    iov[0].iov_len = sizeof(initial_request);
    if (recvmsg(known_sock,&msg,0)<0)
```
/* receive message sent from client.
    1st parm is socket file descriptor,
    2nd parm is pointer to msghdr,
    3rd value is flags */
```
    {
      perror("Receive Message");
      exit(1);
    } /* end if */
initial_request.new_port = get_new_port(initial_request);
```
/* assign value associated with this "dr_id"
    with initial_request.new_port to notify
    client which port to hook up on to
    complete the request with a server thread.
    Must be done initially to enter the while
    loop. All following will occur inside while
    loop. */
```
while (initial_request.new_port != 99999)
```
/* continue accepting requests from clients
    until server sends a message with "master"
    as the surgeon ID (get_new_port returns 99999)
    when this occurs, exit thread as soon as all
    mutex's are under this thread's control */
```
  {
    iov[0].iov_base = &initial_request;
```
/* assign address of the initial_request to be sent */
```
    iov[0].iov_len = sizeof(initial_request);
```

```
if (sendmsg(known_sock,&msg,0) < 0)
```
            /* send message to client, indicating
            new port value to reconnect with in
            msghdr iovec.
            1st parm is socket file descriptor,
            2nd parm is pointer to msghdr,
            3rd value is flags */
```
  {
    perror("Sendmsg");
    exit(1);
  } /* end if */
  if ((new_addr = (int*) malloc (sizeof(int))) == NULL)
```
            /* get memory for new_port */
```
  {
    perror ("malloc");
    exit(1);
  } /* end if */
 *new_addr = initial_request.new_port;
 error_num =
  (pthread_create(&surgeon_thread,NULL,(void
*)run_request,new_addr));
   if(error_num != 0)
```
            /* create a thread to execute function run-request.
            this thread will now handle the client request to
            completion.
            The 1st parameter is a pointer to the thread ID.
            The 2nd parameter is a pointer to thread
              attributes, in this case default values are
              are used with "NULL".
            The 3rd parameter indicates the function to
              to be called immediately following thread creation.
            The 4th parameter contains a pointer to arguments. */
```
     {
       printf("pthread create failed error: %d \n ",
       error_num);
       exit(1);
     } /* end if */
 if (recvmsg(known_sock,&msg,0)<0)
```
            /* receive message sent from client.
            1st parm is socket file descriptor,
            2nd parm is pointer to msghdr,
            3rd value is flags */
```
  {
```

```
      perror("Receive Message");
      exit(1);
    } /* end if */
   initial_request.new_port = get_new_port(initial_request);
               /* update port number with the port assigned
                  for this client. */
  } /* end while */
               /* for while loop to exit, a datagram must have been
                  sent indicating to shutdown the server. This function
                  is responsible to ensure that all critical sections
                  are locked before server shutdown. Lock all critical
                  sections so that server will not be shut down with
                  any file open. */
pthread_mutex_lock(&neuro_room_mutex);
pthread_mutex_lock(&cardio_room_mutex);
pthread_mutex_lock(&plastic_room_mutex);
pthread_mutex_lock(&ortho_room_mutex);
iov[0].iov_base = &initial_request;
               /* assign address of the initial_request to be sent */
iov[0].iov_len = sizeof(initial_request);
if (sendmsg(known_sock,&msg,0) < 0)
   {
    perror("Sendmsg Exit of server init ");
    exit(1);
   } /* end if */
               /* send the reply  to the client identifying
                  that all critical sections have been locked.
                  The first parameter identifies the file
                  descriptor of the socket (established with
                  "socket" call previously). The second parameter
                  is a pointer to the message to be sent. 3rd
                  is flags, set to 0, NULL value */
close(known_sock);
               /* close this socket from accepting any more
                  surgeon requests */
pthread_exit((void*)0);
               /* exit this thread, user has requested shutdown.*/
  } /* end function serversetup */
```

A.7.4 Hospital.c

/* "hospital.c" maintains functions used exclusively in the

server for the Surgical Scheduling Program.
Functions included:
  get_new_port(),
  run_request(),
  review_rooms(),
  select_room(),
  stop_server(),
  print_files(),
  test_pend(),
  update_stat(),
  select_stat(),

*/

```
#include  "commonh.h"
                /* local file kept for all common include files
                    and definitions. */
#include  "hospital.h"
                /* local file kept for all include files and
                    definitions exclusive to the server (hospital) */

/*************** get_new_port ******************/
    int get_new_port(struct initial_connect update_port)
                /* function used to maintain list of valid surgeons
                    and return the port reserved for them on the system.
                    pre - function is passed struct initial connect
                        which lists the enumerated type of "dr_id".
                    post - function returns the port number which
                        is identified for this client.
                    Note: This is an example of a simplified demo
                        non-industrial appraoch. Generally a more
                        complex algorithm would select ports since ports
                        are limited and would need to maintain list of
                        available and used port numbers in order to determine
                        selection.*/
    {
      int new_port;
      switch (update_port.dr_name)
      {
        /*case williams:
          new_port = 20001;
          break;*/
        case jones:
```

```
             new_port = 20002;
             break;
         case smith:
             new_port = 20003;
             break;
         case johnson:
             new_port = 20004;
             break;
         case master:
             new_port = 99999;
             break;
         default:
             new_port = 30000;
             break;
     } /* end switch */
     return (new_port);
   }; /* end function get_new_port */


/************** run_request *****************/
    void run_request(int  *new_addr)
                /* function handles client request to completion.
                   pre - function is passed port value to dedicate to
                       this request used for binding with
                       server socket.
                   post -struct day_request is passed back and forth
                       between client and server. available rooms
                       are passed to the client, client selects,
                       updates are made to files, confirmation is
                       returned to client. */
     {
      int thread_sock,
                /* used to identify this particular socket */
            server_len,
                        /* used to identify length of server
                           and client information */
            client_len;
      struct day_request request;
                /* struct format used to pass request from client
                   to server and return */
      struct sockaddr_in server,
                /* used to produce internet version of port for
                   both server, */
                client;
```

```
                    /* and client */
struct msghdr msg;
                    /* declare struct to be used in sendmsg */
struct iovec iov[1];
                    /* declare struct to be used to hold values
                       for data and length of data for sendmsg */
if ((thread_sock = socket(AF_INET, SOCK_DGRAM, 0)) < 0)
                    /* create a handle for this connection.
                       domain of connection is AF_INET used for
                       connection between different machines.
                       SOCK_DGRAM is the style of communication,
                       using datagrams versus stream. Connection is
                       "connectionless". The third parameter is the
                       protocol to be used, 0 indicates default value */
    {
      perror("Server Socket Error");
      exit(1);
    } /* end if */
server.sin_family = AF_INET;
                    /* establish this connection as internet type */

server.sin_port = htons(*new_addr); /*fix (* new_port) */
                    /* assign port number passed to function */
server.sin_addr.s_addr = inet_addr(SERVER_HOST);
                    /* lookup inet adress, actual value for this
                       host was given in the commonh.h file */
if (bind(thread_sock, (struct sockaddr *) &server,
            sizeof(server)) <0)
                    /* bind the socket values to this socket.
                       thread_sock is the value of this socket,
                       &server is the server information, family
                       name and protocol. third parameter is the number
                       of bytes in the address. */
  {
    perror("Server Bind Error");
    exit(1);
  } /* end if */
client_len = sizeof(client);
msg.msg_name = (char *) &client;
msg.msg_namelen = sizeof(client);
msg.msg_iov = iov;
msg.msg_iovlen = 1 ;
msg.msg_control = NULL;
```

```
msg.msg_controllen = 0;
                /* assign values for msg struct and iov for sendmsg.
                    msg_name is optional, carries address of the
                        receiver. (not required on connection  protocol.
                    msg_namelen = length of name.
                    msg_iov = array of input/output buffer.
                    msg_iovlen = number of elements in msg_iov.
                    msg_control = ancillary data, set to NULL.
                    msg_controllen = value result arg for recvmsg. */
iov[0].iov_base = &request;
                /* assign address of the initial_request to be sent */
iov[0].iov_len = sizeof(request);
if (recvmsg(thread_sock,&msg,0)<0)
                /* receive message sent from client.
                    1st parm is socket file descriptor,
                    2nd parm is pointer to msghdr,
                    3rd value is flags */
  {
   perror("Receive Message");
   exit(1);
  }
review_rooms(&request);
                /* update current request with room availability */
if (sendmsg(thread_sock,&msg,0) < 0)
                /* send message to client, indicating
                    times available for the day selected.
                    1st parm is socket file descriptor,
                    2nd parm is pointer to msghdr,
                    3rd value is flags */
  {
   perror("Sendmsg");
   close(thread_sock);
   exit(1);
  }
 if (recvmsg(thread_sock,&msg,0)<0)
                /* receive message sent from client.
                    value of request should indicate
                    client's selection.
                    1st parm is socket file descriptor,
                    2nd parm is pointer to msghdr,
                    3rd value is flags */
  {
    perror("Receive Message");
```

```
         exit(1);
       }
    select_room(&request);
                    /* send request to be evaluated for validity,
                       update respective files, and update request
                       with confirm status if the selection is
                       confirmed. */
    if (sendmsg(thread_sock,&msg,0) < 0)
                    /* send message to client, indicating
                       times available for the day selected.
                       1st parm is socket file descriptor,
                       2nd parm is pointer to msghdr,
                       3rd value is flags */
      {
       perror("Sendmsg");
       close(thread_sock);
       exit(1);
      }
    close(thread_sock);
                    /* close the connection with this socket file
                       descriptor */
    pthread_exit(new_addr);
                    /* exit this thread and call thread exit handlers */
    } /* end function run_request */


/*************** review_rooms *******************/
   int review_rooms(struct day_request *request)
                    /* function will identify which hospital rooms are
                       available for the day surgeon requests to
                       schedule surgery
                       pre - function is passed pointer to the current
                          request with all hours to be reviewed in
                          open status.
                       post - function will update the current request
                          with those times which are not available,
                          leaving available times in open status. */
   {
     int i;                    /* used to traverse array */
     struct timeval current_time;
                    /* declare var for use to identify current time
                       and check pending time for > 10 minutes. */
     char roomtype[25];
                    /* array used to build string to identify
```

```
                              which file to read from for current array */
FILE *room_file;
struct room_struct init_room[366];
                    /* build array of room_structs from file to read
                    and update as required */
switch (request->surgery_name)
                    /* identify which room type the surgeon requires.
                    then open the file based on this room type
                    also set mutex lock based on which file is
                    being read */
 {
   case neuro:
                    strcpy(roomtype, "neuro_rooms.dat");
                    pthread_mutex_lock(&neuro_room_mutex);
           break;
   case cardio:
                    strcpy(roomtype, "cardio_rooms.dat");
                    pthread_mutex_lock(&cardio_room_mutex);
           break;
   case plastic:
                    strcpy(roomtype, "plastic_rooms.dat");
                    pthread_mutex_lock(&plastic_room_mutex);
           break;
   case ortho:
                    strcpy(roomtype, "ortho_rooms.dat");
                    pthread_mutex_lock(&ortho_room_mutex);
           break;
   default:
                    printf("invalid surgery name \n");
                    exit(1);
   } /*end switch */
                    /* open the file and build an array of
                    struct room_struct */
if ((room_file = fopen (roomtype, "r")) == (FILE *) NULL)
    {
       printf("%s didn't open: %d \n", roomtype, errno);
    } /* end if */
for (i = 1; 365 >= i ; i++)
             /* build array from file of room_struct list */
    {
      fread(&init_room[i], sizeof(init_room[i]), 1, room_file);
    } /* end for */
i = request->julian_date;
```

```
                          /* set i to value of day selected (less typing) */
gettimeofday(&current_time,NULL);
                          /* get current time of day to use as reference to
                          identify if pending status has expired. */
test_pend(&init_room[i].status0800, &init_room[i].ptime0800 );
                          /* Pass values to function test_pend to identify
                          if the value for the requested room is pending
                          and update values. Function will
                          check to identify if the request is over
                          ten minutes old. If so, then update the
                          array with status "open", since time expired for
                          the request which put the timeslot in pending status.
                          If not pending, or pending status is less than
                          ten minutes old, update the request with the current
                          status from the array. This will identify which
                          times are available to the client when passed
                          back */
test_pend(&init_room[i].status0900, &init_room[i].ptime0900);
test_pend(&init_room[i].status1000, &init_room[i].ptime1000);
test_pend(&init_room[i].status1100, &init_room[i].ptime1100);
test_pend(&init_room[i].status1200, &init_room[i].ptime1200);
test_pend(&init_room[i].status1300, &init_room[i].ptime1300);
test_pend(&init_room[i].status1400, &init_room[i].ptime1400);
test_pend(&init_room[i].status1500, &init_room[i].ptime1500);
test_pend(&init_room[i].status1600, &init_room[i].ptime1600);
update_stat(&request->status0800,
                &init_room[i].status0800,
                 &init_room[i].ptime0800,
                  &request->dr_name,
                   &init_room[i].dr0800);
                          /* call function update_stat to evaluate file status.
                          If the file does not have this slot available,
                          (open status), then function will update the file
                          status to the request. This will indicate to the client
                          that the room is not available for selection.
                          If the status of the room IS  open,
                          and the request has not been previously changed from
                          open, write pending to the array, as the surgeon has
                          been advised that this timeslot is available. The
                          client(surgeon) now has ten minutes to respond to the
                          request or may lose it. Also update the file with
                          the name of the surgeon for whom the slot is being
                          held. The name will allow ONLY that surgeon access for
```

```
                10 minutes  */
update_stat(&request->status0900,
              &init_room[i].status0900,
               &init_room[i].ptime0900,
                &request->dr_name,
                  &init_room[i].dr0900);
update_stat(&request->status1000,
              &init_room[i].status1000,
               &init_room[i].ptime1000,
                &request->dr_name,
                  &init_room[i].dr1000);
update_stat(&request->status1100,
              &init_room[i].status1100,
               &init_room[i].ptime1100,
                &request->dr_name,
                  &init_room[i].dr1100);
update_stat(&request->status1200,
              &init_room[i].status1200,
               &init_room[i].ptime1200,
                &request->dr_name,
                  &init_room[i].dr1200);
update_stat(&request->status1300,
              &init_room[i].status1300,
               &init_room[i].ptime1300,
                &request->dr_name,
                  &init_room[i].dr1300);
update_stat(&request->status1400,
              &init_room[i].status1400,
               &init_room[i].ptime1400,
                &request->dr_name,
                  &init_room[i].dr1400);
update_stat(&request->status1500,
              &init_room[i].status1500,
               &init_room[i].ptime1500,
                &request->dr_name,
                  &init_room[i].dr1500);
update_stat(&request->status1600,
              &init_room[i].status1600,
               &init_room[i].ptime1600,
                &request->dr_name,
                  &init_room[i].dr1600);
fclose(room_file);
                /* close the file from read status, and
```

```
                        reopen to write updated array. */
    if ((room_file = fopen (roomtype, "w")) == (FILE *) NULL)
        {
            printf(" %s didn't open: %d \n",roomtype, errno);
        } /* end if */
    for (i = 1; 365 >= i ; i++)
                    /* write updated array back to file */
      {
        fwrite(&init_room[i], sizeof(init_room[i]), 1, room_file);
      } /* end for */
    fclose(room_file);
    switch (request->surgery_name)
                    /* identify which file was required.
                       unlock the mutex for this file
                       to allow access by other threads. */
      {
      case neuro:
                    pthread_mutex_unlock(&neuro_room_mutex);
            break;
      case cardio:
                    pthread_mutex_unlock(&cardio_room_mutex);
            break;
      case plastic:
                    pthread_mutex_unlock(&plastic_room_mutex);
            break;
      case ortho:
                    pthread_mutex_unlock(&ortho_room_mutex);
            break;
        default:
                    printf("invalid surgery name \n");
                    exit(1);
      } /*end switch */
    return (0);
  } /* end function review_rooms */


/*************** select_room ******************/
    int select_room(struct day_request *request)
                    /* function will update room_file for day
                       and time client requests the room.
                       pre - function is passed pointer to
                         struct day request with one time
                         in select status.
                       post - function will verify that this
```

request is authorized for selected time
and will update the file with the time
reserved. Also update the request with
"confirmed" for surgeon to know that his
request has been satisfied. */

```
{
 int i;                      /* used to traverse array */
 char roomtype[25];
              /* array used to build string to identify
                 which file to read from for current array */
 FILE *room_file;
 struct room_struct init_room[366];
              /* build array of room_structs from file to read
                 and update as required */
 switch (request->surgery_name)
              /* identify which room type the client requires.
                 then open the file based on this room type
                 also set mutex lock based on which file is
                 being read */
  {
   case neuro:
                strcpy(roomtype, "neuro_rooms.dat");
                pthread_mutex_lock(&neuro_room_mutex);
        break;
   case cardio:
                strcpy(roomtype, "cardio_rooms.dat");
                pthread_mutex_lock(&cardio_room_mutex);
        break;
   case plastic:
                strcpy(roomtype, "plastic_rooms.dat");
                pthread_mutex_lock(&plastic_room_mutex);
        break;
   case ortho:
                strcpy(roomtype, "ortho_rooms.dat");
                pthread_mutex_lock(&ortho_room_mutex);
        break;
   default:
                printf("invalid surgery name \n");
                exit(1);
  } /*end switch */
 if ((room_file = fopen (roomtype, "r")) == (FILE *) NULL)
    {
      printf("%s didn't open: %d \n",
```

```
                        roomtype,errno);
            }  /* end if */

     for (i = 1; 365 >= i ; i++)
                       /* build array from file of room_struct list */
        {
          fread(&init_room[i], sizeof(init_room[i]), 1, room_file);
        }  /* end for */
     i = request->julian_date;
                      /* set i to value of day selected (less typing) */
     if (request->status0800 == Select)
                      /* if the value of the request for this time is
                         selected, then check for status of the array.
                         If this "dr_id" is the last ID for this time,
                         then update this time to busy status leaving
                         this "dr_id". note:regardless of the status,
                         if this "dr_id" is on the timeslot, it is
                         safe to assign the room. No one has requested it
                         since this client or the name should change.
                         Also, a room should never be in open status once
                         it has been selected the first time. Only the
                         "dr_id" should change on pending status. further
                         note that "else if" is used, so only one selection
                         per request is allowed. */
        {
          select_stat(&request->status0800,
                        &init_room[i].status0800,
                         &request->dr_name,
                           &init_room[i].dr0800);
        }  /* end if */
     else if (request->status0900 == Select)
        {
          select_stat(&request->status0900,
                        &init_room[i].status0900,
                         &request->dr_name,
                           &init_room[i].dr0900);
        }  /* end else if */
     else if (request->status1000 == Select)
        {
          select_stat(&request->status1000,
                        &init_room[i].status1000,
                         &request->dr_name,
                           &init_room[i].dr1000);
```

```
      } /* end else if */
    else if (request->status1100 == Select)
      {
        select_stat(&request->status1100,
                    &init_room[i].status1100,
                    &request->dr_name,
                    &init_room[i].dr1100);
      } /* end else if */
    else if (request->status1200 == Select)
      {
        select_stat(&request->status1200,
                    &init_room[i].status1200,
                    &request->dr_name,
                    &init_room[i].dr1200);
      } /* end else if */
    else if (request->status1300 == Select)
      {
        select_stat(&request->status1300,
                    &init_room[i].status1300,
                    &request->dr_name,
                    &init_room[i].dr1300);
      } /* end else if */
    else if (request->status1400 == Select)
      {
        select_stat(&request->status1400,
                    &init_room[i].status1400,
                    &request->dr_name,
                    &init_room[i].dr1400);
      } /* end else if */
    else if (request->status1500 == Select)
      {
        select_stat(&request->status1500,
                    &init_room[i].status1500,
                    &request->dr_name,
                    &init_room[i].dr1500);
      } /* end else if */
    else if (request->status1600 == Select)
      {
        select_stat(&request->status1600,
                    &init_room[i].status1600,
                    &request->dr_name,
                    &init_room[i].dr1600);
      } /* end else if */
```

```
      fclose(room_file);
                   /* close the file in read status and reopen
                       to write updated array. */
      if ((room_file = fopen (roomtype, "w")) == (FILE *) NULL)
          {
            printf(" %s didn't open: %d \n",
                     roomtype,errno);
          } /* end if */
      for (i = 1; 365 >= i ; i++)
                   /* write updated array back to file */
        {
          fwrite(&init_room[i], sizeof(init_room[i]), 1, room_file);
          } /* end for */
      fclose(room_file);
      switch (request->surgery_name)
                   /* identify which file was required.
                       unlock the mutex for this file
                       to allow access by other threads. */
        {
         case neuro:
                       pthread_mutex_unlock(&neuro_room_mutex);
              break;
         case cardio:
                       pthread_mutex_unlock(&cardio_room_mutex);
              break;
         case plastic:
                       pthread_mutex_unlock(&plastic_room_mutex);
              break;
         case ortho:
                       pthread_mutex_unlock(&ortho_room_mutex);
              break;
           default:
                       printf("invalid surgery name \n");
                       exit(1);
          } /*end switch */
       return (0);
       } /* end function select_room */


/*************** stop_server *******************/
    int stop_server(int addr_num)
                   /* function used to stop the server.
                       pre - function is passed well known port value
                           used for binding  with server socket.
```

```
                        post -function passes "master" as dr_name
                        which indicates to the server to
                        shutdown when it has access to all
                        critical sections. All files are closed.
                        function waits in receive mode for
                        return value which indicates that server
                        has shut down. */
{
  struct initial_connect stop_request;
                /* struct passed to server requesting server
                   shutdown. */
  int known_sock,
              /* used to identify this particular socket */
      server_len;
                /* used to identify length of server information */
  struct sockaddr_in server,
                /* used to produce internet version of port
                    for both server*/
                client;
                /* and client */
  struct msghdr msg;
                /* declare struct to be used in sendmsg */
  struct iovec iov[1];
                /* declare struct to be used to hold values
                    for data and length of data for sendmsg */
  stop_request.dr_name = master;
                /* establish the name master which indicates to server to
                    shut down when it has access to all critical sections.
                    Therefore, All files are closed. */
  stop_request.new_port = 0;
                /* initialize request for new_port to 0 prior
                    to sending request to server just to give it some
                    value. */
  server.sin_family = AF_INET;
                /* establish this connection as internet type */
  server.sin_port = htons(addr_num);
                /* assign port number passed to function */
  server.sin_addr.s_addr = inet_addr(SERVER_HOST);
                /* lookup inet adress, actual value for this
                    host was given in the commonh.h file */
  if ((known_sock = socket(AF_INET, SOCK_DGRAM, 0)) < 0)
                /* create a handle for this connection.
                    domain of connection is AF_INET used for
```

connection between different machines.
SOCK_DGRAM is the style of communication,
using datagrams versus stream. Connection is
"connectionless". The third parameter is the
protocol to be used, 0 indicates default value */

```
    {
       perror("Server Socket Error");
       exit(1);
    } /* end if */
client.sin_family = AF_INET;
            /* establish this connection as internet type */
client.sin_addr.s_addr = inet_addr(SERVER_HOST);
            /* address is set to SERVER_HOST, same
               machine used as client and server. */
client.sin_port = htons(0);
            /* default value 0 allows connection to any port. */
if (bind(known_sock, (struct sockaddr *) &client,
        sizeof(client)) <0)
            /* bind the socket values to this socket.
               known_sock is the value of this socket,
               &client is the client information, family
               name and protocol. third parameter is the
               number of bytes in the address.
               Note: At this time, the server is acting
               as a client from this function, and as
               the server from the main_thread */
  {
     perror("Server Bind Error");
     exit(1);
  } /* end if */
msg.msg_name = (char *) &server;
msg.msg_namelen = sizeof(server);
msg.msg_iov = iov;
msg.msg_iovlen = 1;
msg.msg_control = NULL;
msg.msg_controllen = 0;
            /* assign values for msg struct and iov for sendmsg.
               msg_name is optional, carries address of the
                 receiver. (not required on connection  protocol.
               msg_namelen = length of name.
               msg_iov = array of input/output buffer.
               msg_iovlen = number of elements in msg_iov.
               msg_control = ancillary data, set to NULL.
```

```
                        msg_controllen = value result arg for recvmsg. */
        iov[0].iov_base = &stop_request;
                        /* assign address of the initial_request to be sent */
        iov[0].iov_len = sizeof(stop_request);
    if (sendmsg(known_sock,&msg,0) < 0)
                        /* send message to server, requesting
                        shutdown with "dr_id" "master".
                        Also pass struct
                        client for return confirmation.
                        1st parm is socket file descriptor,
                        2nd parm is pointer to msghdr,
                        3rd value is flags */
        {
        perror("Sendmsg in stop_server");
        exit(1);
        }
    if (recvmsg(known_sock, &msg ,0) < 0)
                        /* receive message sent from server.
                        This message holds port value 99999
                        indicating server has shutdown and
                        locked all critical sections.
                        1st parm is socket file descriptor,
                        2nd parm is pointer to msghdr,
                        3rd value is flags */
        {
        perror ("Client Recvmsg Error");
        close(known_sock);
        exit(1);
        } /* end if */
    close(known_sock);
                        /* close socket, no longer used for this client
                        transaction */
    return(stop_request.new_port);
                        /* return value of 99999 which is flag
                        indicating "master" "dr_id"
                        to stop server operation */
    } /* end function stop_server */


/*************** print_files ******************/
    int print_files()
                        /* this function is used to print files from
                        the server site.
                        pre - function is called and files are built.
```

```
                       post - user is given selection of which room type
                           and day they would like printed. Respective
                           information is printed to screen. */
{
  enum surgery_type surg_type;
                           /* used to later print file type for user */
  char user_select[1],
       null_value[1] ;
                           /* used to accept user input */
  int i;                   /* used to traverse array */
  FILE *room_file;
  char this_file[25];
               /* used to read name of file*/
  struct room_struct init_room[366];
               /* struct format used to save room available
                  status. */
  do                       /* continue loop until user requests to exit */
  {
    do                     /* continue loop until user selects a valid option */
    {
       printf("Which file would you like to print
               from? \n");
       printf("Please enter the appropriate character
               : \n");
       printf("
               A = Neurological Rooms \n
               B = Cardiovascular Rooms \n
               C = Orthopedic Rooms \n
               D = Plastics Rooms \n
               Z = EXIT \n");
       scanf("%s",user_select);
       user_select[0] = toupper(user_select[0]);
       switch(user_select[0])
               /* based on user input, assign surg_type and
                  copy correct name of file to open. */
       {
         case 'A': strcpy(this_file,"neuro_rooms.dat");
                   surg_type = neuro;
               break;
         case 'B': strcpy(this_file,"cardio_rooms.dat");
                   surg_type = cardio;
               break;
         case 'C': strcpy(this_file,"ortho_rooms.dat");
```

```
                    surg_type = ortho;
            break;
    case 'D': strcpy(this_file,"plastic_rooms.dat");
                    surg_type = plastic;
            break;
    case 'Z': printf("Exiting Print Program \n");
            break;
    default:  printf("This Option is Invalid \n");
            break;
  } /* end switch */
} /* end do-while */
while((user_select[0] != 'A')
            /* continue to loop until valid selection
              is chosen */
      && (user_select[0] != 'B')
      && (user_select[0] != 'C')
      && (user_select[0] != 'D')
      && (user_select[0] != 'Z')   );
            /* open the appropriate file and build an array to
              allow selection of day and print data.*/
if ( user_select[0] != 'Z')
 {
  if ((room_file = fopen (this_file, "r")) == (FILE *) NULL)
    {
      printf("%s didn't open: %d \n ", this_file,errno);
    } /* end if */
  for (i = 1; 365 >= i ; i++)
    {
      fread(&init_room[i], sizeof(init_room[i]), 1, room_file);
    } /* end for */
  do
   {
      printf("What day would you like to look at? \n");
      scanf("%d", &i);
   } /* end do-while */
   while( (i < 1) || ( i > 365));
            /* get user selection for day to print, while loop
              ensures that day is between day 1 and 365. i=1
              equals day 1 of Julian year. */
            /* print requested data calling necessary functions */
  printf("Surgery date: %d ", init_room[i].julian_date);
  printf(" Room Type ");
  print_type(surg_type);
```

```
printf("Room Status: \n ");
printf(" 08:00 - ");
print_status(init_room[i].status0800);
printf("Dr. ");
print_dr(init_room[i].dr0800);
printf(" 09:00 - ");
print_status(init_room[i].status0900);
printf("Dr. ");
print_dr(init_room[i].dr0900);
printf(" 10:00 - ");
print_status(init_room[i].status1000);
printf("Dr. ");
print_dr(init_room[i].dr1000);
printf(" 11:00 - ");
print_status(init_room[i].status1100);
printf("Dr. ");
print_dr(init_room[i].dr1100);
printf(" 12:00 - ");
print_status(init_room[i].status1200);
printf("Dr. ");
print_dr(init_room[i].dr1200);
printf(" 13:00 - ");
print_status(init_room[i].status1300);
printf("Dr. ");
print_dr(init_room[i].dr1300);
printf(" 14:00 - ");
print_status(init_room[i].status1400);
printf("Dr. ");
print_dr(init_room[i].dr1400);
printf(" 15:00 - ");
print_status(init_room[i].status1500);
printf("Dr. ");
print_dr(init_room[i].dr1500);
printf(" 16:00 - ");
print_status(init_room[i].status1600);
printf("Dr. ");
print_dr(init_room[i].dr1600);
printf(" \n This is the status of the room you requested.");
printf("ENTER any character to continue \n");
scanf("%s",null_value);
printf("\n\n\n");
fclose(room_file);
            /* after room_struct is printed, re-enter do-while loop
```

```
                         allow user to select another day and type or quit.
                    */
         }  /* end if */
      }  /* end do-while */
      while (user_select[0] != 'Z');
      return (0);
   }  /* end function print_files */


/*************** test_pend ******************/
      int test_pend (enum room_status *this_room_status,
                          long int *this_time)
                  /* This function will review status of the room passed,
                     and update if pending status has expired.
                     pre - function is passed a pointer to enum room
                         status and a pointer to the time room was put in
                         that status.
                     post - Time is check to identify if the request is over
                         ten minutes old. If so, then update the
                         file with status "open", since time expired for
                         the request which put the timeslot in pending
                         status.
                         If not pending, or pending status is less than
                         ten minutes old, leave status as is. */
   {
      struct timeval current_time;
                  /* declare var for use to identify current time
                     and check pending time for > 10 minutes. */
      gettimeofday(&current_time,NULL);
                  /* get current time of day to use as reference to
                     identify if pending status has expired. */
      if (* this_room_status == pending)
                  /* if the value for the requested room is pending,
                     check time to identify if the request is over
                     ten minutes old. If so, then update the
                     file with status "open", since time expired for
                     the request which put the timeslot in pending status.
                     If not pending, or pending status is less than
                     ten minutes old, update the request with the current
                     status from the array. This will identify which
                     times are available to the client when passed
                     back */
        {
          if ((current_time.tv_sec - *this_time) > 600)
```

```
                  /* If over 10 minutes has elapsed since the
                     room was put into pending status, then
                     update status to open and update the timestamp
                     to reflect the current time.  */
            {
               *this_time = current_time.tv_sec;
               *this_room_status = open;
            } /* end if */
        } /* end if */
      return(0);
   } /* end function test_pend */


/************** update_stat *******************/
   int update_stat(enum room_status *request_room_status,
                        enum room_status *file_room_status,
                          long int *this_time,
                            enum "dr_id" *request_dr,
                              enum "dr_id" *file_dr)
                /* Function will update status of request room status
                   and request "dr_id" based on data file status.
                   pre - function is passed a pointer to request
                        room status, request "dr_id", and file
                        timestamp, file room_status.
                   post - function updates these values based
                        on the value of the file_room_status. */
    {
       struct timeval current_time;
                    /* declare var for use to identify current time
                       and check pending time for > 10 minutes. */
       gettimeofday(&current_time,NULL);
                    /* get current time of day to use as reference to
                       timestamp pending status */
      if (*file_room_status != open)
                    /* If the file does not have this slot available,
                       (open status), then update the current status
                       to the request. This will indicate to the client
                       tha the room is not available for selection. */
          {
               *request_room_status = *file_room_status;
          } /* end if */
      else if (*file_room_status == open)
                    /* else if the status of the room is open,
                       and the request has not been previously changed from
```

open, write pending to the array, as the surgeon has
been advised that this timeslot is available. The
client(surgeon) now has ten minutes to respond to the
request or may lose it. Also update the file with
the name of the surgeon for whom the slot is being
held. The name will allow ONLY that surgeon access for
10 minutes */

```
    {
        *file_room_status = pending;
        *this_time = current_time.tv_sec;
        *file_dr = *request_dr;
    } /* end if */
  return(0);
} /* end function update_stat */
```

```
/*************** select_stat ******************/
    int select_stat(enum room_status *request_room_status,
                    enum room_status *file_room_status,
                        enum "dr_id" *request_dr,
                           enum "dr_id" *file_dr)
            /* Function will update the values if status when
               sent info regarding a room which is in "select"
               status.
               pre- function is passed pointers to
                   the pertinant parameters
                   of a room_status which is "select" status.
               post- function updates the parameters based on
                   the following:
                   if the value of the request for this time is
                   selected, then check for status of the array.
                   If this "dr_id" is the last ID for this time,
                   then update this time to busy status leaving
                   this "dr_id". */
    {
        if (*file_dr == *request_dr)
          {
            *file_room_status = busy;
            *request_room_status = confirm;
          } /* end if */
        else
          {
            *request_room_status = busy;
          } /* end else */
```

```
    return(0);
  } /* end function select_stat */
```

A.8 COMMON SOURCE CODE

A.8.1 Commonh.h

/* "commonh.h" file used to maintain common include files and
   definitions for both client and server in the Surgical Scheduling
   Program.
   Written by John A. Fritz under the direction of Dr. D. L. Galli
*/

```
#include <pthread.h>
#include <stdio.h>
#include <stdlib.h>
#include <unistd.h>
#include <errno.h>
#include <string.h>
#include <sys/socket.h>
#include <sys/types.h>
#include <netinet/in.h>
#include <arpa/inet.h>
#include <netdb.h>
#include <sys/time.h>
#define SERVER_HOST "???.?.?.?"
```
            /* IP address of the host to be used as the hospital
               server.: YOU MUST FILL THIS IN!*/
```
#define KNOWN_PORT 20000
```
            /* known port value for connection with the
               server */
```
enum surgery_type {neuro, cardio, plastic, ortho};
```
            /* types of surgery for which a room can be
               requested. */
```
enum "dr_id" {williams, jones, smith, johnson, master, none};
```
            /* identifiers of those doctors which are allowed
                to practice in the hospital. master is used by
                the main hospital program to indicate to the
                server to shut down. */
```
enum room_status {busy, open, pending, Select, confirm};
```

```
                    /* possible status for a time.
                       time could be already committed "busy"
                       time could be available "open"
                       time could be held waiting for another
                          surgeon to respond "pending"
                       "select" is used for request from surgeon
                          to hospital identifying which time
                          they selected based on availability.
                       "confirm" is used to notify a surgeon
                          that the hospital has processed the
                          selection and it is confirmed for
                          that surgeon.  */
struct initial_connect
                    /* struct format used to pass initial request from
                       the client */
  {
    enum "dr_id" dr_name;
                    /* id of the client making the request */
      int new_port;    /* value of port for reconnection will be
                       returned to the client from the server.
                       when first sent to the server it should
                       be initialized to zero */
  };
struct day_request
                    /* struct format used to pass request from client
                       to server and return */
  {
    enum "dr_id" dr_name;
                    /* id of the client making the request */
    enum surgery_type surgery_name;
                    /* name of surgery being performed */
    int julian_date;
                    /* date requested for the surgery */
    enum room_status status0800;
                    /* status of availability at a specific time */
    enum room_status status0900;
    enum room_status status1000;
    enum room_status status1100;
    enum room_status status1200;
    enum room_status status1300;
    enum room_status status1400;
    enum room_status status1500;
    enum room_status status1600;
```

```
    };
int print_day_request(struct day_request request);
                /* function is used to print a request of
                   type day_request.
                   pre - function is passed a var of type
                       day_request.
                   post - status of the request is printed
                */
int print_status(enum room_status this_room_status);
                /* function prints status of the room.
                   pre- function is passed struct room_status.
                   post - function prints status. */
int print_dr(enum "dr_id" this_dr);
                /* function prints dr_name.
                   pre- function is passed enum type "dr_id".
                   post - function prints dr name. */
int print_type(enum surgery_type this_type);
                /* function prints type of surgery.
                   pre- function is passed struct surgery_type.
                   post - function prints the surgery type. */
```

A.8.2 Commonc.c

```
/* "commonc.c" file used to maintain common functions of client and
   server in the Surgical Scheduling Program.
   Functions included:
   print_day_request(),
   print_status(),
   print_dr(),
   print_type().
*/

    #include "commonh.h"
    int print_day_request(struct day_request request)
                /* function is used to print a request of
                   type day_request.
                   pre - function is passed a var of type
                       day_request.
                   post - status of the request is printed
                */
    {
       printf("\n\n\n\n Surgeon Name: Dr. ");
```

```
        print_dr(request.dr_name);
        printf("Surgery Type: ");
        print_type(request.surgery_name);
        printf("Surgery date: %d \n ", request.julian_date);
```
                /* print room status "shell", and pass
                    room status enumerated type to function
                    print_status. */
```
        printf("Room Status: \n ");
        printf(" 08:00 - ");
        print_status(request.status0800);
        printf(" 09:00 - ");
        print_status(request.status0900);
        printf(" 10:00 - ");
        print_status(request.status1000);
        printf(" 11:00 - ");
        print_status(request.status1100);
        printf(" 12:00 - ");
        print_status(request.status1200);
        printf(" 13:00 - ");
        print_status(request.status1300);
        printf(" 14:00 - ");
        print_status(request.status1400);
        printf(" 15:00 - ");
        print_status(request.status1500);
        printf(" 16:00 - ");
        print_status(request.status1600);
    return (0);
} /* end function print_day_request */
int print_status(enum room_status this_room_status)
```
                /* function prints status of the room.
                    pre- function is passed struct room_status.
                    post - function prints status. */
```
{
    switch (this_room_status)
```
                /* evaluate room_status and print the appropriate
                    name. if name is not listed, error is not
                    serious, program not exited. status will
                    simply be blank */
```
    {
      case busy: printf("Busy \n");
                break;
      case open: printf("Open \n");
                break;
```

```
          case pending: printf("Pending \n");
                    break;
          case Select: printf("Select \n");
                    break;
          case confirm: printf("Confirmed \n");
                    break;
     } /* end switch */
   return(0);
 } /* end function print_status */
int print_dr(enum "dr_id" this_dr)
```
          /* function prints dr_name.
               pre- function is passed enum type "dr_id".
               post - function prints dr name. */
```
 {
   switch (this_dr)
```
               /* evaluate dr_name and print the appropriate
               name. if name is not listed, then error is
               serious, and files need to be updated
               exit the program. Obviously, this would need
               enhancement to be industrial strength. This is
               a very elementary approach for the sake of simplicity
               and space. */
```
     {
     case smith : printf("Smith \n");
                    break;
     case jones : printf("Jones \n");
                    break;
     case johnson : printf("Johnson \n");
                     break;
     case williams : printf("Williams \n");
                      break;
    case none : printf("None \n");
                    break;
     default: printf("Invalid Dr name \n");
                     exit(1);
    } /* end switch */
   return (0);
 } /* end function print_dr */
int print_type(enum surgery_type this_type)
```
          /* function prints type of surgery.
               pre- function is passed struct surgery_type.
               post - function prints the surgery type. */
```
 {
```

```
    switch (this_type)
                /* evaluate surgery_name and print the appropriate
                   name. if name is not listed, then error is
                   serious, and files need to be updated
                   exit the program. */
      {
        case neuro : printf("Neurological \n");
                     break;
        case cardio : printf("Cardio Vascular \n");
                      break;
        case plastic : printf("Plastic \n" );
                        break;
        case ortho : printf("Orthopedic \n");
                        break;
        default: printf("Invalid Surgery Type \n");
                        exit(1);
      } /* end switch */
      return(0);
    } /* end function print_type */
```

A.9 FILE INITIALIZATION SOURCE CODE: WRITE_CA.C

```
/* "write_ca.c" file used to maintain program for initializing data
   files for server use in the Surgical Scheduling Program.
   Program will build array of room_struct and write to user
   selected file.
   pre- none.
   post- files are built.
   Written by John A. Fritz under the direction of Dr. D. L. Galli
*/

    #include "commonh.h"
                /* local file kept for all common include files
                   and definitions. */
    #include "hospital.h"
                /* local file kept for all include files and
                   definitions exclusive to the server (hospital) */

/***************** main ********************/
    void main()
    {
```

```
char user_select[1],
            /* for user input */
        this_file[25];
            /* used to identify file name string */
    int i;              /* used to traverse array */
    struct timeval current_time;
            /* declare var of type struct to hold value of
                current time */
    FILE *room_file;
    struct room_struct init_room[366];
            /* struct format used to save room available
                status. */
printf("\n\n\n "Which file would you like to initialize? \n");
do                      /* continue loop until user requests to exit */
{
  do                        /* continue loop until user selects a valid option */
  {
    printf("Please enter the appropriate character: \n ");
    printf("
            A = Neurological Rooms \n
            B = Cardiovascular Rooms \n
            C = Orthopedic Rooms \n
            D = Plastics Rooms \n
            Z = EXIT \n");
    scanf("%s",user_select);
            /* retrieve user input and set to uppercase */
    user_select[0] = toupper(user_select[0]);
    switch(user_select[0])
            /* allow user to select file to initialize, and copy
                name of file to this_file. this_file will be used to
                open the file and write. */
      {
        case 'A': strcpy(this_file,"neuro_rooms.dat");
            break;
        case 'B': strcpy(this_file,"cardio_rooms.dat");
            break;
        case 'C': strcpy(this_file,"ortho_rooms.dat");
            break;
        case 'D': strcpy(this_file,"plastic_rooms.dat");
            break;
        case 'Z': printf("Exiting File Init Program \n");
            break;
        default:  printf("This Option is Invalid \n");
```

```
                     break;
          } /* end switch */
        } /* end do-while */
   while((user_select[0] != 'A')
                /* continue to loop until valid selection
                   is chosen */
             && (user_select[0] != 'B')
             && (user_select[0] != 'C')
             && (user_select[0] != 'D')
             && (user_select[0] != 'Z')   );
   if ( user_select[0] != 'Z')
                /* to get this far, selection must be valid.
                   if not 'Z', then open the file, build the array
                   and write it. */
     {
       if ((room_file = fopen (this_file, "w")) ==
           (FILE *) NULL)
       {
         printf(" %s didn't open %d \n",
                  this_file,errno);
         exit(1);
       } /* end if */
       for ( i = 1 ; 365 >= i ; i++)
       {
       init_room[i].julian_date = i;
                /* date requested for the surgery fill julian date for
                   1 total year. (leap year is not addressed.) */
       init_room[i].status0800 = open ;
                /* status of availability at a specific time
                   initialize all to open status.will be updated
                   with current values when program is run. Updated
                   values will then be written to the file. */
       init_room[i].status0900 = open ;
       init_room[i].status1000 = open ;
       init_room[i].status1100 = open ;
       init_room[i].status1200 = open ;
       init_room[i].status1300 = open ;
       init_room[i].status1400 = open ;
       init_room[i].status1500 = open ;
       init_room[i].status1600 = open ;
       gettimeofday(&current_time,NULL);
                /* call function to retrieve current time of day
                   to place SOME value in the time slot */
```

```
        init_room[i].ptime0800 = current_time.tv_sec;
            /* used to identify timestamp of when room
                was put into "pending status "
                If time stamp is > than 10 minutes,
                will reset value with next request for
                availability at that time. initialize
                to current time, so SOMETHING will be in
                there. */
        init_room[i].ptime0900 = current_time.tv_sec;
        init_room[i].ptime1000 = current_time.tv_sec;
        init_room[i].ptime1100 = current_time.tv_sec;
        init_room[i].ptime1200 = current_time.tv_sec;
        init_room[i].ptime1300 = current_time.tv_sec;
        init_room[i].ptime1400 = current_time.tv_sec;
        init_room[i].ptime1500 = current_time.tv_sec;
        init_room[i].ptime1600 = current_time.tv_sec;
        init_room[i].dr0800 = none   ;
            /* "dr_id" at a specific time. Initialize
                all to "none" status.will be updated
                with current values when program is run. Updated
                values will then be written to the file.  */
        init_room[i].dr0900 = none ;
        init_room[i].dr1000 = none ;
        init_room[i].dr1100 = none ;
        init_room[i].dr1200 = none ;
        init_room[i].dr1300 = none ;
        init_room[i].dr1400 = none ;
        init_room[i].dr1500 = none ;
        init_room[i].dr1600 = none ;
        fwrite(&init_room[i], sizeof(init_room[i]), 1,
                room_file);
      } /* end for */
    printf("\n\n\n %s has been initialized \n", this_file);
    printf("Would you like to initialize another? \n ");
    fclose(room_file);
    } /* end if */
  } /* end do-while */
  while (user_select[0] != 'Z');
            /* continue initializing files until user requests to
                exit */
} /* end main */
```

List of Acronyms

AAL: ATM Adaptation Layer

ACID: Atomicity, Consistency, Isolation, Durability (properties of a transaction)

ACL: Access Control Lists

ACM: Association for Computing Machinery

ACPI: Advanced Configuration and Power Interface

AFS: Andrew File System

API: Application Programming Interface

APM: Advanced Power Management

APPN: Advanced Peer-to-Peer Network

ARPANET: Advanced Army Research Projects Network

ASCII: American Standard Code of Information Interchange

ATM: Asynchronous Transfer Mode

BOA: Basic Object Adapter (CORBA)

BSD: Berkeley Software Distribution

CCITT: Intl. Telegraph & Telephone Consultative Committee (now ITU-T)

CDFS: Compact Disk File System

COM: Component Object Model

COOL: Chorus Object-Oriented Layer

CORBA: Common Object Request Broker Architecture

CSMA/CD: Carrier Sensitive Multiple Access with Collision Detection

DAP: Directory Access Protocol

DARPA: Defense Advanced Research Projects Agency

DCE: Distributed Computing Environment

DCOM: Distributed Component Object Model

DNS: Directory Name Service

DES: Data Encryption Standard

DFS: Distributed File System (Windows 2000)

DIB: Directory Information Base (X.500)

DISP: Directory Information Shadowing Protocol

DIT: Directory Information Tree (X.500)

DLL: Dynamic Link Library

DNS: Distributed Name System

DNS: Domain Name System (or Server)

DoD: Department of Defense

DSM: Distributed Shared Memory

DSP: Directory System Protocol

DPC: Deferred Procedure Call (Windows 2000)

DVD: Officially not an acronym, although once stood for Digital Video Disk

EBCDIC: Extended Binary-Coded Decimal Interchange Code

EDR: External Data Representation

EFS: Encrypting File System (Windows 2000)

FAT: File Allocation Table

FAQ: Frequently Asked Questions

FDO: Functional Device Objects (Windows 2000)

FDDI: Fiber Distributed Data Interface

FEK: File Encrypting Key

FIFO: First In First Out

FTP: File Transfer Protocol

GEOS: Geostationary Operational Environmental Satellites

GSM: Global System for Mobile Communications

GUI: Graphical User Interface

HAL: Hardware Abstraction Layer (Windows 2000)

HTML: HyperText Markup Language

HTTP: Hypertext Transfer Protocol

ICMP: Internet Control Message Protocol

IDL: Interface Definition Language

IETF: Internet Engineering Task Force

IGMP: Internet Group Management Protocol

IIS: Internet Information Service

IP: Internet Protocol

IPC: InterProcess Communication

IRP: I/O Request Packets

ISO/OSI: International Standards Organization/Open System Internconnection

ITU-T: International Telecommunications Union-Telecommunication (sector)

IVR: Interactive Voice Response

KDBM: Kerberos Database Management System

LDAP: Lightweight Directory Access Protocol

LPC: Local Procedure Call

MIMD: Multiple Instruction Stream, Multiple Data Stream

MISD: Multiple Instruction Stream, Single Data Stream

MMC: Microsoft Management Console

MMU: Memory Management Unit

NBS: National Bureau of Standards (now NIST)

NCP: Network Control Program

NCSC: National Computer Security Center

NFS: Network File System

NIS: Network Information Services

NIST: National Institute of Standards and Technology

NORMA: NO Remote Memory Access (multiprocessor)

NRU: Not Recently Used

NSA: National Security Administration

NSF: National Science Foundation (USA)

NSP: Name Server Protocol

NT: New Technology

NTFS: NT File System

NTP: Network Time Protocol

NUMA: Non-Uniform Memory Access (multiprocessor)

OEM: Original Equipment Manufacturers

OMG: Object Management Group

ONC: Open Network Computing (from Sun)

ORG: Object Request Broker

OSF: Open Software Foundation

OU: Organizational Units (Windows 2000)

PAID: Prevent, Avoid, Ignore or Detect (methods for handling deadlocks)

PDO: Physical Device Objects (Windows 2000)

POA: Portable Object Adapter (CORBA)

PRAM: Pipelined Random Access Memory (a consistency model)

PSTN: Public-Switched Telephone Network

RAM: Random Access Memory

RCP: Remote CoPy

RDN: Relative Distinguished Name (X.500)

RFC: Request for Comments

ROT: Running Object Table (DCOM)

RPC: Remote Procedure Call

RSA: Rivest, Shamir, and Adleman (their public-key encryption algorithm)

SCSI: Small Computer Systems Interface

SDDL: Security Descriptor Definition Language (Windows 2000)

SDK: Software Developer's Kit (Windows 2000)

SIGOPS: Special Interest Group in Operating Systems (ACM)

SIMD: Single Instruction Stream, Multiple Data Stream

SISD: Single Instruction Stream, Multiple Data Stream

SMTP: Simple Mail Transfer Protocol

SNMP: Simple Network Management Protocol

SNTP: Simple Network Time Protocol

SOP: Subject-Oriented Programming

SSL: Secure Socket Layer

SSPI: Security Support Provider Interface (Windows 2000)

TCP: Transmission Control Protocol

TIG: Task Interaction Graph

TI-RPC: Transport-Independent Remote Procedure Call

TNI: Trusted Network Interpretation

UDF: Universal Disk Format

UDP: User Datagram Protocol

UMA: Uniform Memory Access (multiprocessor)

USN: Update Sequence Number (Windows 2000)

URL: Uniform Resource Locator

UTC: Universal Time Coordinator

VLM: Very Large Memory (64-bit address space)

VLSI: Very Large Scale Integration

VRU: Voice Response Unit

WDM: Win32 Device Manager

Glossary of Terms

access control: preventing unwanted access and tampering to your computer resources and files.

access list: a form of access control whereby each file or resource maintains a list of who may access the resource and what type of access is permitted.

access matrix: a two-dimensional array utilized to store the access list information for a system.

ACID properties: properties of a transaction that, when observed, can ensure proper transaction handling. The ACID properties include Atomicity, Consistency, Isolation, and Durability and were first proposed in [HaRe83].

acquire access: a synchronization primitive utilized in release consistency when performing a read that forces the local system to update its copies of shared data.

acyclic directory structure: a directory structure where a file or directory is allowed to have multiple parents thereby allowing the possibility of cycles within the structure.

adaptive schedulers: schedulers that permit a process to be rescheduled after it has commenced execution at a particular location in order to accommodate system needs. Thus, such schedulers allow a process to migrate at any time during execution.

address space: a portion of the entire system's memory that is allocated for a particular process.

application layer: the seventh layer in the ISO/OSI reference model. This layer not only focuses on the user interface but also focuses on establishing authority and availability of network-based applications.

assignment graph: a graph utilized to represent possible process assignments for the purpose of distributed scheduling.

asymmetric encryption: encryption that involves two keys. One key encrypts the plain text while the other key is used to decrypt the ciphertext.

asynchronous: events that do not occur at regular intervals and are typically generated from external sources.

asynchronous primitive: see non-blocking primitive.

atomic action: a series of actions that are indivisible and occur as if they were a single action.

atomicity property: a transaction property requiring an all actions within a transaction to appear as a single action throughout the distributed system.

authentication: act of verifying an identity.

automaton vector: a vector whose values represent the various overall load states of a distributed system. This vector is utilized with stochastic learning for distributed scheduling.

backbone: a network used to connect multiple networks together. Generally, the only 'hosts' on the backbone are other networks.

barriers: employed for synchronization in order to provide release consistency. It is utilized to distinguish various phases of execution.

bastion host: an exposed gateway machine that is exposed to the Internet. It is the main point of contact and the system vulnerable to attack. Named after the fortified medieval castle walls.

block caching: remote copy for portions of a file in terms of blocks.

blocking primitives: a type of message passing primitive in which the kernel does not return control to the process until the primitive is completed. This is also known as a synchronous primitive since the communicating processes become synchronized as a result.

bridge: a device two connect multiple networks that implement the same network protocols. Only packets of data meant for or required to pass through a particular network are forwarded onto that network.

bus-contention: the overuse of a bus caused by several processors utilizing the same bus to retrieve information from shared memory; thus, causing the system to be less efficient and effective.

busy wait: a continuous loop executed by a process (spinning) that is waiting for the value of a variable (spinlock) to change.

capability: something presented to a resource by a valid user of the resource to indicate permission for said usage.

casual consistency model: a consistency model that requires all casually related events to be viewed in the same order by all participants of the distributed system.

casual related events: events that change the same set of shared data.

certificate authority: someone who is in charge of issuing and verifying digital certificates; the electronic equivalence to the US Passport Agency for passports or the State Department of Motor Vehicles for driver's licenses.

certificate list: one method of providing authentication. The list contains certificates of various users. A service must check with the list to verify public keys.

child process allowance: a method for handling orphan processes whereby a child process must continually ask for a time allowance to continue executing. If the parent is dead, it will not distributed a time allowance and the child process will terminate execution.

ciphertext: plain text that has been encrypted or disguised.

change journal: a method to record and track changes to the contents of files and directories.

class: the abstract definition of an object.

clock skew: the difference in time between two clocks due to drifting

cluster: an abstraction of a scalable service that allows relative location independence and is able to provide redundancy and fault tolerance within itself through the coordination of multiple physical servers to perform the required services.

communication deadlock: a deadlock involving communication buffers.

compound transaction: a transaction that consists of more than one sub-transactions. Sub-transactions must be organized in a hierarchical structure. The compound transaction and all nested sub-transactions must adhere to the ACID properties individually and collectively.

computationally secure: a message encrypted by the algorithm cannot be broken by systematic analysis with available resources.

concurrent-copy: a method of memory migration that copies the entire virtual memory and other information related to the migrating process while concurrently executing that process at the original location.

condition variable: global variables within a monitor used to control processes wishing to be active within the monitor and ensure only one process is active.

consistency: the process of attempting to maintain multiple copies of data, which are manipulated by many locations, each having an acceptable copy of the data.

consistency model: a set of defined consistency rules that all participants in a distributed system must adhere to, including user applications.

consistency property: a transaction property requiring all transactions to leave the system in a consistent state according to the system defined consistency model.

constructor: in object based development, an instantiation of a method when multiple instantiations are allowed. Instantiations do not need to be unique. Thus, what is known as function overloading may be permitted.

copy-on-reference: a method of memory migration that only copies pages of virtual memory of a migrated process when the migration destination references said pages.

copy set: utilized in distributed shared data method of memory management for maintaining a list of all system participants who hold a copy of a particular block of data.

critical region: the portion of a program that is accessing a shared resource.

cryptography: art of making secure ciphertext.

cutset: a set of edges that when removed, turn a connected graph to a disconnected graph meaning that it has two or more components that are not connected via an edge.

cyclic directory structure: a directory structure where a file or directory is allowed to have multiple parents thereby allowing the possibility of cycles within the structure. Furthermore, a child may become the parent of one of its parents thereby creating a cyclic structure.

data link layer: the second layer in the ISO/OSI reference model. This layer is divided into two sub-layers: medium access control and logical link control.

deadlock: a resource allocation problem that has resulted in a allocation that prohibits two or more processes from making progress.

decryption: making a message readable by applying the appropriate algorithm with the appropriate key to the message.

digest function: a function who's input is a document and output is a unique value used as a digital signature. These functions are also known as hash functions.

digital certificate: an electronic, verifiable, piece of identification; an electronic equivalence to a passport or driver's license.

digital signature: a technique to ensure the identity of the origin or contents when working in a distributed environment.

directory service: part of a distributed file system that provides the user interface to the file system and is responsible for the overall structure of the system.

direct store-and-forward deadlock: a communication deadlock involving exactly two locations.

dispersion: the maximum error allowable for a local clock relative to the primary reference clock in NTP. A higher dispersion factor indicates less reliable clock information.

distributed system: a collection of heterogeneous systems connected via a network that present a global unified view of the system and its resources.

divisible process: a process which can be subdivided into smaller sub-processes or tasks based on characteristics of the process. These tasks may be independently scheduled.

domino effect: the result of a transaction aborting if other transactions wrongfully relied on results from the aborted transaction. In this situation, all other transactions must abort as well as any transactions that relied on those transactions.

drifting: the gradual misalignment of once synchronized clocks.

dual-homed host: a computer system attached to at least two networks.

durability property: a transaction property requiring a committed server to complete a transaction even if it suffers a system failure. All results of the transaction must be permanent.

dynamic binding: processes that are not bound to a particular location for execution when the executable image is created.

economic usage points: a variation to the usage points approach to distributed scheduling where points reflect the value of remote execution based on a systems load and possibly other characteristics.

embedded real-time system: a real-time system in installed in a larger system and is used to control specialized hardware.

encryption: making a message unreadable by applying an algorithm and a key to the message.

entry release consistency: a consistency model based upon release consistency that also requires all variables to be synchronization variables or to be associated with a synchronization mechanism such as a lock or barrier.

executive: implements the system services within Windows NT kernel.

external fragmentation: wasted memory space within physical memory between various units (such as segments) of memory.

explicit addressing: an addressing mechanism for message passing in which the calling process specifies the exact process with which they wish to communicate.

false sharing: this occurs when separate locations in a distributed system are thrashing over a page yet do not share any of the data structures on the page.

file access semantics: the method for performing notification to participants in the distributed system when changes are made to shared files.

file handle: information given to a file user regarding a file's location and may include permission to access said file.

file service: the portion of a distributed file system that is responsible for operations on a particular file.

file system: an important subsystem of an operating system responsible for maintaining directories, files, as well as managing the name space.

firewall: designed to protect your internal computer resources from external threats; provides access control.

firm-real-time system: a real-time system that can tolerate a low probability of missing a deadline.

flow control: the term used to describe network functions which regulate the amount of data transmitted and the frequency of transmission which is regulated in order to prevent 'overwhelming' network resources.

freeze time: the execution time wasted between the time a process is stopped and restarted at its migration location.

function overloading: when multiple definitions for a function is allowed. All functions defined utilize the same exact name but differ by the list of arguments and behavior.

gang scheduling: a scheduling strategy that allows all related processes/threads to be scheduled together.

global naming: a system where each file or object has a unique name within a distributed system. Global naming does *not* imply name transparency.

global scheduler: the scheduler responsible for allocating a process to a processor within the distributed system.

global order: the concept of being able to uniquely identify the order of all events in a distributed system.

global time: the concept of having all clocks throughout a distributed system synchronized.

happen-before relationship: the relationship utilized for obtaining relative partial ordering in a distributed environment. It is used to identify casual relationships and was first proposed by Lamport [Lam78].

hard real-time system: a system that must satisfy bounded response-time constraints or suffer severe, possibly life threatening, consequences.

hash function: see digest function.

heuristics: rules that will generally lead to desired results. These rules are not necessarily provable or directly quantifiable but generally lead to satisfactory results in an efficient manner.

hierarchical directory structure: a tree-like directory structure where a given file or directory is only allowed to have one parent.

host: any computer system attached to a network.

immediate notification: a type of modification notification whereby every change to a file is immediately communicated to the distributed system participants.

immutable files: a file whose contents cannot be changed; that is, modifications are not permitted.

implicit addressing: an addressing mechanism for message passing in which the calling process specifies the service they wish to communicate with instead of explicitly naming the exact process.

incidental ordering: a form of many-to-many message ordering that only requires messages that are incidentally related to be received in the correct order.

indirect store-and-forward deadlock: a communication deadlock involving more than two locations.

indivisible process: a process which cannot be further subdivided into sub-processes or tasks and must be processed on a single processor.

inheritance: the allowance of an object to define itself in terms of other another object.

internal fragmentation: wasted memory space within a block of memory.

interprocess communication: the means of which two or more processes may communicate in order to accomplish a common goal.

interrupt: a means in which a process may signal an operating system that the process requires some sort of service.

isochronous: a sub-category of asynchronous events for events that may not occur at precise intervals allowing them to be categorized as synchronous but do occur within regular intervals possible due to some type of network latency.

isolation property: a transaction property requiring transactions to be performed in an 'all or nothing' manner, other participants are not allowed access to intermediate results.

ISO/OSI reference model: a seven-layer reference model established as a standard to base system comparisons on in different distributed/network environments.

job: a program in execution. This term generally refers to the system view of a process.

kernel: the privileged portion of the operating system that executes with complete access privileges for all resources.

lazy release consistency: release consistency that only propagates writes or performs updates on demand.

leap second: the addition or removal of a second within a particular minute employed to keep UTC time, an atomic based time, accurate with Astrological time

load balancing: a load distribution policy that strives to maintain an *even* load throughout the system through migration.

load sharing: a load distribution policy that assists *overworked resources* through migration.

local scheduler: the scheduler in charge of scheduling a process to the actual CPU at a particular location. The local scheduler is only responsible for scheduling at one location and is not involved with scheduling at remote locations.

location resolution: the mapping of a global file name to the file's location.

logical clocks: clocks that are employed for the determination of the relative order of events. Logical clocks are not concerned with 'people' time.

logical link control: a sub-layer of the data link layer in the ISO/OSI reference model. The dominating functions include error control and flow control.

lost update: a potential problem that can occur in shared data if transactions are not handled atomically. In particular, it involves multiple transactions all copying the same shared data in order to change the value. When the results are returned, each return value overwrites the previous transaction; thereby, loosing the results of entire previous transaction.

mandatory schedulers: distributed schedulers that mandate that every location within the distributed system participate in distributed scheduling and allow remote processes to execute locally.

marshalling: the name of the function performed on the parameters within a remote procedure call that flattens the data into a form for quick communication across a network.

maximum flow of a graph: a subgraph of a graph that contains the edges with the largest weighting.

medium access control: a sub-layer of the data link layer in the ISO/OSI reference model. This LAN centered sub-layer focuses on appropriate usage of the shared broadcast network.

memory management unit: the virtual memory manager which maps virtual memory to physical memory and disk.

message digest: the result of applying a digest function to a document. This digest may then be utilized to verify that the contents of the document have not been altered.

message passing: a form of interprocess communication that allows two processes, possibly on different machines, to communicate by sending a message containing shared data.

midware: a distributed operating system that runs on top of the local or base centralized operating system.

migration: the act of relocating a process and all related information to another processor possibly at a remote location.

min-cut: a minimum cutset for a graph; that is, a cutset with the lowest possible cost. The cost of a cutset is determined by summing the weights of the cut edges.

modification notification: utilized to notify distributed system participants that changes have been made to a file in a distributed file system.

moniker: an object instance in DCOM. The interface to a moniker is an Imoniker.

monitor: a language construct that utilizes compiler support to ensure mutual exclusion. A monitor is an abstract data type and contains variables, procedures and data structures.

multicast: a message intended for a subset of all participants connected to a network.

multicomputers: a parallel computer in which each processor has its own local memory.

multiple inheritance: the allowance of an object to define itself in terms of multiple existing objects.

multi-threaded: an environment that allows a process to execute more than one 'thread of computation concurrently.

multi-processors: a parallel computer in which all processors share the same memory.

mutual exclusion: ensures that multiple processes do not simultaneously utilize a shared resource.

named pipes: a form of interprocess communication for use with related processes.

name resolution: the mapping of a human (character based) file name to a global (binary) name.

name service: a part of a file system responsible for mapping file names to file locations. In a distributed environment it may also be responsible for mapping local names to global names and computer generated names to human-friendly names.

Name space: the entire collection of viable names for files, directories and components within a system. This collection is frequently confined due to naming rules implemented by the name service for a given system.

nested transaction: see sub-transaction.

network layer: the third layer in the ISO/OSI reference model that is responsible for routing. This layer is a null layer for LANs.

network system: a heterogeneous collections of computers connected via a network. The heterogeniality of the system is exposed and there a very little constraints put on the participating computers.

non-blocking primitives: a type of message passing primitive in which the kernel immediately returns control to the process and does not wait until the primitive is completed. This is also known as a asynchronous primitive.

nonce: a random integer value used in an authentication challenge. If received, correct nonce value must be included in all messages back to challenger.

non-repudiation: ensures that one cannot deny that they signed and sent a digital message after the fact.

NORMA multiprocessor: a multiprocessor where each processor has its own local memory and the processors do not share memory.

notification on close: a type of modification notification whereby members of the distributed system are only notified of changes when a participant closes a file that they have changed.

notification on transaction completion: a type of modification notification whereby transactions are employed and members of the distributed system are only notified of changes when a participant completes a transaction.

NP-Hard: problems that are computationally intractable and no known polynomial-time algorithm solutions exist.

NUMA multiprocessor: a multiprocessor with shared memory where the access time to this memory varies due to its association with only a sub-group of the processors.

object: a development abstraction that encapsulates all related services and data.

object-based system: a system designed and defined utilizing objects.

object behavior: defined by the complete collection of functions that can be performed by a particular object.

object-oriented system: a system designed and defined utilizing objects and permitting object inheritance.

one-time assignment schedulers: schedulers that are not involved or permit process migration after a process has been designated to execute a particular location.

optimal scheduling algorithm: a scheduling algorithm that is able to determine the best possible solution in terms of a particular metric.

orphan clean up: a method for handling orphan processes whereby the system of the dead parent process terminates orphan processes when the system is rebooted.

orphan process: a process that is remotely executing in a distributed system whose parent has premature died, probably due to a system crash.

packet: the primary unity of communication on the Internet. Messages are divided up into packets.

packet-filtering gateway: a firewall that selectively controls or `filters' data coming into and leaving your internal network. It attempts to protect your network from attack.

page: a concept for dividing blocks of memory up into blocks of equal size. Paging systems suffer from internal fragmentation but not external fragmentation.

page fault: when a process requires a page of memory that does not currently reside in the physical memory. The page fault causes the system to fetch the page from disk or another host within the distributed system via the network.

page scanner: a system daemon utilized in shared memory models that monitors the frequency in which a page of memory is being non-locally accessed.

parallel system: a collection of homogeneous processors and memory modules contained in a single computer.

peer-to-peer layers: functions in these layers of the ISO/OSI reference model are only performed at the source and destination.

pipes: a form of interprocess communication for use when processes at least share a common file system.

physical clocks: clocks used to report and maintain 'people' time as contrasted with logical clocks.

physical layer: the lowest of the seven layers of the ISO/OSI reference model. This layer concerns issues such as putting the bits on the network and determining connection physical interfaces.

plaintext: the information you want to disguise.

plug and play: requires hardware and software support and enables computer devices connected to a system to change and be recognized without user intervention and configuration.

point-to-point layers: functions in these layers of the ISO/OSI reference model are not only performed at the source and destination but also at the possibly thousands of locations on the network between the source and destination.

polled-loop scheduler: a scheduler that requires processes to be asked by the scheduler if it needs service from the system. The requests operate in a round-robin fashion.

PRAM consistency model: the pipelined random access memory consistency model requires all write operations performed by a single process to be viewed by other processes in the order that they were performed.

presentation layer: the sixth layer in the ISO/OSI reference model. This layer deals with the syntax of the messages including ASCII to EBCDIC conversion, compression, encryption and so on.

processor consistency model: a consistency model that requires PRAM consistency in addition to memory coherence.

private key cryptography: a single key is used for encryption and decryption. It must be kept secret.

process: an abstraction of a program in execution.

process migration: relocating a process and all related state information to another processor, possibly at a remote location.

process version number: a method for handling orphan processes whereby a child process is always accompanied with a version number. When the parent system is rebooted, it utilizes a new version number and announces the new version number to members of the distributed system. Any processes executing with an out-of-date version number must terminate.

protected variables: variables designated to comply with release consistency.

proxy-service firewall: replaces services with more secure versions for use with external networks; specifically, it deals with external servers on behalf of internal clients instead of the clients dealing directly with the servers. Helps guard against the consequences of a compromised gateway.

public key cryptography: two keys, a public and private key exist. If one key encrypts a message, the other key can decrypt the message. The private key is kept secret.

race condition: when the output is dependent on the exact timing of the arrival of the input values.

reactive real-time system: a real-time system which reacts to constant interactions with its environment.

real-time system: a system that must satisfy bounded response-time constraints or suffer sever consequences (see soft-real-time and hard-real-time).

release access: a synchronization primitive utilized in release consistency employed when performing a final write operation. It forces changes to shared data to propagate throughout the system.

release consistency model: a consistency model that employs acquire access and release access synchronization primitives.

remote access: a type of distributed file service where clients do not transfer files locally but rather conduct all file access on the actual file server.

remote copy: a type of distributed file service where clients transfer a copy of the file to their location.

remote procedure calls: (RPC) a form of interprocess communication using the familiar procedural format. This method also allows the called process to return a value not just an acknowledgement.

reparse tags: designate that a reparse point has been reached and is applicable to the given file.

reparse points: a method that allows file system filters to change how a file is handled through the use of designated filters specified in the file name and designated through reparse tags.

retrieval disparity: a potential problem that can occur in shared data if transactions are not handled atomically and in isolation. In particular, it involves the retrieval of data that does not reflect the latest transaction.

repeater: a device to connect two networks that implement the same protocol. Every packet of data on one network is repeated onto the other network.

request: in object based development, the manner in which one can call upon the services of an object.

router: a device to connect two networks that implement possibly different protocols.

session layer: the fifth layer in the ISO/OSI reference model which is responsible for the synchronization of the communication between the source and destination.

segments: a type of memory block that is variable in size. Segments suffer from external fragmentation as well as minor internal fragmentation.

sequential consistency model: a consistency model that requires all participants to share the same global view regarding the order of transactions.

shared memory model: a model of memory management in a distributed computing environment in which processes communicate through the utilization of common data structures.

simple memory model: a model of memory management utilized by parallel UMA architectures which is directly based on the memory management of a centralized system.

snoopy cache: a cache consistency model in which processors snoop on the shared bus for information regarding changes to data that they currently have a copy of in their local cache.

stateful file service: a type of distributed file service where the file server maintains state information regarding all clients and their list of files they are accessing as well as their position within a given file.

stateless file service: a type of distributed file service where the file server does not maintain any state information for the clients. All client requests must contain complete information regarding their particular request.

static binding: processes that are immediately bound to a particular location for execution when the executable image is created.

status state: a value that represents the load on a particular system within a distributed system. Some implementations utilize two states: under-loaded and over-loaded while others also utilize suitably-loaded as a third state.

stratum: the term used in NTP to refer to the level of a client or server in the tree based architecture.

stochastic learning: an approach to distributed scheduling whereby the algorithm receives feedback from previous choices and utilizes this information to improve future choices.

strict consistency model: a consistency model that requires all reads to return the value from the most recent write operation.

structured files: a method of file storage whereby each file is broken down into various records. These records may be supported by the file system by an external index.

socket: a method for interprocess communication that requires the communicating processes to be bound to common endpoints.

soft real-time system: a system that must satisfy bounded response time constraints or suffer consequences such as degradation of performance.

spinlock: a variable that is continuously checked by looping or spinning. Spinlocks are often utilized for busy waits.

spinning: continuously looping to check the value of a variable in a busy wait.

stop-and-copy: a method of memory migration that stops execution, copies the entire virtual memory associated with the migrating process and then restarts execution at the migration destination.

sub-optimal approximate scheduling algorithms: scheduling algorithms that utilize 'short cuts' on optimal solutions to quickly obtain sub-optimal solutions.

sub-optimal heuristic scheduling algorithms: scheduling algorithms that utilize basic intuition considering rules that will generally lead to better overall system performance. These rules are not necessarily provable or directly quantifiable in terms of how system performance is affected.

sub-optimal scheduling algorithms: scheduling algorithms that attempt to find very good solutions when measured by a particular metric, but not necessarily the best solution. Sub-optimal solutions tend to execute much faster than optimal solutions.

sub-transaction: a transaction that is part of a larger, compound transaction also referred to as a nested transaction.

symmetric encryption: encryption that involves a single key. Specifically, the same key encrypts the plain text and is also used to decrypt the ciphertext.

synchronization variable: used for synchronizing memory and maintaining weak consistency.

synchronous: events occurring at precise, regular, predictable intervals generally originating from an attached component in an real-time system.

synchronous primitive: see blocking primitive.

Task Interaction Graph: a graph whose vertices represent related processes and edges represent the interaction between the processes. This graph is utilized to represent modularly divisible loads.

thrashing: a term in memory management to describe a system in a constant state of fetching and moving pages of memory to the point of serious degradation of performance.

thread: short for a thread of execution that represents a path through a program.

time provider: a commercial device that is capable of directly receiving information from a UTC server and making appropriate adjustments due to communication delays

transaction: a set of operations on shared data that are grouped together and treated as single action.

transaction management: the service employed to ensure proper transaction handling.

transport layer: the fourth layer in the ISO/OSI reference model. This layer is where the class of service for communications is established. Class of service may be connection oriented or connectionless.

two-phase commit protocol: a protocol for implementing transactions. The protocol is divided into a prepare to commit phase and a commit phase and adheres to the ACID properties of a transaction.

unnamed pipes: a form of interprocess communication for use when possibly unrelated processes share a common file system.

UMA multiprocessor: a multiprocessor where all processors share memory and the access time is uniform (the same) for accessing any memory module.

uniform ordering: a form of many-to-many message ordering that mandates that all messages are received by all receiver processes uniformly. All participants receive them in the same order that may be a different order then sent.

universal numbers: telephone numbers that do not depend on area codes and exhibit location independence.

universal ordering: a form of many-to-many message ordering that mandates and ensures that all messages are received in exactly the same order as sent.

usage table: the location on a centralized server that maintains the running total of usage points for all participants in a distributed system.

update sequence number: a number that represents a specific change to a file or directory within a change journal.

usage points: an approach to distributed scheduling that charges points against a location for utilizing outside resources and credits a location for allowing remote locations to utilize local resources.

very large memory: address space capable of supporting 64-bit addresses.

virtual memory: a memory management concept that allows a process to believe it has all the memory available to it that it needs, even if this amount of memory is larger than the actual physical memory.

voluntary schedulers: scheduling algorithms that do not mandate that every location in the distributed system allow remote processes to execute locally. Participation in distributed scheduling is strictly voluntary.

weak consistency model: a consistency model that employs synchronization variables. When a synchronization variable is utilized, all local writes must be propagated throughout the system and a location must update all changes made to data for which it holds a copy.

whole file caching: a type of distributed file service where clients transfer a copy of the file to their location also known as remote copy.

Bibliography

[AAO92] Abrossimov, A., F. Armand, and M. Ortega. "A Distributed Consistency Server for the CHORUS System." *Proceedings of SEDMS III, Symposium on Experience with Distributed and Multiprocessor Systems.* USENIX, pp. 129-148: 1992.

[ABCLMN98] Anderson, R., F. Bergadano, B. Crispo, J. Lee, C. Manifavas, and R. Needham. "A New Family of Authentication Protocols." *Operating Systems Review.* ACM SIGOP Press. Vol 32, Num 4, pp. 9-20: 1998.

[ABLL91] Anderson, T., B. Bershad, E. Lazowska, and H. Levy. "Scheduler Activations: Effective Kernel Support for the User Level Management of Parallelism." *ACM Transactions on Computer Systems*, Vol. 10, No. 1, pp. 53-79: 1991.

[AbPo86] Abrams, M. and H. Podell. *Tutorial: Computer and Network Security.* IEEE Computer Society Press., Washington D.C., 1986.

[ADFS98] Arbaugh, W., J. Davin, D. Farber, and J. Smith. "Security for Virtual Private Intranets." *IEEE Computer.* Vol. 31, No. 9, pp. 48-55: 1998.

[AdHi90] Adve, S. and M. Hill. "Weak Ordering: A New Definition." *Proceedings of the 17th IEEE Annual International Symposium on Computer Architecture.* pp. 2-14: 1990.

[AgAb91] Agarwal, D. and A. El Abbadi. "An Efficient and Fault-Tolerant Solution of Distributed Mutual Exclusion." *ACM Transactions on Computer Systems.* Vol. 9, pp. 1-20: 1991.

[AGGL86] Armand, F., M. Gien, M. Guillemont, and P. Leonard. "Towards' a Distributed UNIX System – The CHORUS Approach." *Proceedings of the EUUG Autumn '86 Conference.* Manchester, England, Autumn 1986.

[AGS83] Ames, S., M. Gasser, and R. Schell. "Security Kernel Design and Implementation: An Introduction", *IEEE Computer.* Vol. 16, No. 7, pp. 14-22: 1983.

[AJP95] Abrams, M., Jajodia, and H. Podell (Eds). *Information Security: An Integrated Collection of Essays.* IEEE Computer Society Press., Washington D.C., 1995.

[Akl97] Akl, S. *Parallel Computation: Models and Methods.* Prentice Hall, Englewood Cliffs, New Jersey, 1997.

[AKZ96] Awad, M., J. Kuusela, and J. Ziegler. *Object-Oriented Technology for Real-Time Systems.* Prentice Hall, Englewood Cliffs, New Jersey, 1996.

[And94] Anderson, R. "Why Cryptosystems Fail." *Communications of the ACM.* Vol. 37, No. 11, pp. 32-40: 1994.

[ArFi89] Artsy, Y., and R. Finkel. "Designing a Process Migration Facility." *IEEE Computer.* Vol. 22, No. 9, pp. 47-56: 1989.

[ARJ97] Anderson, J., S. Ramamurthy, and K. Jeffay. "Real-Time Computing with Lock-Free Shared Objects." *ACM Transactions on Computer Systems.* Vol. 15, No. 2, pp. 134-165: 1977.

[ARS89] Abrossimov, V., M. Rozier, and M. Shapiro. "Generic Virtual Memory Management for Operating System Kernels." *Proceedings of the 12th ACM Symposium on Operating Systems Principles.* Pp. 123-136: 1989.

[BaHa87] Bacon, J. and K. Hamilton. *Distributed Computing with RPC: The Cambridge Approach.* The University of Cambridge Computer Laboratory Technical Report No. 117, England: 1987.

[BAN90] Burrows, M., M. Abadi, and R. Needham. "A Logic of Authentication." *ACM Transactions on Computer Systems.* Vol. 8, No. 1, pp. 18-36: 1990.

[BALL90] Bershad, B., T. Anderson, E. Lazowska, and H. Levy. "Lightweight Remote Procedure Call." *ACM Transactions on Computer Systems.* Vol. 8, No. 1, pp. 37-55: 1990.

[BBF83] Bauer, R., T. Berson, and R. Feirtag. "A Key Distribution Protocol Using Event Markers." *ACM Transactions on Computer Systems.* Vol. 1, No. 3, pp. 249-255: 1983.

[BCEF94] Bauer, M., N. Coburn, D. Erickson (Galli), P. Finnigan, J. Hong, P. Larson, J. Pachl, J. Slonim, D. Taylor, and T. Teorey. "A Distributed System Architecture for a Distributed Application Environment." *IBM Systems Journal.* Vol. 33, No. 3, pp. 399-425: 1994.

[BeFe91] Berthome, P. and A. Ferreira. "On Broadcasting Schemes in Restricted Optical Passive Star Systems." *Interconnection Networks and Maping and Scheduling Parallel Computations.* D. Hsu (ed.) DIMACS Series in Discrete Mathematics and Theoretical Computer Science, Volume 21, pp. 19-30: 1991.

[Ber92] Berson, A. *Client/Server Architecture.* McGraw Hill, New York, New York, 1992.

[BeZe91] Bershad, B. and M. Zekauskas. *Midway: Shared Memory Parallel Programming with Entry Consistency for Distributed Memory Multiprocessors.* Carnegie Mellon University Technical Report: CMU-CS-91: 1991.

[BFMV84] Blake, I., R. Fuji-Hara, R. Mullin, and S. Vanstone. Computing Logarithms in Finite Fields of Characteristic Two. *Siam Journal of Algorithms for Discrete Mathematics*, pp. 276-285, 1984.

[BGGLOR94] Bricker, A., M. Gien, M. Guillemont, J. Lipkis, D. Orr, and M. Rozier. "A New Look at Mircro-kernel Based UNIX Operating Systems:

Lessons in Performance and Compatibility." *Distributed Open Systems*, IEEE Computer Society Press, Los Alamitos, California, pp. 31-48: 1994.

[BGMR96] Bharadwaj, V., D. Ghose, V. Mani, and T. Robertazzi. *Scheduling Divisible Loads in Parallel and Distributed Systems.* IEEE Computer Society Press, Los Alamitos, California, 1996.

[BiJo87] Birman, K. and T. Joseph. "Reliable Communication in the Presence of Failures." *ACM Transactions on Computer Systems.* Vol. 5, No. 1, pp. 47-76: 1987.

[Bir85] Birrell, A. "Secure Communication Using Remote Procedure Calls." *ACM Transactions on Computer Systems.* Vol. 3, No. 1, pp. 1-14: 1985.

[BKT85] Brown, M., K. Kolling, and E. Taft. "The Alpine File System." *ACM Transactions on Computer Systems.* Vol. 3, No. 4, pp. 261-293: 1985.

[BGMR96] Bharadwaj, V., D. Ghose, V. Mani, and T. Robertazzi. *Scheduling Divisible Loads in Parallel and distributed Systems.* IEEE Computer Society Press, Los Alamitos, California, 1996.

[Bla90] Black, D. "Scheduling Support for Concurrency and Parallelism in the Mach Operating system." *IEEE Computer*, Vol 23, No. 5, pp. 35-43:1990

[Bla96] Black, U. *Mobile and Wireless Networks.* Prentice Hall, Englewood Cliffs, New Jersey, 1996.

[Blo92] Bloomer, J. *Power Programming with RPC.* O'Reilly & Associates, Inc; Sebastopol, California, 1992.

[BLPv93] Barnett, M., R. Littlefield, D. Payne, and R. van de Geijn. "Efficient Communication Primitives on Mesh Architectures with Hardware Routing." *Proceedings of the Sixth SIAM Conference on Parallel Processing for Scientific Computing.* R. Sincovec, K. Keyes, M. Leuze, L. Petzold, and D. Reed (eds.) Vol. II, pp. 943-948: 1993.

[Bra80] Braun, W. "Short Term Frequency Effects on Networks of Coupled Oscillators." *IEEE Transactions on Communications.* Vol. Com-28, No. 8, pp. 1269-1275: 1980.

[Bra95] Braun, C. *UNIX System Security Essentials.* Addison Wesley; Reading, Massachusetts, 1995.

[Bri75] Brinch Hansen, P., "The Programming Language Concurrent Pascal." *IEEE Transactions on Software Engineering.* Vol. SE-1, No. 6, pp. 199-207: 1975.

[BrJo94] Brazier, F. and D. Johansen Eds. *Distributed Open Systems.* IEEE Press, Los Alamitos, California, 1994.

[BSCEFHLS93] Bauer, M., E. Strom, N. Coburn, D. Erickson (Galli), P. Finnigan, J. Hong, P. Larson, and J. Slonim. "Íssues in Distributed Architectures: A Comparison of Two Paradigms." *Proceedings of the 1993 International Conference on Open Distributed Processing.* Berlin, Germany, pp. 411-418: 1993.

[BuScSu97] Buttazzo, T. and S. Scuola Superiore. *Hard Real-Time Computing Systems: Predictable Scheduling Algorithms and Applications.* Kluwer Academic Publishers, Hingham, MA: 1997.

[BZS93] Bershad, B., M. Zekauskas, and W. Sawdon. "The Midway Distributed Shared Memory System." *Proceedings of the IEEE COMPCON Conference.* pp. 528-537: 1993.

[CAKLMS92] Chutani, S., O. Anderson, M. Kazar, B. Leverett, W. Mason, and R. Sidebothan. "The Episode File System." *Proceedings of the 1992 USENIX Winter Conference.* pp. 43-60: 1992.

[CaKu88] Casavant, T. and J. Kuhl. "A Taxonomy of Scheduling in General-Purpose Distributed Computing Systems." *IEEE Transactions on Software Engineering.* Vol. 14, No. 2, pp. 141-154: 1988.

[CaMu94] Casavant, T. and M. Singhal (Eds.). *Readings in Distributed Computing Systems.* IEEE Press, Los Alamitos, California, 1994.

[CAPK98] Cabrera, L., B. Andrew, K. Peltonen, and N. Kusters. "Advanced in Windows NT Storage Management." *IEEE Computer.* Vol. 31, No. 10, pp. 48-54: 1998.

[Car95] Carter, D. *Computer Crime in America.* Technical Report, Michigan State University, 1995.

[CaRo83] Carvallo, O. and G. Roucairol. "On Mutual Exclusion in Computer Networks." *Communications of the ACM.* Vol. 26, No. 2, pp. 146-147: 1983.

[CBE95] Chen, K., R. Bunt, and D. Eager. "Write Caching in Distributed File Systems." *Proceedings of the 15th IEEE International Conference on Distributed Computing Systems.* IEEE Press, New York, New York: 1995.

[Cha97] Chan, T. *UNIX System Programming Using C++.* Prentice Hall PTR; Upper Saddle River, New Jersey, 1996.

[ChBe94] Cheswick, W. and S. Bellovin. *Firewalls and Internet Security: Repelling the Wily Hacker.* Addison-Wesley Publishing Co.; Reading, Massachusetts, 1994

[ChZw95] Chapman, D. and E. Zwicky. *Building Internet Firewalls.* O'Reilly & Associates, Inc; Sebastopol, California, 1995.

[CIRM93] Campbell, R., N. Islam, D. Raila, and P. Madany. "Designing and Implementing Choices: An Object-Oriented System in C++." *Communications of the ACM.* Vol. 36, No. 9, pp. 117-126: 1993.

[Cla85] Clark, D. "The Structuring of Upcalls." *Proceedings of the Tenth ACM Symposium on Operating Systems Principles.* Pp. 171-180: 1985.

[ClHo94] Clark, P. and L. Hoffman. "BITS: A Smartcard protected Operating System." *Communications of the ACM.* Vol. 37, No. 11, pp. 66-70: 1994.

[Cou98] Courtois, T. *JAVA: Networking & Communications.* Prentice Hall, Englewood Cliffs, New Jersey: 1998.

[Cri89] Cristian, F. "Probabilistic Clock Synchronization." *Distributed Computing.* Vol 3, pp. 146-158: 1989.

[Cve87] Cvetanovic, Z. "The Effects of Problem Partitioning, Allocation, and Granularity on the Performance of Multiple-Processor Systems." *IEEE Transactions on Computers*. Vol. C-36, No. 4, pp. 421-432: 1987.

[DaBu85] Davcev, D. and W. Burkhard. "Consistency and Recovery Control for Replicated Files." *Proceedings of the 10th ACM Annual Symposium on Operating Systems Principles*. pp. 87-96: 1985.

[DDK94] Coulouris, G., J. Dollimore, and T. Kindberg. *Distributed Systems: Concepts and Design Second Edition*. Addison Wesley, Reading, Massachusetts, 1994.

[DeDe94] Deitel, H. and P. Deitel. *C++ How to Program*. Prentice Hall, Englewood Cliffs, New Jersey: 1994.

[DeDe98] Deitel, H. and P. Deitel. *Java How to Program*. Prentice Hall, Englewood Cliffs, New Jersey: 1998.

[DeSa81] Denning, D. and G. Sacco. "Timestamps in Key Distribution Protocols." *Communications of the ACM*. Vol. 24, No. 8, pp. 533-536: 1981.

[DH76] Diffie, W. and M. Hellman. "New Directions in Cryptography." *IEEE Transactions on Information Theory*. Vol. IT-11, No. 11, pp. 644-654: 1976.

[Dij65] Dijkstra, E. "Co-operating Sequential Processes." *Programming Languages*. F. Genuys (Ed.) Academic Press, London: 1965.

[Dio80] Dion, J. "The Cambridge File Server." *ACM Operating Systems Review*. Vol. 14, No. 4, pp. 26-35: 1980.

[DLAR91] Dasgupta, P., R. LeBlanc Jr., M. Ahamad, and U. Ramachandran. "The Clouds Distributed Operating System." *IEEE Computer*. Vol. 24, No. 11, pp. 34-44: 1991.

[DoMc98] Dowd, P. and J. McHenry. "Network Security: It's Time to Take it Seriously." *IEEE Computer*. Vol. 31, No. 9, pp. 24-28: 1998.

[DSB86] Dubois, M., C. Scheurich, and F. Briggs. "Memory Access Bufering in Multiprocessors." *Proceedings of the 13th ACM Annual International Symposium on Computer Architecture*. Pp. 434-442: 1986.

[DSB88] Dubois, M., C. Scheurich, and F. Briggs. "Synchronization, Coherence, and Event Ordering in Multiprocessors." *IEEE Computer*. Vol. 21, No. 2, pp. 9-21: 1988.

[ErCo93a] Erickson (Galli), D. and C. Colbourn, *Combinatorics and the Conflict-Free Access Problem*, Congressus Numerantium, Vol. 94, pp. 115-121, December 1993.

[ErCo93b] Erickson (Galli), D. and C. Colbourn, *Conflict-Free Access for Collections of Templates*, Proceedings of the Sixth SIAM Conference on Parallel Processing for Scientific Computing, Vol. II, pp. 949-952, March 1993.

[Erick93a] Erickson (Galli), D. *Threshold Schemes with Hierarchical Information*, Technical Report #CS-93-23, University of Waterloo, Department of Computer Science, ftp only. (ftp://cs-archive.uwaterloo.ca/cs-archive/CS-93-23/23Th.Z) 81 pages, 1993.

[Erick93b] Erickson (Galli), D. *Conflict-Free Access to Rectangular Subarrays in Parallel Memory Modules*, Technical Report #CS-93-24, University of Waterloo, Department of Computer Science, ftp only. (ftp://cs-archive.uwaterloo.ca/cs-archive/CS-93-24/Thesis.Z) 102 pages, 1993.

[ErCo92] Erickson (Galli), D. and C. Colbourn, *Conflict-Free Access to Rectangular Subarrays*, Congressus Numerantium, Vol. 90, pp. 239-253, November 1992.

[ELZ86] Eager, D., E. Lazowska, and J. Zahorjan. "Adaptive Load Sharing in Homogeneous Distributed Systems." *IEEE Transactions on Software Engineering*. Vol. SE-12, No. 5, pp. 662-675: 1986.

[EAL95] El-Rweini, H., H. Ali, and T. Lewis. "Task Scheduling in Multiprocesing Systems." *IEEE Computer*. Vol. 28, No. 12, pp. 27-37: 1995.

[ELZ86] Eager, D., E. Lazowska, and J. Zahorjan. "Adaptive Load Sharing in Homogeneous Distributed Systems." *IEEE Transactions on Software Engineering*. Vol. SE-12, No. 5, pp. 662-675: 1986.

[Esk89] Eskicioglu, M. "Design Issues of Process Migration Facilties in Distributed Systems." *IEEE Technical Committee on Operating Systems Newsletter*. Vol. 4, No. 2, pp. 3-13: 1989.

[Esk95] Eskicioglu, M., B. Shirazi, A. Hurson, and K. Kavi (Eds.) "Design Issues of Process Migration Facilties in Distributed Systems." *Scheduling and Load Balancing in Parallel and Distributed Systems*. IEEE Computer Society Press, Los Alamitos, California, pp. 414-424: 1995.

[Fer89] Fernandez-Baca, D. "Allocating Modules to Processors in a Distributed System." *IEEE Transactions on Software Engineering*. Vol. 15, No. 11, pp. 1427-1436: 1989.

[Fer95] Ferrari, D. "A New Admission Control Method for Real-Time Communication in an Internetwork." *Advances in Real-Time Systems*. S. Son (ed.) Prentice Hall PTR; Upper Saddle River, New Jersey, 1995.

[FeZh87] Ferrari, D. and S. Zhou. "An Empirical Investigation of Load Indices for Load Balancing Applications." *Proceedings Performance '87, The 12th Annual International Symposium on Computer Performance Modeling, Measurement and Evaluation*. North Holland Publishers, The Netherlands. Pp. 515-528: 1987.

[Fla96] Flanagan, D. *Java in a Nutshell*. O'Reilly & Associates, Inc.; Sebastopol, California, 1996.

[FrOl85] Fridrich, M. and W. Older. "Helix: the Architecture of the XMS Distributed File System." *IEEE Computer*. Vol. 18, No. 1, pp. 21-29: 1985.

[Fer89] Fernandez-Baca, D. "Allocating Modules to Processors in a Distributed System." *IEEE Transactions on Software Engineering*. Vol. 15, No. 11, pp. 1427-1436: 1989.

[Fu97] Fu, S. "A Comparison of Mutual Exclusion Algorithms for Distributed Memory Systems." *IEEE Newsletter of the Technical Committee on Distributed Processing.* pp. 15-20, Summer 1997.

[FYN88] Ferguson, D., Y. Yemini, and C. Nikolaou. "Microeconomic Algorithms for Load Balancing in Distributed Computer Systems." *Proceedings of the Eight IEEE International Conference on Distributed Computing Systems.* pp. 491-499: 1988.

[GaCo95] Galli, D. and C. Colbourn, *Conflict-Free Access to Constant-Perimeter Rectangular Subarrays* (Book Chapter), edited by F. Hsu, DIMACS Series in Discrete Mathematics and Theoretical Computer Science, Vol. 21, pp. 105-124, 1995.

[Gar82] Garcia-Molina, H. "Elections in a Distributed computing System." *IEEE Transactions on Computers.* Vol. 31, No. 1, pp. 48-59: 1982.

[GaSp91] Garcia-Molina, H. and A. Spauster. "Ordered and Reliable Multicast Communication." *ACM Transactions on Computer Systems.* Vol. 9, No. 3, pp. 242-271: 1991.

[GaShMa98] Gamache, R., R. Short, and M. Massa. "The Windows NT Clustering Service." *IEEE Computer.* Vol. 31, No. 10, pp. 55-62: 1998.

[GaSp96] Garfinkel, S. and G. Spafford. *Practical UNIX & Internet Security.* O'Reilly & Associates, Inc., Cambridge,1996.

[Gen81] Gentleman, W. M. "Message Passing Between Sequential Processes: The Reply Primitive and the Administrator Concept." *Software-Practice and Experience.* Vol. II, pp. 435-466: 1981.

[GeYa93] Gerasoulis, A. and T. Yang. "On the Granularity and Clustering of Directed Acyclic Task Graphs." *IEEE Transactions on parallel and Distributed Systems.* Vol. 4, No. 6, pp. 686-701: 1993.

[GGH91] Gharachorloo, K., A. Gupta, and J. Hennessy. "Performance Evaluations of Memory Consistency Models for Shared-Memory Multiprocessors." *Proceedings of the 4th ACM Symposium on Architectural Support for Programming Languages and Operating Systems.* Pp. 245-257: 1991.

[GhSc93] Gheith, A. and K. Schwan. "Chaos^{arc}: Kernel SupporT FOR Multi-WEIGHT Objects, Invocations and Atomicity in Real-Time Multiprocessor Applications." *ACM Transactions on Computer Systems.* Vol. 11, No. 1, pp. 33-72: 1993.

[Gib87] Gibbons, P. "A Stub Generator for Multi-Language RPC in Heterogeneous Environment." *IEEE Transactions on Software Engineering.* Vol. SE-13, No. 1, pp. 77-87: 1987.

[GiGl88] Gifford, D. and N. Glasser. "Remote Pipes and Procedures for Efficient Distributed Communication." *ACM Transactions on Computer Systems.* Vol. 6, No. 3, pp. 258-283: 1988.

[GLLGGH90] Gharachorloo, K., D. Lenoski, J. Laudon, P. Gibbons, A. Gupta, and J. Hennessy. "Memory Consistency and Event Ordering in Scalable Shared-Memory Processors." *Proceedings of the 17ᵗʰ ACM Annual International Symposium on Computer Architecture*. pp. 15-26: 1990.

[GNS88] Gifford, D., R. Needham, and M. Schroeder. "The Cedar File System." *Communications of the ACM*. Vol. 31, No. 3, pp. 288-298: 1988.

[Goo89] Goodman, J. *Cache Consistency and Sequential Consistency.* Technical Report No. 61, IEEE Scalable Coherent Interface Working Group, IEEE, New York: 1989.

[Gra78] Gray, J. "Notes on Database Operating Systems." R. Bayer, R. Graham, and G. Seegmuller (eds.) *Operating Systems: An Advance Course.* Springer-Verlag, Berlin, Germany: pp. 394-481: 1978.

[Gra97] Gray, J. *Interprocess Communications in UNIX: The Nooks & Crannies.* Prentice Hall PTR; Upper Saddle River, New Jersey, 1996.

[GrRe93] Gray, J., and A. Reuter. *Transaction Processing: Concepts and Techniques.* Morgan Kaufmann, San Francisco, California: 1993.

[GuZa89] Gusella, R. and S. Zatti. "The Accuracy of the Clock synchronization Achieved by TEMPO in Berkely UNIX 4.3 BSD." *IEEE Transactions on Software Engineering.* Vol. SE-15, No. 7, pp. 847-853: 1989.

[Hal96] Halsall, F. *Data Communications, Computer Networks, and Open Systems.* Addison Wesley, Reading Massachusetts, 1996.

[HaOs93] Harrison, W. and H. Ossher, *Subject-Oriented Programming (A Critique of Pure Objects)*, Proceedings of the conference on object-oriented programming: Systems, languages, and applications, Washington, D.C., ACM: pp. 411-428, 1993

[HaRe83] Harder, T. and A. Teuter. "Principles of Transaction-Oriented Database Recover." *ACM Computing Surveys.* Vol. 15, No. 4: 1983.

[HaSe98] Haggerty, P. and K. Seetharaman. "The Benefits of CORBA-Based Network Management." *Communications of the ACM.* Vol. 41, No. 10, pp: 73-79: 1998.

[Hel78] Hellman, M. "An Overview of Public-Key Cryptography." *IEEE Transactions on Computers.* Vol. C-16, No. 6, pp. 24-31: 1978.

[Hen98] Henning, M. "Binding, Migration, and Scalability in CORBA." *Communications of the ACM.* Vol. 41, No. 10, pp: 62-72: 1998.

[Her94] Herbert, A. "Distributing Objects." Brazier and Johansen (Eds.) *Distributed Open Systems*, IEEE Computer Society Press, Los Alamitos, California, pp. 123-133: 1994.

[HKMNSSW88] Howard, H., M. Kazar, S. Menees, D. Nichols, M. Satyanarayanan, R. Sidebotham, and M. West. "Scale and Performance in a Distributed File System." *ACM Transactions on Computer Systems.* Vol. 6, No. 1, pp. 51081: 1988.

[Hoa74] Hoare, C. A. R. "Monitors, An Operating System Structuring Concept." *Communications of the ACM*. Vol. 17, No 10, pp. 549-557: 1974.

[HSSD84] Halpern, J., B. Simons, R. Strong, and D. Dolly. "Fault-tolerant Clock Synchronization." *Proceedings of the Third Annual ACM Symposium on Distributed Systems*. pp. 89-102: 1984.

[Hu95] Hunter, P. *Network Operating Systems: Making the Right Choices.* Addison Wesley; Reading, Massachusetts, 1994.

[HuAh90] Hutto, P. and M. Ahamad. "Low Memory: Weakening Consistency to Enhance Cponcurrency in distributed Shared Memories." *Proceedings of the 10th IEEE International Conference on Distributed Computing Systems*. Pp. 302-311: 1990.

[HuPe91] Hutchinson, N. and L. Peterson. "The X-Kernel: An Architecture for Implementing Network Protocols." *IEEE Transactions on Software Engineering*. Vol. 17, No.1, pp. 64-76: 1991.

[ISL96] Iftode, L., J. Pal Singh, and K. Li. "Scope Consistency: A Bridge between Release Consistency and Entry Consistency." *Proceedings of the 8th Annual Symposium on Parallel Algorithms and Architecture*. pp. 277-287: 1996.

[IEEE85a] Institute of Electrical and Electronics Engineers. *802.3 CSMA/CD Access Method and Physical Layer Specifications*. IEEE, Standard 802.3, 1985.

[IEEE85b] Institute of Electrical and Electronics Engineers. *802.5 Token Ring Access Method and Physical Layer Specifications*. IEEE, Standard 802.5, 1985.

[ISO84] International Standards Organization. "Open System Interconnection". ISO Number 7498: 1984.

[Jal94] Jalote, P. *Fault Tolerance in Distributed Systems*. Prentice Hall, Englewood Cliffs, New Jersey: 1994.

[Joh95] Johnson, T. "A Performance Comparison of Fast Distributed Mutual Exclusion Algorithms." *Proceedings of the 9th International Parallel Processing Symposium*. Pp. 258-264: April 1995.

[JoHa97] Johnson, T. and K. Harathi. "A Prioritized Multiprocessor Spin Lock." *IEEE Transactions on Paralle and Distributed Systems*. Vol. 8, No. 9. Pp. 926-933: 1997.

[KCZ92] Keleher, P., A. Cox, W. Zwaenepoel. "Lazy Release Consistency." *Proceedings of the 19th ACM International Symposium on Computer Architecture*. pp. 13-21:1992.

[KeLi89] Kessler, R. and M. Livney. "An Analysis of Distributed Shared Memory Algorithms." *Proceedings Ninth International Conference on Distributed Computing Systems*. CS Press, pp. 498-505: 1989.

[Kim97] Kim, K. H. "Object Structures for Real-Time Systems and Simulators." *IEEE Computer*. Vol. 30, No. 8, pp. 62-70: 1997.

[KiPu95] Kim, T. and J. Purtilo. "Configuration-Level Optimization of RPC-Based Distributed Programs." *Proceedings of the 15th International Conference on distributed Computing Systems*. IEEE Press, Piscataway, New Jersey: 1995.

[KJAKL93] Kranz, D., K. Johnson, A. Agarwal, J. Kubiatowicz, and B. Lim. "Integrating Message Passing and Shared Memory: Early Experiences." *Proceedings of the 4ᵗʰ Symposium on Principles and Practice of Parallel Programming (ACM)*. pp. 54-63: 1993.

[Klu94] Kluepfel, H. "Securing a Global village and Its Resources." *IEEE Communications Magazine*. pp. 82-89: September 1994.

[Kna87] Knapp, E., "Deadlock Detection in Distributed Databases." *ACM Computing Surveys*. Vol. 19, No. 4, pp. 303-328: 1987.

[KoOc87] Kopertz, H. and W. Ochsenreiter. "Clock Synchronization in Distributed Real-time Systems." *IEEE Transactions on Computers*. Vol. C-36, No. 8, pp. 933-939: 1987.

[Kop97] Kopetz, H. *Real-Time Systems Design Principles for Distributed Embedded Applications*. Kluwer Academic Publishers, Hingham, MA: 1997.

[KPS95] Kaufman, C., R. Perlman, and M. Speciner. *Network Security: PRIVATE Communication in a PUBLIC World*. Prentice Hall, Upper Saddle River, New Jersey: 1995.

[Kri89] Krishnamurthy, E. *Parallel Processing: Principles and Practice*. Addison Wesley, Reading Massachusetts, 1989.

[KrLi87] Krueger, P. and M. Livney. "The Diverse Objectives of Distributed Scheduling Policies." *Proceedings IEEE 7ᵗʰ International Conference on Distributed Computing Systems*. Pp. 242-249: 1987.

[KSS97] Kleiman, S. , D. Shah, and B. Smaalders. *Programming with Threads*. SunSoft Press: A Prentice Hall Title: Sun Microsystems, Mountain View California: 1997.

[Kum91] Kumar, A., "Hierarchical Quorum Consensus: A New Algorithms for Managing Replicated Data." *IEEE Transactions on Computers*. Vol. 40, No. 9, pp. 996-1004: 1991.

[Kun91] Kunz, T. "The Influence of Different Workload Descriptions on Heuristic Load Balancing Scheme." *IEEE Transactions on Software Engineering*. Vol. 17, No.' 7, pp. 725-730: 1991.

[LABW94] Lampson, B., M. Abadi, M. Burrows, and W. Wobber. "Authentication in distributed Systems: Theory and Practice." *ACM Transactions on Computer Systems*. Vol. 10, No. 4, pp. 265-310: 1992.

[LaEl91] LaRowe, R. and C. Ellis. "Experimental Comparison of Memory Management Policies for NUMA Multiprocessors." *ACM Transactions on Computer Systems*. Vol. 9, pp. 319-363: 1991.

[Lai92] Lai, X. *On the Design and Security of Block Ciphers: Series in Information Processing*. Hartung-Corre Verglag, Konstanz, Germany: 1992.

[Lam78] Lamport, L. "Time, Clocks, and the Ordering of Events in a Distributed System." *Communications of the ACM*. Vol. 8, No. 7, pp. 558-564: 1978.

[Lam79] Lamport, L. "How to Make a Multiprocessor Computer That Correctly Executes Multiprocess Programs." *IEEE Transactions on Computers*. Vol. C-28, No. 9, pp. 690-691: 1979.

[Lam81] Lampson, B. "Atomic Transactions in Distributed Systems - Architecture and Implementation." *An Andvanced Course, Lecture Notes in Computer Science Vol. 105*. B. Lampson, M. Paul and H. Siegart (Eds.) Springer-Verlag, New York, pp. 246-264.

[LaMe85] Lamport, L. and P. Melliar-Smith. "Clock Synchronization in the Presence of Faults." *Journal of the ACM*. Vol. 32, No. 1, pp. 52-78: 1985.

[Lap92] Laplante, P. *Real-Time Systems Design and Analysis: An Engineer's Handbook*. IEEE Press, Piscataway, New Jersey: 1992.

[Lap97] Laplante, P. *Real-Time Systems Design and Analysis: An Engineer's Handbook, Second Edition*. IEEE Press, Piscataway, New Jersey: 1997.

[LeBe96] Lewis, B. and D. Berg. *THREADS PRIMER: A guide to multithreaded Programming*. SunSoft Press: A Prentice Hall Title: Sun Microsystems, Mountain View California: 1997.

[Lee97] Lee, P. "Efficient Algorithms for Data Distribution on Distributed Memory Parallel Computers." *IEEE Transactions on Parallel and Distributed Systems*. Vol 8, No. 8, pp. 825-839: 1997.

[LEK91] LaRowe, R., C. Ellis, and L. Kaplan. "The Robustness of NUMA Memory Management." *Proceedings of the 13th ACM Symposium on Operating System Principles*. pp. 137-151: 1991.

[LeSi90] Levy, E. and A. Silberschatz. "Distributed File Systems: Concepts and Examples." *ACM Computing Surveys*. Vol. 22, No. 4, pp. 321-374: 1990.

[LHWS96] Loh, P. K. K., W. J. Hsu, C. Wentong, and N. Sriskanthan. "How Network Topology Affects Dynamic Load Balancing." *IEEE Parallel & Distributed Technology: Systens and Applications*. Vol. 4, No. 3, pp. 25-35: 1996.

[LiHu89] Li, K. and P. Hudak. "Memory Coherence in Shared Virtual Memory Systems." *ACM Transactions on Computer Systems*. Vol. 7, pp. 321-359: 1989.

[LiKa80] Lindsay, W. and A. Kantak. "Network Synchronization of Random Signals. *IEEE Transactions on Communications*. Vol. Com-28, No. 8, pp. 1260-1266: 1980.

[Lin95] Lin, K. J. "Issues on Real-Time Systems Programming: Language, Compiler, and Object Orientation." In Son, S. H. (Ed.) *Advances in Real-Time Systems*. Prentice Hall, Englewood Cliffs, New Jersey, 1995.

[LiSa88] Lipton, R. and J. Sandberg. *PRAM: A Scalable Shared Memory*. Princton University Computer Science Technical Report: CS-TR-180-88: 1988.

[LJP93] Lea, R., C. Jacquemot, and E. Pillevesse. "COOL: System Support for Distributed Programming." *Communications of the ACM*. Vol. 36, No. 9, pp. 37-46: 1993.

[LoKi97] Lopes, C. and D. Kiczales. *A Language For Distributed Programming*, Xerox Palo Alto Research Center, Palo Alto, CA, 1997.

[Lo88] Lo, V. M. "Heuristic Algorithms for Task Assignment in Distributed Systems." *IEEE Transactions on Computers*. Vol. 37, No. 11, pp. 1384-1397: 1988.

[LuLy84] Lundelius, J. and N. Lynch. "A New Fault Tolerant Algorithm for Clock Synchroniztion." *Proceedings of the Third Annual ACM Symposium on Principles of Distributed Computing*. Pp. 75-88: 1984.

[LZCZ86] Lazowska, E., J. Zahorjan, D. Cheriton, and W. Zwaenepoel. "File Access Performance of Diskless Workstations." *ACM Transactions on Computer Systems*. Vol. 4, No. 3, pp. 238-268: 1986.

[MaOw85] Marzullo, K., and S. Owicki. "Maintaining Time in a Distributed System." *ACM Operating Systems Review*. Vol. 19, No. 3, pp. 44-54: 1985.

[MaSm88] Maguire, G. Jr., and J. Smith. "Process Migration: Effects on Scientific Computation." *ACM SIGPLAN Notices*. Vol. 23, No. 3, pp. 102-106: 1988.

[Makk94] Makki, K. "An Efficient Token-based Distributed Mutual Exclusion Algorithm." *Journal of Computer and Software Engineering*. December 1994.

[McC98] McCarthy, L. *Intranet Security: Stories from the Trenches*. Prentice Hall, Upper Saddle River, New Jersey: 1998.

[MDGM99] McReynolds, D., S. Duggins, D. Galli, and J. Mayer. "Distributed Characteristics of Subject Oriented Programming: An Evaluation with the Process and Object Paradigms." *Proceedings of the ACM SouthEastern Regional Conference*, ACM, Mobile Alabama: to appear 1999.

[Micr98] Microsoft Corporation. *NT White Paper Series*. www.microsoft.com/ntserver, accessed 1998.

[MiDi82] Mitchell, J. and J. Dion. "A Comparison of Two Network Based File Servers." *Coommunications of the ACM*. Vol. 25, No. 4, pp. 233-245: 1982.

[Mil88] Mills, D. "The Fuzzball." *Proceedings of ACM's SIGCOMM Symposium*. Pp. 115-122: 1988.

[Mil90] Mills, D. "Measured Performance of the Network Time Protocol in the Internet System." *ACM Computer Communication Review*. Vol. 20, No. 1, pp. 65-75: 1990.

[Mil91a] Mills, D. "Internet Time Synchronization: The Network Time Protocol." *IEEE Transactions on Communications*. Vol. 39, No. 10, pp. 1482-1493: 1991.

[Mil91b] Mills, D. "On the Chronology and Metrology of Computer Network Timescales and their Application to the Network Time Protocol." *ACM Computer Communications Review*. Vol. 21, No. 5, pp. 8-17: 1991.

[Mil92] Mills, D. "Network Time Protocol Version 3: Specification, Implementation and Analysis." *Network Working Group Request For Comments*. No. 1305: March, 1992.

[Mil95] Mills, D. "Simple Network Time Protocol (SMTP)." *Network Working Group Request For Comments*. No. 1769: March, 1995.

[Mit80] Mitra, D. "Network Synchronization: Analysis of a Hybrid of Master/Slave Synchronization." *IEEE Transactions on Communications*. Vol. Com-28, No. 8, pp. 1245-1258: 1980.

[MoPu97] Morin, C. and I. Puaut. "A Survey of Recoverable Distributed Shared Virtual Memory Systems." *IEEE Transactions on Parallel and Distributed Systems*. Vol. 8, No. 9, pp. 959-969: 1997.

[MSCHRS86] Morris, J., M. Satyanarayanan, M. Conner, J. Howard, D. Rosenthal, and F. Smith. "Andrew: A Distributed Personal Computing Environment." *Communications of the ACM*. Vol. 29, No. 3, pp. 184-201: 1986.

[Mul93a] Mullender, S. (Ed.). *Distributed Systems: Second Edition*. ACM Press, New York, New York, 1993.

[Mul93b] Mullender, S. "Kernel Support for Distributed Systems." *Distributed Systems: Second Edition*. ACM Press, New York, New York, pp. 385-410: 1993.

[MuLi87] Mutka, M. and M. Livney. "Scheduling Remote Processor Capacity in a Workstation-Processor Bank Network." *Proceedings of the Seventh IEEE International Conference on Distributed Computing Systems*. Pp. 2-9: 1987.

[MVTVV90] S. Mullender, G. VanRossum, A. Tanenbaum, R. VanRenesse, and H. VanStaveren. "Amoeba: A Distributed Operating System for the 1990's," *IEEE Computer*, Vol 23, No. 5, pp. 44-53:1990.

[NeBi84] Nelson, B. and A. Birrell. "Implementing Remote Procedure Calls." *ACM Transactions on Computer Systems*. Vol. 1, No. 2, pp. 39-59: 1984.

[NeTs94] Neuman, C. and T. Ts'O. "Kerberos: An Authentication Service for Computer Networks." *IEEE Communications*, Vol. 32, No. 9, pp. 33-38: 1994.

[NCSC94] National Computer Security Center, *Final Evaluation Report: Cray Research Incorporated Trusted UNICOS 8.0*. CSC-EPL-94/002, C-Evaluation No. 27/94. Fort George G. Meade, Maryland, March, 1994.

[Nel81] Nelson, B. *Remote Procedure Call*. Ph.D. Thesis, Carnegie-Mellon University: 1981.

[Nes83] Nessett, D. "A Systematic methodology for analyzing Security Threats to Interprocess' Communications in a Distributed System." *IEEE Transactions on Communications*. Vol. COM-31, pp. 1065-1063: 1983.

[Nev95] Nevison, C. "Parallel Computing in the Undergraduate Curriculum." *IEEE Computer*. Vol. 28, No. 12: pp. 51-56: 1995.

[NiPe96] Niemeyer, P. and J. Peck. *Exploring Java*. O'Reilly & Associates, Inc.; Sebastopol, California, 1996.

[NIST77] NIST. *Data Encryption Standard*. Federal Information Processing Standards publication 46, January 15, 1977.

[NIST93a] NIST (J. Barkley). *Comparing Remote Procedure Calls.* National Institute for Standards and Technology Information Report 5277: 1993.

[NIST93b] NIST. *Secure Hash Standard (SHS).* Federal Information Processing Standards publication 180: 1993.

[NIST94a] NIST. *Escrowed Encryption Standard.* Federal Information Processing Standards publication 185: 1994.

[NIST94b] NIST. *Digital Signature Standard (DSS).* Federal Information Processing Standards publication 186: 1994.

[NWO88] Nelson, M., B. Welch, and J. Ousterhout. "Caching in the Sprite Network File System." *ACM Transactions on Computer Systems.* Vol. 6, No. 1, pp. 134-154: 1988.

[OMG97] Object Management Group. *The Common Object Request Broker: Architecture and Specification: Version 2.1.* OMG, Framingham, Massachusetts, August 1997.

[OMG98a] Object Management Group. *The Common Object Request Broker: Architecture and Specification: Version 2.2.* OMG, Framingham, Massachusetts, February 1998.

[OMG98b] Object Management Group. *CORBAtelecoms: Telecommunications Domain Specifications: Version.1.* OMG, Framingham, Massachusetts, June 1998.

[Opp97] Oppliger, R. "Internet Security: Firewalls and Beyond." *Communications of the ACM.* Vol. 40, No. 5, pp. 92-102: 1997.

[Opp98] Oppliger, R. "Security at the Internet Layer." *IEEE Computer.* Vol. 31, No. 9, pp. 43-47: 1998.

[OsHa95] Ossher, H. and W. **????**, *Subject-Oriented Programming: Supporting Decentralized Development of Objects*, Research Report RC 20004, IBM Thomas J. Watson Research Center, Yorktown Heights, NY March 1995.

[Ous82] Ousterhout, J. "Scheduling Techniques for Concurrent systems" *Proceedings of the Third International Conference on Distributed Computing Systems*: Ft. Lauderdale, FL, IEEE Computer Science Press, pp: 22-30.

[PaSh88] Panzieri, F. and S. Shrivastava. "Rajdoot: A Remote Procedure Call Mechanism with Orphan Detection and Killing." *IEEE Transactions on Software Engineering.* Vol. 14, No. 1, pp. 30-37: 1988.

[PaSh98] Patiyoot, D., and S. Shepherd. "Techniques for Authentication Protocols and Key Distribution on Wireless ATM Networks." *Operating Systems Review.* ACM SIGOP Publication. Vol. 32, No. 4, pp. 25-32: 1998.

[Pfl97] Pfleeger, C. *Security in Computing: Second Edition.* Prentice Hall, Upper Saddle River, New Jersey: 1997.

[Pow95] Power, R. *Current and Future Danger: A CSI Primer on Computer Crime and Information Warfare*? Computer Security Institute, 1995.

[Prim95] Primatesta, F. *Tuxedo: An Open Approach to OLTP, 1/e*. Prentice Hall, Upper Saddle River, New Jersey: 1995.

[PTM96] Protic, J., M. Tomasevic, and V. Milutinovic. "Distributed Shared Memory: Concepts and Systems." *IEEE Parallel & Distributed Technology: Systems & Applications*. Vol. 4, No. 2, pp. 63-79: 1996.

[PTM98] Protic, J., M. Tomasevic, and V. Milutinovic. *Distributed Shared Memory: Concepts and Systems*. IEEE Computer Society Press, Los Alamitos, California: 1998.

[PTS88] Pulidas, S., D. Towsley, and J. Stankovic. "Imbedding Gradient Estimators in Load Balancing Algorithms." *Proceedings IEEE 8th International Conference on Distributed Systems*. Pp. 482-490: 1988.

[QuSh95] Quinn, B. and D. Shute. *Windows Sockets Network Programming*. Addison Wesley; Reading, Massachusetts, 1995.

[RaCh96] Ramamritham, K. and P. Chrysanthis (Eds.) *Advances in Concurrency Control and Transaction Processing*, IEEE Computer Society Press, Los Alamitos, California: 1996.

[RaSh92] Ramanthan, P. and K. Shin. "Delivery of Time-Critical Messages Using a Multiple Copy Approach." *ACM Transactions on Computer Systems*. Vol. 10, pp. 144-166: 1992.

[RiAg81] Ricard, G. and A. Agrawala. "An Optimal Algorithms for Mutual Exclusion in Computer Networks." *Communications of the ACM*. Vol. 34, No. 2, pp. 9-17: 1981.

[Ric88] Rickert, N. "Non-Byzantine Clock Synchronization: A Programming Experiment." *ACM Operating Systems Review*. Vol. 22, No. 1, pp. 73-78: 1988.

[RoRo96] Robbins, K. and S. Robbins. *Practical Unix Programming: A Guide to Concurrency, Communication, and Multithreading*. Prentice Hall PTR; Upper Saddle River, New Jersey, 1996.

[RSA78] Rivest, R., A. Shamir, and L. Adleman. "A Method for Obtaining Digital Signatures and Public-Key Cryptosystems." *Communications of the ACM*. Vol. 21, No. 2, pp. 120-126: 1978.

[RuGe98] Rubin, A. and D. Geer Jr. "A Survey of Web Security." *IEEE Computer*. Vol. 31, No. 9, pp. 34-41: 1998.

[San87] Sandberg, R. "The Sun Network File System: Design, Implementations and Experience." *Proceedings of the USENIX Summer Conference*. pp. 300-314: 1987.

[Sat90a] Satyanarayanan, M. "A Survey of Distributed File Systems." *Annual Review of Computer Science*. Vol. 4, pp. 73-104: 1990.

[Sat90b] Satyanarayanan, M. "Scalable, Secure, and Highly Available Distributed File System Design." *IEEE Transactions on Software Engineering*. Vol. 18, No. 1: 1992.

[ScBu89] Schroeder, M. and M. Burrows. "Performance of the Firefly RPC." *Twelfth ACM Symposium on Operating System Principles*. Pp. 83-90: 1989.

[Sch98] Schmidt, D. "Evaluating Architectures for Multithreaded Object Request Brokers." *Communications of the ACM*. Vol. 41, No. 10, pp: 54-61: 1998.

[Schn98] Schneier, B. "Cryptographic Design Vulnerabilities." *IEEE Computer*. Vol. 31, No. 9, pp. 29-33: 1998.

[ScPu94] Schwartz, M. and C. Pu. "Applying an Information Gathering Architecture to Netfind: A White Pages Tool for Changing and Growing Internet." *IEEE/ACM Transactions on Networking*. Vol. 2, No. 5, pp. 426-439: 1994.

[Sha77] Shankar, K. "The Total Computer Security Problem: An Overview." *IEEE Computer*. Vol. 10, pp. 50-62,' 71-73: 1977.

[SHFECB93] Slonim, J., J. Hong, P. Finnigan, D. Erickson (Galli), N. Colburn, and M. Bauer. "Does Midware Provide an Adequate Distributed Application Environment?" *Proceedings of the 1993 International Conference on Open Distributed Processing*. Berlin, Germany. Pp. 34-46: 1993.

[SHK95] Shirazi, B., A. Hurson, and K. Kavi. *Scheduling and Load Balancing in Parallel and Distributed Systems*. IEEE Computer Society Press, Los Alamitos, California: 1995.

[ShSn88] Shasha, D. and M. Snir. "Efficient and Correct Execution of Parallel Programs that Share Memory." *ACM Transactions on Programming Languages and Systems*. Vol. 10, No. 2, pp. 282-312: 1988.

[Sie98] Siegel, J. "OMG Overview: CORBA and the OMA in Enterprise Computing." *Communications of the ACM*. Vol. 41, No. 10, pp: 37-43: 1998.

[Sim92] Simmons, G. (Ed). *Contemporary Cryptography*. IEEE, New York, 1992.

[Sin97] Sinha, P. *Distributed Operating Systems: Concepts and Design*. IEEE Computer Society Press, New York, 1977.

[SKS92] Shivaratri, N., P. Krueger, and M. Singhal. "Load Distribution for Locally Distributed Systems." *IEEE Computer*, Vol. 25, No. 12. pp. 33-44: 1992.

[SMI80] Sturgis, H., J. Mitchell, and J. Israel. "Issues in the Design and Use of a Distributed File System." *ACM Operating Systems Review*. Vol. 14, No. 3, pp. 55-69: 1980.

[SOL98] Solomon, D. A. "The Windows NT Kernel Architecture." *IEEE Computer*. Vol. 31, No. 10, pp. 40-47: 1998.

[Son95] Son, S.H. (Ed.) *Advances in Real-Time Systems*. Prentice Hall, Englewood Cliffs, New Jersey, 1995.

[SrPa82] Srivastava, S. and F. Panzieri. "The Design of Reliable Remote Procedure Call Mechanism." *IEEE Transactions on Computers*. Vol. C-31, No. 7: 1982.

[SSF97] Shuey, R., D. Spooner, and O. Frieder. *The Architecture of Distributed Computing Systems*. Addison Wesley; Reading, Massachusetts, 1997.

[SSRB98] Stankovic, J., M. Spuri, K. Ramamritham, and G. Buttazzo. *Deadline Scheduling for Real-Time Systems: EDF and Related Algorithms.* Kluwer Academic Publishers, Hingham, MA, 1998.

[Sta95] Stallings, W. *Network and Internetwork Security: Principles and Practice.* Prentice Hall, Englewood Cliffs, New Jersey, 1995.

[Sta97] Stallings, W. *Data and Computer Communications: Fifth Edition.* Prentice Hall, Englewood Cliffs, New Jersey, 1997.

[Ste94] Stevens, W.R. *TCP/IP Illustrated, Vol. 1: The Protocols.* Addison Wesley, Reading Massachusetts, 1994.

[StZh90] Stumm, M. and S. Zhou. "Algorithms Implementing Distributed Shared Memory." *IEEE Computer.* Vol. 23, No. 5, pp. 54-64: 1990.

[Sun88] Sun Microsystems, Inc. *RPC: Remote Procedure Call: Protocol Specification Version 2.* Request for Comments 1057: 1988.

[SuZu96] Sun, X.H. and J. Zhu. "Performance Prediction: A Case Study Using a Scalable Shared-Virtual-Memory Machine." *IEEE Parallel & Distributed Technology.* Vol. 4, No. 4, pp. 36-49: 1996.

[SWP90] Shirazi, B., M. Wang, and G. Pathak. "Analysis and Evaluation of Heuristic Methods for Static Task Scheduling." *Journal of Parallel and Distributed Computing.* Vol. 10, pp. 222-232: 1990.

[TaAn90] Tay, F. and A. Ananda. "A Survey of Remote Procedure Calls." *Operating Systems Review.* Vol. 24, pp. 68-79: 1990.

[TaKa94] Tanenbaum, A. and M. F. Kaashoek., Brazier and Johansen (Eds.) "The Amoeba Microkernel." *Distributed Open Systems*, IEEE Computer Society Press, Los Alamitos, California, pp. 11-30B: 1994.

[Tan95] Tanenbaum, A. *Distributed Operating Systems.* Prentice Hall, Englewood Cliffs, New Jersey, 1995.

[Tan96] Tanenbaum, A. *Computer Networks: Third Ed.* Prentice Hall, Englewood Cliffs, New Jersey, 1996.

[Tho79] Thomas, R. "A Majority Consensus Approach to Concurrency Control for Multiple Copy Databases." *ACM Transactions on Database Systems.* Vol. 4, No. 2, pp. 180-209: 1979.

[THPSW98] Tarman, T., R. Hutchinson, L. Pierson, P. Sholander, and E. Witzke. "Algorithm-Agile Encryption in ATM Networks." *IEEE Computer.* Vol. 31, No. 9, pp. 57-64: 1998.

[TLC85] Theimer, M., K. Lantz, and D. Cheriton. "Preemptive Remote Execution Facilities for the V System." *Proceedings of the 10th ACM Symposium on Operating System Principles*: 1985.

[Vin98] Vinoski, S. "New Features for CORBA 3.0." *Communications of the ACM.* Vol. 41, No. 10, pp: 44-53: 1998.

[VLL90] Veltman, B., B. Lageweg, and J. Lenstra. "Multiprocessor Scheduling with Communication Delays." *Parallel Computing*, Vol. 16, pp. 173-182: 1990.

[WaMo85] Wang, Y. and R. Morris. "Load Sharing in Distributed Systems." *IEEE Transactions on Computers*. Vol. C-35, No. 3, pp. 204-217: 1985.

[Wei91] Weihl, W. "Transaction-Processing Techniques." *Distributed Systems: 2nd Edition*. S. Mullender (Ed.). Association for Computing Machinery, New York, New York: pp. 329-352: 1993.

[Wei93] Weikum, G., "Principles and Realization of Multilevel Transaction Management." *ACM Transactions on Database Systems*. Vol. 16, No. 1, pp. 132-140: 1991.

[Wil94] Williams, D. *Authentication Protocols in Distributed Computer Networks*. Master's Thesis, Southern College of Technology: Dept. of Computer Science; Marietta, Georgia, 1994.

[WoLa92] Woo, T. and S. Lam. "Authentication for Distributed Systems." *IEEE Computer*. Vol. 25, No. 1, pp. 39-52: 1992.

[WuSa93] Wu, K. and Y. Saad. "Performance of the CM-5 and Message Passing Primitives." *Proceedings of the Sixth SIAM Conference on Parallel Processing for Scientific Computing*. R. Sincovec, K. Keyes, M. Leuze, L. Petzold, and D. Reed (eds.) Vol. II, pp. 937-942: 1993.

[YSL97] Yang, C., S. Shi, and F. Liu. "The Design and Implementation of a Reliable File Server." *IEEE Newsletter of the Technical Committee on Distributed Processing*. Summer 1997.

[Zay87] Zayas, E. "Attacking the Process Migration Bottleneck." *Proceedings of the ACM Symposium on Operating Systems Principles*. Pp. 13-24: 1987.

Index

*D*oreen **L. Galli** received a highest honors BS degree from Eckerd College with a triple major in Computer Science, Mathematics, and Business Management. Her M.Math. degree as well as her Ph.D. are both in Computer Science and were awarded from the renown University of Waterloo with research in cryptography and parallel memory management respectively.

Dr. Galli has authored over a dozen technical and research articles in the industry's most respected journals in addition to countless internal technical reports, executive technical recommendations, and white papers. Her experience in telecommunications includes unified messaging, voice messaging, enhanced calling card services, and interactive voice response systems. She has also been heavily involved in network operations, as well as Internet and web technology including portal development and deployment. Her experience has included roles such as a software engineer, architect, configuration and release manager, and project lead for the likes of IBM Center for Advanced Studies, Premiere Technologies, to leading the successful system deployment for the Centennial Olympic Games. Currently, Dr. Galli is a technical executive at USWeb/CKS in her roll as a Director of Technology.

In addition to Dr. Galli's considerable industry experience, she has taught in academia as an Associate Professor of Computer Science. In this capacity, she has been recognized by Who's Who Among America's Teachers on multiple occasions, supervised over 20 students, and taught more than 35 graduate and undergraduate courses with a primary focus on advanced system and network technologies. She has also served as an external examiner for doctoral candidates and has delivered numerous invited colloquiums. The one common thread throughout her career has always been networks and distributed technology.

Dr. Galli is an active member of IEEE, IEEE Computer Society, IEEE Communications Society, ACM, ACM SIGCOMM, ACM SIGOPS, Systers, and NAFE.